# A THEOLOGY
# OF LIBERATION

*GUSTAVO GUTIÉRREZ*

# A THEOLOGY OF LIBERATION

## History, Politics, and Salvation

Revised Edition
with a New Introduction

*Translated and edited by*
*Sister Caridad Inda and John Eagleson*

ORBIS BOOKS
Maryknoll, New York 10545

The Catholic Foreign Mission Society of America (Maryknoll) recruits and trains people for overseas missionary service. Through Orbis Books Maryknoll aims to foster the international dialogue that is essential to mission. The books published, however, reflect the opinions of their authors and are not meant to represent the official position of the society.

Originally published as *Teología de la liberación, Perspectivas* by CEP, Lima, 1971

The text of this book is a revised version of the original English-language translation © 1973 Orbis Books, Maryknoll, NY 10545; the present book contains a new introduction by the author, translation © 1988 Orbis Books

Manuscript editor and indexer: William E. Jerman

New introduction and revisions to this edition translated by Matthew J. O'Connell

Nineteenth Printing, April 2007

**LIBRARY OF CONGRESS**
**Library of Congress Cataloging-in-Publication Data**


Gutiérrez, Gustavo 1928-
     [Teología de la liberación. English]
     A theology of liberation: history, politics and salvation/
Gustavo Gutiérrez; translated and edited by Sister Caridad Inda and
John Eagleson.
          p.          cm.
     Translation of: Teología de la liberación.
     Originally published: Maryknoll, N.Y.: Orbis, 1973. With new
introd.
     Includes bibliographical references and index.
     ISBN 0-88344-543-3.          ISBN 0-88344-542-5 (pbk.)
     1. Liberation theology.          I. Title.
BT83.57.G88313 1988
230′ .2—dc19
                                        87-34793
                                        CIP

*To*
*José María Arguedas*
*and Henrique Pereira Neto*

Nunca quiso ayudar a la misa en las fiestas principales de la comunidad. El cura de un distrito vecino que venía a celebrarlas le pidió que hiciera de sacristán, le exigió muchas veces. Lahuaymarca tenía un sacristán indio.

—Ése no sabe. Repite las palabras como loro, no entiende; casi no es cristiano. Tú eres mestizo, organista, contestas en latín. La misa será más grande contigo—le dijo el cura en la víspera de una fiesta grande.

—Quemado yo padre. Mi iglesia dentro de mi pecho, quemado. ¿Cómo voy a cantar? La Gertrudis igual que ángel canta. El sacristán contesta.

—La Gertrudis no piensa en Dios; canta triste, sí, porque es deforme.

—Padrecito, tú no entiendes el alma de indios. La Gertrudis, aunque no conociendo a Dios, de Dios es. ¿Quién, si no, le dio esa voz que limpia el pecado? Consuela al triste, hace pensar al alegre; quita de la sangre cualquier suciedad.

—Bueno, terco. No puedo obligarte. Esa "Kurku" tiene algo, algo extraño, duele.

—El Dios, pues, padrecito. Ella ha sufrido entre los señores. Dios de los señores no es igual. Hace sufrir sin consuelo.

. . . Ha llegado amarillo, rotoso, sin chullu siquiera. Ha regresado igual de su ropa, pero en su ojo había Dios . . .

—¿Qué Dios? ¿Cómo sabes?

—Dios es esperanza. Dios alegría. Dios ánimo. Llegó "unpu," enjuermo, agachadito. Salió tieso, juirme, águila. Era mozo no más. Dios hay aquí, en Lahuaymarca. De San Pedro se ha ido, creo para siempre.

—Tú tampoco eres cristiano verdadero, hijo. ¡Tantos años de sacristán! Y piensas como brujo. Dios está en todas partes, en todas partes . . .

El viejo sacristán de San Pedro movía negativamente la cabeza.

¿Había Dios en el pecho de los que rompieron el cuerpo del inocente maestro Bellido? ¿Dios está en el cuerpo de los inginieros que están matando "La Esmeralda"? ¿De señor autoridad que quitó a sus dueños ese maizal donde jugaba la Virgen con su Hijito, cada cosecha? No me hagas llorar, padrecito. Yo también como muerto ando. Don Demetrio tiene Dios, en la "Kurku" está Dios, cantando; en don Bruno pelea Dios con el demonio; para mí no hay consuelo, de nadies.

JOSÉ MARÍA ARGUEDAS
*Todas las sangres*

# CONTENTS

# INTRODUCTION TO THE ORIGINAL EDITION

This book is an attempt at reflection, based on the gospel and the experiences of men and women committed to the process of liberation in the oppressed and exploited land of Latin America. It is a theological reflection born of the experience of shared efforts to abolish the current unjust situation and to build a different society, freer and more human. Many in Latin America have started along the path of a commitment to liberation, and among them is a growing number of Christians; whatever the validity of these pages, it is due to their experiences and reflections. My greatest desire is not to betray their experiences and efforts to elucidate the meaning of their solidarity with the oppressed.

My purpose is not to elaborate an ideology to justify postures already taken, or to undertake a feverish search for security in the face of the radical challenges that confront the faith, or to fashion a theology from which political action is "deduced." It is rather to let ourselves be judged by the word of the Lord, to think through our faith, to strengthen our love, and to give reason for our hope from within a commitment that seeks to become more radical, total, and efficacious. It is to reconsider the great themes of the Christian life within this radically changed perspective and with regard to the new questions posed by this commitment. This is the goal of the so-called *theology of liberation.*[1]

Many significant efforts along these lines are being made in Latin America. Insofar as I know about them, they have been kept in mind and have contributed to this study. I wish to avoid, however, the kind of reflection that— legitimately concerned with preventing the mechanical transfer of an approach foreign to our historical and social coordinates—neglects the contribution of the universal Christian community. It seems better, moreover, to acknowledge explicitly this contribution than to introduce surreptitiously and uncritically

---

The present study is based on a paper presented at the *Encuentro Nacional del Movimiento Sacerdotal ONIS*, July 1968, in Chimbote, Peru, published by the MIEC Documentation Service in Montevideo (1969) with the title *Hacia una teología de la liberación*. The original lecture was updated for a presentation at the Consultation of Theology and Development organized by SODEPAX, November 1969, in Cartigny, Switzerland, and published as "Notes on a Theology of Liberation," in *In Search of a Theology of Development: A Sodepax Report* (Lausanne, 1970). This study follows the same line of thought.

certain ideas elaborated in another context—ideas that can be fruitful among us only if they undergo a healthy and frank scrutiny.

A reflection on the theological meaning of the process of human liberation throughout history demands methodologically that I define my terms. The first part of this book is devoted to that purpose. This will enable me to indicate why I pay special attention in this work to the critical function of theology with respect to the presence and activity of humankind in history. The most important instance of this presence in our times, especially in underdeveloped and oppressed countries, is the struggle to construct a just and fraternal society, where persons can live with dignity and be the agents of their own destiny. It is my opinion that the term *development* does not well express these profound aspirations. *Liberation,* on the other hand, seems to express them better. Moreover, in another way the notion of liberation is more exact and all-embracing: it emphasizes that human beings transform themselves by conquering their liberty throughout their existence and their history. The Bible presents liberation—salvation—in Christ as the total gift, which, by taking on the levels I indicate, gives the whole process of liberation its deepest meaning and its complete and unforeseeable fulfillment. Liberation can thus be approached as a single salvific process. This viewpoint, therefore, permits us to consider *the unity, without confusion*, of the various human dimensions, that is, one's relationships with other humans and with the Lord, which theology has been attempting to establish for some time; this approach will provide the framework for our reflection.

It is fitting, secondly, to show that the problem that the theology of liberation poses is simultaneously traditional and new. This twofold characteristic will be more evident if I analyze the different ways in which theology has historically responded to this problem. This will lead me to conclude that because the traditional approaches have been exhausted, new areas of theological reflection are being sought. My examination should help me remove the obstacles from my path and move ahead more quickly. The second part of the work deals with this matter.

The preceding analysis leads me to reconsider the "practice" of the church in today's world. The situation in Latin America, the only continent among the exploited and oppressed peoples where Christians are in the majority, is especially interesting. An attempt to describe and interpret the forms under which the Latin American church is present in the process of liberation—especially among the most committed Christian groups—will allow me to establish the questions for an authentic theological reflection. These will be the first efforts along these lines. The third part of this treatise is devoted to this attempt.

The previous remarks make it clear that the question regarding the theological meaning of liberation is, in truth, a question *about the very meaning of Christianity and about the mission of the church*. There was a time when the church responded to any problem by calmly appealing to its doctrinal and vital resources. Today the seriousness and scope of the process that we call liberation is such that Christian faith and the church are being radically challenged. They are being asked to show what significance they have for a human task that has reached adulthood. The greater part of my study is concerned with this aspect. I approach the subject within the framework of the unity and, at the same time, the complexity of the process of liberation centered in the salvific work of Christ. I am aware, however, that I can only sketch these considerations, or more precisely, outline the new questions—without claiming to give conclusive answers.

The novelty and shifting quality of the problems posed by the commitment to liberation make the use of adequate language and sufficiently precise concepts rather difficult. Nevertheless, I present this study in the hope that it will be useful, and especially because I am confident that the confrontation necessarily implied in publishing will allow me to improve and deepen these reflections.

# INTRODUCTION TO THE REVISED EDITION: EXPANDING THE VIEW

In 1968 the Latin American bishops wrote this description of the new phase of history that was dawning among us:

> Latin America is obviously under the sign of transformation and development; a transformation that, besides taking place with extraordinary speed, has come to touch and influence every level of human activity, from the economic to the religious.
>
> This indicates that we are on the threshold of a new epoch in this history of Latin America. It appears to be a time of zeal for full emancipation, of liberation from every form of servitude, of personal maturity and of collective integration [Medellín, "Introduction," 4].

This was a vision of a new historical era to be characterized by a radical aspiration for integral liberation. However painful the Latin American situation is (and it was painful in 1968), the vision is still valid. During the intervening years much has happened to change the history of the region and bring it across the threshold of which the bishops spoke and into an ever-accelerating process.

All this creates a new challenge for those who are trying to draw inspiration for their lives from him who "dwelt among us" (John 1:14). The perspective given by faith should help us see what is at stake in the present stage of history. In this context the bishops at Medellín observed:

> We cannot fail to see in this gigantic effort toward a rapid transformation and development an obvious sign of the Spirit who leads the history of humankind and of the peoples toward their vocation. We cannot but discover in this force, daily more insistent and impatient for transformation, vestiges of the image of God in human nature as a powerful incentive. This dynamism leads us progressively to an even greater control of nature, a more profound personalization and fellowship, and an encounter with the God who ratifies and deepens those values attained through human efforts [Medellín, ibid.].

My reason for beginning with these lengthy citations is that they express so well both the historical situation of liberation theology and the perspective of faith in which it interprets this situation. (The name and reality of "liberation theology" came into existence at Chimbote, Peru, in July 1968, only a few months before Medellín.)[1] Ever since Medellín, the development of liberation theology in Latin America has been accompanied by a continual awareness that we have entered into a new historical stage in the life of our peoples and by a felt need of understanding this new stage as a call from the Lord to preach the gospel in a way that befits the new situation. Both of these factors condition the thinking of liberation theology, requiring that it maintain a twofold fidelity: to the God of our faith and to the peoples of Latin America. Therefore we cannot separate our discourse about God from the historical process of liberation.

In the years since Medellín there has been an inevitable clarification of this theological undertaking. Liberation theology has been welcomed with sympathy and hope by many and has contributed to the vitality of numerous undertakings in the service of Christian witness. At the same time it has stimulated an interest in reflection on the Christian faith—an interest previously unknown in Latin American intellectual circles, which have traditionally been cool toward Christianity or even hostile to it. The years have also brought serious and relevant critiques that have helped this theological thinking to reach maturity. On the other hand, the theology of liberation has also stirred facile enthusiasms that have interpreted it in a simplistic or erroneous way by ignoring the integral demands of the Christian faith as lived in the communion of the church. Finally, there has been the foreseeable resistance of some.

There are various reasons for these several responses. But rather than point out the responsibilities of others, let me say simply that it is not easy to deal with sensitive and conflictual themes—like the very reality we are attempting to penetrate with the eyes of faith—and to find immediately and for good the clearest and most balanced formulas in which to express theological reflection on these themes. All language is to some extent a groping for clarity; it is therefore necessary to deal respectfully with other persons and with what they think they find in works written from this theological perspective. Readers have rights that authors neither can nor ought to deny. At every stage, therefore, we must refine, improve, and possibly correct earlier formulations if we want to use language that is understandable and faithful both to the integral Christian message and to the reality we experience.[2]

Recent years have witnessed an important debate on the theology of liberation in the context of the Catholic Church. It has meant some painful moments at the personal level, usually for reasons that eventually pass away. The important thing, however, is that the debate has been an enriching spiritual experience. It has also been an opportunity to renew in depth our fidelity to the church in which all of us as a community believe and hope in the Lord, as well as to reassert our solidarity with the poor, those privileged members of the reign of God. The theological labor must continue, but in pursuing it we now have some important documents of the magisterium that advise us about the path to be followed and in various ways spur us on in our quest.[3]

The passage of time has caused essentials to become clearer. Secondary elements have lost the importance they seemed to have at an earlier period. A process of maturation has been under way. But the temporal *factor* is not the only one affecting the course of liberation theology during these years. There has also been a *spatial* extension. Within the different Christian confessions and their respective traditions, thinkers have adopted the liberation perspective suggested by the message of God's reign. In this development, theological influences (which in some cases were evidently nonexistent at the beginning) have played a less important role than the impulse given by a situation of fundamental oppression and marginalization that the Christian conscience rejects and in response to which it proclaims the total gospel in all its radicalness.

Black, Hispanic, and Amerindian theologies in the United States, theologies arising in the complex contexts of Africa, Asia, and the South Pacific, and the especially fruitful thinking of those who have adopted the feminist perspective—all these have meant that for the first time in many centuries theology is being done outside the customary European and North American centers. The result in the so-called First World has been a new kind of dialogue between traditional thinking and new thinking. In addition, outside the Christian sphere efforts are underway to develop liberation theologies from Jewish and Muslim perspectives.[4]

We are thus in the presence of a complex phenomenon developing on every side and representing a great treasure for the Christian churches and for their dialogue with other religions. The clarification I mentioned earlier is thus not limited to the Latin American context but affects a process and a search that are being conducted on a very broad front today.

These considerations should not make us forget, however, that we are not dealing here solely with an intellectual pursuit. Behind liberation theology are Christian communities, religious groups, and peoples, who are becoming increasingly conscious that the oppression and neglect from which they suffer are incompatible with their faith in Jesus Christ (or, speaking more generally, with their religious faith). These concrete, real-life movements are what give this theology its distinctive character; in liberation theology, faith and life are inseparable. This unity accounts for its prophetic vigor and its potentialities.

It is not possible, when speaking of liberation theology, to pass over in silence this broad movement of Christian and religious experiments and commitments that feed reflection. In these pages I must nonetheless deal especially with the Latin American world, for it is the world closest to me and the one in which I have made my own contribution and experienced my own development.

Now that twenty years have passed since the beginning of liberation theology, it may be appropriate to review the ways in which it has found expression and the paths it has followed. I shall not try to rewrite past essays, such as those in this book, in the light of my present concerns and perspectives. I do, however, think it important and useful to call attention to what I regard as the most important points, to anticipate ambiguous interpretations, revise and make more accurate certain formulations I now consider unsatisfactory, leave aside what time has undermined, and point out some of the new and promising themes developed in recent years. The task is an extensive one; it has been begun and is underway. My intention here is to indicate some important points in that program.[5]

The "new epoch in the history of Latin America," of which Medellín spoke, continues to be our vital context. In the language of the Bible, we are in a *kairos*, a propitious and demanding time in which the Lord challenges us and we are called upon to bear a very specific witness. During this *kairos* Latin American Christians are experiencing a tense and intense period of *solidarity*, *reflection*, and *martyrdom*. This direct, real-life setting enables me to go more deeply into the three points that I have for some time regarded as basic to liberation theology and have also been the primary ones in the chronological development of this theology: the viewpoint of the poor; theological work; and the proclamation of the kingdom of life. I should like to explain here what is permanent in each of these, the enrichments each has received, the development and maturation that time has effected, and the resultant evolution of ideas in the theological perspective that I have adopted.

## A NEW PRESENCE

What we have often called the "major fact" in the life of the Latin American church—the participation of Christians in the process of liberation—is simply an expression of a far-reaching historical event: *the irruption of the poor*. Our time bears the imprint of the new presence of those who in fact used to be "absent" from our society and from the church. By "absent" I mean: of little or no importance, and without the opportunity to give expression themselves to their sufferings, their comraderies, their plans, their hopes.

This state of affairs began to change in Latin America in recent decades, as a result of a broad historical process. But it also began to change in Africa (new nations) and Asia (old nations obtaining their independence), and among racial minorities (blacks, Hispanics, Amerindians, Arabs, Asiatics) living in the rich countries and in the poor countries as well (including Latin American countries). There has been a further important and diversified movement: the new presence of women, whom Puebla described as "doubly oppressed and marginalized" (1134, note) among the poor of Latin America.

As a result of all this it can be said that:

The powerful and almost irresistible aspiration that persons have for liberation constitutes one of the principal signs of the times that the church has to examine and interpret in the light of the gospel. This major phenomenon of our time is universally widespread, though it takes on different forms and exists in different degrees according to the particular people involved. It is, above all, among those who bear the burden of misery and in the heart of the disinherited classes that this aspiration expresses itself with the greatest force [*Libertatis Nuntius*, I, 1].

Liberation theology is closely bound up with this new presence of those who in the past were always absent from our history.[6] They have gradually been turning into active agents of their own destiny and beginning a resolute process that is changing the condition of the poor and oppressed of this world. Liberation theology (which is an expression of the right of the poor to think out their own faith) has not been an automatic result of this situation and the changes it has undergone. It represents rather an attempt to accept the invitation of Pope John XXIII and the Second Vatican Council and interpret this sign of the times by reflecting on it critically in the light of God's word. This theology should lead us to a serious discernment of the values and limitations of this sign of the times.

### A Complex World

"Dominated peoples," "exploited social classes," "despised races," and "marginalized cultures" were formulas often used in speaking of the poor in the context of liberation theology (there was repeated reference also to discrimination against women). The point of these formulas was to make it clear that the poor have a social dimension. But the turbulent situation in Latin America has caused many to place an almost exclusive emphasis on the social and economic aspect of poverty (this was a departure from the original insight). I am indeed convinced that it is still necessary to call atttention to this dimension of poverty if we are to do more than touch the surface of the real situation of the poor, but I also insist that we must be attentive to other aspects of poverty as well.

As a matter of fact, the increasingly numerous commitments being made to the poor have given us a better understanding of how very complex their world is. For myself, this has been the most important (and even crushing) experience of these past years. The world of the poor is a universe in which the socio-economic aspect is basic but not all-inclusive. In the final analysis, poverty means death: lack of food and housing, the inability to attend properly to health and education needs, the exploitation of workers, permanent unemployment, the lack of respect for one's human dignity, and unjust limitations placed on personal freedom in the areas of self-expression, politics, and religion. Poverty is a situation that destroys peoples, families, and individuals; Medellín and Puebla called it "institutionalized violence" (to which must be added the equally unacceptable violence of terrorism and repression).

At the same time, it is important to realize that being poor is a way of living, thinking, loving, praying, believing, and hoping, spending leisure time, and struggling for a livelihood. Being poor today is also increasingly coming to mean being involved in the struggle for justice and peace, defending one's life and freedom, seeking a more democratic participation in the decisions made by society, organizing "to live their faith in an integral way" (Puebla, 1137), and being committed to the liberation of every human being.

All this, I repeat, goes to make up the complex world of the poor.[7] The fact that misery and oppression lead to a cruel, inhuman death, and are therefore contrary to the will of the God of Christian revelation who wants us to live, should not keep us from seeing the other aspects of poverty that I have mentioned. They reveal a human depth and a toughness that are a promise of life. This perception represents one of the most profound changes in our way of seeing the reality of poverty and consequently in the overall judgment we pass on it.

The same period, meanwhile, has seen a converging process in which we have become more aware that there is a racial problem among us. One of our social lies has been the claim that there is no racism in Latin America. There may indeed be no racist laws as in some other countries, but there are very rigid racist customs that are no less serious for being hidden. The marginalization of Amerindian and black populations, and the contempt in which they are held, are situations we cannot accept as human beings, much less as Christians. These populations themselves are becoming increasingly aware of their situation and are beginning to claim their most basic human rights; this new attitude carries the promise of fruitful results.

The racial question represents a major challenge to the Christian community, and one to which we are only now beginning to respond.[8] The approaching five-hundredth anniversary of the evangelization of Latin America should be the occasion for an examination of conscience regarding the immense human cost historically connected with that evangelization—I mean the destruction of individuals and cultures. Such an examination will help us define a commitment of the church to races that have for centuries been neglected and mistreated. The bold efforts of Bartolomé de Las Casas and so many others past and present are there to point a way we must follow in accordance with our present historical situation.

I referred above to the conditions in which women live. We in Latin America are only now beginning to wake up to the unacceptable and inhuman character of their situation. One thing that makes it very difficult to grasp its true character is its hiddenness, for it has become something habitual, part of everyday life and cultural tradition. So true is this that when we point it out we sound a bit like foreigners bent on causing trouble. The issue was hardly raised at Medellín. Puebla, however, did initiate reflection on it (see 834–49 and 1134). A growing number of persons are committed to the restoration of women's rights, even as we realize more and more clearly how intolerable the situation of women really is.

The situation of racial and cultural minorities and of women among us is a challenge to pastoral care and to commitment on the part of the Christian churches; it is therefore also a challenge to theological reflection. In this area we have a long way to go, but a good beginning is being made as cultural and racial and feminist themes are addressed more and more frequently in liberation theology. The most important part will have to be played by persons who themselves belong to these groups, despite the difficulties in the way of their doing so. It is not possible for others simply to stand up and effectively play the part of a protagonist. But the voices of these groups are beginning to be heard, and this development is promising. This will certainly be one of the richest veins to be mined by liberation theology in years ahead.

In this whole matter I have found it very helpful to enter into dialogue with theologies developed in settings different from our own. Through direct contacts with Christian groups in other countries and continents (as well as through meetings with those who are trying to reflect theologically in those contexts) I have learned much about situations different from the Latin American. At the same time, I have gained a better understanding and appreciation of aspects of our people that had been clear in theory but had little or no consequence in practice. As a result, I have come to see with new eyes our racial and cultural world, and the discrimination against women.

Perhaps the most important fruit derived from dialogues among Third World theologians (organized principally by the Ecumenical Association of Third World Theologians—EATWOT) and from related activities has been a better and deeper understanding of the world of the poor. Closely connected as we are with our peoples, we brought to these meetings a desire to speak about the world from which we come, with its experiences and its thinking, but little by little we learned that it was more important to listen to what others had to say about their respective situations. Captivated as we are by the life and death of the poor of Latin America and by the riches to be found in the Christian communities that come into existence there and bear witness—even to the point of martyrdom—to the Lord in their midst, we have perhaps tended to focus our attention too much on these things. I must admit, therefore, that from these contacts with these other theologians I have grown in hope and have become more sensitive to the suffering of human groups geographically and culturally far removed from us.

The predominant characteristics of this complex and widespread world of the poor are, on the one hand, its unimportance in the eyes of the great powers that rule today's wider world and, on the other, its vast human, cultural, and religious wealth, and especially its capacity for creating new forms of solidarity in these areas.

All this takes us far from the simplistic position we were perhaps in danger of initially adopting in analyzing the situation of poverty. A fundamental point has become clear: it is not enough to describe the situation; its *causes* must also be determined. Medellín, Puebla, and John Paul II in his encyclical on work and, more recently, on social concerns, as well as in other writings, have made a forceful analysis of these causes. Structural analysis has thus played an important part in building up the picture of the world to which liberation theology addresses itself. The use of this analysis has had its price, for although the privileged of this world can accept the existence of human poverty on a massive scale and not be overawed by it (after all, it is something that cannot be hidden away in our time), problems begin when the *causes* of this poverty are pointed out to them. Once causes are determined, then there is talk of "social injustice," and the privileged begin to resist. This is especially true when to structural analysis there is added a concrete historical perspective in which personal responsibilities come to light. But it is the conscientization and resultant organization of poor sectors that rouse the greatest fears and the strongest resistance.

The tools used in this analysis vary with time and according to their proven effectiveness for gaining knowledge of social reality and finding solutions for social problems. Science is by its nature critical of its own presuppositions and achievements; it moves on to new interpretive hypotheses. It is clear, for example, that the theory of dependence, which was so extensively used in the early years of our encounter with the Latin American world, is now an inadequate tool, because it does not take sufficient account of the internal dynamics of each country or of the vast dimensions of the world of the poor. In addition, Latin American social scientists are increasingly alert to factors of which they were not conscious earlier and which show that the world economy has evolved.

Problems like unpayable foreign debt, to give but one example, are drawing attention, sharpening awareness of what lies behind them, and refining the available analytical tools (it is worth mentioning here that Medellín in 1968 called attention to the dangers of foreign indebtedness; see "Peace," 9d). It is in fact impossible to deal effectively with the poverty experienced in Latin America without following the development of the most urgent problems and without attending to factors that enable us to locate these problems in a broad and complex international context.

All this requires that we refine our analytical tools and develop new ones. The socio-economic dimension is very important but we must go beyond it. In recent years there has been an insistent emphasis, and rightly so, on the contrast between a Northern world developed and wealthy (whether it be capitalist or socialist) and a Southern world underdeveloped and poor. This approach yields a different view of the world scene, one in which it is not enough to focus on ideological confrontations or give a narrow interpretation of opposition between social classes. It also brings out the radical opposition that is the setting for the confrontation of East and West.[9] Diverse factors are making us aware of the different kinds of opposition and social conflict that exist in the modern world.

As far as poverty is concerned, an important transformation is undoubtedly taking place in the social analysis on which liberation theology depends to some extent. The change has led liberation theology to incorporate beneficial perspectives and new sources of knowledge from the human sciences (psychology, ethnology, anthropology) for its study of a reality that is intricate and shifting. To incorporate does not mean simply to add on without interrelating. Attention to cultural factors will help us to enter into mentalities and basic attitudes that explain important aspects of the reality with which we are faced. The economic dimension itself will take on a new character once we see things from the cultural point of view; the converse will also certainly be true.

There is no question of choosing among the tools to be used; poverty is a complex human condition, and its causes must also be complex. The use of a variety of tools does not mean sacrificing depth of analysis; the point is only not to be simplistic but rather to insist on getting at the deepest causes of the situation, for this is what it means to be truly radical. Responsiveness to new challenges requires changes in our approach to the paths to be followed in really overcoming the social conflicts mentioned earlier and in building a just and fraternal world, as the gospel calls upon us to do.

If we were simply to adopt the traditional approach, we would be taking the course that has always been taken in the social sciences in their contribution to analysis. But we also know that the sciences and, for a number of reasons, the social sciences in particular, are not neutral. They carry with them ideological baggage requiring discernment; for this reason the use of the sciences can never be uncritical (see the Introduction of *Libertatis Nuntius*). In consequence, both the scientific outlook itself and the Christian conception of the world call for a rigorous discernment of scientific data—discernment, but not fear of the contributions of the human disciplines.[10] We need to make an unruffled but critical use of mediations that can help us to understand better where and how the Lord is challenging us as we face the life (and death) of our brothers and sisters.[11]

### Opting for the God of Jesus

Important though it is to acquire a substantial knowledge of the poverty in which the vast majority of Latin Americans live and of the causes from which it springs, theological work proper begins when we try to interpret this reality in the light of Christian revelation.

The meaning given to poverty in the Bible is therefore a cornerstone of liberation theology. The problem of poverty is an ancient one in Christian thought, but the new presence of the poor to which I have referred gives it a new urgency. An essential clue to the understanding of poverty in liberation theology is the distinction, made in the Medellín document "Poverty of the Church," between three meanings of the term "poverty": real poverty as an evil—that is something that God does not want; spiritual poverty, in the sense of a readiness to do God's will; and solidarity with the poor, along with protest against the conditions under which they suffer.

This is the context of a theme that is central in liberation theology and has now been widely accepted in the universal church: the preferential option for the poor. Medellín had already spoken of giving "preference to the poorest and most needy sectors and to those segregated for any cause whatsoever" ("Poverty," 9). The very word "preference" denies all exclusiveness and seeks rather to call attention to those who are the first—though not the only ones—with whom we should be in solidarity. In the interests of truth and personal honesty I want to say that from the very beginning of liberation theology, as many of my writings show, I insisted that the great challenge was to maintain both the universality of God's love and God's predilection for those on the lowest rung of the ladder of history. To focus exclusively on the one or the other is to mutilate the Christian message. Therefore every attempt at such an exclusive emphasis must be rejected.

During the difficult decade of the 1970s this attitude gave rise to many experiences and resultant theological reflections in the Latin American church. In the process, formulas intended to express commitment to the poor and oppressed proliferated. This became clear at Puebla, which chose the formula "preferential option for the poor" (see the Puebla Final Document, part 4, chapter 1). It was a formula that theologians in Latin America had already begun to use in preceding years. The Puebla Conference thus gave it a major endorsement and importance.

The term "option" has not always been correctly understood. Like every term, it has its limitations; the intention in using it is to emphasize the freedom and commitment expressed in a decision. The commitment to the poor is not "optional" in the sense that a Christian is free to make or not make this option, or commitment, to the poor, just as the love we owe to all human beings without exception is not "optional." Neither, on the other hand, does the term "option" suppose that those making it do not themselves belong to the world of the poor. In very many instances, of course, they do not, but it must be said at the same time that the poor too have an obligation to make this option.

The expression "preferential option for the poor" had an important and significant predecessor. I refer to John XXIII's statement, a month before the opening of Vatican II, that the church is called upon to be a church of the poor. The reader will probably be familiar with the passage: "In face of the underdeveloped countries, the church is, and wants to be, the church of all and especially the church of the poor" (address of September 11, 1962). Let me say only that we have here two aspects of the church's life that are both demanding and inseparable: universality and preference for the poor.

In recent years the central teaching authority of the Catholic Church has issued important documents that echo the outlook of the Latin American church and use the expression "preferential option for the poor." John Paul II has used it repeatedly.[12] It is also to be found in the second Instruction of the Congregation for the Doctrine of the Faith on liberation theology (*Libertatis Conscientia*, 68). In addition, the extraordinary Synod of Bishops held in 1985 spoke as follows in its final report:

> Following the Second Vatican Council the church became more aware of its mission in the service of the poor, the oppressed, and the outcast. In this preferential option, which must not be understood as exclusive, the true spirit of the gospel shines forth. Jesus Christ declared the poor

blessed (Matt. 5:3; Luke 6:20), and he himself wished to be poor for us (2 Cor. 8:9).[13]

The experience and thinking of the Latin American church have undoubtedly played a very important role in this growth of consciousness.

At both ends of the spectrum of positions on these subjects, there are those who claim that the magisterium has been trying to substitute "preferential love" for "preferential option." It seems to me, however, that any doubt on this point has been removed by John Paul II's encyclical *Sollicitudo Rei Socialis*. Speaking of "characteristic themes and guidelines" of the magisterium in the recent years, the pope says:

> Here I would like to indicate one of them: the option or love of preference for the poor. This is an option or special form of primacy in the exercise of Christian charity to which the whole tradition of the church bears witness. It affects the life of the each Christian inasmuch as he or she seeks to imitate the life of Christ, but it applies equally to our social responsibilities and hence to our manner of living, and to the logical decisions to be made concerning the ownership and use of goods [*Sollicitudo Rei Socialis,* 42].

In the final analysis, an option for the poor is an option for the God of the kingdom whom Jesus proclaims to us; this is a point that I myself have developed and discussed in depth on various occasions.[14] The entire Bible, beginning with the story of Cain and Abel, mirrors God's predilection for the weak and abused of human history. This preference brings out the gratuitous or unmerited character of God's love. The same revelation is given in the evangelical Beatitudes, for they tell us with the utmost simplicity that God's predilection for the poor, the hungry, and the suffering is based on God's unmerited goodness to us.

The ultimate reason for commitment to the poor and oppressed is not to be found in the social analysis we use, or in human compassion, or in any direct experience we ourselves may have of poverty. These are all doubtless valid motives that play an important part in our commitment. As Christians, however, our commitment is grounded, in the final analysis, in the God of our faith. It is a theocentric, prophetic option that has its roots in the unmerited love of God and is demanded by this love. Bartolomé de Las Casas, who had direct experience of the terrible poverty and decimation of Latin American Amerindians, explained it by saying: "God has the freshest and keenest memory of the least and most forgotten."[15] The Bible has much to say to us about this divine remembering, as the works of J. Dupont, among others, have made clear to us.

This same perception was confirmed by the experience of the Christian communities of Latin America and reached Puebla via the document that the Peruvian bishops prepared for the CELAM meeting. Puebla asserted that simply because of God's love for them as manifested in Christ "the poor merit preferential attention, whatever may be the moral or personal situation in which they find themselves" (no. 1142). In other words, the poor deserve preference not because they are morally or religiously better than others, but because God is God, in whose eyes "the last are first." This statement clashes with our narrow understanding of justice; this very preference reminds us, therefore, that God's ways are not ours (see Isa. 55:8).

There have certainly been misunderstandings of the preferential option for the poor, as well as tendencies, sociological and spiritualist, to play it down, and this on the part both of those who claim to favor it and those who are expressly opposed to it. It can be said, nonetheless, that the option is now an essential element in the understanding that the church as a whole has of its task in the present world. This new approach is pregnant with consequences; it is also, we must say, only in its beginnings.

## THE ROLE OF REFLECTION

The rich, troubled, and creative life that the Latin American church is living as it tries to respond to the challenge set for it by the new presence of the poor calls for a deeper understanding of its own faith in the Lord Jesus. For a long time, as a result of a Latin American cultural tradition imposed by colonization, theology as practiced among us simply echoed the theology developed in Europe. Latin American theologians had recourse to European theology without any reference to its intellectual and historical context, with the result that their theology easily became a set of abstract propositions. Or else they made a painful effort to adapt European theology to a new reality, but were unable to explain the reasons for its themes and priorities or for the development of this kind of thinking, as long as the effort was undertaken in a North Atlantic framework.

The quest for models or guidelines outside itself was long characteristic of Latin American thinking, and indeed still is in some circles. But the urgency and rich resources of the commitment that many Christians were beginning to make to the process of popular liberation during the 1960s raised new questions based on Latin American reality, and they pointed to new and fruitful ways for theological discourse. Liberation theology is one manifestation of the adulthood that Latin American society, and the church as part of it, began to achieve in recent decades. Medellín took note of this coming of age and in turn made a major contribution to its historical significance and importance.

All this reminds us that this theological perspective is explicable only when seen in close conjunction with the life and commitments of Christian communities. This connection was present at the historical beginnings of liberation theology in the 1960s and is still fully operative today. It is the basis for the familiar distinction between the two phases of theological work: Christian life and reflection in the strict sense. The way in which a people lives its faith and hope and puts its love to work is the most important thing in God's eyes and is also, or ought to be, the most important in discourse about God and God's saving will.

I have already pointed out the important role played in Christian consciousness by the irruption of the poor into our history. In the development of liberation theology our awareness of this new presence has made us aware that our partners in dialogue are the poor, those who are "nonpersons"—that is, those who are not considered to be human beings with full rights, beginning with the right to life and to freedom in various spheres. Elsewhere, on the other hand, the best modern theology has been sensitive rather to the challenge posed by the mentality that asserted itself at the European Enlightenment; it is therefore responsive to the challenges posed by the nonbeliever or by Christians under the sway of modernity.

The distinction between these two approaches is not an attempt to juxtapose two theological perspectives. It tries only to be clear on their respective starting points, to see their differences, and then correctly to define relationships between the two. If we follow this line, we will avoid yielding to a tendency found in some academic settings: the tendency to regard liberation theology as the radical, political wing of European progressive theology. Such a view of liberation theology is clearly a caricature for anyone with a good knowledge of the subject. It is true, of course, that in a world of increasingly rapid communication it is not possible to do theology in a manner free of all contacts and influences; it is, however, both possible and necessary to be clear on the perduring basis and inspiration of our theological thinking. Only on that condition can there be dialogue among the various theologies that share a concern to speak of God in our day.

### The Life of a People

One of the first statements of my way of understanding the theological task was that liberation theology is "a critical reflection on Christian praxis in light of the word of God." The point of this was not to try to reduce the riches of a quest to a short definition, but rather to point out a path to be followed.

In many and very different ways the Bible shows us that the doing of God's will is the main demand placed on believers. Karl Barth echoed this thought when he said that "the true hearer of the word is the one who puts it into practice." In liberation theology I accepted this traditional datum of Christian revelation because I was moved by the witness of those who were beginning to commit themselves ever more fully to the process of freeing the poor from the various servitudes from which they suffer.

This commitment reflected the experience of the oppressed themselves, who were beginning to become the agents of their own destiny. During the 1950s and 60s we saw the first steps being taken in conscientization, and we saw the poor beginning to organize themselves in the defense of their right to life, in the struggle for dignity and social justice, and in a commitment to their own liberation. As a result, they were beginning to play a major active role that would become stronger with the passing years and that is still intensifying today amid advances and regressions. Many Christians played a part in this process. It is therefore wrong to say that theological thinking on liberation originated in the middle classes and that only years later did it open itself to the experience of the poor themselves. No, this experience played its part from the outset—at the level it had reached at that time. To be ignorant of this is to be mistaken about what happened at that time or even to give an explicitly false picture of it; the facts reject any such interpretation.

The praxis on which liberation theology reflects is a praxis of solidarity in the interests of liberation and is inspired by the gospel. It is the activity of "peacemakers"—that is, those who are forging shalom. Western languages translate this Hebrew word as "peace" but in doing so, diminish its meaning. Shalom in fact refers to the whole of life and, as part of this, to the need of establishing justice and peace. Consequently, a praxis motivated by evangelical values embraces to some extent every effort to bring about authentic fellow-ship and authentic justice. For faith shows us that in this commitment the grace of Christ plays its part, whether or not those who practice it are aware of this fact.

This liberating praxis endeavors to transform history in the light of the reign of God. It accepts the reign now, even though knowing that it will arrive in its fullness only at the end of time. In this practice of love, social aspects have an important place on a continent in which socio-economic structures are in the service of the powerful and work against the weak of society. But in my understanding of it, "praxis" is not reducible to "social aspects" in this narrow sense. The complexity of the world of the poor and lowly compels us to attend to other dimensions of Christian practice if it is to meet the requirements of a total love of God.

In saying this I am not trying to make the Christian commitment less demanding and radical, but only to bring out the breadth of vision and the courage needed if we are to enter into the world of the poor and respond to their varied aspirations for justice and freely given friendship. As I have traveled this road, I have learned much in recent years; various experiences of being a part of the world of the poor have brought me to a less theoretical knowledge of that world and to a greater awareness of simple but profoundly human aspects of it, apart from which there is no truly liberating commitment.[16] The struggles of those who reject racism and machismo (two attitudes so deeply rooted in the culture and custom of peoples and individuals), as well as of those who oppose the marginalization of the elderly, children, and other "unimportant" persons in our society, have made me see, for example, the importance of gestures and ways of "being with" that some may regard as having little political effective-ness.

In addition, the experience of these years has shown me that generous solidarity with the poor is not exempted from the temptation of imposing on them categories foreign to them and from the risk of dealing with them in an impersonal way. Sensitivity to these and other dangers is part of a human and Christian praxis whose truly liberating effects extend to those also who are trying to carry on such a praxis for the benefit of the poor and exploited. If there is no friendship with them and no sharing of the life of the poor, then there is no authentic commitment to liberation, because love exists only among equals. Any talk of liberation necessarily refers to a comprehensive process, one that embraces everyone. This is an insight that has been repeated again and again since the beginnings of liberation theology and that in my own case has become much more firmly established and has acquired a much greater importance with the passage of the years.

Christian life is commitment in the form of an acceptance of the gift of the reign of God. It is also, and necessarily, prayer. There is no life of faith that does not have its contemplative dimension. The Latin Americans who are struggling for justice are also persons who believe and hope. They are oppressed persons, but also Christians who, like Mary in her Magnificat, remember their obligations of thankfulness and of surrender to God in prayer.

This outlook is characteristic of the faith of our Latin Americans. They cultivate a form of prayer that the modern mind is likely to regard as primitive if not downright superstitious. But, although it is true that various factors play a part in this way of living the faith, it would be a serious mistake to stop at a superficial analysis and not to discern the profound sense of God that this prayer manifests in ways that are perhaps not very enlightened but that are not therefore any less legitimate. Deeply rooted as it is in this popular devotion, while also drawing nourishment from the wellspring of protest against repression and the demand for freedom, the prayer life of the Christian communities that are engaged in the process of liberation possesses great creativity and depth. Those who have claimed from time to time that Latin America has been losing the spirit of prayer have shown only that they themselves are remote from the everyday life of the poor and committed sectors of our peoples.

Those working at a theology of liberation in the Asian context have likewise tried to bring out the deeply contemplative side of that continent on which ancient and magnificent religions of the human race have left such a profound imprint. Aloysius Pieris, theologian of Sri Lanka, describes the Asian peoples as both poor and religious.[17] Both of these conditions point the way to a radical and complete liberation.[18] Meanwhile, black theology in the United States has drawn fruitfully on the liberating and religious perspectives that find expression in black music.[19] Theology done in the African context has likewise always been open to the cultural riches of the African peoples; religion is an essential element of this cultural treasure.

Prayer is a privileged way of being in communion with Christ and of "keeping all these things in our heart," as his mother did (see Luke 2:51). The Gospels tell us of various occasions when the Lord went apart to pray. Contemplation was an essential part of his life. At one of the most difficult times in his experience, he rebuked his disciples for having been unable to persevere with him during his final prayer, which had turned into a difficult struggle for him. Luke tells us that he was "in an agony" as he struggled for his life, so that his sweat "became like great drops of blood" (22:44-45). Our communion with the prayer of Jesus must reach this point of "agony"—that is, of combat (that is what the Greek word *agōnia* means). But this requirement is not difficult for those to understand who are putting their own lives on the line as they share the lot of the stripped and impoverished of Latin America.

Those, therefore, who adopt the liberation perspective must have the sensitivity that is needed for understanding and cultivating the celebratory and contemplative dimension of peoples who find in the God of their faith the source of their demand for life and dignity. Nothing could be further from my mind, however, than to defend in this context the kind of spiritualism that serves as a refuge from the troubles and sufferings of daily life. I am referring rather to the desire and determination to live simultaneously, and to the reciprocal enrichment of each, two pursuits that the Western mind often separates. The Western mind persistently applies this dichotomy in interpreting both the more spontaneously unified behavior of other peoples and cultures, and the theological efforts made in that context.

I am, of course, not speaking of syntheses that are fully successful and without defects, but rather of a process whereby one achieves a diversified presence that is open to a variety of experiences and that progresses only amid setbacks; that develops gradually and deploys creativity. It is a matter of honesty to recognize this fact, as well as of respect for those who bear this witness. We find ourselves, then, in the presence of a process that locates us at a point at which it is impossible to separate solidarity with the poor *and* prayer. This means that we are disciples of Christ, who is both God and a human being.

What we see here is an authentic spirituality—that is, a way of being Christian. It is from this rich experience of the following of Jesus that liberation theology emerges; the following constitutes the practice—at once commitment and prayer—on which liberation theology reflects. The increasing number of Latin American theological works on spirituality in recent years are not as it were an appendix to works on other themes; they represent rather a deeper penetration of the very wellspring from which this kind of theological thinking flows.

The work done on spirituality will help to develop, more than has hitherto been done, a traditional aspect of theology (one whose existence was acknowledged at an early date in the perspective I am adopting here)—namely, its function as wisdom. Discourse on faith is knowledge that brings with it a taste for its object; it is a spiritual tasting of the word of the Lord, and, as such, it nourishes our life and is the source of our joy.

In liberation theology the way to rational talk of God is located within a broader and more challenging course of action: the following of Jesus. Talk of God supposes that we are living in depth our condition as disciples of him who said in so many words that he is the Way (see John 14:6). This fact has led me to the position that in the final analysis the method for talking of God is supplied by our spirituality. In other words, the distinction of two phases in theological work is not simply an academic question; it is, above all, a matter of lifestyle, a way of living the faith. Being part of the life of our people, sharing their sufferings and joys, their concerns and their struggles, as well as the faith and hope that they live as a Christian community—all this is not a formality required if one is to do theology; it is a requirement for being a Christian. For that reason, it also feeds the very roots of a reflection that seeks to explain the God of life when death is all around.

### The Locus of Reflection

The historical womb from which liberation theology has emerged is the life of the poor and, in particular, of the Christian communities that have arisen within the bosom of the present-day Latin American church. This experience is the setting in which liberation theology tries to read the word of God and be alert to the challenges that faith issues to the historical process in which that people is engaged. Revelation and history, faith in Christ and the life of a people, eschatology and praxis: these are the factors that, when set in motion, give rise to what has been called the hermeneutical circle. The aim is to enter more deeply into faith in a God who became one of us, and to do so on the basis of the faith-filled experience and commitment of those who acknowledge this God as their liberator.[20]

The major challenges to which theology must respond will come, therefore, from the demands of the gospel as seen today in the development of an oppressed but Christian people. Since liberation theology is a critical reflection on the word of God received in the church, it will make explicit the values of faith, hope, and love that inspire the praxis of Christians. But it will also have to help in correcting possible deviations on the part of those who reject the demands for participation in history and the promotion of justice that follow from faith in the God of life, and also on the part of those who run the risk of forgetting central aspects of Christian life, because they are caught up in the demands of immediate political activity.

Because liberation theology takes a critical approach, it refuses to serve as a Christian justification of positions already taken. It seeks to show that unless we make an ongoing commitment to the poor, who are the privileged members of the reign of God, we are far removed from the Christian message. It also wants to help make the commitment to liberation increasingly evangelical, effective, and integral. Theology is at the service of the evangelizing mission of the Christian community; it develops therefore as an ecclesial function. Its task is one that locates it within the church, for it is there that it receives revelation and there that it is nourished by the charisms of prophecy, government, and teaching that reside in the church and guide its efforts.

It is clear from what I have been saying that when I call reflection in the strict sense a *second* stage of theological work, I am by no means saying that is *secondary*. Discourse about God comes second because faith comes first and is the source of theology; in the formula of St. Anselm, we believe in order that we may understand (*credo ut intelligam*). For the same reason, the effort at reflection has an irreplaceable role, but one that is always subordinate to a faith that is lived and receives guidance within the communion of the church.

The first stage or phase of theological work is the lived faith that finds expression in prayer and commitment. To live the faith means to put into practice, in the light of the demands of the reign of God, these fundamental elements of Christian existence. Faith is here lived "in the church" and geared to the communication of the Lord's message. The second act of theology, that of reflection in the proper sense of the term, has for its purpose to read this complex praxis in the light of God's word. There is need of discernment in regard to the concrete forms that Christian commitment takes, and this discernment is accomplished through recourse to the sources of revelation.[21] The ultimate norms of judgment come from the revealed truth that we accept by faith and not from praxis itself. But the "deposit of faith" is not a set of indifferent, catalogued truths; on the contrary, it lives in the church, where it rouses Christians to commitments in accordance with God's will and also provides criteria for judging them in the light of God's word.

For all these reasons, a principal task of "reflection on praxis in the light of faith" will be to strengthen the necessary and fruitful links between ortho-praxis and orthodoxy. The necessity of this circular relationship between the two is a point frequently underscored in liberation theology; as is always the case in dealing with essential dimensions of one and the same reality, it is not possible to accept the one and belittle the other. More than that, any attempt to focus on only one means the loss of both; orthopraxis and orthodoxy need one another, and each is adversely affected when sight is lost of the other.[22] The polemical manner in which this subject is sometimes treated (whether for or against the union of orthopraxis and orthodoxy) should not make one forget that fidelity to the message of Jesus requires one not to impoverish or mutilate it by choosing where no choice is possible. In a key passage of Mark's Gospel (8:27–33) he speaks in an incisive way of the necessity of this enriching circular relationship.[23] Theology as critical reflection must make its contribution to this profound unity.

Starting from Christian praxis (commitment and prayer), theology seeks to provide a language for speaking about God. It deals with a faith that is inseparable from the concrete conditions in which the vast majority and, in a sense, even all the inhabitants of Latin America live. Among us the great pastoral, and therefore theological, question is: How is it possible to tell the poor, who are forced to live in conditions that embody a denial of love, that God loves them? This is equivalent to asking: How can we find a way of talking about God amid the suffering and oppression that is the experience of the Latin American poor? How is it possible to do theology "while Ayacucho lasts"?[24] As the church, the assembly of the disciples of Jesus, we must proclaim his resurrection to a continent scarred by "inhuman" (Medellín, "Poverty," 1) and "antievangelical" (Puebla, 1159) poverty. As I said earlier, in the final analysis poverty means death. Liberation theology had its origin in the contrast between the urgent task of proclaiming the life of the risen Jesus and the conditions of death in which the poor of Latin America were living.

Theology done in such a setting has something in common with all theology: dialogue with the prevailing culture or, in our case, with the various cultures to be found in Latin America. This dialogue has barely begun, and it has a long way to go. In conducting it, we will be greatly helped if we adopt the view of theology as wisdom, which I mentioned above—that is, if we see theology as knowledge shot through with the "savored" experience first of God but then also of the people and culture to which we belong. In the contributions that I myself have been able to make to liberation theology, my frequent references to Felipe Guamán Poma de Ayala, César Vallejo, José Carlos Mariátegui, and José María Arguedas, among others, have had the purpose precisely of communicating some of this "savor." These men are all Peruvians who have experienced their own time in depth; they have been deeply involved in the sufferings and hopes of our peoples and have been able to express, as few others have, the soul of the nation, its Amerindians and mestizos. But, I repeat, this is an area in which far more remains to be done than has so far been accomplished.

This approach makes it urgent that we acquire a better understanding of our history. A people that knows the past that lies behinds its sufferings and hopes is in a better position to face and reflect on the present. Furthermore, we must learn from the attempts made to understand the faith by Christians who are able to face up intensely to their times and to appeal to the gospel with clarity and courage. These men and women try to see clearly amid the changes of history and, in many cases, try to oppose the interests of the powerful. I am thinking here of the witness given by many sixteenth-century missionaries who did not forget the demands of the kingdom of life when they were faced with cruel exploitation and death being inflicted on the Amerindians. Among those missionaries, Bartolomé de Las Casas was perhaps the one who saw most deeply into the situation and best articulated a theological reflection based on it. He was, however, only *primus inter pares,* for he had many companions who shared his commitment and his hope. The witness of all those persons should feed the life of the Christian community today, for it is one tributary of the great ecclesial tradition within which every sound theology is located.

Although theology is a language for communicating God, in every place it must display the inflections given it by those who formulate it and those to whom it is directed. Every language has a number of dialects. The language of Jesus the Nazarene (like that of Peter, his disciple, to whom they said: "Your accent betrays you": Matt. 26:73) undoubtedly showed him to be a native of Galilee and seemed odd to the inhabitants of Jerusalem. Our theological language is subject to the same rule; it takes its coloring from our peoples, cultures, and racial groupings, and yet we use it in an attempt to proclaim the universality of God's love. This accent may not be to the liking of those who until now have regarded themselves the proprietors of theology and are not conscious of their own accent (to which, of course, they have every right) when they speak of God.

This dialogue between faith and culture in Latin America is accompanied by another, which is different in character but highly important and derives its tone from the first. I am referring to the encounter in recent years of theologies springing from human contexts unlike our own. I mentioned earlier the dialogue between the theologies of the Third World, in which the theologies emerging from minorities in different countries all participate on an equal footing. But this further dialogue does not stop at the borders of the Third World. There have also been very profitable meetings with representatives of types of theological thinking that originate in Europe and North America. Then there is the encounter with the feminist perspective in theology and with the new and challenging contribution this is making.[25] My impression is that the deeper importance of this dialogue is to be found, not in the coming together of theologians, but in the communication established among Christian communities and their respective historical, social, and cultural contexts, for these communities are the real subjects who are actively engaged in these discourses of faith.

In my view, the fact that any understanding of the faith has its roots in the particularity of a given situation should not cause us to neglect the comparison of what we are doing with efforts being made at the level of the universal church. Particularity does not mean isolation. It is true, of course, that each type of theological thinking cannot, and ought not, be applied mechanically to situations different from that in which it arose; whence the foolishness of attempts to do just that with liberation theology, as if it resembled a pharmaceutical prescription. But it is no less true that any theology is discourse about a universal message. For this reason, and to the extent that it springs from an experience that is both deeply human and deeply Christian, every theology also has a universal significance; or, to put it more accurately, every theology is a question and challenge for believers living other human situations.

Authentic universality does not consist in speaking precisely the same language but rather in achieving a full understanding within the setting of each language. The book of the Acts of the Apostles tells us that the reason for the astonishment felt by the speakers of different languages who were gathered in Jerusalem on Pentecost was not that the apostles all spoke in a unique tongue but that "we hear, all of us in *our own native language*" (Act 2:6–8). The goal, then, is not uniformity but a profound unity, a communion or *koinōnia*. One element in this Christian *koinōnia* (which extends far beyond mere intellectual dialogue) is the understanding that the various forms of theology exist within a profound ecclesial communion and give a richly diversified expression to the truth proclaimed by the Only Son.

## FRIENDS OF LIFE

Christians are witnesses of the risen Christ. It is this testimony that calls us together in a permanent way as the church and at the same time is the very heart of the church's mission. The realization that life and not death has the final say about history is the source of the joy of believers, who experience thereby

God's unmerited love for them. To evangelize is to communicate this joy; it is to transmit, individually and as a community, the good news of God's love that has transformed our lives.

Theology is at the service of this proclamation of the reign of love and justice. Nothing human falls outside the purview of the reign, which is present in history and is transforming it, while also leading it beyond itself. Liberation theology made this perspective its starting point as it attempted to show the meaning of the proclamation of the gospel for the history of Latin America. This is indeed the most important point in this type of theological thinking— namely, that its major concern is with the proclamation of the gospel to the peoples of Latin America. This concern gave birth to it and continues to nourish its efforts.

The major achievement of the Latin American church from 1968 to 1988 was that it renewed with unwonted energy its mission of evangelization and, ultimately, of liberation. It is in this context that we must understand what the preferential option for the poor means. As a result, throughout Latin America (including sectors that used to regard themselves as estranged from the church) and on the international stage, the church has acquired a presence it never had before. Various factors have played a part in producing this result (which is in fact an ongoing process); one of them is liberation theology, which has in large measure articulated the way in which the Latin American Christian community now proclaims its message.

The witness given by Christians has, of course, inevitably elicited resistance and painful hostility. One thing is nonetheless certain: the commitment made by a church that is conscious of the necessity of proclaiming and building a peace based on justice for all, but especially for those who today suffer more from despoliation and mistreatment, has left its mark on the history of Latin America during these years. The Latin American church has made this commitment in many forms throughout the length and breadth of the region, and it has even begun to make its voice heard outside its own borders. Echoing the gospel itself, the Second Vatican Council called on the entire church to make such a commitment. It is the special characteristic of the Christian community that it goes out into the world to "make disciples of all nations" (Matt. 28:20) and is therefore never satisfied with successes already obtained. It must continually go out of itself and look forward in expectation of the Lord's coming.

### To Liberate = To Give Life

The historical process in which Latin America has been involved, and the experiences of many Christians in this process, led liberation theology to speak of salvation in Christ in terms of liberation. This approach meant listening to the "muted cry [that] wells up from millions of human beings, pleading with their pastors for a liberation that is nowhere to be found in their case" (Medellín, "Poverty," 2). Puebla added that this cry "might well have seemed muted back then" but today it is "loud and clear, increasing in volume and intensity, and at times full of menace" (no. 89). In speaking thus, the two episcopal conferences were displaying a manifest fidelity to the message of the God who acts in history to save a people by liberating it from every kind of servitude. Continuing in the line of Medellín and Puebla, Pope John Paul II addressed these strong and sensitive words to the bishops of Brazil: "The poor of this country, whose pastors you are, and the poor of this continent are the first to feel the urgent need of this *gospel of* radical and integral *liberation*. To conceal it would be to cheat them and let them down" (letter of April 1986; emphasis added).

The combination of these two factors—the message that is at the heart of biblical revelation, and the profound longing of the Latin American peoples—led us to speak of liberation in Christ and to make this the essential content of evangelization. Something similar has been happening in other sectors of the human race and in the Christian churches present in their midst. There is a longing for liberation that wells up from the inmost hearts of the poor and oppressed of this world and opens them to receive the saving love of God. This longing is a sign of the active presence of the Spirit. The various theologies of liberation to which I have referred are meeting the challenge and giving expression to the experience and its potentialities.

From the outset, liberation was seen as something comprehensive, an integral reality from which nothing is excluded, because only such an idea of it explains the work of him in whom all the promises are fulfilled (see 2 Cor. 1:20). For that reason I distinguished three levels or dimensions of liberation in Christ, and Puebla made the distinction its own (nos. 321-29). First, there is liberation from social situations of oppression and marginalization that force many (and indeed all in one or another way) to live in conditions contrary to God's will for their life. But it is not enough that we be liberated from oppressive socio-economic structures; also needed is a personal transformation by which we live with profound inner freedom in the face of every kind of servitude, and this is the second dimension or level of liberation.

Finally, there is liberation from sin, which attacks the deepest root of all servitude; for sin is the breaking of friendship with God and with other human beings, and therefore cannot be eradicated except by the unmerited redemptive love of the Lord whom we receive by faith and in communion with one another. Theological analysis (and not social or philosophical analysis) leads to the position that only liberation from sin gets to the very source of social injustice and other forms of human oppression and reconciles us with God and our fellow human beings.

This idea of total liberation was inspired by that of integral development that Paul VI set down in *Populorum Progressio* (no. 21). With the help of this concept the pope showed how it is possible, without confusing the various levels, to affirm the deeper unity of a process leading from less human to more human conditions. Among the "more human" conditions he listed "finally and above all: faith, a gift of God accepted by human good will, and unity in the charity of Christ, who calls us all to share as offspring in the life of the living God, the Father of all human beings."[26] The pope was obviously speaking of human possibilities in a broad sense, not disregarding the gratuitousness of faith and love.

There is no slightest tinge of immanentism in this approach to integral liberation. But if any expression I have used may have given the impression that there is, I want to say here as forcefully as I can that any interpretation along those lines is incompatible with my position. Moreover, my repeated emphasis (in my writings) on the gratuitousness of God's love as the first and last word in biblical revelation is reliable evidence for this claim. The saving, all-embracing love of God is what leads me to speak of history as profoundly one (in saying this, I am not forgetting the distinctions also to be found within history). What I want to say when I speak of history has been expressed with all desirable exactness by the Peruvian bishops:

> If we mean by the "history of salvation" not only those actions that are properly divine—creation, incarnation, redemption—but the actions of human beings as they respond to divine initiatives (either accepting them or rejecting them), then there is in fact only one history, for the uncertain endeavors of human beings, whether they like it or not, whether they even know it or not, have their place in the divine plan [*Documento sobre teología de la liberación,* October 1984].

History is, after all, the field where human beings attain to fulfillment as persons and in which, in the final analysis, they freely say yes or no to God's saving will.[27]

Liberation theology is thus intended as a theology of salvation. Salvation is God's unmerited action in history, which God leads beyond itself. It is God's gift of definitive life to God's children, given in a history in which we must build fellowship. Filiation and fellowship are both a grace and a task to be carried out; these two aspects must be distinguished without being separated, just as, in accordance with the faith of the church as definitively settled at the Council of Chalcedon, we distinguish in Christ a divine condition and a human condition, but we do not separate the two.

This christological truth enables us to determine what gives unity and what creates duality in the process of liberation—that is, in the saving work that God calls us to share. Puebla makes the distinction in carefully worded language at the end of its lengthy section on the three dimensions or levels of liberation:

> We are liberated by our participation in the new life brought to us by Jesus Christ, and by communion with him in the mystery of his death and resurrection. But this is true only on condition that we live out this mystery on the three planes described above, without focusing exclusively on any one of them. Only in this way will we avoid reducing the

mystery to the verticalism of a disembodied spiritual union with God, or
to the merely existential personalism of individual or small-group ties, or
to one or another form of social, economic, or political horizontalism
[no. 329].

The very complexity of the concept of liberation prevents us from reducing it to
only one of its aspects.

In this view of the matter, a key point—not always assigned its proper
value—is consideration of the "second level," that of human liberation. I
myself have always emphasized its necessity in my writings. This emphasis
reflected an effort to avoid the narrow approach taken to liberation when only
two levels, the political and the religious, are distinguished. The political and
the religious are certainly basic aspects of liberation, but exclusive attention to
them often led to a simple juxtaposition of them, thus impoverishing both, or
else to an identification of the two, thus perverting the meaning of both. From
the theological standpoint, emphasis on the mediation of aspects of the human
that are not reducible to the socio-political made it easier to think of the unity
of all the aspects without confusing them; it also made it possible to speak of
God's saving action as all-embracing and unmerited, without reducing it to a
purely human set of activities, as well as to interrelate the political and the
religious dimensions while also incorporating the needed ethical perspective.
Inertia, however, caused some to interpret the three dimensions distinguished
by liberation theology and later by Puebla in the more common, but theologically different, perspective: the relationship between only two of the levels or
dimensions.

In his Apostolic Exhortation *Evangelii Nuntiandi* Paul VI made this very
careful statement:

We must . . . say the following about the liberation that evangelization
proclaims and endeavors to bring about:

a) It cannot be limited purely and simply to the economic, social, and
cultural spheres but must concern the whole person in all dimensions,
including the relationship to an "absolute" and even to *the* Absolute,
which is God.

b) It is based, therefore, on *a conception of human nature*, an anthropology, which can never be sacrificed to the requirements of some
strategy or other, or to practice, or to short-term effectiveness.[28]

As a matter of fact, in the measure that we acquire a more complete vision of
the process of liberation, its humblest level—the second—helps us understand
better the process in the light of faith.

All that has been said shows that liberation, understood as an integral whole
(as it is in liberation theology and in the Medellín documents), is the central
theme of evangelization. It is at the heart of the Lord's saving work and of the
kingdom of life; it is what the God of the kingdom seeks.

### On the Way of Poverty and Martyrdom

It is general knowledge that, inspired by John XXIII, Cardinal Lercaro and other fathers of the Vatican Council wanted to make the evangelization of the poor the main focus of their discussions. A passage of the Constitution on the Church (*Lumen Gentium*), a document that bears witness to this desire, says that the church, like its founder, lives "in poverty and oppression" (no. 8). And one of the richest documents issued by the council says that the church, like its Lord, must walk the "way of poverty" (decree *Ad Gentes*, on the Missionary Activity of the Church, 5).

Living as it does in a part of the world marked by massive poverty and by the premature and unjust death of multitudes, the Latin American church made its own the outlook of Pope John and pleaded at Medellín that "the church in Latin America should be manifested, in an increasingly clear manner, as truly *poor, missionary, and paschal*, separate from all temporal power and courageously committed to the liberation of each and every person" ("Youth," 14, emphasis added).

Evangelizing means proclaiming, by word and action, that Christ has set us free, but evangelization is always an ecclesial task. The church must be a sign of the kingdom within human history. Medellín saw that the sign must take the form of being poor, missionary, and paschal. Puebla thought that what Medellín wanted was beginning to come about: "Bit by bit the church has been dissociating itself from those who hold economic or political power, freeing itself from various forms of dependence, and divesting itself of privileges" (no. 623).[29]

John XXIII, whom we can never forget, called the church "the church of the poor," and John Paul II has forcefully repeated the phrase on various occasions. The church is to be a poor church at the service of all, but paying special attention to the lowly of this world. The base-level ecclesial communities, which Paul VI greeted as "a real hope for the church" (*Evangelii Nuntiandi*, 58) and which Puebla described as "an important ecclesial event that is peculiarly ours" (no. 629), are a manifestation of the presence of the church of the poor in Latin America. These communities are a major source of vitality within the larger Christian community and have brought the gospel closer to the poor and the poor closer to the gospel—and not only the poor but, through them, all who are touched by the church's action, including those outside its boundaries.

This entrance into the world of the poor has had numerous consequences for the mission of the Latin American church. Among others, it has made it possible to discern new dimensions in the part to be played by the poor themselves in the work of evangelization and in meeting the challenges that this raises. This has been a foundational experience that has nourished reflection within the framework of liberation theology and to which Puebla referred in an often cited passage:

Commitment to the poor and oppressed and the rise of grassroots communities have helped the church to discover the evangelizing potential of the poor. For the poor challenge the church at all times, summoning it to conversion; and many of the poor incarnate in their lives the evangelical values of solidarity, service, simplicity, and openness to accepting the gift of God [no. 1147].

On the other hand, if we view the church as the people of God—that is, as the sum total of Christians—we must acknowledge that the effort to see the Lord's features in the faces of the Latin American poor (see Puebla, 31–40) has also brought difficulties within the church itself. Some have felt their interests adversely affected by the challenges the bishops have issued, and they have tried to draw a curtain of silence around these alerts. Others have gone further: from their positions of power they have openly violated the human rights defended in the documents of the church and have struck hard at Christians who were trying to express their solidarity with the poor and oppressed. These latter cases have led bishops (in Paraguay, Brazil, and Chile, for example) to adopt means not often used in our day, such as the excommunication of those who claimed to be Christians but disrespected the most basic demands of the gospel message.

Others have claimed to be in solidarity with the poor and oppressed but have acted impetuously, not respecting their slower pace or making them uneasy, and have therefore often met with rejection.

The various forms of de facto opposition are typical in periods of difficulty and change. At such times it becomes even more urgent to try to strengthen the unity that is the church's fundamental vocation. Such is the commandment and prayer of the Lord: that we may be one as the Father and the Son are one with each other and in us, in a unity that we must live out while not withdrawing from a world in which the forces of evil tend to divide us (see John 17). This communion—common union—is at once a gift of God and a task set for us.

The growing solidarity of the Latin American church with the poor and oppressed has at times raised concerns about the religious outlook at work in this movement. Is this commitment causing the church to lose its identity? The matter is important because the preservation of identity by each partner in a dialogue is undoubtedly an indispensable condition for the authenticity of dialogue itself. The church's raison d'être is to be found in the mission that Christ gave it: the mission of preaching the gospel. Only if the church maintains this identity can it engage in a dialogue that is fruitful for salvation.

Today, perhaps more than at other periods, certain tendencies within the church make it necessary to strengthen our ecclesial identity in fidelity to the Lord and in the determination to serve those to whom we preach the word. But a proper involvement in the world of the poor by no means detracts from the church's mission; rather in such involvement the church finds its full identity as a sign of the reign of God to which all human beings are called but in which the lowly and the "unimportant" have a privileged place. Solidarity with the poor does not weaken the church's identity but strengthens it. Paul VI gave memorable expression to this truth in his address at the close of the council, when he answered criticisms of its alleged excessive humanism.[30]

It is true, however, that we must pay a high price for being an authentic church of the poor. I am referring not to the cost entailed in the manner of life and action proper to the church, but to that inflicted by the hostile reactions that the church meets in its work. In present-day Latin America this means frequent attacks on the church and its representatives and, more concretely, the determination to hamper their mission, undermine their reputation, violate their personal freedom, deny them the right to live in their own country, and make attempts against their physical integrity, even to the point of assassination. The experience of the cross marks the daily life of many Christians in Latin America.

The murder of Archbishop Oscar Romero was undoubtedly a milestone in the life of the Latin American church. This great bishop risked his life in his Sunday homilies (the same was true of Bishop Angelelli in Argentina) and in interventions that responded to First World pressures by continually calling for a peace founded on justice. He received several death threats. The murder of six priests in El Salvador during the preceding years was already a warning close to home. A month before his own death he said with reference to those in power in his country: "Let them not use violence to silence those of us who are making this demand; let them not continue killing those of us who are trying to bring about a just distribution of power and wealth in our country." Calmly and courageously he continued: "I speak in the first person because this week I received a warning that I am on the list of those to be eliminated next week. But it is certain that no one can kill the voice of justice."

He died—they killed him—for bearing witness to the God of life and to his predilection for the poor and the oppressed. It was because he believed in this God that he uttered an anguished, demanding cry to the Salvadoran army: "In the name of God and of this suffering people whose wailing mounts daily to heaven, I ask and beseech you, I order you: stop the repression!" The next evening his blood sealed the covenant he had made with God, with his people, and with his church. Martyrdom (in the broad sense of the term) is the final accomplishment of life; in this case, it was a concrete gesture toward the poor and thereby an utterly free encounter with the Lord.

Those who have given and are now giving their lives for the gospel demonstrate the consistency that the gospel demands. The Apostle St. James (1:8 and 4:8) warns us against the danger of being "double-minded" (*dipsychos*)—that is, of speaking in one way and acting in another. What brought Jesus to his death, and is bringing his present-day followers to their death, is precisely the coherence of message and commitment. It has traditionally been said that the church is enriched by the blood of the martyrs; the present vitality, amid distress, of the people of God in Latin America is due in great part to the same experience.

The testimony given by martyrdom shows clearly how ignoble are the maneuverings of the powerful, their accusations, and their fears, and how far removed from the gospel they are. The men and women—and there are many of them today in Latin America—who bear witness to their faith in the resurrection of the Lord are proof that they who sow death will depart empty-handed and that only they who defend life have their hands filled with history.

## CONCLUSION

In speaking of liberation theology I have been referring to a vast movement now to be found in various parts of the world. The longing for liberation from every form of servitude (which John Paul II has once again called "something noble and legitimate": *Sollicitudo Rei Socialis*, 46), as well as the active presence of the gospel in Christians who share this longing, have given rise to a quest and a praxis; these in turn are the soil in which is rooted an understanding of the faith at the service of the church's mission of evangelization.

Twenty years after the beginning of liberation theology in Latin America and, more importantly, twenty years after the decisive event of Medellín, new challenges face us. This is the best reason for deepening our fidelity to the God of life, to the church that is called to be a sign of the reign of God, and to the oppressed who are struggling for their liberation. In his letter to the bishops of Brazil (April 1986) John Paul II said:

Liberation theology is not only timely but useful and necessary. It should be seen as a new stage, closely connected with earlier ones, in the theological reflection that began with the apostolic tradition and has continued in the great fathers and doctors, the ordinary and extraordinary exercise of the church's teaching office, and, more recently, the rich patrimony of the church's social teaching as set forth in documents from *Rerum Novarum* to *Laborem Exercens*.

Liberation theology is in fact "a new stage" and, as such, strives to be in continuity with the teaching of the church. This theology, in my understanding of it, does indeed seek to be "closely connected" with the church's teaching. In my opinion, its power and importance are due to a *freshness* or newness that derives from attention to the historical vicissitudes of our peoples, for these are authentic signs of the times through which the Lord continually speaks to us. At the same time, its power and importance are due to the *continuity* that leads it to sink its roots deep in scripture, tradition, and the magisterium. These factors play a determining role in the continuing evolution of a theology that aims at being "a reflection on praxis in the light of faith." I have been discussing this evolution in the preceding pages, and it is within it that I locate myself.

In connection with the fifth centenary of the coming of the gospel to these lands, John Paul II has spoken of the need for "a new evangelization." The expression has far-reaching implications. The preaching of the reign of God is always something new, just as the commandment of love which Christ left us is continually new (see John 13:34). But there are many other reasons for speaking of a renewed evangelization in Latin America. The cumulative experience and reflections of the last few decades can serve as a springboard capable of giving a major impetus to this task.

One of the great achievements of these years has been the vital presence of the gospel in our midst. The change begun at Medellín and ratified at Puebla gave many a new vision of the church in Latin America. Despite our tremendous problems and the especially painful conditions in which the vast majority of Latin Americans live, it can be asserted that the Christian community in Latin America is experiencing a fruitful and vital period, a period that is certainly not any easy one to deal with but that is heavy with promise. It is therefore cause for concern, and sometimes for anguish, to see the resistances and hostilities of some among us to the most fruitful trends in pastoral practice and in theology.

The challenges we face in Latin America are, of course, very great, and the changes needed are radical, even within the church. That is why Puebla several times called for the conversion of all Christians and of the church as a whole in face of the poverty prevalent throughout the region (see part 4, chapter 1, "A Preferential Option for the Poor"). We must nevertheless face our new situations with faith and love; according to the Bible, fear is the opposite of both. In the Gospels the words "Have no fear" are a response to a "man of little faith" (Matt. 14:26–31). St. John, for his part, tells us that where there is love there is no fear (1 John 4:18).

I am not saying that we should urge imprudence and thoughtlessness, but only that we should be convinced that the Spirit will lead us to the whole truth (see John 16:13). His presence is visible in the new face of the Christian community in Latin America: the face of a church that is poor, missionary, and paschal. We would betray and sin against the Spirit if we were to lose what has been gained in these years by Latin American Christians and non-Christians.

John XXIII has left a standard in this area, one that cannot be bettered. In a passage that reflects his strong sense of the God who "makes all things new" (Rev. 21:5) and his deep spirit of hope, the pope said with crystal clarity:

> Today more than ever, certainly more than in previous centuries, we are called to serve humankind as such, and not merely Catholics; to defend above all and everywhere the rights of the human person, and not merely those of the Catholic Church. Today's world, the needs made plain in the last fifty years, and a deeper understanding of doctrine have brought us to a new situation, as I said in my opening speech to the Council. It is not that the Gospel has changed: it is that we have begun to understand it better. Those who have lived as long as I have were faced with new tasks in the social order at the start of the century; those who, like me, were twenty years in the East and eight in France, were enabled to compare different cultures and traditions, and know that the moment has come to

discern the signs of the times, to seize the opportunity and to expand the view.[31]

To expand our view—beyond our little world, our ideas and discussions, our interests, our hard times, and—why not say it?—beyond our reasons and legitimate rights. The church in Latin America must combine its forces and not wear itself out in discussions from which it derives little strength. In this way it will be able to "seize the opportunity" for a new evangelization to be carried on in solidarity with all, beginning with the poorest and least important in our midst. To this end we must hear the Lord speaking to us in the signs of the times; they call for interpretation but, more than anything else, they call for a commitment to others that will make us friends of him who is "the friend of wisdom" (Wisd. 11:26).

Allow me to end with a personal story. Some years ago, a journalist asked whether I would write *A Theology of Liberation* today as I had two decades earlier. In answer I said that though the years passed by, the book remained the same, whereas I was alive and therefore changing and moving forward thanks to experiences, to observations made on the book, and to lectures and discussions. When he persisted, I asked whether in a love letter to his wife today he would use the same language he used twenty years ago; he said he would not, but he acknowledged that his love perdured. My book is a love letter to God, to the church, and to the people to which I belong. Love remains alive, but it grows deeper and changes its manner of expression.

LIMA
FEBRUARY 1988

*—Translated by Matthew J. O'Connell*

# A THEOLOGY
# OF LIBERATION

# PART 1

# THEOLOGY AND LIBERATION

Theology and liberation are terms subject to a variety of interpretations. In order to present our study properly and clearly, we must examine critically the notion of theology which we will use throughout. Likewise, it is necessary to determine, at least in rough outline, what it is we understand by liberation. As we progress, various shades of meaning and deeper levels of understanding will complement this initial effort.

*Chapter One*

# THEOLOGY:
# A CRITICAL REFLECTION

Theological reflection—that is, the understanding of the faith—arises spontaneously and inevitably in the believer, in all those who have accepted the gift of
the Word of God. Theology is intrinsic to a life of faith seeking to be authentic
and complete and is, therefore, essential to the common consideration of this
faith in the ecclesial community. There is present in *all believers*—and more so
in every Christian community—a rough outline of a theology. There is present
an effort to understand the faith, something like a pre-understanding of that
faith which is manifested in life, action, and concrete attitude. It is on this
foundation, and only because of it, that the edifice of theology—in the precise
and technical sense of the term—can be erected. This foundation is not merely
a jumping-off point, but the soil into which theological reflection stubbornly
and permanently sinks its roots and from which it derives its strength.[1]

But the focus of theological work, in the strict sense of the term, has
undergone many transformations throughout the history of the Church.
"Bound to the role of the Church, theology is dependent upon its historical
development," writes Christian Duquoc.[2] Moreover, as Congar observed recently, this evolution has accelerated to a certain extent in recent years: "The
theological work has changed in the past twenty-five years."[3]

## THE CLASSICAL TASKS OF THEOLOGY

Theological study has fulfilled different functions throughout the history of
the Christian community, but this does not necessarily mean that any of these
different approaches has today been definitively superseded. Although expressed in different ways, the essential effort to understand the faith has
remained. Moreover, the more penetrating and serious efforts have yielded
decisive gains, opening paths along which all subsequent theological reflection
must travel. In this perspective it is more accurate to speak of permanent
tasks—although they have emerged at different moments in the history of the

3

Church—than of historically successive stages of theology. Two of these functions are considered classical: theology as wisdom and theology as rational knowledge.

### Theology as Wisdom

In the early centuries of the Church, what we now term theology was closely linked to the spiritual life.[4] It was essentially a meditation on the Bible,[5] geared toward spiritual growth. Distinctions were made between the "beginners," the faithful, and the "advanced," who sought perfection.[6] This theology was above all monastic and therefore characterized by a spiritual life removed from worldly concerns;[7] it offered a model for every Christian desirous of advancing along the narrow path of sanctity and seeking a life of spiritual perfection.

Anxious to dialogue with the thought of its time, this theology used Platonic and Neoplatonic categories. In these philosophies it found a metaphysics which stressed the existence of a higher world and the transcendence of an Absolute from which everything came and to which everything returned.[8] The present life, on the other hand, was regarded as essentially contingent and was not valued sufficiently.

It is important to remember, however, that at this same time the reflections of the Greek Fathers on the theology of the world—cosmos and history—go well beyond a mere personal spiritual meditation and place theology in a wider and more fruitful context.

Around the fourteenth century, a rift appears between theologians and masters of the spiritual life. This division can be seen, for example, in such books as *The Imitation of Christ*, which has made a deep impact upon Christian spirituality during past centuries. We are suffering from this dichotomy even today, although it is true that Biblical renewal and the need to reflect upon lay spirituality are providing us with the broad outlines of what might be considered a new spiritual theology.[9]

The spiritual function of theology, so important in the early centuries and later regarded as parenthetical, constitutes, nevertheless, a permanent dimension of theology.[10]

### Theology as Rational Knowledge

From the twelfth century on, theology begins to establish itself as a science: "The transition has been made from *sacra pagina* to *theologia* in the modern sense which Abelard . . . was the first to use."[11] The process culminated with Albert the Great and Thomas Aquinas. On the basis of Aristotelian categories, theology was classified as a "subaltern science."[12] St. Thomas's view, nevertheless, was broad and synthetical: theology is not only a science, but also wisdom flowing from the charity which unites a person to God.[13] But this balance is lost when the above-mentioned separation appears between theology and spirituality in the fourteenth century.

The Thomistic idea of science is unclear today because it does not correspond to the definition generally accepted by the modern mind. But the essential feature of St. Thomas Aquinas's work is that theology is an intellectual discipline, born of the meeting of faith and reason.[14] From this point of view, therefore, it is more accurate to regard the theological task not as a science, but as rational knowledge.

The function of theology as rational knowledge is also permanent—insofar as it is a meeting between faith and reason, not exclusively between faith and any one philosophy, nor even between faith and philosophy in general. Reason has, especially today, many other manifestations than philosophical ones. The understanding of the faith is also following along new paths in our day: the social, psychological, and biological sciences. The social sciences, for example, are extremely important for theological reflection in Latin America. Theological thought not characterized by such a rationality and disinterestedness would not be truly faithful to an understanding of the faith.

But it is well to remember, especially with respect to the outdated views which still persist in some quarters, that in Scholastic theology after the thirteenth century there is a degradation of the Thomistic concept of theology.[15] There arises at that time, regardless of outward appearances, a very different way of approaching the theological task. The demands of rational knowledge will be reduced to the need for systematization and clear exposition.[16] Scholastic theology will thus gradually become, especially after the Council of Trent, an ancillary discipline of the magisterium of the Church. Its function will be "(1) to define, present, and explain revealed truths; (2) to examine doctrine, to denounce and condemn false doctrines, and to defend true ones; (3) to teach revealed truths authoritatively."[17]

In summary, theology is of necessity both spirituality and rational knowledge. These are permanent and indispensable functions of all theological thinking. However, both functions must be salvaged, at least partially, from the division and deformations they have suffered throughout history. A reflective outlook and style especially must be retained, rather than one or another specific achievement gained in a historical context different from ours.

## THEOLOGY AS CRITICAL REFLECTION ON PRAXIS

The function of theology as critical reflection on praxis has gradually become more clearly defined in recent years, but it has its roots in the first centuries of the Church's life. The Augustinian theology of history which we find in *The City of God,* for example, is based on a true analysis of the signs of the times and the demands with which they challenge the Christian community.

### Historical Praxis

For various reasons the existential and active aspects of the Christian life have recently been stressed in a different way than in the immediate past.

In the first place, *charity* has been fruitfully rediscovered as the center of the Christian life. This has led to a more Biblical view of the faith as an act of trust, a going out of one's self, a commitment to God and neighbor, a relationship with others.[18] It is in this sense that St. Paul tells us that faith works through charity: love is the nourishment and the fullness of faith, the gift of one's self to the Other, and invariably to others. This is the foundation of the *praxis* of Christians, of their active presence in history. According to the Bible, faith is the total human response to God, who saves through love.[19] In this light, the understanding of the faith appears as the understanding not of the simple affirmation—almost memorization—of truths, but of a commitment, an over-all attitude, a particular posture toward life.

In a parallel development, Christian *spirituality* has seen a significant evolu-tion. In the early centuries of the Church there emerged the primacy, almost exclusiveness, of a certain kind of contemplative life, hermitical, monastic, characterized by withdrawal from the world, and presented as the model way to sanctity. About the twelfth century the possibility of sharing contemplation by means of preaching and other forms of apostolic activity began to be considered. This point of view was exemplified in the mixed life (contemplative and active) of the mendicant orders and was expressed in the formula: *contem-plata aliis tradere* ("to transmit to others the fruits of contemplation").[20] Viewed historically this stage can be considered as a transition to Ignatian spirituality, which sought a difficult but fruitful synthesis between contempla-tion and action: *in actione contemplativus* ("contemplative in action").[21] This process, strengthened in recent years by the search for a spirituality of the laity, culminates today in the studies on the religious value of the profane and in the spirituality of the activity of the Christian in the world.[22]

Moreover, today there is a greater sensitivity to the *anthropological aspects* of revelation.[23] The Word about God is at the same time a promise to the world. In revealing God to us, the Gospel message reveals us to ourselves in our situation before the Lord and with other humans. The God of Christian revelation is a God incarnate, hence the famous comment of Karl Barth regarding Christian anthropocentrism, "Man is the measure of all things, since God became man."[24] All this has caused the revaluation of human presence and activity in the world, especially in relation to other human beings. On this subject Congar writes: "Seen as a whole, the direction of theological thinking has been characterized by a transference away from attention to the being *per se* of supernatural realities, and toward attention to their relationship with man, with the world, and with the problems and the affirmations of all those who for us represent the *Others*."[25] There is no *horizontalism* in this ap-proach.[26] It is simply a question of the rediscovery of the indissoluble unity of humankind and God.[27]

On the other hand, *the very life of the Church* appears ever more clearly as a *locus theologicus*. Regarding the participation of Christians in the important social movements of their time, Chenu wrote insightfully more than thirty years ago: "They are active *loci theologici* for the doctrines of grace, the

Incarnation, and the redemption, as expressly promulgated and described in detail by the papal encyclicals. They are poor theologians who, wrapped up in their manuscripts and scholastic disputations, are not open to these amazing events, not only in the pious fervor of their hearts but formally in their science; there is a theological datum and an extremely fruitful one, in the *presence* of the Spirit."[28] The so-called new theology attempted to adopt this posture some decades ago. The fact that the life of the Church is a source for all theological analysis has been recalled to mind often since then. The Word of God gathers and is incarnated in the community of faith, which gives itself to the service of all.

Vatican Council II has strongly reaffirmed the idea of a Church of service and not of power. This is a Church which is not centered upon itself and which does not "find itself" except when it "loses itself," when it lives "the joys and the hopes, the griefs and the anxieties of persons of this age" (*Gaudium et spes*, no. 1). All of these trends provide a new focus for seeing the presence and activity of the Church in the world as a starting point for theological reflection.

What since John XXIII and Vatican Council II began to be called a theology of the *signs of the times*[29] can be characterized along the same lines, although this takes a step beyond narrow ecclesial limits. It must not be forgotten that the signs of the times are not only a call to intellectual analysis. They are above all a call to pastoral activity, to commitment, and to service. Studying the signs of the times includes both dimensions. Therefore, *Gaudium et spes*, no. 44, points out that discerning the signs of the times is the responsibility of every Christian, especially pastors and theologians, to hear, distinguish, and interpret the many voices of our age, and to judge them in the light of the divine Word. In this way, revealed truths can always be more deeply penetrated, better understood, and set forth to greater advantage. Attributing this role to every member of the People of God and singling out the pastors—charged with guiding the activity of the Church—highlights the call to commitment which the signs of the times imply. Necessarily connected with this consideration, the function of theologians will be to afford greater clarity regarding this commitment by means of intellectual analysis. (It is interesting to note that the inclusion of theologians in the above-mentioned text met opposition during the conciliar debates.)

Another factor, this time of a *philosophical* nature, reinforces the importance of human action as the point of departure for all reflection. The philosophical issues of our times are characterized by new relationships of humankind with nature, born of advances in science and technology. These new bonds affect the awareness that persons have of themselves and of their active relationships with others.

Maurice Blondel, moving away from an empty and fruitless spirituality and attempting to make philosophical speculation more concrete and alive, presented it as a critical reflection on action. This reflection attempts to understand the internal logic of an action through which persons seek fulfillment by constantly transcending themselves.[30] Blondel thus contributed to the elaboration of a new *apologetics* and became one of the most important thinkers of contemporary theology, including the most recent trends.

To these factors can be added the influence of *Marxist thought*, focusing on praxis and geared to the transformation of the world.[31] The Marxist influence began to be felt in the middle of the nineteenth century, but in recent times its cultural impact has become greater. Many agree with Sartre that "Marxism, as the formal framework of all contemporary philosophical thought, cannot be superseded."[32] Be that as it may, contemporary theology does in fact find itself in direct and fruitful confrontation with Marxism, and it is to a large extent due to Marxism's influence that theological thought, searching for its own sources, has begun to reflect on the meaning of the transformation of this world and human action in history.[33] Further, this confrontation helps theology to perceive what its efforts at understanding the faith receive from the historical praxis of humankind in history as well as what its own reflection might mean for the transformation of the world.

Finally, the rediscovery of the *eschatological dimension* in theology has also led us to consider the central role of historical praxis. Indeed, if human history is above all else an opening to the future, then it is a task, a political occupation, through which we orient and open ourselves to the gift which gives history its transcendent meaning: the full and definitive encounter with the Lord and with other humans. "To do the truth," as the Gospel says, thus acquires a precise and concrete meaning in terms of the importance of action in Christian life. Faith in a God who loves us and calls us to the gift of full communion with God and fellowship with others not only is not foreign to the transformation of the world; it leads necessarily to the building up of that fellowship and communion in history. Moreover, only by doing this truth will our faith be "verified," in the etymological sense of the word. From this notion has recently been derived the term *orthopraxis*, which still disturbs the sensitivities of some. The intention, however, is not to deny the meaning of *orthodoxy*, understood as a proclamation of and reflection on statements considered to be true. Rather, the goal is to balance and even to reject the primacy and almost exclusiveness which doctrine has enjoyed in Christian life and above all to modify the emphasis, often obsessive, upon the attainment of an orthodoxy which is often nothing more than fidelity to an obsolete tradition or a debatable interpretation. In a more positive vein, the intention is to recognize the work and importance of concrete behavior, of deeds, of action, of praxis in the Christian life.[34] "And this, it seems to me, has been the greatest transformation which has taken place in the Christian conception of existence," said Edward Schillebeeckx in an interview. "It is evident that thought is also necessary for action. But the Church has for centuries devoted its attention to formulating truths and meanwhile did almost nothing to better the world. In other words, the Church focused on orthodoxy and left orthopraxis in the hands of nonmembers and nonbelievers."[35]

In the last analysis, this concern for praxis seeks to avoid the practices which gave rise to Bernanos' sarcastic remark: "God does not choose the same ones to keep his Word as to fulfill it."[36]

### Critical Reflection

All the factors we have considered have been responsible for a more accurate understanding that communion with the Lord inescapably means a Christian life centered around a concrete and creative commitment of service to others. They have likewise led to the rediscovery or explicit formulation of the function of theology as critical reflection. It would be well at this point to define further our terms.

Theology must be critical reflection on humankind, on basic human principles. Only with this approach will theology be a serious discourse, aware of itself, in full possession of its conceptual elements. But we are not referring exclusively to this epistemological aspect when we talk about theology as critical reflection. We also refer to a clear and critical attitude regarding economic and socio-cultural issues in the life and reflection of the Christian community. To disregard these is to deceive both oneself and others. But above all, we intend this term to express the theory of a definite practice. Theological reflection would then necessarily be a criticism of society and the Church insofar as they are called and addressed by the Word of God; it would be a critical theory, worked out in the light of the Word accepted in faith and inspired by a practical purpose—and therefore indissolubly linked to historical praxis.[37]

By preaching the Gospel message, by its sacraments, and by the charity of its members, the Church proclaims and shelters the gift of the Kingdom of God in the heart of human history."[38] The Christian community professes a "faith which works through charity." It is—at least ought to be—real charity, action, and commitment to the service of others. Theology is reflection, a critical attitude. Theology *follows*; it is the second step.[39] What Hegel used to say about philosophy can likewise be applied to theology: it rises only at sundown. The pastoral activity of the Church does not flow as a conclusion from theological premises. Theology does not produce pastoral activity; rather it reflects upon it. Theology must be able to find in pastoral activity the presence of the Spirit inspiring the action of the Christian community.[40]

A privileged *locus theologicus* for understanding the faith will be the life, preaching, and historical commitment of the Church.[41]

To reflect upon the presence and action of the Christian in the world means, moreover, to go beyond the visible boundaries of the Church. This is of prime importance. It implies openness to the world, gathering the questions it poses, being attentive to its historical transformations. In the words of Congar, "If the Church wishes to deal with the real questions of the modern world and to attempt to respond to them, . . . it must open as it were a new chapter of theologico-pastoral epistemology. Instead of using only revelation and tradition as starting points, as classical theology has generally done, it must start with facts and questions derived from the world and from history."[42] It is precisely this opening to the totality of human history that allows theology to fulfill its critical function vis-à-vis ecclesial praxis without narrowness.

This critical task is indispensable. Reflection in the light of faith must constantly accompany the pastoral action of the Church. By keeping historical events in their proper perspective, theology helps safeguard society and the Church from regarding as permanent what is only temporary. Critical reflection thus always plays the inverse role of an ideology which rationalizes and justifies a given social and ecclesial order. On the other hand, theology, by pointing to the sources of revelation, helps to orient pastoral activity; it puts it in a wider context and so helps it to avoid activism and immediatism. Theology as critical reflection thus fulfills a liberating function for humankind and the Christian community, preserving them from fetishism and idolatry, as well as from a pernicious and belittling narcissism. Understood in this way, theology has a necessary and permanent role in liberation from every form of religious alienation—which is often fostered by the ecclesiastical institution itself when it impedes an authentic approach to the Word of the Lord.

As critical reflection on society and the Church, theology is an understanding which both grows and, in a certain sense, changes. If the commitment of the Christian community in fact takes different forms throughout history, the understanding which accompanies the vicissitudes of this commitment will be constantly renewed and will take untrodden paths. A theology which has as its points of reference only "truths" which have been established once and for all—and not the Truth which is also the Way—can be only static and, in the long run, sterile. In this sense the often-quoted and misinterpreted words of Bouillard take on new validity: "A theology which is not up-to-date is a false theology."[43]

Finally, theology thus understood, that is to say as linked to praxis, fulfills a prophetic function insofar as it interprets historical events with the intention of revealing and proclaiming their profound meaning. According to Cullmann, this is the meaning of the prophetic role: "The prophet does not limit himself as does the fortune-teller to isolated revelations, but his prophecy becomes preaching, proclamation. He explains to the people the true meaning of all events; he informs them of the plan and will of God at the particular moment."[44] But if theology is based on this observation of historical events and contributes to the discovery of their meaning, it is with the purpose of making Christians' commitment within them more radical and clear. Only with the exercise of the prophetic function understood in this way, will the theologian be—to borrow an expression from Antonio Gramsci—a new kind of "organic intellectual."[45] Theologians will be personally and vitally engaged in historical realities with specific times and places. They will be engaged where nations, social classes, and peoples struggle to free themselves from domination and oppression by other nations, classes, and peoples. In the last analysis, the true interpretation of the meaning revealed by theology is achieved only in historical praxis. "The hermeneutics of the Kingdom of God," observed Schillebeeckx, "consists especially in making the world a better place. Only in this way will I be able to discover what the Kingdom of God means."[46] We have here a political hermeneutics of the Gospel.[47]

## CONCLUSION

Theology as a critical reflection on Christian praxis in the light of the Word does not replace the other functions of theology, such as wisdom and rational knowledge; rather it presupposes and needs them. But this is not all. We are not concerned here with a mere juxtaposition. The critical function of theology necessarily leads to redefinition of these other two tasks. Henceforth, wisdom and rational knowledge will more explicitly have ecclesial praxis as their point of departure and their context. It is in reference to this praxis that an understanding of spiritual growth based on Scripture should be developed, and it is through this same praxis that faith encounters the problems posed by human reason. Given the theme of the present work, we will be especially aware of this critical function of theology with the ramifications suggested above. This approach will lead us to pay special attention to the life of the Church and to commitments which Christians, impelled by the Spirit and in communion with others, undertake in history. We will give special consideration to participation in the process of liberation, an outstanding phenomenon of our times, which takes on special meaning in the so-called Third World countries.

This kind of theology, arising from concern with a particular set of issues, will perhaps give us the solid and permanent albeit modest foundation for the *theology in a Latin American perspective* which is both desired and needed. This Latin American focus would not be due to a frivolous desire for originality, but rather to a fundamental sense of historical efficacy and also—why hide it?—to the desire to contribute to the life and reflection of the universal Christian community. But in order to make our contribution, this desire for universality—as well as input from the Christian community as a whole—must be present from the beginning. To concretize this desire would be to overcome particularistic tendencies—provincial and chauvinistic—and produce something *unique*, both particular and universal, and therefore fruitful.[48]

"The only future that theology has, one might say, is to become the theology of the future," Harvey Cox has said.[49] But this theology of the future must necessarily be a critical appraisal of historical praxis, of the historical task in the sense we have attempted to sketch. Moltmann says that theological concepts "do not limp after reality . . . . They illuminate reality by displaying its future."[50] In our approach, to reflect critically on the praxis of liberation is to "limp after" reality. The present in the praxis of liberation, in its deepest dimension, is pregnant with the future; hope must be an inherent part of our present commitment in history. Theology does not initiate this future which exists in the present. It does not create the vital attitude of hope out of nothing. Its role is more modest. It interprets and explains these as the true underpinnings of history. To reflect upon a forward-directed action is not to concentrate on the past. It does not mean being the caboose of the present. Rather it is to penetrate the present reality, the movement of history, that which is driving history toward the future. To reflect on the basis of the historical praxis of liberation is to reflect in the light of the future which is believed in and hoped for. It is to reflect with a view to action which transforms the present. But it does not mean doing this from an armchair; rather it means sinking roots where the pulse of history is beating at this moment and illuminating history with the Word of the Lord of history, who irreversibly committed himself to the present moment of humankind to carry it to its fulfillment.

It is for all these reasons that the theology of liberation offers us not so much a new theme for reflection as a *new way* to do theology. Theology as critical reflection on historical praxis is a liberating theology, a theology of the liberating transformation of the history of humankind and also therefore that part of humankind—gathered into *ecclesia*—which openly confesses Christ. This is a theology which does not stop with reflecting on the world, but rather tries to be part of the process through which the world is transformed. It is a theology which is open—in the protest against trampled human dignity, in the struggle against the plunder of the vast majority of humankind, in liberating love, and in the building of a new, just, and comradely society—to the gift of the Kingdom of God.

*Chapter Two*

# LIBERATION AND DEVELOPMENT

The world today is experiencing a profound and rapid socio-cultural transformation. But the changes do not occur at a uniform pace, and the discrepancies in the change process have differentiated the various countries and regions of our planet.

Contemporary thinkers have become clearly aware of this unequal process of transformation, of its economic causes, and of the basic relationships which combine to determine conditions and approaches. They examine their own circumstances and compare them to those of others; since they live in a world where communication is fast and efficient, the conditions in which others live are no longer distant and unknown. But thinkers go beyond the limited expectations which such a comparison might create. They see the process of transformation as a quest to satisfy the most fundamental human aspirations—liberty, dignity, the possibility of personal fulfillment for all. Or at least they would like the process to be moving toward these goals. They feel that the satisfaction of these aspirations should be the purpose of all organization and social activity. They know also that all their plans are possible, able to be at least partially implemented.

Finally, history demonstrates that the achievements of humanity are cumulative; their effects and the collective experience of the generations open new perspectives and allow for even greater achievements in the generations yet to come.

The phenomenon of the awareness of differences among countries characterizes our era, due to the bourgeoning of communications media; it is particularly acute in those countries less favored by the evolution of the world economy—the poor countries where the vast majority of humans live. The inhabitants of these countries are aware of the unacceptable living conditions of most of their fellow citizens. They confirm the explanation that these inequalities are caused by a type of relationship which often has been imposed upon them. For these reasons, the efforts for social change in these areas are characterized both by a great urgency and by conflicts stemming from differences of expectations, degrees of pressure, and existing systems of relationships and power. It is well to clarify, on the one hand, that the current (and very recent) level of expectations of the poor countries goes far beyond a mere imitation of the rich countries and is of necessity somewhat indistinct and imprecise. On the other hand, both the internal heterogeneity and the presence of external determinants in these societies contribute to defining different needs in different groups. All of this causes a dynamics of action which is inevitably conflictual.

The poor countries are not interested in modeling themselves after the rich countries, among other reasons because they are increasingly more convinced that the status of the latter is the fruit of injustice and coercion. It is true that the poor countries are attempting to overcome material insufficiency and misery, but it is in order to achieve a more human society.

## THE CONCEPT OF DEVELOPMENT

The term *development* seems tentatively to have synthesized contemporary aspirations for more human living conditions. The term itself is not new, but its current usage in the social sciences is new, for it responds to a different set of issues which has emerged only recently. Indeed, the old wealth-poverty antinomy no longer expresses all the problems and contemporary aspirations of humankind.

### Origin

For some, the origin of the term *development* is, in a sense, negative. They consider it to have appeared in opposition to the term *underdevelopment*, which expressed the situation—and anguish—of the poor countries compared with the rich countries.[1]

It would perhaps be helpful to recall some of the more important trends which helped clarify the concept of development.

First of all, there is the work of Joseph A. Schumpeter,[2] the first economist after the English classics and Marx to concern himself with long-term processes. Schumpeter studied a capitalism characterized by a "circular flow," that is, a system which repeats itself from one period to the next and does not suffer appreciable structural change. The element which breaks this equilibrium and introduces a new dynamism is an *innovation*. Innovations are on the one hand technico-economic, since they are supposed to have originated in these areas; but they are simultaneously politico-social, because they imply contradicting and overcoming the prevailing system. Schumpeter calls this process *Entwicklung*, which today is translated as "development," although earlier renderings were "evolution"[3] or "unfolding."[4]

The work of the Australian economist Colin Clark represents another important contribution.[5] Clark affirms that the objective of economic activity is not wealth, but well-being, a term understood to mean the satisfaction derived from the resources at one's disposal. He proposes to measure well-being by making comparisons in time and space. The differences among countries are shown by various indicators. His calculations show that the highest levels of well-being are found in the industrialized countries. Clark designated the road toward industrialization which poor countries are to follow as "progress" (not development).

The Bandung Conference of 1955 also played an important role in the evolution of the term, although on a different level. A large number of countries met there, especially Asian and African countries. They recognized their common membership in a Third World—underdeveloped and facing two developed worlds, the capitalist and the socialist. This conference marked the beginning of a policy which was supposed to lead out of this state of affairs. Although the deeds that followed did not always correspond to the expectations aroused, Bandung nevertheless signalled a deepened awareness of the fact of underdevelopment and a proclamation of its unacceptability.[6]

### Approaches

The concept of development has no clear definition;[7] there are a variety of ways to regard it. Rather than reviewing them all at length, we will recall briefly the general areas involved.

Development can be regarded as purely economic, and in that sense it would be synonymous with *economic growth.*

The degree of development of a country could be measured, for example, by comparing its gross national product or its per capita income with those of a country regarded as highly developed. It is also possible to refine this gauge and make it more complex, but the presuppositions would still be the same: development consists above all in increased wealth or, at most, a higher level of well-being.

Historically, this is the meaning which appears first. What led to this point of view was perhaps the consideration of the process in England, the first country to develop and, understandably enough, the first to be studied by economists. This viewpoint was later reinforced by the mirage which the well-being of the rich nations produced.

Those who champion this view today, at least explicitly, are few in number.[8] Currently its value lies in serving as a yardstick to measure more integral notions. However, this focus continues to exist in a more or less subtle form in the capitalistic view of development.

The deficiencies of the above-mentioned view have led to another more important and more frequently held one. According to it, development is a *total social process*, which includes economic, social, political, and cultural aspects. This notion stresses the interdependence of the different factors. Advances in one area imply advances in all of them and, conversely, the stagnation of one retards the growth of the rest.[9]

A consideration of development as a total process leads one to consider also all the external and internal factors which affect the economic evolution of a nation as well as to evaluate the distribution of goods and services and the system of relationships among the agents of its economic life. This has been carefully worked out by social scientists concerned with so-called Third World countries. They have reached the conclusion that the dynamics of world economics leads simultaneously to the creation of greater wealth for the few and greater poverty for the many.[10]

From all this flows a strategy of development which, taking into account the different factors, will allow a country to advance both totally and harmoniously and to avoid dangerous setbacks.

To view development as a total social process necessarily implies for some an ethical dimension, which presupposes a concern for human values. The step toward an elaboration of a *humanistic perspective* of development is thus taken unconsciously, and it prolongs the former point of view without contradicting it.

François Perroux worked consistently along these lines. Development for him means "the combination of mental and social changes of a people which enable them to increase, cumulatively and permanently, their total real production." Going even further, he says, "Development is achieved fully in the measure that, by reciprocity of services, it prepares the way for reciprocity of consciousness."[11]

It would be a mistake to think that this point of view, which is concerned with human values, is the exclusive preserve of scholars of a Christian inspiration. Converging viewpoints are found in Marxist-inspired positions.[12]

This humanistic approach attempts to place the notion of development in a wider context: a historical vision in which humankind assumes control of it own destiny.[13] But this leads precisely to a change of perspective which—after certain additions and corrections—we would prefer to call liberation. We shall attempt to clarify this below.

## THE PROCESS OF LIBERATION

### From the Critique of Developmentalism to Social Revolution

The term *development* has synthesized the aspirations of poor peoples during the last few decades. Recently, however, it has become the object of severe criticism due both to the deficiencies of the development policies proposed to the poor countries to lead them out of their underdevelopment and also to the lack of concrete achievements of the interested governments. This is the reason why *developmentalism (desarrollismo)*, a term derived from *development (desarrollo)*, is now used in a pejorative sense, especially in Latin America.[14]

Much has been said in recent times about development. Poor countries competed for the help of the rich countries. There were even attempts to create a certain development mystique. Support for development was intense in Latin America in the '50s, producing high expectations. But since the supporters of development did not attack the roots of the evil, they failed and caused instead confusion and frustration.[15]

One of the most important reasons for this turn of events is that development—approached from an economic and modernizing point of view—has been frequently promoted by international organizations closely linked to groups and governments which control the world economy.[16] The changes encouraged were to be achieved within the formal structure of the existing institutions without challenging them. Great care was exercised, therefore, not to attack the interests of large international economic powers nor those of their natural allies, the ruling domestic interest groups. Furthermore, the so-called changes were often nothing more than new and underhanded ways of increasing the power of strong economic groups.

*Developmentalism* thus came to be synonymous with *reformism* and modernization, that is to say, synonymous with timid measures, really ineffective in the long run and counterproductive to achieving a real transformation. The poor countries are becoming ever more clearly aware that their underdevelopment is only the by-product of the development of other countries, because of the kind of relationship which exists between the rich and the poor countries. Moreover, they are realizing that their own development will come about only with a struggle to break the domination of the rich countries.

This perception sees the conflict implicit in the process. Development must attack the root causes of the problems and among them the deepest is economic, social, political, and cultural dependence of some countries upon others—an expression of the domination of some social classes over others. Attempts to bring about changes within the existing order have proven futile. This analysis of the situation is at the level of scientific rationality. Only a radical break from the status quo, that is, a profound transformation of the private property system, access to power of the exploited class, and a social revolution that would break this dependence would allow for the change to a new society, a socialist society—or at least allow that such a society might be possible.[17]

In this light, to speak about the process of *liberation* begins to appear more appropriate and richer in human content.[18] Liberation in fact expresses the inescapable moment of radical change which is foreign to the ordinary use of the term *development*. Only in the context of such a process can a policy of development be effectively implemented, have any real meaning, and avoid misleading formulations.

### Humankind, the Agent of Its Own Destiny

To characterize the situation of the poor countries as dominated and oppressed leads one to speak of economic, social, and political liberation. But we are dealing here with a much more integral and profound understanding of human existence and its historical future.

A broad and deep aspiration for liberation inflames the history of humankind in our day, liberation from all that limits or keeps human beings from self-fulfillment, liberation from all impediments to the exercise of freedom. Proof of this is the awareness of new and subtle forms of oppression in the heart of advanced industrial societies, which often offer themselves as models to the underdeveloped countries. In them subversion does not appear as a protest against poverty, but rather against wealth.[19] The context in the rich countries, however, is quite different from that of the poor countries: we must beware of all kinds of imitations as well as new forms of imperialism—revolutionary this time—of the rich countries, which consider themselves central to the history of humankind. Such mimicry would only lead the revolutionary groups of the Third World to a new deception regarding their own reality. They would be led to fight against windmills.

But, having acknowledged this danger, it is important to remember also that the poor countries would err in not following these events closely since their future depends at least partially upon what happens on the domestic scene in the dominant countries. Their own efforts at liberation cannot be indifferent to that proclaimed by growing minorities in rich nations. There are, moreover, valuable lessons to be learned by the revolutionaries of the countries on the periphery, who could in turn use them as corrective measures in the difficult task of building a new society.

What is at stake in the South as well as in the North, in the West as well as the East, on the periphery and in the center, is the possibility of enjoying a truly human existence, a free life, a dynamic liberty which is related to history as a conquest. We have today an ever-clearer vision of this dynamism and this conquest, but their roots stretch into the past.

The fifteenth and sixteenth centuries are important milestones in human self-understanding. Human relationship with nature changed substantially with the emergence of experimental science and the techniques of manipulation derived from it. Relying on these achievements, humankind abandoned its former image of the world and itself. Gilson expresses this idea in a well-known phrase: "It is because of its physics that metaphysics grows old." Because of science humankind took a step forward and began to regard itself in a different way.[20] This process indicates why the best philosophical tradition is not merely an armchair product; it is rather the reflective and thematic awareness of human experience of human relationships with nature and with other persons. And these relationships are interpreted and at the same time modified by advances in technological and scientific knowledge.[21]

Descartes is one of the great names of the new physics which altered human relationship to nature. He laid the cornerstone of a philosophical reflection which stressed the primacy of thought and of "clear and distinct ideas," and so highlighted the creative aspects of human subjectivity.[22] Kant's "Copernican Revolution" strengthened and systematized this point of view. For him our concept ought not to conform to the objects but rather "the objects . . . must conform to my conceptions." The reason is that "we only cognize in things *a priori* that which we ourselves place in them."[23] Kant was aware that this leads to a "new method" of thought, to a knowledge which is critical of its foundations and thus abandons its naiveté and enters an adult stage.

Hegel followed this approach, introducing with vitality and urgency the theme of history.[24] To a great extent his philosophy is a reflection on the French Revolution. This historical event had vast repercussions, for it proclaimed the right of all to participate in the direction of the society to which they belong. For Hegel one is aware of oneself "only by being acknowledged or 'recognized' " by another consciousness. But this being recognized by another presupposes an initial conflict, "a life-and-death struggle," because "solely by risking life that freedom is obtained."[25]

Through the lord-bondsman dialectic (resulting from this original confrontation), the historical process will then appear as the genesis of consciousness and therefore of the gradual liberation of humankind.[26] Through the dialectical process humankind constructs itself and attains a real awareness of its own being; it liberates itself in the acquisition of genuine freedom which through work transforms the world and educates the human species.[27] For Hegel "world history is the progression of the awareness of freedom." Moreover, the driving force of history is the difficult conquest of freedom, hardly perceptible in its initial stages. It is the passage from awareness of freedom to real freedom. "It is Freedom in itself that comprises within itself the infinite necessity of bringing itself to consciousness and thereby, since knowledge about itself is its very nature, to reality."[28] Thus human nature gradually takes hold of its own destiny. It looks ahead and turns towards a society in which it will be free of all alienation and servitude. This focus will initiate a new dimension in philosophy: social criticism.[29]

Marx deepened and renewed this line of thought in his unique way.[30] But this required what has been called an "epistemological break" (a notion taken from Gaston Bachelard) with previous thought. The new attitude was expressed clearly in the famous *Theses on Feuerbach*, in which Marx presented concisely but penetratingly the essential elements of his approach. In them, especially in the First Thesis, Marx situated himself equidistant between the old materialism and idealism; more precisely, he presented his position as the dialectical transcendence of both. Of the first he retained the affirmation of the objectivity of the external world; of the second he kept the transforming capacity of human nature. For Marx, to know was something indissolubly linked to the transformation of the world through work. Basing his thought on these first intuitions, he went on to construct a scientific understanding of historical reality. He analyzed capitalistic society, in which were found concrete instances of the exploitation of persons by their fellows and of one social class by another. Pointing the way towards an era in history when humankind can live humanly, Marx created categories which allowed for the elaboration of a science of history.[31]

The door was opened for science to help humankind take one more step on the road of critical thinking. It made humankind more aware of the socioeconomic determinants of its ideological creations and therefore freer and more lucid in relation to them. But at the same time these new insights enabled humankind to have greater control and rational grasp of its historical initiatives. (This interpretation is valid unless of course one holds a dogmatic and mechanistic interpretation of history.) These initiatives ought to assure the change from the capitalistic mode of production to the socialistic mode, that is to say, to one oriented towards a society in which persons can begin to live freely and humanly. They will have controlled nature, created the conditions for a socialized production of wealth, done away with private acquisition of excessive wealth, and established socialism.

But modern human aspirations include not only liberation from *exterior* pressures which prevent fulfillment as a member of a certain social class, country, or society. Persons seek likewise an interior liberation, in an individual and intimate dimension; they seek liberation not only on a social plane but also on a psychological. They seek an interior freedom understood, however, not as an ideological evasion from social confrontation or as the internalization of a situation of dependency.[32] Rather it must be in relation to the real world of the human psyche as understood since Freud.

A new frontier was in effect opened up when Freud highlighted the unconscious determinants of human behavior, with repression as the central element of the human psychic make-up. Repression is the result of the conflict between instinctive drives and the cultural and ethical demands of the social environment.[33] For Freud, unconscious motivations exercise a tyrannical power and can produce aberrant behavior. This behavior is controllable only if the subject becomes aware of these motivations through an accurate reading of the new language of meanings created by the unconscious. Since Hegel we have seen conflict used as a germinal explanatory category and awareness as a step in the conquest of freedom. In Freud, however, they appear in a psychological process which ought also to lead to a fuller liberation of humankind.

The scope of liberation on the collective and historical level does not always and satisfactorily include psychological liberation. Psychological liberation includes dimensions which do not exist in or are not sufficiently integrated with collective, historical liberation.[34] We are not speaking here, however, of facilely separating them or putting them in opposition to one another. "It seems to me," writes David Cooper, "that a cardinal failure of all past revolutions has been the dissociation of liberation on the mass social level, i.e. liberation of whole classes in economic and political terms, and liberation on the level of the individual and the concrete groups in which he is directly engaged. If we are to talk of revolution today our talk will be meaningless unless we effect some union between the macro-social and micro-social, and between 'inner reality' and 'outer reality.' "[35] Moreover, alienation and exploitation as well as the very struggle for liberation from them have ramifications on the personal and psychological planes which it would be dangerous to overlook in the process of constructing a new society and a new person.[36] These personal aspects— considered not as excessively privatized, but rather as encompassing all human dimensions—are also under consideration in the contemporary debate concerning greater participation of all in political activity. This is so even in a socialist society.[37]

In this area, Marcuse's attempt, under the influence of Hegel and Marx, to use the psychoanalytical categories for social criticism is important. Basing his observations on a work which Freud himself did not hold in high regard, *Civilization and its Discontents*,[38] Marcuse analyzes the *over-repressive* character of the affluent society and envisions the possibility of a non-repressive society,[39] a possibility skeptically denied by Freud. Marcuse's analyses of advanced industrial society, capitalistic or socialistic, lead him to denounce the emergence of a one-dimensional and oppressive society.[40] In order to achieve this non-repressive society, however, it will be necessary to challenge the values espoused by the society which denies human beings the possibility of living freely. Marcuse labels this the Great Refusal: "the specter of a revolution which subordinates the development of the productive forces and higher standards of living to the requirements of creating solidarity for the human species, for abolishing poverty and misery beyond all national frontiers and spheres of interest, for the attainment of peace."[41]

We are not suggesting, of course, that we should endorse without question every aspect of this development of ideas. There are ambiguities, critical observations to be made, and points to be clarified. Many ideas must be reconsidered in the light of a history that advances inexorably, simultaneously confirming and rejecting previous assertions. Ideas must be reconsidered too in light of praxis, which is the proving ground of all theory, and in light of socio-cultural realities very different from those from which the ideas emerged. But all this should not lead us to an attitude of distrustful reserve toward these ideas; rather it should suggest that the task to be undertaken is formidable. And the task is all the more urgent because these reflections are attempts to express a deeply-rooted sentiment in today's masses: the aspiration to liberation. This aspiration is still confusedly perceived, but there is an ever greater awareness of it. Furthermore, for many persons in various ways this aspiration—in Vietnam or Brazil, New York or Prague—has become a norm for their behavior and a sufficient reason to lead lives of dedication. Their commitment is the backbone which validates and gives historical viability to the development of the ideas outlined above.

To conceive of history as a process of human liberation is to consider freedom as a historical conquest; it is to understand that the step from an abstract to a real freedom is not taken without a struggle against all the forces that oppress humankind, a struggle full of pitfalls, detours, and temptations to run away. The goal is not only better living conditions, a radical change of structures, a social revolution; it is much more: the continuous creation, never ending, of a new way to be human, a *permanent cultural revolution*.

In other words, what is at stake above all is a dynamic and historical conception of the human person, oriented definitively and creatively toward the future, acting in the present for the sake of tomorrow.[42] Teilhard de Chardin has remarked that humankind has taken hold of the reins of evolution. History, contrary to essentialist and static thinking, is not the development of potentialities preexistent in human nature; it is rather the conquest of new, qualitatively different ways of being a human person in order to achieve an ever more total and complete fulfillment of the individual in solidarity with all humankind.

### The Concept of Liberation Theologically Considered

Although we will consider liberation from a theological perspective more extensively later,[43] it is important at this time to attempt an initial treatment in the light of what we have just discussed.

The term *development* is relatively new in the texts of the ecclesiastical magisterium.[44] Except for a brief reference by Pius XII,[45] the subject is broached for the first time by John XXIII in the encyclical letter *Mater et Magistra*.[46] *Pacem in terris* gives the term special attention. *Gaudium et spes* dedicates a whole section to it, though the treatment is not original. All these documents stress the urgency of eliminating the existing injustices and the need for an economic development geared to the service of humankind. Finally, *Populorum progressio* discusses development as its central theme. Here the language and ideas are clearer; the adjective *integral* is added to development, putting things in a different context and opening new perspectives.

These new viewpoints were already hinted at in the sketchy discussion of Vatican Council II on dependence and liberation. *Gaudium et spes* points out that "nations on the road to progress . . . continually fall behind while very often their *dependence* on wealthier nations deepens more rapidly, even in the economic sphere" (no. 9). Later it acknowledges that "although nearly all peoples have gained their independence, it is still far from true that they are free from excessive inequalities and from every form of *undue dependence*" (no. 85).

These assertions should lead to a discernment of the need to be free from dependence, to be liberated from it. The same *Gaudium et spes* on two occasions touches on liberation and laments the fact that it is seen exclusively as the fruit of human effort: "Many look forward to a genuine and total *emancipation* of humanity wrought solely by human effort. They are convinced that the future rule of man over the earth will satisfy every desire of his heart" (no. 10). Or it is concerned that liberation be reduced to a purely economic and social level: "Among the forms of modern atheism is that which anticipates the *liberation* of man especially through his economic and social emancipation" (no. 20).[47] These assertions presuppose, negatively speaking, that liberation must be placed in a wider context; they criticize a narrow vision. They allow, therefore, for the possibility of a "genuine and total" liberation.

Unfortunately, this wider perspective is not elaborated. We find some indications, however, in the texts in which *Gaudium et spes* speaks of the birth of a "new humanism, one in which man is defined first of all by his responsibility toward his brothers and toward history"(no. 55). There is a need for persons who are makers of history, "who are truly new and artisans of a new human-ity" (no. 30), persons moved by the desire to build a really new society. Indeed, the conciliar document asserts that beneath economic and political demands "lies a deeper and more widespread longing. Persons and societies thirst for a full and free life worthy of man—one in which they can subject to their own welfare all that the modern world can offer them so abundantly" (no. 9).

All this is but a beginning. It is an oft-noted fact that *Gaudium et spes* in general offers a rather irenic description of the human situation; it touches up the uneven spots, smooths the rough edges, avoids the more conflictual aspects, and stays away from the sharper confrontations among social classes and countries.

The encyclical *Populorum progressio* goes a step further. In a somewhat isolated text it speaks clearly of "building a world where every man, no matter what his race, religion, or nationality, can live a fully human life, freed from servitude imposed on him by other men or by natural forces over which he has not sufficient control" (no. 47).[48] It is unfortunate, however, that this idea was not expanded in the encyclical. From this point of view, *Populorum progressio* is a transitional document. Although it energetically denounces the "interna-tional imperialism of money," "situations whose injustice cries to heaven," and the growing gap between rich and poor countries, ultimately it addresses itself to the great ones of this world urging them to carry out the necessary changes.[49] The outright use of the language of liberation, instead of its mere suggestion, would have given a more decided and direct thrust in favor of the oppressed, encouraging them to break with their present situation and take control of their own destiny.[50]

The theme of liberation appears more completely discussed in the message from eighteen bishops of the Third World, published as a specific response to the call made by *Populorum progressio*.[51] It is also treated frequently—almost to the point of being a synthesis of its message—in the conclusions of the Second General Conference of Latin American Bishops held in Medellín, Colombia, in 1968,[52] which have more doctrinal authority than the eighteen bishops' message. In both these documents the focus has changed. The situa-tion is not judged from the point of view of the countries at the center, but rather of those on the periphery, providing insiders' experience of their anguish and aspirations.

The product of a profound historical movement, this aspiration to liberation is beginning to be accepted by the Christian community as a sign of the times, as a call to commitment and interpretation. The Biblical message, which presents the work of Christ as a liberation, provides the framework for this interpretation. Theology seems to have avoided for a long time reflecting on the conflictual character of human history, the confrontations among individ-uals, social classes, and countries. St. Paul continuously reminds us, however, of the paschal core of Christian existence and of all of human life: the passage from the old to the new person, from sin to grace, from slavery to freedom.

"For freedom Christ has set us free" (Gal. 5:1), St. Paul tells us. He refers here to liberation from sin insofar as it represents a selfish turning in upon oneself. To sin is to refuse to love one's neighbors and, therefore, the Lord himself. Sin—a breach of friendship with God and others—is according to the Bible the ultimate cause of poverty, injustice, and the oppression in which persons live. In describing sin as the ultimate cause we do not in any way negate the structural reasons and the objective determinants leading to these situations. It does, however, emphasize the fact that things do not happen by chance and that behind an unjust structure there is a personal or collective will responsible—a willingness to reject God and neighbor. It suggests, likewise, that a social transformation, no matter how radical it may be, does not automatically achieve the suppression of all evils.

But St. Paul asserts not only that Christ liberated us; he also tells us that he did it in order that we might be free. Free for what? Free to love. "In the language of the Bible," writes Bonhoeffer, "freedom is not something man has for himself but something he has for others. . . . It is not a possession, a presence, an object, . . . but a relationship and nothing else. In truth, freedom is a relationship between two persons. Being free means 'being free for the other,' because the other has bound me to him. Only in relationship with the other am I free."[53] The freedom to which we are called presupposes the going out of oneself, the breaking down of our selfishness and of all the structures that support our selfishness; the foundation of this freedom is openness to others. The fullness of liberation—a free gift from Christ—is communion with God and with other human beings.

## CONCLUSION

Summarizing what has been said above, we can distinguish three reciprocally interpenetrating levels of meaning of the term *liberation*, or in other words, three approaches to the process of liberation.

In the first place, *liberation* expresses the aspirations of oppressed peoples and social classes, emphasizing the conflictual aspect of the economic, social, and political process which puts them at odds with wealthy nations and oppressive classes. In contrast, the word *development*, and above all the policies characterized as developmentalist (*desarrollista*), appear somewhat aseptic, giving a false picture of a tragic and conflictual reality. The issue of development does in fact find its true place in the more universal, profound, and radical perspective of liberation. It is only within this framework that *development* finds its true meaning and possibilities of accomplishing something worthwhile.

At a deeper level, *liberation* can be applied to an understanding of history. Humankind is seen as assuming conscious responsibility for its own destiny. This understanding provides a dynamic context and broadens the horizons of the desired social changes. In this perspective the unfolding of all the dimensions of humanness is demanded—persons who make themselves throughout their life and throughout history. The gradual conquest of true freedom leads to the creation of a new humankind and a qualitatively different society. This vision provides, therefore, a better understanding of what in fact is at stake in our times.

Finally, the word *development* to a certain extent limits and obscures the theological problems implied in the process designated by this term.[54] On the contrary the word *liberation* allows for another approach leading to the Biblical sources which inspire the presence and action of humankind in history. In the Bible, Christ is presented as the one who brings us liberation. Christ the Savior liberates from sin, which is the ultimate root of all disruption of friendship and of all injustice and oppression. Christ makes humankind truly free, that is to say, he enables us to live in communion with him; and this is the basis for all human fellowship.[55]

This is not a matter of three parallel or chronologically successive processes, however. There are three levels of meaning of a single, complex process, which finds its deepest sense and its full realization in the saving work of Christ. These levels of meaning, therefore, are interdependent. A comprehensive view of the matter presupposes that all three aspects can be considered together. In this way two pitfalls will be avoided: first, *idealist* or *spiritualist* approaches, which are nothing but ways of evading a harsh and demanding reality, and second, shallow analyses and programs of short-term effect initiated under the pretext of meeting immediate needs.[56]

# PART 2

# POSING THE PROBLEM

The foregoing comments lead us to reflect, in the light of the Word of the Lord, on the complex process of liberation which we have attempted to sketch; that is to say, they lead us to a *theology of liberation*.

This reflection must be rooted in the presence and action of Christians—in solidarity with others—in the world today, especially as participants in the process of liberation which is being effected in Latin America. But first we will attempt to state the problem we are considering as precisely as possible. Throughout the life of the Church, this problem has received different responses which are still in one way or another significant because of the part they play in the concrete activity of many Christians. An analysis of these responses can therefore help us to understand the features which currently characterize the problem.

# Chapter Three

# THE PROBLEM

To speak about a theology of liberation is to seek an answer to the following question: what relation is there between salvation and the historical process of human liberation? In other words, we must attempt to discern the interrelationship among the different meanings of the term *liberation* which we indicated above. The scope of the problem will be clarified in the course of this work, but it might be helpful to point out at this stage some of its fundamental features.

The question is essentially traditional. Theological reflection has always at least implicitly addressed itself to it. In recent years the theology of temporal realities[1]—an expression which was never fully accepted—attempted to deal with it in its own way. Other attempts have been the theology of history[2] and, more recently, the theology of development.[3] From another viewpoint, the question is also considered by "political theology";[4] and it is partially treated by the much-debated—and debatable—theology of revolution.[5]

We are dealing here with the classic question of the relation between faith and human existence, between faith and social reality, between faith and political action, or in other words, between the Kingdom of God and the building up of the world. Within the scope of this problem the classical theme of the Church-society or Church-world relationship is also considered.

Its perennial quality, however, must not make us forget the new aspects which the traditional question takes on today.

Under new forms it maintains all its topicality. J.B. Metz asserted recently that, "despite the many discussions about the Church and the world, there is nothing more unclear than the nature of their relationship to one another."[6] But if this is so, if the problem continues to be current and yet the attempted responses are not wholly satisfactory, it is perhaps because as traditionally stated the problem has become tangential to a new and changing reality; as traditionally stated the problem does not go deep enough. In studying these questions, the texts and especially the spirit of Vatican II are undoubtedly necessary as points of reference. Nevertheless, the new design of the problem was—and could only be—partially present in the conciliar documents. "It seems to me of utmost importance," said Karl Rahner recently, "to agree on the fact that the ideas explicitly considered during Vatican Council II do not actually represent the central problems of the postconciliar Church."[7] It is not enough to say that Christians should not "shirk" their earthly responsibilities or that these have a "certain relationship" to salvation. *Gaudium et spes* itself sometimes gives the impression of remaining at this level of generalization.[8] More regrettably, the same is true of a considerable number of commentators. The task of contemporary theology is to elucidate the current state of these problems, drawing with sharper lines the terms in which they are expressed.[9] Only thus will it be possible to confront the concrete challenges of the present.[10]

In the current statement of the problem, one fact is evident: the social praxis of contemporary humankind has begun to reach maturity. It is the behavior of a humankind ever more conscious of being an active subject of history, ever more articulate in the face of social injustice and of all repressive forces which stand in the way of its fulfillment; it is ever more determined to participate both in the transformation of social structures and in effective political action. It was above all the great social revolutions—the French and the Russian, for example, to mention only two important milestones—together with the whole process of revolutionary ferment that they initiated which wrested—or at least began to—political decisions from the hands of an elite who were "destined" to rule. Up to that time the great majority of people did not participate in political decisions or did so only sporadically and formally. Although it is true that the majority of people are far from this level of awareness, it is also certain that they have had confused glimpses of it and are oriented in its direction. The phenomenon that we designate with the term "politicization"—which is increasing in breadth and depth in Latin America—is one of the manifestations of this complex process. And in the struggle for the liberation of the oppressed classes on this continent—which is implicit in the effective and human political responsibility of all—people are searching out new paths.

Human reason has become political reason. For the contemporary historical consciousness, things political are not only those which one attends to during the free time afforded by one's private life; nor are they even a well-defined area of human existence. The construction—from its economic bases—of the "polis," of a society in which people can live in solidarity, is a dimension which encompasses and severely conditions all human activity. It is the sphere for the exercise of a critical freedom which is won down through history. It is the universal determinant and the collective arena for human fulfillment.[11] Only within this broad meaning of the political sphere can we situate the more precise notion of "politics," as an orientation to power. For Max Weber this orientation constitutes the typical characteristics of political activity. The concrete forms taken on by this quest for and exercise of political power are varied. But they are all based on the profound aspiration of a humankind that wants to take hold of the reins of its own life and be the artisan of its own destiny. Nothing lies outside the political sphere understood in this way. Everything has a political color. It is always in the political fabric—and never outside of it—that a person emerges as a free and responsible being, as a person in relationship with other persons, as someone who takes on a historical task. Personal relationships themselves acquire an ever-increasing political dimension. Persons enter into relationships among themselves through political means. This is what Ricoeur calls the "lasting and stable" relationships of the *socius*, as opposed to the "fleeting and fragile" relationships of the neighbor.[12] To this effect, M.D. Chenu writes: "Man has always enjoyed this social dimension, since he is social by his very nature. But today, not accidentally but structurally, the collective event lends scope and intensity to the social dimension. What is collective as such has human value and is, therefore, a means and object of love. Human love treads these 'lasting' paths, these organizations of distributive justice, and these administrative systems."[13]

In addition to this universality of the political sphere, we are faced with an increasing radicalization of social praxis. Contemporary persons have begun to lose their naiveté as they confront economic and socio-cultural determinants; the deep causes of the situation in which they find themselves are becoming clearer. They realize that to attack these deep causes is the indispensable prerequisite for radical change. And so they have gradually abandoned a simple reformist attitude regarding the existing social order, for, by its very shallowness this reformism perpetuates the existing system. The revolutionary situation which prevails today, especially in the Third World, is an expression of this growing radicalization. To support the social revolution means to abolish the present status quo and to attempt to replace it with a qualitatively different one; it means to build a just society based on new relationships of production; it means to attempt to put an end to the domination of some countries by others, of some social classes by others, of some persons by others. The liberation of these countries, social classes, and persons undermines the very foundation of the present order; it is the greatest challenge of our time.

This radicality has led us to see quite clearly that the political arena is necessarily conflictual. More precisely, the building of a just society means the confrontation—in which different kinds of violence are present—between groups with different interests and opinions. The building of a just society means overcoming every obstacle to the creation of authentic peace. Concretely, in Latin America this conflict revolves around the *oppression-liberation axis*. Social praxis makes demands which may seem difficult or disturbing to those who wish to achieve—or maintain—a low-cost conciliation. Such a conciliation can be only a justifying ideology for a profound disorder, a device for the few to keep living off the poverty of the many. But to become aware of the conflictual nature of the political sphere should not mean to become complacent. On the contrary, it should mean struggling—with clarity and courage, deceiving neither oneself nor others—for the establishment of peace and justice among all people.

In the past, concern for social praxis in theological thought did not sufficiently take into account the political dimension. In Christian circles there was—and continues to be—difficulty in perceiving the originality and specific-ity of the political sphere. Stress was placed on private life and on the cultiva-tion of private values; things political were relegated to a lower plane, to the elusive and undemanding area of a misunderstood "common good." At most, this viewpoint provided a basis for "social pastoral planning," grounded on the "social emotion" which every self-respecting Christian ought to experience. Hence there developed the complacency with a very general and "humanizing" vision of reality, to the detriment of a scientific and structural knowledge of socio-economic mechanisms and historical dynamics. Hence also there came the insistence on the personal and conciliatory aspects of the Gospel message rather than on its political and conflictual dimensions. We must take a new look at Christian life; we must see how these emphases in the past have conditioned and challenged the historical presence of the Church. This pres-ence has an inescapable political dimension. It has always been so, but because of new circumstances it is more urgent that we come to terms with it. Indeed, there is a greater awareness of it, even among Christians. It is impossible to think of or live in the Church without taking into account this political dimension.

What we have discussed above leads us to understand why for Christians social praxis is becoming less and less merely a duty imposed by their moral conscience or a reaction to an attack on Church interests. The characteristics of totality, radicalness, and conflict which we have attributed to the political sphere preclude any compartmentalized approach and lead us to see its deepest human dimensions. Social praxis is gradually becoming more of the arena itself in which the Christians work out—along with others—both their destiny as humans and their life of faith in the Lord of history. Participation in the process of liberation is an obligatory and privileged *locus* for Christian life and reflection. In this participation will be heard nuances of the Word of God which are imperceptible in other existential situations and without which there can be no authentic and fruitful faithfulness to the Lord.

If we look more deeply into the question of the value of salvation which emerges from our understanding of history—that is, a liberating praxis—we see that at issue is a question concerning *the very meaning of Christianity*. To be a Christian is to accept and to live—in solidarity, in faith, hope, and charity—the meaning that the Word of the Lord and our encounter with that Word give to the historical becoming of humankind on the way toward total communion. To regard the unique and absolute relationship with God as the horizon of every human action is to place oneself, from the outset, in a wider and more profound context. It is likewise more demanding. We are faced in our day with the bare, central theologico-pastoral question: *What does it mean to be a Christian? What does it mean to be Church in the unknown circumstances of the future?*[14] In the last instance, we must search the Gospel message for the answer to what according to Camus constitutes the most important question facing all persons: "To decide whether life deserves to be lived or not."[15]

These elements lend perhaps greater depth and a new dimension to the traditional problem. Not to acknowledge the newness of the issues raised under the pretext that in one way or another the problem has always been present is to detach oneself dangerously from reality; it is to risk falling into generalities, solutions without commitment, and, finally, evasive attitudes. But, on the other hand, to acknowledge nothing but the new aspects of the contemporary statement of the problem is to forego the contribution of the life and reflection of the Christian community in its historical pilgrimage. Its successes, its omissions, and its errors are our heritage. They should not, however, delimit our boundaries. The People of God march on, "accounting for their hope" toward "a new heaven and a new earth."

The question as it is posed today is not really dealt with by the attempted responses we will look at in the next chapter. But the positive achievements of these efforts with regard to the permanent elements of the problem as well as their deficiencies and limitations can help us to sketch—often by showing us pitfalls to avoid—the itinerary we must follow.

*Chapter Four*

# DIFFERENT RESPONSES

The different responses given throughout history to the question of the relationship between faith and temporal realities, between the Church and the world, are still pertinent in one form or another. It is because they are germane to the ecclesial present and not merely because of their historical interest that we recall these points of view.[1]

## THE CHRISTENDOM MENTALITY

Christendom is not primarily a mental construct. It is above all a fact, indeed the longest historical experience the Church has had. Hence the deep impact it has made on its life and thought.

In the Christendom mentality, and in the point of view which prolongs it, temporal realities lack autonomy. They are not regarded by the Church as having an authentic existence. It therefore uses them for its own ends. This is the sequel of the so-called "Political Augustinism."[2] The plan for the Kingdom of God has no room for a profane, historical plan.[3]

The Church is regarded substantially as the exclusive depository of salvation: "Outside the Church there is no salvation." Because of this exclusiveness, notwithstanding certain qualifications which do not change the overall picture, the Church feels justified in considering itself as the center of the economy of salvation and therefore presenting itself as a powerful force in relation to the world. This power will spontaneously and inevitably seek to express itself in the political arena.

Under these circumstances, participation in temporal tasks has a very precise meaning for the Christian: to work for the direct and immediate benefit of the Church. A historical example typical of this point of view is to be found in the well-known ban (*Non possumus*) upon Italian Catholics, which prohibited them from participating—until a few decades ago—in the political life of their country. "Christian politics," therefore, will mean assisting the Church in its evangelizing mission and safeguarding the Church's interests. This was the mentality which inspired the confessional parties in Europe and Latin America toward the end of the nineteenth century and the beginning of the twentieth.

34

This is the role which in certain places Catholics in public office are still expected to play. The interests of the ecclesiastical institution are represented especially by the bishops and the clergy; lay persons, given their situation in political society, will normally act in an auxiliary capacity.[4]

The theological categories we have mentioned were formulated—at least essentially—in that era of the history of the Christian community characterized by close unity between faith and social life. In our day, since this unity no longer exists, those categories have become dysfunctional and engender pastoral attitudes out of touch with reality;[5] worse yet, they engender conservative political positions, tending towards the restoration of an obsolete social order or the shoring up of what is left of it.

Let us not too easily dismiss this mentality as extinct. It survives today implicitly or explicitly in large and important sectors of the Church. It is the cause of conflict and resistance to change in the Church today which cannot otherwise be explained. The conciliar debates[6] and perhaps above all the postconciliar era provide sufficient proof of this.

## NEW CHRISTENDOM

The grave problems facing the Church which arose from the new historical circumstances of the sixteenth century and were made more acute by the French Revolution slowly gave way to another pastoral approach and another theological mentality. Thanks to Jacques Maritain, this new approach was to be known as New Christendom.[7] It attempted to learn from the separation between faith and social life, which had been so intimately linked during the era of Christendom. This attempt, however, was to use categories which were not able to shake off completely the traditional mentality, as we can see better with the help of hindsight. A century before a similar effort had taken place, although it was perhaps less solid and coherent from a doctrinal point of view. We refer to the so-called Catholic liberalism, which sought to take into account the situation created a short time before by the ideas of French Revolution. Although it created a clamor, this movement was neutralized by the misunderstanding of the majority of the Christian community and the hostility of the ecclesiastical authorities.

The theses of New Christendom mark another stage in the life of the Church. This is a first and well-structured effort, which attempts moreover to root itself in the traditional thought of the Church. If Augustinian theology predominated in the previous approach, Thomism does in the latter. St. Thomas Aquinas's teaching that grace does not suppress or replace nature, but rather perfects it, opened the door to possibilities of a more autonomous and disinterested political action. On this foundation, Maritain fashioned a political philosophy which also sought to integrate certain modern elements.[8] The task of constructing the human city would consist above all in the search for a society based upon justice, respect for the rights of others, and human fellowhip. Its meaning would not flow, as in the approach we considered above, directly from religion or the defense of Church interests. Consequently, the autonomy of the temporal sphere is asserted especially in relation to the ecclesiastical hierarchy, thus preventing their later interference in an area considered outside their competence.[9]

The view of the Church as a power in relation to the world has been profoundly modified. But it continues to be, in a certain way, at the center of the work of salvation. A certain ecclesiastical narcissism is still evident. In fact, this approach seeks—by means of the creation of a just and democratic society—to achieve conditions favorable to the activity of the Church in the world. It is necessary to build a "profane Christendom," in other words, a society inspired by Christian principles.

Once the autonomy of the world is asserted, the lay persons acquire a proper function which was not recognized as theirs before. This function is facilitated by the famous distinction between acting "as a Christian as such" and acting "as a Christian."[10] In the first case, the Christians act as members of the Church, and their actions represent the ecclesial community. (This is what happened with the leaders of "Catholic Action" groups.) In the second case Christians act under the inspiration of Christian principles but assume exclusive personal responsibility for their actions; this gives them greater freedom in their political commitments. Therefore, the special task of lay persons will be to create this New Christendom in the temporal sphere. To this end they will find it useful to join organizations inspired by Christian principles—and carrying a Christian name.[11]

This position represents an initial effort to evaluate temporal tasks with the eyes of faith as well as to situate better the Church in the modern world. This approach led many Christians to commit themselves authentically and generously to the construction of a just society. Those Christians who supported this position often had to endure the enmity of the faithful and Church authorities, both of whom were of a conservative mentality. In fact, nevertheless, this approach amounted only to a timid and basically ambiguous attempt.[12] It gave rise to fundamentally moderate political attitudes—at least in the beginning—which combined a certain nostalgia for the past (reestablishment of guilds, for example) with a modernizing mentality. It is a long way, therefore, from a desire to become oriented towards radically new social forms.

## THE DISTINCTION OF PLANES

The focus provided by New Christendom made possible an advance from the traditional viewpoint towards a position in which the terms of the Church-world relationship are better defined. The first attempt to distinguish these two levels without separating them comes from Maritain. Later the theme was quickly enriched and radicalized, losing every trace of "Christendom." In the years prior to the Council the pastoral and theological thinking of some sectors of the Church tended to draw a very clear distinction between the Church and the world, within the unity of God's plan.[13]

Much more clearly than in the past, the world emerged as autonomous, distinct from the Church and having its own ends.[14] The autonomy of the temporal sphere was asserted not only with regard to ecclesiastical authority but also with regard to the Church's very mission. It was not to interfere, as institution, in temporal matters, except—according to the most venerable tradition—through moral teaching. In practice this would mean, as we will see later, acting through the mediation of the conscience of the individual Christian.[15] The building up of the earthly city, then, is an autonomous endeavor.

As a result, the function of the Church in the world becomes clearer. The Church, it was said, has two missions: evangelization and the inspiration of the temporal sphere.[16] "By converting men to faith and baptizing them," wrote Congar, "according to the mission she has received from the Lord, the Church presents and actualises herself as the 'order apart' of salvation and holiness in the world. By acting in the sphere of civilization, which means in the temporal order and in history, she fulfills her mission to be the soul of human society."[17] The Church is not responsible for constructing the world; hence the lack of sympathy for this point of view from temporal institutions of Christian inspiration, especially those considered "powerful."[18] (Institutions of this sort do in fact give the impression that Christianity is an ideology for the building up of the world.)[19] The planes are thus clearly differentiated. The Kingdom of God provides the unity; the Church and the world, each in its own way, contribute to its edification.[20]

The functions of the clergy and the laity can be differentiated in like manner. The priest breaks off his point of insertion in the world. His mission is identified with that of the Church: to evangelize and to inspire the temporal order. To intervene directly in political action is to betray his function. Lay persons' position in the Church, on the other hand, does not require them to abandon their insertion in the world. It is their responsibility to build up both the Church and the world.[21] In their temporal endeavors, lay persons will seek to create with others, Christian or not, a more just and more human society; they will be well aware that in so doing they are ultimately building up a society in which man will be able to respond freely to the call of God.[22] They will have, nevertheless, the fullest respect for the autonomy of temporal society.

The mission of lay apostolic movements, on the other hand, should not go beyond the mission of the Church and the priest: to evangelize and to inspire the temporal order.[23] To this theology corresponds a *particular way* of approaching the *Révision de Vie* technique, which assures an authentically Christian presence in the world. Christians meet, as Christians, only to share and celebrate their faith and to examine in the light of faith their own political options—or other options, which might be different and even opposing.[24]

This theological perspective predominated in the specialized apostolic movements of Europe, the French in particular, around 1950 and a few years later in the Latin American movements. But in Latin America, contrary to the European experience, this approach did not extend beyond the members of the movements and certain pastoral circles. In practice, the greater part of the

Church remained untouched by this Church-world distinction, for it was contradicted by the strong bonds which consciously or unconsciously tied the Church to the existing social order.

This model has the advantage of being clear and achieving a difficult balance between the unity of God's plan and the distinction between Church and world. By and large, this is the theological approach of many of the texts of Vatican II. There are, however, emphases and insights which go beyond this, for example in *Gaudium et spes*. Congar explains that because the inductive method was used, *Gaudium et spes* does not clearly distinguish between two missions of the Church: this relationship "could have been stated from the beginning after the fashion of a doctrinal thesis," he said.[25] But it is interesting to observe that due precisely to the dynamics of the inductive method, the constitution *Lumen gentium* at times transcends a rigid distinction of planes.[26]

*Chapter Five*

# CRISIS OF THE DISTINCTION OF PLANES MODEL

The acceptance of the New Christendom position entails of course a rejection of previous approaches; it in turn, however, is criticized because of its position on the distinction of planes.

In recent years there has been a questioning of pastoral action and theology based on distinctions which, although they gained ground very slowly, did indeed contribute to the clarification of many problems.[1]

This crisis has become distinctly manifest on two levels: pastoral action and theological reflection.

## THE PASTORAL LEVEL

As we have seen, the model which distinguishes faith and temporal realities, Church and world, leads to the perception of two missions in the Church and to a sharp differentiation between the roles of the priest and the lay person; this model soon began to lose its vitality and to become a hindrance to pastoral action. Two instances can illustrate this point.

### Crisis of the Lay Apostolic Movements

The rise and development of an adult laity has been one of the most important events in the Church in recent decades. Although they foreshadowed a profound ecclesiological and spiritual renewal, the lay apostolic movements as such have nevertheless been experiencing for some time a deep crisis which it would be well to examine and analyze in detail. This crisis, indeed, provides us with a number of lessons and points for reflection.

As we have pointed out, the distinction of planes approach held that the mission of lay apostolic organizations was to evangelize and to inspire the temporal order, without directly intervening. But the life of these movements overflowed this narrow and aseptic conceptual model.

*39*

The movements, especially the youth groups, felt called upon to take ever clearer and more committed positions,[2] that is to say, to take on themselves in greater depth the problems of the milieu in which they supposedly assured "a presence of the Church."

Initially this change was presented as deriving from a pedagogical concern: the youth movements could not separate religious formation from political formation.[3] The question, however, went deeper. At stake was the very nature of these organizations: the fact that they took a stand on the temporal plane meant that the Church (especially the bishops) became committed in an area foreign to it, and this was not acceptable. Simultaneously, because of the very dynamics of the movement, the members felt compelled by circumstances to make ever more definite commitments; this necessarily led to a political radicalization incompatible with an *official* position of the Church which postulated a certain asepsis in temporal affairs. Therefore, frictions and even divisions were inevitable.[4]

Crises have occurred and spread.[5] The lay apostolic movements, *such as they are understood in the distinction of planes model*, seem to have burned themselves out.[6]

### Growing Awareness of an Alienating Situation

The "social problem" or the "social question" has been discussed in Christian circles for a long time, but it is only in the last few years that people have become clearly aware of the scope of misery and especially of the oppressive and alienating circumstances in which the great majority of humankind exists. This state of affairs is offensive to humankind and therefore to God. Moreover, today people are more deeply aware both of personal responsibility in this situation and the obstacles these conditions present to the complete fulfillment of all human beings, exploiters and exploited alike.

People are also more keenly and painfully aware that a large part of the Church is in one way or another linked to those who wield economic and political power in today's world. This applies to its position in the opulent and oppressive countries as well as in the poor countries, as in Latin America, where it is tied to the exploiting classes.

Under these circumstances, can it honestly be said that the Church does not interfere in "the temporal sphere"? Is the Church fulfilling a purely religious role when by its silence or friendly relationships it lends legitimacy to a dictatorial and oppressive government?[7] We discover, then, that the policy of nonintervention in political affairs holds for certain actions which involve ecclesiastical authorities, but not for others. In other words, this principle is not applied when it is a question of maintaining the status quo, but it is wielded when, for example, a lay apostolic movement or a group of priests holds an attitude considered subversive to the established order. Concretely, in Latin America the distinction of planes model has the effect of concealing the real political option of a large sector of the Church—that is, support of the established order. It is interesting to note that when there was no clear under-standing of the political role of the Church the distinction of planes model was disapproved of by both civil and ecclesiastical authorities. But when the system—of which the ecclesiastical institution is a central element—began to be rejected, this same model was adopted to dispense the ecclesiastical institu-tion from effectively defending the oppressed and exploited and to enable it to preach a lyrical spiritual unity of all Christians. The dominant groups, who have always used the Church to defend their interests and maintain their privileged position, today—as they see "subversive" tendencies gaining ground in the heart of the Christian community—call for a return to the purely religious and spiritual function of the Church. The distinction of planes banner has changed hands. Until a few years ago it was defended by the vanguard; now it is held aloft by power groups, many of whom are in no way involved with any commitment to the Christian faith. Let us not be deceived, however. Their purposes are very different. Let us not unwittingly aid the opponent.

Further, in the face of the immense misery and injustice, ought not the Church especially in those areas such as Latin America where it has great social influence—intervene more directly and abandon the field of lyrical pronounce-ments? In fact, the Church has done so at times, but always clarifying that this was a merely supplementary role.[8] The scope and omnipresence of the problem would seem to render this argument inadequate in our day. More recent options, such as that offered at Medellín, have transcended these limitations and now require another theological foundation.

In short, political options have become radicalized, and the specific commit-ments which Christians are assuming demonstrate the inadequacies of the theologico-pastoral model of the distinction of planes.

## THE LEVEL OF THEOLOGICAL REFLECTION

In a development related to these new pastoral experiences of the Church, contemporary theological reflection has also eroded the model of the distinc-tion of planes. It has done so in two apparently contradictory ways.

### An Entirely Worldly World

In all the different responses to the problem we are considering, the world has gradually been acknowledged as existing in its own right. Autonomous with regard to both ecclesiastical authority and the mission of the Church, the world has slowly asserted its secularity. Acknowledgment by the Church of this autonomy manifested itself first with timidity and distrust—hence the expres-sions "healthy," "just," and "legitimate" autonomy which frequently appear in documents from the magisterium of the Church. But gradually and espe-cially in theological circles, the values and irreversibility of the process to which we now refer as secularization have become more obvious.[9]

Secularization appeared as a breaking away from the tutelage of religion, as a desacralization. This is the most common way of characterizing this process. Harvey Cox writes: "We have defined secularization as the liberation of man from religious and metaphysical tutelage, the turning of his attention away from other worlds and toward this one."[10] This is how the process of secularization has historically been presented. It was an initial attempt to deal with the problem, valid albeit incomplete.

There is a second and more positive approach to this subject, which is already suggested in the final part of the text quoted above. Secularization is, above all, the result of a transformation of human self-understanding. From a cosmological vision, humankind moves to an anthropological vision, due especially to scientific developments.[11] We perceive ourselves as a creative subject.[12] Moreover, we become aware—as noted above—that we are agents of history, responsible for our own destiny.[13] Our mind discovers not only the laws of nature, but also penetrates those of society, history, and psychology. This new self-understanding of humankind necessarily brings in its wake a different way of conceiving our relationship with God.[14]

In this sense, secularization—and this has been recalled often lately—is a process which not only coincides perfectly with a Christian vision of human nature, of history, and of the cosmos; it also favors a more complete fulfillment of the Christian life insofar as it offers human beings the possibility of being more fully human.[15] This realization has engendered efforts to search for the Biblical roots of secularization, efforts at times somewhat "concordist." Biblical faith does indeed affirm the existence of creation as distinct from the Creator; it is the proper sphere of humankind, and God has proclaimed humankind lord of this creation. *Worldliness*, therefore, is a must, a necessary condition for an authentic relationship between humankind and nature, among human beings themselves, and finally, between humankind and God.[16]

All this has important ramifications. In the first place, rather than define the world in relation to the religious phenomenon, it would seem that religion should be redefined in relation to the profane. The worldly sphere appears in fact ever more consistent in itself. This is Bonhoeffer's world come of age, *mündig*, the source of his anguished question, "How can we speak about God in this adult world?"[17]

On the other hand—on a very concrete level in which we are particularly interested—if formerly the tendency was to see the world in terms of the Church, today almost the reverse is true: the Church is seen in terms of the world. In the past, the Church used the world for its own ends; today many Christians—and non-Christians—ask themselves if they should, for example, use the influence of the Church to accelerate the process of transformation of social structures.

Secularization poses a serious challenge to the Christian community. In the future it will have to live and celebrate its faith in a *nonreligious* world, which the faith itself has helped create. It becomes ever more urgent that it redefine the formulation of its faith, its insertion in the dynamics of history, its morality, its life-style, the language of its preaching, and its worship. The secularization process is reaching Latin America insofar as the history of humanity becomes unified and global. It is true that some features, and especially some interpretations, are once again only a simple reflection of the European scene, the fruit of a kind of *demonstration effect*. However, this should not mislead us. There is a deep-rooted movement; its characteristics have been poorly studied; because it is peculiar to Latin America, this makes it no less real. Latin Americans, by participating in their own liberation, gradually are taking hold of the reins of their historical initiative and perceiving themselves as artisans of their own destiny. Moreover, in the revolutionary struggle they are freeing themselves in one way or another from the tutelage of an alienating religion which tends to support the status quo.[18]

But the problem is complex. It is not a matter of achieving the same end by other means. Latin America is not purely and simply passing through "less developed" stages of the secularization experienced in Europe. It could rather be said, if we may borrow an expression from another discipline, that in Latin America we are witnessing a secularization process which is "uneven and combined."[19] A rhythm different from Europe's, coexistence with other ways of living religion and of experiencing its relation to the world, the possibility of effectively concretizing the potentialities of the Gospel and the Churches in order to contribute to the liberation of Latin American persons—all these factors suggest an original process which defies any simplistic conceptualization and all extrapolation. A consideration of this process helps explain many attitudes and crises of persons who might not be fully aware of their root causes. The challenge of redefinition with regard to an ever more adult world also faces the Latin American Church, but has very peculiar characteristics.[20]

### One Call to Salvation

The temporal-spiritual and profane-sacred antitheses are based on the natural-supernatural distinction. But the theological evolution of this last term has tended to stress the unity which eliminates all dualism. We will recall briefly the high points of this process.

Concern for preserving the gratuitous quality of the supernatural order led to the formulation of the doctrine of *pure nature*. This completely separated human nature from divine grace; it attributed to human nature not a strong orientation toward grace, but rather a bare "lack of repugnance" for it.[21] There was no interior desire for communion with God, but rather simple passivity. The supernatural was fundamentally alien to human beings, a perfection superimposed upon them. This viewpoint—which goes back to Cajetan, a less-than-faithful interpreter of Thomas Aquinas[22]—dominated Western Catholic theology for a long period. Not foreign to it are an attitude of distrust of the world and ecclesiocentrism (that is, a view of the Church as exclusive repository of grace), which since the sixteenth century until a short time ago were both found among Catholics.

The inadequacies of this position produced impasses which necessitated searching for other answers. The move forward was towards a distinction, not a separation, between the natural and supernatural orders, based on the *infinite openness* of the human spirit to God. In this view there is in human nature something more than a "lack of repugnance" for entering into communion with God; it is a real desire. Some were fearful, however, of not being able sufficiently to assert the gratuitous character of this encounter. And so there were timid references to an "eventual and contingent" natural desire mediated through the orientation of human intelligence to being in general (*ens in communi*). According to this position, this desire only proves that the vision of God is a simple possibility; its contingent realization does not affect human nature in any significant way.[23]

The polemical dialogue between these two positions deepened the reflection and issued in a fruitful return to the original thought of Thomas Aquinas. Now there was mention of the presence in human nature of an *innate desire* to see God. This is at the other extreme "lack of repugnance." Indeed, the orientation towards God is viewed here as a constitutive element of the human spirit: every act of knowing implicitly contains the desire to know God. This desire defines human intellectual dynamism.[24] The grace of the vision of God thus culminates a profound aspiration of the human spirit. Human beings fulfill themselves completely only in this communion, dependent upon God's free initiative. The natural and supernatural orders are therefore intimately unified.

The tendency in this development we are describing is to stress unity beyond all distinctions. But this is still to consider it on a metaphysical, abstract, and essentialist level, involving moreover complicated and ultimately fruitless academic arguments. Once the way was cleared, however, for the elimination of dualism, the problem took a sudden new turn; a significant stage was introduced with the recovery of the *historical and existential* viewpoint. In the concrete situation there is but one vocation: communion with God through grace. In reality there is no pure nature and there never has been; there is no one who is not invited to communion with the Lord, no one who is not affected by grace.

This point of view was first supported by Yves de Montcheuil[25] and Henri de Lubac.[26] The novelty of this view (although thoroughly "traditional") and certain ambiguities in language provoked strong reactions. Rahner continued thinking along these lines, and in order to avoid the difficulties encountered by the authors mentioned above proposed the idea of a "supernatural existential," that is, the universal salvific will of God creates in the human being a deep affinity which becomes a gratuitous ontologico-real determinant of human nature. This is "the central and enduring existential condition of man in the concrete."[27] Blondel, whose influence de Montcheuil and de Lubac have explicitly acknowledged, had attempted something similar. He characterized the human state as "transnatural." Devoid of supernatural life, human beings are nevertheless oriented to it by necessity. They are "highly stimulated in relation to this vocation; after the loss of the initial gift, [they] do not fall back into an undifferentiated nature. Rather [they retain] the mark of the point of insertion ready and as it were in potency to receive the restitution [they need] to attain [their] real and obligatory destiny."[28]

This perspective, which transcends scholastic argumentation and expression, is now generally accepted: historically and concretely we know humanity only as actually called to meet God. All considerations not based on this fact are speculations devoid of any real content. But an even more precise formulation has been sought in an effort to be faithful both to the gratuitous quality of God's gift as well as to its unified and all–embracing character.[29]

With certain important qualifications, this actually had been the line of theological thinking until the rise of the doctrine of pure nature in the sixteenth century. Today this perspective is being revived, due at least in part to a different philosophical and theological context which places more value on what is historical and concrete. The initial and fundamental issue, however, is the unity of the divine vocation and therefore of the destiny of the human person, of all persons. The historical point of view allows us to break out of a narrow, individualistic viewpoint and see with more Biblical eyes that human beings are called to meet the Lord insofar as they constitute a community, a people. It is a question not so much of a vocation to salvation as a convocation.

The rediscovery of this single convocation to salvation has caused the crumbling of barriers erected diligently but artificially by a certain kind of theology. It reaffirms the possibility of the presence of grace—that is, of the acceptance of a personal relationship with the Lord—in all persons, be they conscious of it or not. This in turn has led to the consideration of an anonymous Christianity,[30] in other words, of a Christianity beyond the visible frontiers of the Church.[31] The advent of a "Christendom without the name" has been proclaimed.[32] These expressions are equivocal and the choice of words poor.[33] It will be necessary to refine them so that they will point with greater precision to a reality which is itself indisputable: all persons are in Christ efficaciously called to communion with God. To accept the historical viewpoint of the meaning of human existence is to rediscover the Pauline theme of the universal lordship of Christ,[34] in whom all things exist and have been saved.[35]

These developments have manifested themselves in the gradual forsaking of such expressions as *supernatural end*, *supernatural vocation*, and *supernatural order*[36] and in the ever-increasing use of the term *integral*. Martelet rightly observes regarding *Gaudium et spes*, "This term *integral* is perhaps one of the key words of this constitution. In any case, this is how the Council constantly characterizes its way of approaching the vocation of all persons and of the whole person."[37] *Integral vocation* (for example in *Gaudium et spes*, no. 57; see also nos. 10, 11, 59, 61, 63, 64, 75, 91, and *Ad gentes*, no.8) and *integral development* (*Populorum progressio*, no. 14) are expressions which tend to stress the unity of the call to salvation.[38]

The most immediate consequence of this viewpoint is that the frontiers between the life of faith and temporal works, between Church and world, become more fluid. In the words of Schillebeeckx: "The boundaries between the Church and mankind are fluid not merely in the Church's direction, but also, it may be said, in the direction of mankind and the world."[39] Some even ask if they are really two different things "Is not the Church also world? . . . " Metz asks. "The Church is of the world: in a certain sense the Church is the world: the Church is not Non-World."[40]

But there is another important consequence. This affirmation of the single vocation to salvation, beyond all distinctions, gives religious value in a completely new way to human action in history, Christian and non-Christian alike. The building of a just society has worth in terms of the Kingdom,[41] or in more current phraseology, to participate in the process of liberation is already, in a certain sense, a salvific work.[42]

We are faced on the one hand with the affirmation of an ever more autonomous world, not religious, or in more positive terms, a world come of age. On the other hand we are also faced with this single vocation to salvation which values human history in Christian terms, although in a way different from that of the past.[43] Caught in this pincerlike movement, which was not exempt from misinterpretation and sloppy expression,[44] the distinction of planes appears as a burnt-out model with nothing to say to the advances in theological thinking.

Both on the level of the concrete commitments of Christians in the world and on that of contemporary theological thought, the distinction of planes model was thus inadequate. If at a given moment this theology stimulated and supported the presence of Christians in the building up of the world, today it is rigid, lacking in dynamism in the face of the new questions being posed, and therefore no longer viable. Whatever was valid in those distinctions can be maintained only within a radical change of perspective.

# PART 3

# THE OPTION BEFORE THE LATIN AMERICAN CHURCH

We have seen that one of the most fruitful functions of theology—and one in which we are particularly interested in this work—is critical reflection, the fruit of a confrontation between the Word accepted in faith and historical praxis.

Historical developments can help us to discover unsuspected facets of revelation as well as to understand the nature of the Church in greater depth, express it better, and adjust it more successfully to our times (*Gaudium et spes*, no. 44). For this reason the commitment of Christians in history constitutes a true *locus theologicus*.

In this connection it is useful to recall, at least in broad outline, the new awareness of the reality of the continent which Latin Americans have acquired as well as the way in which they understand their own liberation. We will also look at the options which important sectors of the Church are making here in the only predominantly Christian continent among those inhabited by oppressed peoples. The Latin American Church indeed faces peculiar and acute problems related to the process of liberation.

*Chapter Six*

# THE PROCESS OF LIBERATION
# IN LATIN AMERICA

*Dependence* and *liberation* are correlative terms. An analysis of the situation of dependence leads one to attempt to escape from it. But at the same time participation in the process of liberation allows one to acquire a more concrete living awareness of this situation of domination, to perceive its intensity, and to want to understand better its mechanisms. This participation likewise highlights the profound aspirations which play a part in the struggle for a more just society.

## A NEW AWARENESS
## OF THE LATIN AMERICAN REALITY

After a long period of real ignorance of its own reality (except for a brief period of optimism induced by vested interests) Latin America is now progressing from a partial and anecdotal understanding of its situation to a more complete and structural one.

The most important change in the understanding of the Latin American reality lies, first, in going beyond a simple, tearful description with an attendant accumulation of data and statistics, and, second, in having no false hopes regarding the possibility of advancing smoothly and by pre-established steps towards a more developed society. The new approach consists in paying special attention to the root causes of the situation and considering them from a historical perspective. This is the point of view which Latin Americans are beginning to adopt in the face of the challenge of an ever more difficult and contradictory situation.

### *The Decade of Developmentalism*

Latin America in the '50s was characterized by great optimism regarding the possibility of achieving self-sustained economic development. To do this it was necessary to end the stage of *foreign-oriented growth* (exportation of primary products and importation of manufactured products), which made the Latin American countries dependent exclusively upon foreign trade. The more developed countries in the area had already begun to do this. There would then begin an *inward development*. The substitution of imports, expansion of the internal market, and full industrialization, would lead to an independent society. Fernando Henrique Cardoso and Enzo Faletto wrote that "it could not be denied that at the beginning of the decade of the '50s some of the necessary preconditions were present for this new stage in the Latin American economy, at least in countries such as Argentina, Mexico, Chile, Colombia, and Brazil."[1] This approach was based on a favorable set of historical circumstances and was theoretically formulated in serious economic studies.[2] In the political sphere, it was adopted by the populist movements which at different times and with varying influence arose in Latin America.

The developmentalist policies current at that time were supported by international organizations.[3] From their point of view—characterized by structural-functionalist categories—to develop meant to be oriented towards a model abstracted from the more developed societies in the contemporary world. This model was considered to be "modern society" or "industrial society." In achieving this goal, social, political, and cultural obstacles originating from the archaic political structures proper to underdeveloped countries—also referred to as "traditional societies" or "transitional societies"—had to be overcome. The underdeveloped countries thus were considered backward, having reached a lower level than the developed countries. They were obligated, therefore, to repeat more or less faithfully the historical experience of the developed countries in their journey towards modern society. For those located in the heart of the Empire, this modern society was characterized by high mass consumption.[4]

Underdevelopment and development constituted a *continuum*. Dysfunctional groups would arise within the social system of traditional societies, leading to the creation of social forces opposed to the existing order. "At first, the accumulated pressures would produce partial changes and later the modification of society as a whole. According to this model, social systems were regarded as unstable and their transformation would result from the cumulative effect of tension between opposing forces."[5] With the inevitable qualifications and variations, this theory yielded a model and an ideology of modernization which explained the transition of Latin American societies from traditionalism to modernism, from underdevelopment to development.

This point of view sanctioned timid and in the long run deceitful efforts which tended to achieve an ever-greater efficiency. Not only have they failed to eliminate the prevailing economic system, however; they have contributed to its consolidation.[6] Developmentalist policies did not yield the expected results. One of their proponents acknowledged that "after more than half of the decade of the '60s has passed, the *gap* between the two worlds is growing bigger, rather than slowly decreasing as was expected. . . . While from 1960 to

1970 the developed nations will have increased their wealth by 50 percent, the developing countries, two-thirds of the world's population, will continue to struggle in poverty and frustration."[7] The developmentalist approach has proven to be unsound and incapable of interpreting the economic, social, and political evolution of the Latin American continent. According to Cardoso and Faletto, "One gets the initial impression that the interpretative model and the prognoses—which in the light of purely economic factors could be formulated towards the end of the 1940s—were not sufficient to explain the later course of events."[8]

A change of attitude occurred in the '60s. A pessimistic diagnosis of economic, social, and political realities replaced the preceding optimism.[9] Today it is evident that the developmentalist model suffered from grave problems of perspective. It did not sufficiently take into account political factors,[10] and worse, stayed on an abstract and ahistorical level. Underdeveloped, backward societies were statically juxtaposed to modern, developed societies. But, as Theotonio Dos Santos has pointed out, "There is no historical possibility that they will become societies reaching the same stage of development as the developed ones. Historical time is not unilinear. There is no possibility that a contemporary society could evolve to levels achieved earlier by existing societies. All peoples move concurrently and in a parallel fashion towards a new society."[11]

The developmentalist and modernizing approach made it impossible to appreciate both the complexity of the problem and the inevitable conflictual aspects of the process taken as a whole.

### The Theory of Dependence

For some time now, another point of view has been gaining ground in Latin America. It has become ever clearer that underdevelopment is the end result of a process. Therefore, it must be studied from a historical perspective, that is, in relationship to the development and expansion of the great capitalist countries. The underdevelopment of the poor countries, as an overall social fact, appears in its true light: as the historical by-product of the development of other countries.[12] The dynamics of the capitalist economy lead to the establishment of a center and a periphery, simultaneously generating progress and growing wealth for the few and social imbalances, political tensions, and poverty for the many.

Latin America was born and developed in this context. "Latin American societies entered into the history of the development of the universal system of interdependence as dependent societies due to Iberian colonization. Their history can be traced to a large extent as the history of the successive modifications of their condition of dependence. The different societies of the region have reached different positions without having been able, up to this time, to break away from the general framework."[13] This initial situation of dependence is the basis for a correct understanding of underdevelopment in Latin

America.[14] The Latin American countries are "from the beginning and constitutively dependent."[15] For this reason their social structure is very different from that of the center countries. It is necessary to determine carefully the differences between these two societies and to reformulate the concept which will allow us to analyze the situation and even the internal social structure of the peripheral countries. In regard to the peripheral countries there is reference to development that is "uneven and combined." (This is in opposition to the unilinear process of the developed countries.) The study of the dynamics proper to dependence, their current modalities, and their consequences, is undoubtedly the greatest challenge the social sciences face in Latin America.

The notion of dependence emerges therefore as a key element in the interpretation of the Latin America reality. Cardoso defines it thus: "The relationships of dependence presuppose the insertion of specifically unequal structures. The growth of the world market created relationships of dependence (and domination) among nations. Differences were thus established within the unity comprised by the international capitalist system."[16] But we are not dealing with a purely external factor: "The system of *external* domination, from one country to another, cuts through the dependent structure and interpenetrates it. To the extent that it does, the external structure is experienced as internal."[17] During the past few years we have witnessed in Latin America an acceleration of the process which Cardoso and Faletto call "internationalization of the internal market"[18] and which José Nun refers to as "internalization of dependence."[19] The old forms of imperialistic presence by means of the enclave economy (mining centers and plantations), simple prolongations of the central economies, still exist.[20] But currently foreign investment is gravitating towards the modern sector of the economy, that is to say, towards the more dynamic elements of budding native industry, binding it ever more closely to international capitalism. In this way a new kind of dependence arises, less apparent, but no less real.[21]

This new form of dependence not only does not necessitate defending the status quo. It even includes fostering change in the social situation of the Latin American countries, especially the most backward ones. Modernization and the introduction of greater rationality into the economies is required by the vested interests of new economic groups.[22] These groups are increasingly less tied to any one country and are gradually acquiring the character of great multinational corporations.[23]

It is necessary, therefore, to place in a single perspective the expansion of the developed nations. We must follow the new modalities very closely. These points were originally treated by authors such as Hobson and from another point of view by Rosa Luxemburg, Lenin, and Bukharin, who formulated the theory of imperialism and colonialism.[24] But despite occasional references (especially in Lenin), their point of view was fundamentally that of the capitalist countries. Franz Hinkelammert writes, "These are authors who live in the centers of the capitalist world and who deal with the problem of imperialism from the point of view of these centers. They experience the expansive strength of capitalism in these centers; they experience the economic crises of the centers and the ramifications which these phenomena have on the dependent periphery which is exploited by the centers. . . . But what happens in the underdeveloped world itself is not analyzed beyond determining the effects of the exploitation of such countries."[25] Latin American social scientists are determined to study the problem from the point of view of the dominated countries, which will allow them to illuminate and to deepen the theory of dependence. This perspective has been overlooked until now; it should lead to a reformulation of the theory of imperialism.[26]

The imbalance between developed and underdeveloped countries—caused by the relationships of dependence—becomes more acute if the cultural point of view is taken into consideration. The poor, dominated nations keep falling behind; the gap continues to grow. The underdeveloped countries, in relative terms, are always farther away from the cultural level of the center countries; for some it is difficult ever to recover the lost ground. Should things continue as they are, we will soon be able to speak of two human groups, two kinds of people: "Not only sociologists, economists, and political theorists, but also psychologists and biologists have pointed with alarm to the fact that the incessant widening of the distance between the developed and the underdeveloped countries is producing a marked separation of two human groups; this implies the appearance, in a short time, of a true anthropological differentiation. . . . At each level of progress and each stage of development, the industrialized countries advance and accumulate strength which allows them to reach new collective goals of a number and degree much higher than those attainable by the underdeveloped countries."[27]

These new insights must not cause us to forget, however, how much needs to be done in working out an adequate theory of dependence. The Latin American social sciences work under the pressure of concern for immediate political action. This pressure is at the same time their strength and their weakness.[28] It provides a solid starting point, a permanent stimulus to reflection, and the guarantee that this reflection will contribute effectively to social change. But this pressure, which contains intuitive and ideological elements, can also endanger the efforts of the social sciences to acquire a sufficiently scientific character and thus provide an authentic framework—broad and detailed at the same time—for interpreting reality. There is urgent need for a purification to eliminate the less scientific approaches, for a clarification of terms used, for an application of the general categories to ever more complex and constantly evolving realities. "A systematic analysis of the forms dependence has taken in Latin America is still to be made," writes Cardoso, "an analysis which will have to consider, on the one hand, the connection among the particular ways in which Latin American economies are tied to the world market, and on the other, the political structures of domination, both internal and external. Without this analysis and without specifying the kinds of dependence, the use of the term can camouflage new equivocations. For one can have recourse to the idea of dependence as a way of 'explaining' internal processes of the dependent societies by a purely 'external' variable—not readily identifiable but omnipresent—which is regarded as a cause. The importance of analyzing the problems of the peripheral countries in terms of dependence, as we understand it, requires an effort to avoid new reifications, which transform concepts into real factors without any precise identification of their real nature."[29] This task is imperative if we wish to make fertile theses effective and avoid pseudo interpretations and facile solutions.[30]

But only a class analysis will enable us to see what is really involved in the opposition between oppressed countries and dominant peoples. To take into account only the confrontation between nations misrepresents and in the last analysis waters down the real situation. Thus the theory of dependence will take the wrong path and lead to deception if the analysis is not put within the framework of the worldwide class struggle.

The perception of the fact of dependence and its consequences has made possible a new awareness of the Latin American reality.[31] It is now seen clearly that in addition to economic factors, it is also necessary to take into consideration political factors. Development theory must now take into account the situation of dependence and the possibility of becoming free from it. Only in this context can the theory make any sense and have any possibility of being implemented. Studies made along these lines lead one to conclude that autonomous Latin American development is not viable within the framework of the international capitalist system.[32]

## THE LIBERATION MOVEMENT

To characterize Latin America as a dominated and oppressed continent naturally leads one to speak of liberation and above all to participate in the process. Indeed, *liberation* is a term which expresses a new posture of Latin Americans.

The failure of reformist efforts has strengthened this attitude. Among more alert groups today, what we have called a new awareness of Latin American reality is making headway. They believe that there can be authentic development for Latin America only if there is liberation from the domination exercised by the great capitalist countries, and especially by the most powerful, the United States of America.[33] This liberation also implies a confrontation with these groups' natural allies, their compatriots who control the national power structure. It is becoming more evident that the Latin American peoples will not emerge from their present status except by means of a profound transformation, *a social revolution,* which will radically and qualitatively change the conditions in which they now live. The oppressed sectors within each country are becoming aware—slowly, it is true—of their class interests and of the painful road which must be followed to accomplish the breakup of the status quo. Even more slowly they are becoming aware of all that the building of a new society implies.

Because of urbanization and increased industrialization, the Latin American popular movement grew from 1930 on, demanding greater participation in the economic and political life of its respective countries. Political parties of a populist bent capitalized on this basically urban movement. But the crisis of developmentalist policies to which we have referred, the rise of multinational businesses and their growing control of the economy of Latin America, and the appearance of militant peasant masses on the political scene—all these were responsible for the loss of political leadership, at different times in different countries, which the different forms of populism held up to that point. After a period of disorientation, an intense process of political radicalization began.[34] In this regard, the Cuban revolution has played a catalytic role. With certain qualifications, this revolution serves as a dividing point for the recent political history of Latin America.[35] One final factor in all this is the Sino-Soviet split, which among other things has accelerated the internal breakup of the classical communist parties and precipitated the birth of new and more radical revolutionary groups.

Guerrilla groups appeared, intending quickly to mobilize the masses: they did this by urging them to follow a radical line more than through an organization really representing their interests. Military defeats followed each other. The political lessons are nevertheless important.[36] Revolutionary political action has diversified in recent years. It has gone from outbreaks of a leftist nationalism in search of definite options—under the pressure of radicalized groups and the masses—through in-depth connections with the popular masses and even the much-discussed "electoral path," to subversion under new forms of armed struggle. Moreover, it is becoming more obvious that the revolutionary process ought to embrace the whole continent. There is little chance of success for attempts limited to a national scope.

This radicalization has brought about a reaction—both domestically and overseas—on the part of the defenders of the established order. This has in turn frequently led to working outside existing institutions and legal norms and to clandestine, even violent, political activity. The reaction becomes even more belligerent and in many cases resorts to severe and brutal forms of repression.[37] The effect is what Dom Helder Câmara refers to graphically as "the spiral of violence."[38]

In Latin America we are in the midst of a full-blown process of revolutionary ferment. This is a complex and changing situation which resists schematic interpretations and demands a continuous revision of the postures adopted. Be that as it may, the untenable circumstances of poverty, alienation, and exploitation in which the greater part of the people of Latin America live urgently demand that we find a path toward economic, social, and political liberation. This is the first step towards a new society.

These groups and individuals who have raised the banner of Latin American liberation are most frequently of socialist inspiration; socialism, moreover, represents the most fruitful and far-reaching approach. There is, however, no monolithic orientation. A theoretical and practical diversity is emerging. Strategies and tactics are different and in many cases even contrary. Theoretical approaches also vary. This can be a result both of different interpretations of reality and of conscious or unconscious imitation of others' approaches. Indeed, cultural dependence has a role to play even here. Nevertheless, the search for indigenous socialist paths continues. In this field the outstanding figure of José Carlos Mariátegui, despite the inconclusiveness of his work, continues to chart the course. "We certainly do not wish," he wrote in an often-quoted text, "for socialism in America to be an exact copy of others' socialism. It must be a heroic creation. We must bring Indo-American socialism to life with our own reality, in our own language. This is a mission worthy of a new generation."[39] According to Mariátegui, Marxism is not "a body of principles which can be rigidly applied the same way in all historical climates and all social latitudes. . . . Marxism, in each country, for each people, works and acts on the situation, on the milieu, without overlooking any of its modalities."[40] For Mariátegui as for many today in Latin America, historical materialism is above all "a method for the historical interpretation of society."[41] All his work, thought, and action—although not exempt from understandable limitations— was characterized by these concerns. His socialism was creative because it was fashioned in loyalty.[42] He was loyal to his sources, that is, to the central intuitions of Marx, yet was beyond all dogmatism; he was simultaneously loyal to a unique historical reality.[43]

However—and Mariátegui predicted this—only a sufficiently broad, rich, and intense revolutionary praxis, with the participation of people of different viewpoints, can create the conditions for fruitful theory. These conditions are beginning to appear. Without any loss of militancy or radicalness in the theory, they will undoubtedly lead to greater modifications than envisioned by those who sought refuge in easy solutions or in the excommunication of those who did not accept their pat answers, schematizations, and uncritical attitudes toward the historical expressions of socialism.[44] One of the great dangers which threaten the building of socialism in Latin America—pressed as it is by immediate concerns—is the lack of its own solid theory. And this theory must be Latin American, not to satisfy a desire for originality, but for the sake of elementary historical realism.[45]

There is also present in this process of liberation, explicitly or implicitly, a further ramification which it is well to keep in mind. The liberation of our continent means more than overcoming economic, social, and political dependence. It means, in a deeper sense, to see the becoming of humankind as a process of human emancipation in history. It is to see humanity in search of a qualitatively different society in which it will be free from all servitude, in which it will be the artisan of its own destiny.[46] It is to seek the building up of *a new humanity*. Ernesto Che Guevara wrote: "We revolutionaries often lack the knowledge and the intellectual audacity to face the task of the development of a new human being by methods different from the conventional ones, and the conventional methods suffer from the influence of the society that created them."[47]

This vision is what in the last instance sustains the liberation efforts of Latin

Americans. But in order for this liberation to be authentic and complete, it has to be undertaken by the oppressed themselves and so must stem from the values proper to them. Only in this context can a true cultural revolution come about.

From this point of view, one of the most creative and fruitful efforts implemented in Latin America is the experimental work of Paulo Freire, who has sought to establish a "pedagogy of the oppressed."[48] By means of an unalienating and liberating "cultural action," which links theory with praxis, the oppressed perceive—and modify—their relationship with the world and with other persons. They thus make the transfer from a "naive awareness"— which does not deal with problems, gives too much value to the past, tends to accept mythical explanations, and tends toward debate—to a "critical awareness"—which delves into problems, is open to new ideas, replaces magical explanations with real causes, and tends to dialogue. In this process, which Freire calls "conscientization," the oppressed reject the oppressive consciousness which dwells in them, become aware of their situation, and find their own language. They become, by themselves, less dependent and freer, as they commit themselves to the transformation and building up of society.[49] Let us specify, also, that this critical awareness is not a state reached once and for all, but rather a permanent effort of those who seek to situate themselves in time and space, to exercise their creative potential, and to assume their responsibilities. Awareness is, therefore, relative to each historical stage of a people and of humankind in general.

Freire's ideas and methods continue to be developed. All the potentialities of conscientization are slowly unfolding, as well as its limitations. It is a process which can be deepened, modified, reorientated, and extended. This is the task in which in the first place the founder of this movement, as well as many of those who in one way or another have participated in it, are involved.[50]

*Chapter Seven*

# THE CHURCH IN THE PROCESS OF LIBERATION

The Latin American Church has lived and to a large extent continues to live as a ghetto church. The Latin American Christian community came into being during the Counter-Reformation and has always been characterized by its defensive attitude as regards the faith. This posture was reinforced in some cases by the hostility of the liberal and anticlerical movements of the nineteenth century and, more recently, by strong criticism from those struggling to transform the society to which the Church is so tightly linked.

This hostility led the Church to seek the support of the established order and economically powerful groups in order to face its adversaries and assure for itself what it believed to be an opportunity to preach the Gospel peacefully.

But for some time now, we have been witnessing a great effort by the Church to rise out of this ghetto power and mentality and to shake off the ambiguous protection provided by the beneficiaries of the unjust order which prevails on the continent.[1] Individual Christians, small communities, and the Church as a whole are becoming more politically aware and are acquiring a greater knowledge of the current Latin American reality, especially in its root causes. The Christian community is beginning, in fact, to read *politically* the signs of the times in Latin America. Moreover, we have witnessed the taking of positions which could even be characterized as daring, especially compared with previous behavior. We have seen a commitment to liberation which has provoked resistance and mistrust.

All this has required a task of reflection on the questions posed by this new attitude; hence the new theological thinking now occurring in Latin America comes more from the Christian groups committed to the liberation of their people than from the traditional centers for the teaching of theology. The fruitfulness of reflection will depend on the quality of these commitments.

The process is complex and things are changing before our very eyes. Here we focus our attention on participation in the process of liberation and thus do not concern ourselves with other aspects of the life of the Church. It will be helpful to point out some of the highlights which characterize the new situation now being created.[2]

## THE COMMITMENT OF CHRISTIANS

The different sectors of the People of God are gradually committing themselves in different ways to the process of liberation. They are becoming aware that this liberation implies a break with the status quo, that it calls for a social revolution. In relation to the entire Latin American Christian community it must be acknowledged that the number of persons involved is small. But the numbers are growing and active and every day they are acquiring a larger hearing both inside and outside the Church.

### Lay Persons

What we have referred to as the pastoral approach of "New Christendom" brought about, among large groups of Christians, a political commitment to the creation of a more just society. In the past, the lay apostolate movements, especially among youth, have given a considerable number of their better leaders to the political parties of socio-Christian inspiration.[3] The "distinction of planes" stage allowed for purification of the motivation of these commitments as well as for the discovery of new perspectives for the action of Christians in the world, in collaboration with persons of different points of view.[4] Today, apostolic youth movements have radicalized their political options. It has been true for some time now that in most Latin American countries young militants do not share the orientation of moderate renewal groups.[5]

The ever more revolutionary political options of Christian groups—especially students, workers, and peasants—have frequently been responsible for conflicts between lay apostolic movements and the hierarchy. These options have likewise caused the movement members to question their place in the Church and have been responsible for the severe crises experienced by some of them.[6]

Moreover, many have discovered in these movements evangelical demands for an ever more resolute commitment to the oppressed peoples of this exploited continent. But the inadequacy of the theologico-pastoral plans which until recently were considered viable by these movements, the perception of the close ties which unite the Church to the very social order which the movements wish to change, the urgent albeit ambiguous demands of political action, the impression of dealing with the "concrete" in the revolutionary struggle—all these factors have caused many gradually to substitute working for the Kingdom with working for the social revolutions[7]—or, more precisely perhaps, the lines between the two have become blurred.

In the concrete, all this has often meant a commitment to revolutionary political groups.[8] The political situation in Latin America, together with the subversion of the status quo advocated by these groups, force them to become at least partially clandestine. Moreover, as awareness of existing legalized violence grows, the problem of counterviolence is no longer an abstract ethical concern. It now becomes very important on the level of political efficacy. Perhaps more accurately, it is on this latter level that the question of human nature is concretely considered.[9] Under these conditions, the political activity of Christians takes on new dimensions which have caught by surprise not only the ecclesial structures but also the most advanced pedagogical methods of the lay apostolic movements. It is clear, for example, that the kind of apostolic movement represented by the Catholic Action groups among the French workers—that is, communities of Christians with different political options who meet for a *révision de vie* in the light of the faith—is, as such, not viable. Among other reasons, this is so because political radicalization tends to lead to united—and impassioned—positions and because the kind of activity which develops does not allow for entirely free expression of ideas. The model of the Workers' Catholic Action is valid in a more or less stable society where political commitments can be lived out publicly. This model presupposes and facilitates, moreover, a theoretical dialogue with Marxism in a way which holds little interest for Latin America. On this continent, the oppressed and those who seek to identify with them face ever more resolutely a common adversary, and therefore, the relationship between Marxists and Christians takes on characteristics different from those in other places.[10]

On the other hand, meetings between Christians of different confessions but of the same political option are becoming more frequent. This gives rise to ecumenical groups, often marginal to their respective ecclesiastical authorities, in which Christians share their faith and struggle to create a more just society. The common struggle makes the *traditional* ecumenical programs seem obsolete (a "marriage between senior citizens" as someone has said) and impels them to look for new paths toward unity.[11]

A profound renewal or renaissance of various lay apostolic movements is nevertheless apparent. After the initial impact of a radical *politicization* for which they were inadequately prepared theologically, pedagogically, and spiritually, everything seems to indicate that they are beginning to find new approaches.[12] There are also arising new kinds of groups[13] as well as close collaboration among existing movements. These go beyond any particular specialization, yet recognize the need for specialized pedagogies and are oriented toward a specific social milieu; the "cement" holding them together is their particular posture within the Church and within the Latin American political process. A clear option in favor of the oppressed and their liberation leads to basic changes in outlook; there emerges a new vision of the fruitfulness and originality of Christianity and the Christian community's role in this liberation. This is not a matter merely of a reaffirmation of a choice but also of concrete experiences of how to witness to the Gospel in Latin America today. But many questions remain unanswered. The new vitality that can be foreseen does not have before it a completely clear path.

### Priests and Religious

A clearer perception of the tragic realities of the continent, the clear options which political polarization demand, the climate of more active participation in the life of the Church created by Vatican II, and the impulse provided by the Latin American Bishops' Conference at Medellín—all these factors have made priests and religious today one of the most dynamic and restless groups in the Latin American Church.[14] Priests and religious in ever increasing proportions seek to participate more actively in the pastoral decisions of the Church. But, above all, they want the Church to break its ties with an unjust order, and they want it—with renewed fidelity to the Lord who calls it and to the Gospel which it preaches—to cast its lot with those who suffer from misery and deprivation.

In a considerable number of countries, we observe the creation of groups of priests—with characteristics not foreseen by canon law!—who have organized to channel and reinforce their growing concern.[15] These groups are characterized by their determination to commit themselves to the process of liberation and by their desire for radical change both in the present internal structures of the Latin American Church as well as in the manner in which the Church is present and active on this continent of revolution.

These concerns, as well as other factors, have led in many cases to friction with local bishops and apostolic nuncios.[16] We can say that unless deep changes take place this conflictual situation will spread and become more serious in the immediate future.

Moreover, there are many priests who consider it a duty to adopt clear and committed personal positions in the political arena. Some participate actively in politics,[17] often in connection with revolutionary groups. As a matter of fact, this participation is not essentially something new. In many ways the clergy has played and still plays a direct participation in political life (barely veiled in some cases under pretexts of a religious nature). The new dimension is that many priests clearly admit the need and obligation to make such a commitment and above all that their options in one way or another place them in a relationship of subversion regarding the existing social order.

There are other factors: for example, the effects of a certain weariness caused by the intensity of the resistance that must be overcome within the Church; and then there is the disenchantment caused by the apparent futility of work regarded as "purely religious," which has little contact with the reality and social demands of the continent. We are facing an "identity crisis." For some this means a reassessment of the current lifestyle of the clergy; and for others it means even a reevaluation of the meaning of the priesthood itself. On the other hand, the numbers are growing of those who have found a renewed meaning for their priesthood or religious life in the commitment to the oppressed and their struggle for liberation. For them, the Gospel, the Word of the Lord, the message of love, is a liberating force which attacks the roots of all injustice. This leads them to put in second place the questions now being debated—with different priorities in other parts of the world—regarding the priestly or religious life.[18]

Frequently in Latin America today certain priests are considered "subversive." Many are under surveillance or are being sought by the police. Others are in prison, have been expelled from their country (Brazil, Bolivia, Colombia, and the Dominican Republic are significant examples), or have been murdered by terrorist anti-communist groups.[19] For the defenders of the status quo, "priestly subversion" is surprising. They are not used to it. The political activity of some leftist groups, we might say, is—within certain limits—assimilated and tolerated by the system and is even useful to it to justify some of its repressive measures; the dissidence of priests and religious, however, appears as particularly dangerous, especially if we consider the role which they have traditionally played.[20]

### Bishops

The new and serious problems which face the Latin American Church and which shape the conflictual and changing reality find many bishops ill-prepared for their function. There is among them, nevertheless, an awakening to the social dimension of the presence of the Church and a corresponding rediscovery of its prophetic mission.

The bishops of the most poverty-stricken and exploited areas are the ones who have denounced most energetically the injustices they witness.[21] But in exposing the deep causes of these injustices, they have had to confront the great economic and political forces of their countries.[22] They naturally leave themselves open to being accused of meddling in affairs outside their competence and even of being friendly to Marxist ideas. Often this accusation is made, and vigorously, in conservative sectors, both Catholic and non-Catholic. Some of these bishops have become almost political personalities in their respective countries. The consequence has been tightened police vigilance and in some cases death threats on the part of groups of the extreme right.

But it is not just a question of isolated personalities. It is often entire conferences of bishops who openly take a position in this arena.[23] We should also mention the efforts of many bishops to make changes—of varying degrees of radicalness—in Church structures. The results are still much below what is desired and necessary. The first steps do appear to have been taken, but the danger of retreat has not been eliminated, and, above all, there is much yet to be done.

In the majority of cases, options at the episcopal level regarding social transformation have been expressed in written statements, but there have also been cases in which these declarations have been accompanied by very concrete actions: direct intervention in workers' strikes, participation in public demonstrations, and so forth.[24]

## STATEMENTS AND ATTEMPTS AT REFLECTION

From these commitments on which we have commented briefly, there have emerged statements explaining them and outlining a theologico-pastoral reflection upon them.[25]

During the past three years there have appeared a great number of public statements by lay movements, groups of priests and bishops, or national conferences of bishops. As regards doctrinal authority and impact, the most important text we will mention is, of course, that of the Episcopal Conference at Medellín (1968). To a certain extent, the others can be ordered around it. But without these others, it would not be possible to grasp accurately the process which led to Medellín or the repercussions flowing from it. These other statements go beyond Medellín. Their options are clearer and less easily neutralized by the system. They are also closer to concrete commitments. Moreover, these statements express the sentiments of large sectors of the People of God. It is a somewhat muffled voice which still does not actually arise from the oppressed—condemned as they have been to a long silence except through many filters. It is, however, a first attempt at speaking out.

From the point of view of the issues being discussed here, we can classify these texts into two necessarily related themes: the transformation of the Latin American reality and the search for new forms of the Church's presence on the contemporary scene.

### Towards a Transformation of the Latin American Reality

One unifying theme which is present throughout these documents and which reflects a general attitude of the Church is the acknowledgment of the *solidarity of the Church* with the Latin American reality. The Church avoids placing itself above this reality, but rather attempts to assume its responsibility for the injustice which it has supported both by its links with the established order as well as by its silence regarding the evils this order implies. "We recognize that we Christians for want of fidelity to the Gospel have contributed to the present unjust situation through our words and attitudes, our silence and inaction," claim the Peruvian bishops.[26] More than two hundred lay persons, priests, and bishops of El Salvador assert that "our Church has not been effective in liberating and bettering the Salvadoran. This failure is due in part to the above-mentioned incomplete concept of human salvation and the mission of the Church and in part to the fear of losing privileges or suffering persecution."[27]

As for the bishops' vision of reality, they describe the misery and the exploitation in Latin America as "a situation of injustice that can be called institutionalized violence";[28] it is responsible for the death of thousands of innocent victims.[29] This view allows for a study of the complex problems of counterviolence without falling into the pitfalls of a double standard which assumes that violence is acceptable when the oppressor uses it to maintain "order" and is bad when the oppressed invoke it to change this "order." Institutionalized violence violates fundamental rights so patently that the Latin American bishops warn that "one should not abuse the patience of a people that for years has borne a situation that would not be acceptable to anyone with any degree of awareness of human rights."[30] An important part of the Latin American clergy request, moreover, that "in considering the problem of violence in Latin America, let us by all means avoid equating the *unjust violence* of the oppressors (who maintain this despicable system) with the *just violence* of the oppressed (who feel obliged to use it to achieve their liberation)."[31] Theologically, this situation of injustice and oppression is characterized as a "sinful situation" because "where this social peace does not exist, there we will find social, political, economic, and cultural inequalities, there we will find the rejection of the peace of the Lord, and a rejection of the Lord Himself."[32] With this in mind, an important group of priests declared, "We feel we have a right and a duty to condemn unfair wages, exploitation, and starvation tactics as clear indications of sin and evil."[33]

The reality so described is perceived ever more clearly as resulting from a situation of dependence, in which the centers of decision-making are to be found outside the continent; it follows that the Latin American countries are being kept in a condition of neocolonialism.[34] It has been asserted that underdevelopment "can be understood only in terms of the *dependency relationship* with the developed world that it results from. In large measure the underdevelopment of Latin America is a *byproduct* of capitalist development in the West."[35] The interpretation of Latin American reality in terms of dependency is adopted and considered valid "insofar as it allows us to seek a causal explanation, to denounce domination, and to struggle to overcome it with a commitment to liberation which will produce a new society."[36] This perspective is also clearly adopted by a seminar on the problems of youth sponsored by the Education Department of the Latin American Episcopal Council. It stresses that "Latin American dependency is not only economic and political but also cultural."[37]

Indeed, in texts of the Latin American Church of varying origins and degrees of authority, in the last few years there has been a significant although perhaps not completely coherent replacement of the theme of *development*[38] by the theme of *liberation*.[39] Both the term and the idea express the aspirations to be free from a situation of dependence; the "Message of the Bishops of the Third World" states that "an irresistible impulse drives these people on to better themselves and to free themselves from the forces of oppression."[40] In the words of 120 Bolivian priests: "We observe in our people a desire for liberation and a movement of struggle for justice, not only to obtain a better standard of living, but also to be able to participate in the socio-economic resources and the decision-making process of the country."[41] The deeper meaning of these expressions is the insistence on the need for the oppressed peoples of Latin America to control their own destiny. Quoting *Populorum progressio*, Medellín advocates therefore a "liberating education." The bishops see this as "the key instrument for liberating the masses from all servitude and for causing them to ascend 'from less human to more human conditions,' bearing in mind that humanity is responsible for and 'the principal author of its success or failure.' "[42] Moreover, liberation from this servitude is considered in an important passage of Medellín as a manifestation of liberation from sin made possible by Christ: "It is the same God who, in the fullness of time, sends his Son in the flesh so that he might come to liberate all persons from the slavery to which sin has subjected them: hunger, misery, oppression and ignorance—in a word, that injustice and hatred which have their origin in human selfishness."[43]

The Church wishes to share in this aspiration of the Latin American peoples; the bishops at Medellín think of themselves as belonging to a people who are "beginning to discover their proper self-awareness and their task in the consort of nations."[44] "We are vitally aware of the social revolution now in progress. We identify with it."[45] Argentinian priests and lay persons also declare their total commitment to the process of liberation: "We wish to express our total commitment to the liberation of the oppressed and the working class and to the search for a social order radically different from the present one, an order seeking to achieve justice and evangelical solidarity more adequately."[46]

Faced with the urgency of the Latin American situation, the Church denounces as insufficient those partial and limited measures which amount only to palliatives and in the long run actually consolidate an exploitive system. Therefore superficial projects that create mirages and cause setbacks are criticized.[47] At a deeper level, considering that the problems are rooted in the structures of capitalist society which produce a situation of dependency, it is stated that "it is necessary to change the very bases of the system,"[48] for "a true solution to these problems can come about only within the context of a far reaching transformation of existent structures."[49] Hence the criticism of "developmentalism," which advocates the capitalist model as a solution,[50] and the calls for a radicalization of reforms which would otherwise "in the long run . . . serve to consolidate new forms of the capitalist system, bringing with them a new dependence less evident but not less real."[51] Hence also the term *social revolution* appears more frequently and opposition to it is less.[52]

For some, participation in this process of liberation means not allowing themselves to be intimidated by the accusation of being "communist."[53] On the positive side it can even mean taking the path of *socialism*. A group of Colombian priests affirmed, "We forthrightly denounce neocolonial capitalism, since it is incapable of solving the acute problems that confront our people. We are led to direct our efforts and actions toward the building of a Socialist type of society that would allow us to eliminate all forms of man's exploitation of his fellow man, and that fits in with the historical tendencies of our time and the distinctive character of Colombians."[54] According to the Argentinian Priests for the Third World, this socialism will be a "Latin American socialism that will promote the advent of the New Humanity."[55]

In a speech which has been bitterly debated and attacked, one of the most influential figures of the Mexican Church, Don Sergio Méndez Arceo, asserted: "Only socialism can enable Latin America to achieve true development. . . . I believe that a socialist system is more in accord with the Christian principles of true fellowship, justice, and peace. . . . I do not know what kind of socialism, but this is the direction Latin America should go. For myself, I believe it should be a democratic socialism."[56] Old prejudices, inevitable ideological elements, and also the ambivalence of the term *socialism* require the use of cautious language and careful distinctions. There is always the risk that statements in this regard may be interpreted differently by different readers.[57] It is therefore important to link this subject to another which enables us at least under one aspect to clarify what we mean. We refer to the progressive radicalization of the debate concerning private property. The subordination of private property to the social good has been stressed often.[58] But difficulties in reconciling justice and private ownership have led many to the conviction that "private ownership of capital leads to the dichotomy of capital and labor, to the superiority of the capitalist over the laborer, to the exploitation of man by man. . . . The history of the private ownership of the means of production makes evident the necessity of its reduction or suppression for the welfare of society. We must hence *opt for social ownership of the means of production*."[59]

The case of Chile is particularly interesting. The electoral victory of a socialist government poses a decisive and potentially very fruitful challenge to Chilean Christians. The first reactions are already being felt, but it is well to remember that they come out of a long tradition of participation by various groups in the struggle for liberation of the oppressed sectors. A group of priests attached to the university parish in Santiago writes: "The capitalist system exhibits a number of elements which are antihuman . . . Socialism, although it does not deliver humanity from injustices caused by personal attitudes or from the ambiguity inherent in all systems, does offer a fundamental equality of opportunity. Through a change in the relationships of production, it dignifies labor so that the worker, while humanizing nature, becomes more of a person. It offers a possibility for the even development of the country for the benefit of all, especially the most neglected. It asserts that the motivation of morality and social solidarity is of higher value than that of individual interest, and so forth." Human transformation emerges as a simultaneous task: "All this can be implemented if together with the transformation of the economic structure, the transformation of humanity is undertaken with equal enthusiasm. We do not believe persons will automatically become less selfish, but we do maintain that where a socio-economic foundation for equality has been established, it is more possible to work realistically toward human solidarity than it is in a society torn asunder by inequity." The attitude of Christians is based on the understanding that the coming of the Kingdom implies the building of a just society. "If our country engages in an all-out struggle against misery, the Christian, who should participate fully in it, will interpret whatever progress is achieved as a first implementation of the Kingdom proclaimed by Jesus. In other words, today the gospel of Christ implies (and is incarnated in) multiple efforts to obtain justice."[60] The MOAC (Workers' Catholic Action Movement) has this to say regarding the victory of the new Chilean regime: "This fact embodies a great hope and a great responsibility for *all* workers and their organizations: active and watchful collaboration to bring about a more just society which will permit the integral liberation of those oppressed by an inhuman and anti-Christian system such as capitalism."[61]

More recently, a large group of priests has taken a clear stand in favor of the socialist process occurring in Chile. "Socialism, characterized by the social appropriation of the means of production, opens the path to a new economy. This economy makes possible an autonomous and more rapid development as well as an overcoming of the division of a society into antagonistic classes. Nevertheless socialism is not only a new economy. It should also generate new values which make possible the emergence of a society of greater solidarity and fellowship in which workers assume with dignity the role which is theirs. We feel committed to this process already underway and wish to contribute to its success." Further they state, "The profound reason for this commitment is our faith in Jesus Christ, which is deepened, renewed, and takes on flesh according to historical circumstances. To be a Christian is to be in solidarity. To be in solidarity at this time in Chile is to participate in the historical task which the people has set for itself."[62] In a document directed to the bishops' synod in Rome, the Peruvian bishops stated: "When governments arise which are trying to implant more just and human societies in their countries, we propose that the Church commit itself to giving them its backing; contributing to the elimination of prejudice; recognizing the aspirations they hold; and encouraging the search for their own road toward a socialist society."[63]

Finally, the process of liberation requires the *active participation of the oppressed*; this certainly is one of the most important themes running through the writings of the Latin American Church. Based on the evidence of the usually frustrated aspirations of the popular classes to participate in decisions which affect all of society,[64] the realization emerges that it is the poor who must be the protagonists of their own liberation. "It is primarily up to the poor nations and the poor of the other nations to effect their own betterment."[65] Rejecting every kind of paternalism, the ONIS priests say, "We believe that social transformation is not simply a revolution for the people, but that the people themselves, especially farmers and working men, exploited and unjustly kept in the background, must take part in their own liberation."[66] The participation of the oppressed presupposes an awareness on their part of their unjust situation. "Justice, and therefore peace," say the Latin American bishops, "conquer by means of a dynamic action of awakening (*concientización*) and organization of the popular sectors which are capable of pressing public officials who are often impotent in their social projects without popular support."[67]

However, existing structures block popular participation and marginate the great majorities, depriving them of channels for expression of their demands.[68] Consequently, the Church feels compelled to address itself directly to the oppressed—instead of appealing to the oppressors—calling on them to assume control of their own destiny, committing itself to support their demands, giving them an opportunity to express these demands, and even articulating them itself.[69] At Medellín a pastoral approach was approved which encourages and favors "the efforts of the people to create and develop their own grass-roots organizations for the redress and consolidation of their rights and the search for true justice."[70]

### A New Presence of the Church in Latin America

A call to struggle against oppressive structures and to construct a more just society would have very little impact, however, if the whole Church did not rise to the level of these demands by means of a profound revision of its presence in Latin America.

a) The first evidence of this revision which can be culled from the texts mentioned is that, having acknowledged the Church's responsibility in the current situation, they strongly insist that the Church and in particular the bishops fulfill a role of *prophetic denunciation* of these grave injustices rampant in Latin America, which have already been characterized as "sinful situations." The bishops at Medellín asserted, "To us, the Pastors of the Church, belongs the duty . . . to denounce everything which, opposing justice, destroys peace."[71] They are moved to make this denunciation by the "duty of solidarity with the poor, to which charity leads us. This solidarity means that we make ours their problems and their struggles, that we know how to speak with them. This has to be concretized in criticism of injustice and oppression, in the struggle against the intolerable situation which a poor person has to tolerate."[72] Even further, the bishops are asked to go "beyond statements about situations . . . to concentrate on concrete events, and . . . to take positions regarding them."[73] The Peruvian bishops commit themselves to denounce injustice, supporting these denunciations, if necessary, "by concrete gestures of solidarity with the poor and the oppressed."[74] Aware of the difficulties which this solidarity with the poor may bring to those who practice it, the bishops assembled in Medellín declared: "We express our desire to be very close always to those who work in the self-denying apostolate with the poor in order that they will always feel our encouragement and know that we will not listen to parties interested in distorting their work."[75] There is likewise an awareness of the political implications of these actions and of the criticisms which arise from certain sectors: "No one should be intimidated," say the Mexican bishops, "by those who—apparently zealous to preserve the 'purity' and 'dignity' of priestly and religious activity—characterize this intervention of the Church as 'political.' Frequently this false zeal veils the desire to impose a law of silence when the real need is to lend a voice to those who suffer injustice and to develop the social and political responsibility of the People of God."[76]

The denunciation of social injustices is certainly the prevailing theme in the texts of the Latin American Church. This denunciation is a manner of expressing the intention of becoming disassociated from the existing unjust order. "When a system ceases to promote the common good and favors special interests, the Church must not only denounce injustice but also break with the evil system."[77] The denunciation of injustice implies the rejection of the use of Christianity to legitimize the established order.[78] It likewise implies, in fact, that the Church has entered into conflict with those who wield power.[79] And finally it leads to acknowledging the need for the separation of Church and state because "this is of primary importance in liberating the Church from temporal ties and from the image projected by its bonds with the powerful. This separation will free the Church from compromising commitments and make it more able to speak out. It will show that in order to fulfill its mission, the Church relies more on the strength of the Lord than on the strength of Power. And the Church will be able to establish . . . the only earthly ties which it should have: communion with the disinherited of our country, with their concerns and struggles."[80]

The prophetic task of the Church is both constructive and critical and is exercised in the midst of a process of change: "The prophetic task of justice demands, on the one hand, that the Church point out those elements within a revolutionary process which are truly humanizing and encourage the determined, dynamic, and creative participation of its members in this process. On the other hand, the Church must point out the dehumanizing elements also to be found in a process of change. But this function is not appropriate if the creative participation of the Christian community within the society has not already occurred. The Cuban Church is called to this twofold task within our revolution."[81]

b) A second thematic line in the texts we have examined is the urgent need for a *conscienticizing evangelization*. "To us, the Pastors of the Church, belongs the duty to educate the Christian conscience, to inspire, stimulate, and help orient all of the initiatives that contribute to the formation of man," asserted the bishops at Medellín.[82] This awareness of being oppressed but nevertheless of being masters of their own destiny is nothing other than a consequence of a well-understood evangelization: "As we see it, a perhaps faulty presentation of the Christian message may have given the impression that religion is indeed the opiate of the people. And we would be guilty of betraying the cause of Peru's development, if we did not stress the fact that the doctrinal riches of the gospel contain a revolutionary thrust."[83] Indeed, "the God whom we know in the Bible is a liberating God, a God who destroys myths and alienations, a God who intervenes in history in order to break down the structures of injustice and who raises up prophets in order to point out the way of justice and mercy. He is the God who liberates slaves (Exodus), who causes empires to fall and raises up the oppressed."[84] The whole climate of the gospel is a continual demand for the right of the poor to make themselves heard, to be considered preferentially by society, a demand to subordinate economic needs to those of the deprived. Was not Christ's first preaching to "proclaim the liberation of the oppressed?"[85] The content of the message itself, the process of liberation in Latin America, and the demands for participation on the part of the people, all determine "the priority of a conscienticizing evangelization. This evangelization will free, humanize, and better man . . . and will be nourished by the recovery of a living faith committed to human society."[86] The same idea appears in another important text: "In Latin America today evangelization in the context of the youth movements is closely linked to conscientization—insofar as this is understood as an analysis of reality which has Christ as its center and which seeks the liberation of the person."[87] At Medellín the bishops have resolved "to be certain that our preaching, liturgy, and catechesis take into account the social and community dimension of Christianity, forming men committed to world peace."[88] Others point out that this conscienticizing evangelization is a form of "service and commitment to the poorest; evangelizing action ought to be directed preferentially to this group, not only because of the need to understand their life, but also to help them become aware of their own mission, by cooperating in their liberation and development."[89] It is then to the oppressed that the Church should address itself and not so much to the oppressors; furthermore, this action will give true meaning to the Church's witness to poverty. "Poverty in the Church will only be truly achieved when the Church focuses on the evangelization of the oppressed as its primary duty."[90]

c) *Poverty* is, indeed, one of the most frequent and pressing demands placed on the Latin American Church. Vatican II asserts that the Church ought to carry out its mission as Christ did "in poverty and under oppression" (*Lumen gentium*, no. 8.). This is not the image given by the Latin American Christian community as a whole.[91] Rather, poverty is an area in which countersigns are rampant: "Instead of talking about the Church of the poor, we must be a poor Church. And we flaunt this commitment with our real estate, our rectories and other buildings, and our whole style of life."[92] At Medellín it was made clear that poverty expresses solidarity with the oppressed and a protest against oppression. Suggested ways of implementing this poverty in the Church are the evangelization of the poor, the denunciation of injustice, a simple lifestyle, a spirit of service, and freedom from temporal ties, intrigue, or ambiguous prestige.[93]

d) The demands placed on the Church by prophetic denunciation, by the conscienticizing evangelization of the oppressed, and by poverty sharply reveal the *inadequacy of the structures of the Church* for the world in which it lives. These structures appear obsolete and lacking in dynamism before the new and serious challenges. "The very structures in which we operate," says a group of Bolivian priests, "often prevent us from acting in a manner that accords with the gospel. This, too, deeply concerns us; for we see that it greatly complicates the chances of bringing the gospel to the people. The Church cannot be a prophet in our day if she herself is not turned to Christ. She does not have the right to talk against others when she herself is a cause of scandal in her interpersonal relations and her internal structures."[94] There arises, therefore, the urgent need for a profound renewal of the present ecclesial structures. It is the opinion of lay movement representatives that "pastoral structures are insufficient and inadequate. The overall pastoral structure must be reworked if it is to be adequate to the sociological situation in which it is to be carried out."[95] This has been the sense of the seminal effort at Medellín; its implementation is urgent.[96]

e) "The profound changes in Latin America today necessarily affect the priest in his ministry and in his lifestyle," assert the Latin American bishops.[97] The need to change the current *lifestyle of the clergy*[98] is to be considered in this light, especially regarding its commitment to the creation of a new society. Although the denunciation of injustice has political overtones, it is first of all a fundamental demand of the gospel, since it concerns, according to a group of Argentinian priests, "the great option of human beings for their rights, their freedom, and their personal dignity as offspring of God. Moreover, we feel that if we did not denounce injustice we would be responsible for and accessory to the injustices being committed. The exercise of our ministry inevitably leads us to commitment and solidarity."[99] There is need for change also with regard to ways of earning a living: "New ways must be found to support the clergy. Those who do not wish to live on stipends or from teaching religion should be allowed to experiment. . . . A secular job could be very healthy: they would find themselves in the real human world (*Presbyterorum ordinis*, no. 8); it would lessen the temptation to servility on the part of those who depend totally on the clerical institution; it would likewise diminish the financial problems of the institutional Church. It would give a great deal more independence from the government and the armed forces; and finally it would contribute in many of us to the development of a strong apostolic vocation disengaged from all unhealthy ties."[100] Changes are also urged regarding greater participation of lay persons, religious, and priests in the pastoral decisions of the Church.[101]

The documents produced by various sectors of the Latin American Church over the last several years are especially abundant and worthy of a more complete and detailed technical analysis.[102] We have recorded here only the most representative texts which fall within the scope of this work. The issues discussed are markedly different from those being dealt with up to a short time ago.[103] Moreover, in the approach to the problems there is apparent a *growing radicalization*. Although there is still a long road ahead, positions are being taken which are no longer so ambiguous or naive. There is a new attitude—ever more lucid and demanding—suggestive of a qualitatively different society and of basically new forms of the Church's presence in it.

*Chapter Eight*

# STATEMENT
# OF THE QUESTIONS

Although until recently the Church was closely linked to the established order, it is beginning to take a different attitude regarding the exploitation, oppression, and alienation which prevails in Latin America.[1] This has caused concern among the beneficiaries and defenders of capitalist society, who no longer can depend on what used to be—whether consciously or unconsciously—one of their mainstays. This concern is reflected, for example, in the *Rockefeller Report*. After asserting that the Church has become a "force dedicated to change—revolutionary change if necessary," it notes apprehensively and patronizingly that the Church "may be somewhat in the same situation as the young—with a profound idealism, but as a result, in some cases, vulnerable to subversive penetration; ready to undertake a revolution if necessary to end injustice, but not clear either as to the ultimate nature of the revolution itself or as to the governmental system by which the justice it seeks can be realized."[2] Certain groups within the Church, as we have noted above, are beginning to be regarded as subversive and are even being harshly repressed. All this creates for the Latin American Church a completely new situation and forces it to face problems for which the Church—and especially ecclesiastical authority—is poorly prepared. "The daily events in the life of the Church," writes César Aguiar, "go far beyond the expectations of the ordinary Christian. Five years ago who would have thought that in our continent priests would be murdered, Christians persecuted, priests deported, the Catholic press silenced and attacked, ecclesiastical premises searched, and so forth? Probably nobody. Five years ago even the most radical Christians viewed events through utopian lenses and did not grasp their dramatic historical implications."[3]

During the last three years, written statements (more moderate than the concrete commitments of many Christians) have multiplied. Many of them are endowed with great doctrinal authority. There is, however, a dangerous disproportion between what is asserted and called for in these documents and the attitudes of the greater part of the Latin American Church. This is particularly serious for a Church which claims to live according to "a truth which is done."[4]

Nevertheless, the commitments of Christians in Latin America and the texts which attempt to explicate them are gradually fashioning an authentic "political" option of the Church on this continent. Many of these actions are ambiguous, romantic, or careless, but this must not distract us from their fundamental direction. It is true that this option is not that of the majority of the Latin American Christian community; it is, however, the option of its most dynamic sectors, which have a growing influence and a promising future. As a whole the Church in the past has reflected—and indeed still reflects—the ideology of the dominant groups in Latin America. This is what has begun to change.

In this context we must include the Medellín Conference as a major event. At Medellín, the Latin American Church, despite the climate created by the Eucharistic Congress held in Bogotá immediately before it, realistically perceived the world in which it was and clearly saw its place in that world. In short, it began to be aware of its own coming of age and to take the reins of its own destiny.[5] Vatican II speaks of the underdevelopment of peoples, of the developed countries and what they can and should do about this underdevelopment; Medellín tries to deal with the problem from the standpoint of the poor countries, characterizing them as subjected to a new kind of colonialism. Vatican II talks about a Church in the world and describes the relationship in a way which tends to neutralize the conflicts; Medellín demonstrates that the world in which the Latin American Church ought to be present is in full revolution. Vatican II sketches a general outline for Church renewal; Medellín provides guidelines for a transformation of the Church in terms of its presence on a continent of misery and injustice.

Medellín, despite its imperfections and lacunae, legitimates newly-created phenomena in the Latin American Church; efforts at renewal now therefore enjoy unexpected support. Above all, Medellín provides an impulse for new commitments. But the Christian community in Latin America is now living in a post-Medellín period, which (like the postconciliar era) is characterized by dwelling on many of the old questions; there is, however, a new and sharper awareness of these questions. In the post-Medellín period (as in the postconciliar one) some groups would like the surprising consequences of positions they took to be forgotten or mitigated. They cannot contradict the letter of what was said, so they try to declare it inapplicable, valid only for special and carefully defined situations. This effort attempts to devalue not only the authority of Medellín but the spirit which it engendered. It is a useless exercise. If and when it should be accomplished, the Medellín texts will be obsolete. We will be facing a completely new situation. Rather than desperately try to protect these statements from erroneous or deliberately exaggerated interpretations, therefore, it is important to work out their exegesis in concrete reality. Their validity will be confirmed in the *praxis* of the Christian community. Only in this way will they have gospel freshness and permanent historical validity.

Here we shall gather under various headings the more important theologico-pastoral questions posed by this new situation. They will be the basis for the rest of the book.

a) The options which Christians in Latin America are taking have brought a fundamental question to the fore: What is the *meaning of the faith* in a life committed to the struggle against injustice and alienation? How do we relate the work of building a just society to the absolute value of the Kingdom? For many the participation in the process of liberation causes a wearying, anguished, long, and unbearable dichotomy between their life of faith and their revolutionary commitment. What is called for is not to accuse them of confusing the Kingdom with revolution, only because they take the latter seriously and because they believe that the Kingdom is incompatible with the present unjust situation and that in Latin America the coming of the Kingdom presupposes the breaking up of this state of affairs; these accusations often come from those who are comfortably established in a very safe "religious" life. Rather, what is called for is to search out theological responses to the problems which arise in the life of a Christian who has chosen for the oppressed and against the oppressors. Moreover, the close collaboration with people of different spiritual outlooks which this option provides leads one to ponder the contribution proper to the faith. This question must be carefully considered in order to avoid the petty ambition of "having more."

b) The problem, however, is not only to find a new theological framework. The *personal and community prayer* of many Christians committed to the process of liberation is undergoing a serious crisis. This could purify prayer life of childish attitudes, routine, and escapes. But it will not do this if new paths are not broken and new spiritual experiences are not lived. For example, without "contemplative life," to use a traditional term, there is no authentic Christian life; yet what this contemplative life will be is still unknown. There is great need for a spirituality of liberation; yet in Latin America those who have opted to participate in the process of liberation as we have outlined it above, comprise, in a manner of speaking, a first Christian generation. In many areas of their life they are without a theological and spiritual tradition. They are creating their own.

(c) The Latin American reality, *the historical moment* which Latin America is experiencing, is *deeply conflictual*. One of Medellín's great merits is to have been rooted in this reality and to have expressed it in terms surprisingly clear and accessible for an ecclesiastical document. Medellín marks the beginning of a new relationship between theological and pastoral language on the one hand and the social sciences which seek to interpret this reality on the other.[6] This relationship gives rise to statements which are to a large extent contingent and provisional; this is the price one must pay for being incisive and contemporary and for expressing the Word *today* in our everyday words. But this language is only a reflection of a deeper process, a new awareness. The commitments and statements referred to in the two preceding chapters are placing us face to face with a new social experience of Latin Americans and with new directions that the Christian community is beginning to take. It is important to be aware of the newness of this phenomenon. It implies a different, very concrete way of looking at the historical process, that is, of perceiving the presence of the Lord in history, who encourages us to be artisans of this process. Moreover, because of close contact with those who see historical development from a Marxist viewpoint, we are led to review and revitalize the eschatological values of Christianity, which stress not only the provisional nature of historical accomplishments, but above all their openness towards the total communion of all human beings with God. We Christians, however, are not used to thinking in conflictual and historical terms. We prefer peaceful conciliation to antagonism and an evasive eternity to a provisional arrangement. We must learn to live and think of peace in conflict and of what is definitive in what is historical. Very important in this regard are collaboration and dialogue with those who from different vantage points are also struggling for the liberation of oppressed peoples. At stake is the meaning of Christian participation in this liberation.

d) The Latin American Church is sharply *divided* with regard to the process of liberation. Living in a capitalist society in which one class confronts another, the Church, in the measure that its presence increases, cannot escape—nor try to ignore any longer—the profound division among its members.[7] Active participation in the liberation process is far from being a uniform position of the Latin American Christian community. The majority of the Church continues to be linked in many different ways to the established order. And what is worse, among Latin American Christians there are not only different political options within a framework of free interplay of ideas; the polarization of these options and the extreme seriousness of the situation have even placed some Christians among the oppressed and persecuted and others among the oppressors and persecutors, some among the tortured and others among the torturers or those who condone torture. This gives rise to a serious and radical confrontation between Christians who suffer from injustice and exploitation and those who benefit from the established order. Under such circumstances, life in the contemporary Christian community becomes particularly difficult and conflictual. Participation in the Eucharist, for example, as it is celebrated today, appears to many to be an action which, for want of the support of an authentic community, becomes an exercise in make-believe.[8]

From now on it is impossible not to face the problems which arise from this division between Christians, which has reached such dramatic proportions. Clarion calls to Christian unity which do not take into account the deep causes of present conditions and the real prerequisites for building a just society are merely escapist. We are moving towards a new idea of unity and communion in the Church. Unity is not an event accomplished once and for all, but something which is always in the process of becoming, something which is achieved with courage and freedom of spirit, sometimes at the price of painful, heartrending decisions. Latin America must brace itself for such experiences.

e) In Latin America, the Church must place itself squarely within the process of revolution, amid the violence which is present in different ways. The Church's *mission* is defined practically and theoretically, pastorally and theologically, in relation to this revolutionary process. That is, its mission is defined more by the political context than by intraecclesiastical problems. Its greatest "omission" would be to turn in upon itself. Because of the options which, with the qualifications we have indicated, the Christian community is making, it is faced ever more clearly with the dilemma now confronting the whole continent: to be for or against the system, or more subtly, to be for reform or revolution. Many Christians have resolutely decided for the difficult path which leads to the latter. Confronted with this polarization, can ecclesiastical authority remain on the level of general statements? On the other hand, can it go beyond them and still remain within what is traditionally considered to be its specific mission?

For the Latin American Church, it is becoming increasingly clearer that to be in the world without being of the world means concretely to be *in* the system without being *of* the system. It is evident that only a break with the unjust order and a frank commitment to a new society can make the message of love which the Christian community bears credible to Latin Americans. These demands should lead the Church to a profound revision of its manner of preaching the Word and of living and celebrating its faith.

f) Closely connected with this problem is another very controversial question: Should *the Church put its social weight* behind social transformation in Latin America? Some are worried that it would be a mistake for the Church to attempt to achieve the necessary and urgent changes.[9] The fear is that the Church will become linked to the future established order, albeit a more just one. There is also a fear that an effort in this direction will end in a noisy failure: the Latin American bishops are not all of one mind and do not have the necessary means at their disposal to orientate Christians as a whole toward social progress.[10]

The relevance of these fears cannot be denied. There is indeed great risk. But the social influence of the Church is a fact. Not to exercise this influence in favor of the oppressed of Latin America is really to exercise it against them, and it is difficult to determine beforehand the consequences of this action. Not to speak is in fact to become another kind of Church of silence, silence in the face of the despoliation and exploitation of the weak by the powerful. On the other hand, would not the best way for the Church to break its links with the existing order—and in the process lose its ambiguous social prestige—be precisely to denounce the fundamental injustice upon which this order is based? Often the Church alone is in a position publicly to raise its voice and its protest. When some churches have attempted to do this, they have been harassed by the dominant groups and repressed by political power.[11] In order to reflect on what action the Latin American Church should take and to act accordingly, it is necessary to consider its historical and social coordinates, its here and now. To neglect doing this is to remain on an abstract and ahistorical theological level; or, perhaps more subtly, it is to remain on the level of a theology more concerned with avoiding past errors than with discovering the originality of the present situation and committing itself to tomorrow.

g) The Latin American Christian community lives on a poor continent, but the image it projects is not, as a whole, that of a *poor Church*. The *Conclusions* of Medellín accurately acknowledge this fact, which can be verified by anyone who takes the time to get to know the impression of the average Latin American. Prejudices and generalizations undoubtedly distort the image, but no one can deny its fundamental validity. The majority of the Church has covertly or openly been an accomplice of the external and internal dependency of our peoples. It has sided with the dominant groups, and in the name of "efficacy" has dedicated its best efforts to them. It has identified with these sectors and adopted their style of life. We often confuse the possession of basic necessities with a comfortable position in the world, freedom to preach the gospel with protection by powerful groups, instruments of service with the means of power. It is nevertheless important to clarify exactly what the witness of poverty involves.

Despite the hopes aroused by the options we have mentioned, many Christians in Latin America regard them very skeptically. They think that these choices have opened up too late and that real changes in the Church will result only from the social transformations which the whole continent is undergoing. Many even fear—as do many non-Christians—that the efforts of the Latin American Church will only make it the Latin American version of di Lampedusa's "Leopard."

This danger is real and we must be aware of it. In any case, by confronting the problems facing it—with all their peculiar characteristics—the Latin American Church ought to be gradually asserting its *own personality*. The situation of dependency which pervades the continent is also present in the ecclesiastical realm. The Latin American Church was born dependent and still remains in circumstances which have prevented it from developing its peculiar gifts.[12] As on the socio-economic and political levels, this dependency is not only an external factor; it molds the structures, life, and thought of the Latin American Church, which has been more a Church-reflection than a Church-source.[13]

This is another of the repeated complaints of lay persons, priests, religious, and bishops in Latin America.[14] Overcoming the colonial mentality is one of the important tasks of the Christian community. In this way, it will be able to make a genuine contribution to the enrichment of the universal Church; it will be able to face its real problems and to sink deep roots into a continent in revolution.[15]

# PART 4

# PERSPECTIVES

It would be well at this point to summarize the questions discussed in the preceding pages and to outline, from a theological point of view, some of the ideas they suggest, or more precisely, to indicate the basic directions of the work to be done in this field.

Attempting to be true to the method suggested in the first part of this study, we will use as our point of departure the questions posed by social praxis in the process of liberation as well as by the participation of the Christian community in this process within the Latin American context. The Latin American experience holds special interest for us. But it is clear that the commitment to the process of liberation occurs also in churches in other places of the world in different forms and with varying degrees of intensity. Any recourse to the Word of the Lord as well as all references to contemporary theology will be made with reference to this praxis.[1]

The most important point seems to be the following: the scope and gravity of the process of liberation is such that to ponder its significance is really to examine the meaning of Christianity itself and the mission of the Church in the world. These questions are posed, explicitly or implicitly, by the commitments which Christians are making in the struggle against an unjust and alienated society. This serious self-examination is occurring in the very midst of the Church. J. B. Metz correctly comments on this point: "Today it is more the person of faith who lives within the Church than he who lives outside it to whom the faith must be justified."[2] The exhortation of Leo the Great, "Christian, know your dignity," is not easily understood and accepted by today's Christian.

Only this approach fully reveals the import of the questions we are considering and allows us to consider in a new way the meaning of the process of liberation in the light of faith.

## Section One

# FAITH AND
# THE NEW HUMANITY

It is not our purpose to deal with all the complex questions which this heading suggests, but only to consider briefly some of the aspects of the subject which concern us.

From the viewpoint of faith, the motive which in the last instance moves Christians to participate in the liberation of oppressed peoples and exploited social classes is the conviction of the radical incompatibility of evangelical demands with an unjust and alienating society. They feel keenly that they cannot claim to be Christians without a commitment to liberation. But the articulation of the way in which this action for a more just world is related to a life of faith belongs to the level of intuition and groping—at times in anguish.

If theology is a critical reflection—in the light of the Word accepted in faith—on historical praxis and therefore on the presence of Christians in the world, it should help us to establish this relationship. Theological reflection should attempt to discern the positive and negative values in this presence. It should make explicit the values of faith, hope, and charity contained in it. And it should contribute to correcting possible aberrations as well as the neglect of other aspects of Christian life, pitfalls into which the demands of immediate political action, regardless of how generous it is, sometimes allow us to fall. This too is the task of critical reflection, which by definition should not be simply a Christian justification a posteriori.[1] Basically this reflection should contribute in one way or another to a more evangelical, more authentic, more concrete, and more efficacious commitment to liberation.

It is important to keep in mind that beyond—or rather, through—the struggle against misery, injustice, and exploitation the goal is the *creation of a new humanity*. Vatican II has declared, "We are witnesses of the birth of a new humanism, one in which man is defined first of all by his responsibility toward his brothers and toward history" (*Gaudium et spes*, no. 55). This aspiration to create a new man is the deepest motivation in the struggle which many have undertaken in Latin America.[2] The fulfillment of this dream (if it can ever be completely fulfilled) can be only vaguely perceived by this generation, but this aspiration even now inspires their commitment.[3]

This quest poses questions and challenges to the Christian faith. What the faith says about itself will demonstrate its relationship to this goal of the people who are struggling for the emancipation of others and of themselves. Indeed, an awareness of the need for self-liberation is essential to a correct understanding of the liberation process. It is not a matter of "struggling for others," which suggests paternalism and reformist objectives, but rather of becoming aware of oneself as not completely fulfilled and as living in an alienated society. And thus one can identify radically and militantly with those—the people and the social class—who bear the brunt of oppression.

In the light of faith, charity, and hope, what then is the meaning of this struggle, this *creation*? What does this option mean? What is the significance of *novelty* in history and of an orientation towards the future? These are three pertinent questions,[4] three indicators which contemporary theology haltingly pursues; but above all, they are three tasks to be undertaken.

*Chapter Nine*

# LIBERATION AND SALVATION

What is the relationship between salvation and the process of human liberation throughout history? Or more precisely, what is the meaning of the struggle against an unjust society and the creation of a new humanity in the light of the Word? A response to these questions presupposes an attempt to define what is meant by salvation, a concept central to the Christian mystery. This is a complex and difficult task which leads to reflection on the meaning of the saving action of the Lord in history. The salvation of the whole man is centered upon Christ the Liberator.

## SALVATION: CENTRAL THEME OF THE CHRISTIAN MYSTERY

One of the great deficiencies of contemporary theology is the absence of a profound and lucid reflection on the theme of salvation.[1] On a superficial level this might seem surprising, but actually it is what often happens with difficult matters: people are afraid to tackle them. It is taken for granted that they are understood. Meanwhile, new edifices are raised on old foundations established in the past on untested assumptions and vague generalities. The moment comes, however, when the whole building totters; this is the time to look again to the foundations. This hour has arrived for the notion of salvation.[2] Recently various works have appeared attempting to revise and deepen our understanding of this idea.[3] These are only a beginning.

We will not attempt to study this criticism in detail, but will only note that a consideration of this question has revealed two focal points; one follows the other in the manner of two closely linked stages.

### *From the Quantitative . . .*

The questions raised by the notion of salvation have for a long time been considered under and limited by the classical question of the "salvation of the pagans." This is the quantitative, extensive aspect of salvation; it is the problem of the number of persons saved, the possibility of being saved, and the role which the Church plays in this process. The terms of the problem are, on the one hand, the universality of salvation, and on the other, the visible Church as the mediator of salvation.

The evolution of the question has been complex and fatiguing.[4] Today we can say that in a way this evolution has ended. The idea of the universality of the salvific will of God, clearly enunciated by Paul in his letter to Timothy, has been established. It has overcome the difficulties posed by various ways of understanding the mission of the Church and has attained definite acceptance.[5] All that is left to do is to consider the ramifications, which are many.[6]

Here we will briefly consider one important point and leave for later a treatment of the repercussions of this idea on ecclesiological matters. The notion of salvation implied in this point of view has two very well-defined characteristics: it is a cure for sin in this life; and this cure is in virtue of a salvation to be attained beyond this life. What is important, therefore, is to know how a person outside the normal pale of grace, which resides in the institutional Church, can attain salvation. Multiple explanations have attempted to show the extraordinary ways by which a person could be assured of salvation, understood above all as life beyond this one. The present life is considered to be a test: one's actions are judged and assessed in relation to the transcendent end. The perspective here is moralistic, and the spirituality is one of flight from this world. Normally, only contact with the channels of grace instituted by God can eliminate sin, the obstacle which stands in the way of reaching that life beyond. This approach is very understandable if we remember that the question of "the salvation of the pagans" was raised at the time of the discovery of people belonging to other religions and living in areas far from those where the Church had been traditionally rooted.

### . . . to the Qualitative

As the idea of the universality of salvation and the possibility of reaching it gained ground in Christian consciousness and as the quantitative question was resolved and decreased in interest, the whole problem of salvation made a qualitative leap and began to be perceived differently. Indeed, there is more to the idea of the universality of salvation than simply asserting the possibility of reaching it while outside the visible frontiers of the Church. The very heart of the question was touched in the search for a means to widen the scope of the possibility of salvation: persons are saved if they open themselves to God and to others, even if they are not clearly aware that they are doing so. This is valid for Christians and non-Christians alike—for all people. To speak about the presence of grace—whether accepted or rejected—in all people implies, on the other hand, to value from a Christian standpoint the very roots of human activity. We can no longer speak properly of a profane world.[7] A *qualitative and intensive* approach replaces a *quantitative and extensive* one. Human existence, in the last instance, is nothing but a yes or a no to the Lord: "Persons already partly accept communion with God, although they do not explicitly confess Christ as their Lord, insofar as they are moved by grace (*Lumen gentium*, no. 16), sometimes secretly (*Gaudium et spes*, nos. 3, 22), renounce their selfishness, and seek to create an authentic fellowship among human beings. They reject union with God insofar as they turn away from the building up of this world, do not open themselves to others, and culpably withdraw into themselves (Mt. 25:31–46)."[8]

From this point of view the notion of salvation appears in a different light. Salvation is not something otherworldly, in regard to which the present life is merely a test. Salvation—the communion of human beings with God and among themselves—is something which embraces all human reality, transforms it, and leads it to its fullness in Christ: "Thus the center of God's salvific design is Jesus Christ, who by his death and resurrection transforms the universe and makes it possible for the person to reach fulfillment as a human being. This fulfillment embraces every aspect of humanity: body and spirit, individual and society, person and cosmos, time and eternity. Christ, the image of the Father and the perfect God-Man, takes on all the dimensions of human existence."[9]

Therefore, sin is not only an impediment to salvation in the afterlife. Insofar as it constitutes a break with God, sin is a historical reality, it is a breach of the communion of persons with each other, it is a turning in of individuals on themselves which manifests itself in a multifaceted withdrawal from others. And because sin is a personal and social intrahistorical reality, a part of the daily events of human life, it is also, and above all, an obstacle to life's reaching the fullness we call salvation.

The idea of a universal salvation, which was accepted only with great difficulty and was based on the desire to expand the possibilities of achieving salvation, leads to the question of the intensity of the presence of the Lord and therefore of the religious significance of human action in history. One looks then to this world, and now sees in the world beyond not the "true life," but rather the transformation and fulfillment of the present life. The absolute value of salvation—far from devaluing this world—gives it its authentic meaning and its own autonomy, because salvation is already latently there. To express the idea in terms of Biblical theology: the prophetic perspective (in which the Kingdom takes on the present life, transforming it) is vindicated before the sapiential outlook (which stresses the life beyond).[10]

This qualitative, intensive approach has undoubtedly been influenced by the factor which marked the last push toward the unequivocal assertion of the universality of salvation, that is, the appearance of atheism, especially in the heart of Christian countries. Nonbelievers are not interested in an otherworldly salvation, as are believers in other religions; rather they consider it an evasion of the only question they wish to deal with: the value of earthly existence. The qualitative approach to the notion of salvation attempts to respond to this problem.[11]

The developments which we have reviewed here have allowed us definitively to recover an essential element of the notion of salvation which had been overshadowed for a long time by the question of the possibility of reaching it. We have recovered the idea that salvation is an intrahistorical reality. Furthermore, salvation—the communion of human beings with God and among themselves—orients, transforms, and guides history to its fulfillment.

## HISTORY IS ONE

What we have recalled in the preceding paragraph leads us to affirm that, in fact, there are not two histories, one profane and one sacred, "juxtaposed" or "closely linked." Rather there is only one human destiny, irreversibly assumed by Christ, the Lord of history. His redemptive work embraces all the dimensions of existence and brings them to their fullness. The history of salvation is the very heart of human history. Christian consciousness arrived at this unified view after an evolution parallel to that experienced regarding the notion of salvation. The conclusions converge. From an abstract, essentialist approach we moved to an existential, historical, and concrete view which holds that the only human being we know has been efficaciously called to a gratuitous communion with God. All reflection, any distinctions which one wishes to treat, must be based on this fact: the salvific action of God underlies all human existence.[12] The historical destiny of humanity must be placed definitively in the salvific horizon. Only thus will its true dimensions emerge and its deepest meaning be apparent. It seems, however, that contemporary theology has not yet fashioned the categories which would allow us to think through and express adequately this unified approach to history.[13] We work, on the one hand, under the fear of falling back again into the old dualities, and, on the other, under the permanent suspicion of not sufficiently safeguarding divine gratuitousness or the unique dimension of Christianity. Although there may be different approaches to understanding it, the fundamental affirmation is clear: there is only one history[14]—a "Christo-finalized" history.

The study of two great Biblical themes will allow us to illustrate this point of view and to understand better its scope. The themes are the relationship between creation and salvation and the eschatological promises.

### Creation and Salvation

The Bible establishes a close link between creation and salvation. But the link is based on the historical and liberating experience of the Exodus. To forget this perspective is to run the risk of merely juxtaposing these two ideas and therefore losing the rich meaning which this relationship has for understanding the recapitulating work of Christ.

#### Creation: the First Salvific Act

The Bible does not deal with creation in order to satisfy philosophic concerns regarding the origin of the world. Its point of view is quite diverse.

Biblical faith is, above all, faith in a God who gives self-revelation through historical events, a God who saves in history. Creation is presented in the Bible, not as a stage previous to salvation, but as a part of the salvific process: "Praise be to God the Father of our Lord Jesus Christ. . . . In Christ he chose us before the world was founded, to be dedicated, to be without blemish in his sight, to be full of love; and he destined us—such was his will and pleasure—to be accepted as his sons through Jesus Christ" (Eph. 1:3-5).[15] God did not create only in the beginning; he also had an end in mind. God creates all to be his children.[16] Moreover, creation appears as the first salvific act: "Creation," writes Von Rad, "is regarded as a work of Yahweh in history, a work within time. This means that there is a real and true opening up of historical prospect. No doubt, creation as the first of Yahweh's works stands at the very remotest beginnings—only, it does not stand alone, other works are to follow."[17] The creation of the world initiates history,[18] the human struggle, and the salvific adventure of Yahweh. Faith in creation does away with its mythical and supernatural character. It is the work of a God who saves and acts in history; since humankind is the center of creation, it is integrated into the history which is being built by human efforts.

Second Isaiah—"the best theologian among Old Testament writers"[19]—is an excellent witness in this respect. His texts are frequently cited as one of the richest and clearest expressions of the faith of Israel in creation. The stress, however, is on the saving action of Yahweh; the work of creation is regarded and understood only in this context: "But now this is the word of the Lord, the word of your creator, O Jacob, of him who fashioned you, Israel: Have no fear; for I have paid your ransom; I have called you by name and you are my own" (43:1; cf. 42:5-6). The assertion is centered on the redemption (or the Covenant). Yahweh is at one and the same time Creator and Redeemer: "For your husband is your maker, whose name is the Lord of Hosts; your ransomer is the Holy One of Israel who is called God of all the earth" (54:5). Numerous psalms sing praise to Yahweh simultaneously as Creator and Savior (cf. Pss. 74, 89, 93, 95, 135, 136). But this is because creation itself is a saving action: "Thus says the Lord, your ransomer, who fashioned you from birth: I am the Lord who made all things, by myself I stretched out the skies, alone I hammered out the floor of the earth" (Isa. 44:24; cf. also Amos 4:12ff.; 5:8ff.; Jer. 33:25ff.; 10:16; 27:5; 32:17; Mal. 2:10). Creation is the work of the Redeemer. Rendtorff says: "A more complete fusion between faith in creation and salvific faith is unimaginable."[20]

### Political Liberation: Human Self-Creation

The liberation from Egypt—both a historical fact and at the same time a fertile Biblical theme—enriches this vision and is moreover its true source.[21] The creative act is linked, almost identified, with the act which freed Israel from slavery in Egypt. Second Isaiah, who writes in exile, is likewise the best witness to this idea: "Awake, awake, put on your strength, O arm of the Lord, awake as you did long ago, in days gone by. Was it not you who hacked the Rahab in pieces and ran the dragon through? Was it not you who dried up the sea, the waters of the great abyss, and made the ocean depths a path for the ransomed?" (51:9-10). The words and images refer simultaneously to two events: creation and liberation from Egypt. Rahab, which for Isaiah symbolizes Egypt (cf. 30:7; cf. also Ps. 87:4), likewise symbolizes the chaos Yahweh had to overcome to create the world (cf. Pss. 74:14; 89:11).[22] The "waters of the great abyss" are those which enveloped the world and from which creation arose, but they are also the Red Sea which the Jews crossed to begin the Exodus. Creation and liberation from Egypt are but one salvific act. It is significant, furthermore, that the technical term *bara*, designating the original creation, was used for the first time by Second Isaiah (43:1, 15; cf. Deut. 32:6) to refer to the creation of Israel. Yahweh's historical actions on behalf of the people are considered creative (41:20; 43:7; 45:8; 48:7).[23] The God who frees Israel is the Creator of the world.

The liberation of Israel is a political action. It is the breaking away from a situation of despoliation and misery and the beginning of the construction of a just and comradely society. It is the suppression of disorder and the creation of a new order. The initial chapters of Exodus describe the oppression in which the Jewish people lived in Egypt, in that "land of slavery" (13:3; 20:2; Deut. 5:6): repression (Exod. 1:10-11), alienated work (5:6-14), humiliations (1:13-14), enforced birth control policy (1:15-22). Yahweh then awakens the vocation of a liberator: Moses. "I have indeed seen the misery of my people in Egypt. I have heard their outcry against their slave-masters. I have taken heed of their sufferings, and have come down to rescue them from the power of Egypt. . . . I have seen the brutality of the Egyptians towards them. Come now; I will send you to Pharaoh and you shall bring my people Israel out of Egypt" (3:7-10).

Sent by Yahweh, Moses began a long, hard struggle for the liberation of the people. The alienation of the children of Israel was such that at first "they did not listen to him; they had become impatient because of their cruel slavery" (6:9). And even after they had left Egypt, when they were threatened by Pharaoh's armies, they complained to Moses: "Were there no graves in Egypt, that you should have brought us here to die in the wilderness? See what you have done to us by bringing us out of Egypt! Is not this just what we meant when we said in Egypt, 'Leave us alone; let us be slaves to the Egyptians'? We would rather be slaves to the Egyptians than die here in the wilderness" (14:11-12). And in the midst of the desert, faced with the first difficulties, they told him that they preferred the security of slavery—whose cruelty they were beginning to forget—to the uncertainties of a liberation in process: "If only we had died at the Lord's hand in Egypt, where we sat round the fleshpots and had plenty of bread to eat" (16:3). A gradual pedagogy of successes and failures would be necessary for the Jewish people to become aware of the roots of their oppression, to struggle against it, and to perceive the profound sense of the liberation to which they were called. The Creator of the world is the Creator and Liberator of Israel, to whom is entrusted the mission of establishing justice: "Thus speaks the Lord who is God, he who created the skies, . . . who fashioned the earth. . . . I, the Lord, have called you with righteous purpose and taken you by the hand; I have formed you, and appointed you . . . to open eyes that are blind, to bring captives out of prison, out of the dungeons where they lie in darkness" (Isa. 42:5-7).

Creation, as we have mentioned above, is regarded in terms of the Exodus, a historical-salvific fact which structures the faith of Israel.[24] And this fact is a political liberation through which Yahweh expresses love for the people and the gift of total liberation is received.

### Salvation: Re-Creation and Complete Fulfillment

Yahweh summons Israel not only to leave Egypt but also and above all to "bring them up out of that country into a fine, broad land; it is a land flowing with milk and honey" (3:8). The Exodus is the long march towards the promised land in which Israel can establish a society free from misery and alienation. Throughout the whole process, the religious event is not set apart. It is placed in the context of the entire narrative, or more precisely, it is its deepest meaning. It is the root of the situation. In the last instance, it is in this event that the dislocation introduced by sin is resolved and justice and injustice, oppression and liberation, are determined. Yahweh liberates the Jewish people politically in order to make them a holy nation: "You have seen with your own eyes what I did to Egypt. . . . If only you will now listen to me and keep my covenant, then out of all peoples you shall become my special possession; for the whole earth is mine. You shall be my kingdom of priests, my holy nation" (19:4-6). The God of Exodus is the God of history and of political liberation more than the God of nature. Yahweh is the Liberator, the *goel* of Israel (Isa. 43:14; 47:4; Jer. 50:34). The Covenant gives full meaning to the liberation from Egypt; one makes no sense without the other: "The Covenant was a historical event," asserts Gelin, "which occurred in a moment of disruption, in an atmosphere of liberation; the revolutionary climate still prevailed: an intense spiritual impulse would arise from it, as often happens in history."[25] The Covenant and the liberation from Egypt were different aspects of the same movement,[26] a movement which led to encounter with God. The eschatological horizon is present in the heart of the Exodus. Casalis rightly notes that "the heart of the Old Testament is the Exodus from the servitude of Egypt and the journey towards the promised land. . . . The hope of the people of God is not to return to the mythological primitive garden, to regain paradise lost, but to march forward towards a new city, a human and comradely city whose heart is Christ."[27]

Yahweh will be remembered throughout the history of Israel by this act which inaugurates its history, a history which is a re-creation. The God who makes the cosmos from chaos is the same God who leads Israel from alienation to liberation. This is what is celebrated in the Jewish passover. André Neher writes: "The first thing that is expressed in the Jewish passover is the certainty of freedom. With the Exodus a new age has struck for humanity: redemption from misery. If the Exodus had not taken place, marked as it was by the twofold sign of the overriding will of God and the free and conscious assent of men, the historical destiny of humanity would have followed another course. This course would have been radically different, as the redemption, the *geulah* of the Exodus from Egypt, would not have been its foundation. . . . All constraint is accidental; all misery is only provisional. The breath of freedom which has blown over the world since the Exodus can dispel them this very day."[28] The memory of the Exodus pervades the pages of the Bible and inspires one to reread often the Old as well as the New Testament.

The work of Christ forms a part of this movement and brings it to complete fulfillment. The redemptive action of Christ, the foundation of all that exists, is also conceived as a re-creation and presented in a context of creation (cf. Col. 1:15-20; 1 Cor. 8:6; Heb. 1:2; Eph. 1:1-22).[29] This idea is particularly clear in the prologue to the Gospel of St. John.[30] According to some exegetes it constitutes the foundation of this whole Gospel.[31]

The work of Christ is a new creation. In this sense, Paul speaks of a "new creation" in Christ (Gal. 6:15; 2 Cor. 5:17). Moreover, it is through this "new creation," that is to say, through the salvation which Christ affords, that creation acquires its full meaning (cf. Rom. 8). But the work of Christ is presented simultaneously as a liberation from sin and from all its consequences: despoliation, injustice, hatred. This liberation fulfills in an unexpected way the promises of the prophets and creates a new chosen people, which this time includes all humanity. Creation and salvation therefore have, in the first place, a Christological sense: all things have been created in Christ, all things have been saved in him (cf. Col. 1:15-20).[32]

Humankind is the crown and center of the work of creation and is called to continue it through its labor (cf. Gen. 1:28)—and not only through its labor. The liberation from Egypt, linked to and even coinciding with creation, adds an element of capital importance: the need and the place for human active participation in the building of society. If faith "desacralizes" creation, making it the area proper for human work, the Exodus from Egypt, the home of a sacred monarchy, reinforces this idea: it is the "desacralization" of social praxis, which from that time on will be the work of humankind.[33] By working, transforming the world, breaking out of servitude, building a just society, and assuming its destiny in history, humankind forges itself. In Egypt, work is alienated and, far from building a just society, contributes rather to increasing injustice and to widening the gap between exploiters and exploited.

To dominate the earth as Genesis prescribed, to continue creation, is worth nothing if it is not done for the good of humanity, if it does not contribute to human liberation, in solidarity with all, in history. The liberating initiative of Yahweh responds to this need by stirring up Moses' vocation. Only the *mediation of this self-creation*—first revealed by the liberation from Egypt—allows us to rise above poetic expressions and general categories and to understand in a profound and synthesizing way the relationship between creation and salvation so vigorously proclaimed by the Bible.

The Exodus experience is paradigmatic. It remains vital and contemporary due to similar historical experiences which the People of God undergo. As

Neher writes, it is characterized "by the twofold sign of the overriding will of God and the free and conscious consent of humans." And it structures our faith in the gift of the Father's love. In Christ and through the Spirit, persons are becoming one in the very heart of history, as they confront and struggle against all that divides and opposes them. But the true agents of this quest for unity are those who today are oppressed (economically, politically, culturally) and struggle to become free.[34] Salvation—totally and freely given by God, the communion of human beings with God and among themselves—is the inner force and the fullness of this movement of human self-generation initiated by the work of creation.

Consequently, when we assert that humanity fulfills itself by continuing the work of creation by means of its labor, we are saying that it places itself, by this very fact, within an all-embracing salvific process. To work, to transform this world, is to become a man and to build the human community; it is also to save. Likewise, to struggle against misery and exploitation and to build a just society is already to be part of the saving action, which is moving towards its complete fulfillment. All this means that building the temporal city is not simply a stage of "humanization" or "pre-evangelization" as was held in theology until a few years ago. Rather it is to become part of a saving process which embraces the whole of humanity and all human history. Any theological reflection on human work and social praxis ought to be rooted in this fundamental affirmation.

### Eschatological Promises

A second important Biblical theme leads to converging conclusions. We refer to the eschatological promises. It is not an isolated theme, but rather, as the former one, it appears throughout the Bible. It is vitally present in the history of Israel and consequently claims its place among the People of God today.

#### Heirs according to the Promise

The Bible is the book of the Promise, the Promise made by God to human beings, the efficacious revelation of God's love and self-communication; simultaneously it reveals humankind to itself. The Greek word which the New Testament uses to designate the Promise is *epangelía*, which also means "word pledged," "announcement," and "notification"; it is related to *evangelion*.[35] This Promise, which is at the same time revelation and Good News, is the heart of the Bible. Albert Gelin says that "this Promise lies behind the whole Bible, and it makes it the book of hope, the slight hope stronger than experience, as Péguy said, which persists through all trials and is reborn to greater strength after every setback."[36] The Promise is revealed, appeals to humankind, and is fulfilled throughout history. The Promise orients all history towards the future and thus puts revelation in an eschatological perspective.[37] Human history is in truth nothing but the history of the slow, uncertain, and surprising fulfillment of the Promise.

The Promise is a gift accepted in faith. This makes Abraham the father of believers. The Promise was first made to him (cf. Gen. 12:1-3; 15:1-16) that he and his posterity would be, as St. Paul says in a vigorous and fertile expression, "the heirs of the world" (Rom. 4:13).[38] For this reason Jesus, John the Baptist (Luke 3:8; 13:16; 16:22; 19:9), and Paul (Gal. 3:16-29; Rom. 4; Heb. 11) place Abraham at the beginning of the work of salvation.[39] This Promise is "given to those who have such faith" in Jesus Christ (Gal. 3:22). The Promise is fulfilled in Christ, the Lord of history and of the cosmos. In him we are "the 'issue' of Abraham, and so heirs by promise" (Gal. 3:29). This is the mystery which remained hidden until "the fullness of time."

But the *Promise* unfolds—becoming richer and more definite—in the *promises* made by God throughout history. "The first expression and realization of the Promise was the Covenant."[40] The kingdom of Israel was another concrete manifestation. And when the infidelities of the Jewish people rendered the Old Covenant invalid, the Promise was incarnated both in the proclamation of a New Covenant, which was awaited and sustained by the "remnant," as well as in the promises which prepared and accompanied its advent. The Promise enters upon "the last days" with the proclamation in the New Testament of the gift of the Kingdom of God.[41]

The Promise is not exhausted by these promises nor by their fulfillment; it goes beyond them, explains them, and gives them their ultimate meaning. But at the same time, the Promise is announced and is partially and progressively fulfilled in them. There exists a dialectical relationship between the Promise and its partial fulfillments. The resurrection itself is the fulfillment of something promised and likewise the anticipation of a future (cf. Acts 13:23); with it the work of Christ is "not yet completed, not yet concluded"; the resurrected Christ "is still future to himself."[42] The Promise is gradually revealed in all its universality and concrete expression: it is *already* fulfilled in historical events, but *not yet* completely; it incessantly projects itself into the future, creating a permanent historical mobility. The Promise is inexhaustible and dominates history, because it is the self-communication of God. With the Incarnation of the Son and the sending of the Spirit of Promise this self-communication has entered into a decisive stage (Gal. 3:14; Eph. 1:13; Acts 2:38-39; Luke 24:29). But by the same token, the Promise illuminates and fructifies the future of humanity and leads it through incipient realizations towards its fullness.[43] Both the present and future aspects are indispensable for tracing the relationships between Promise and history.

### Eschatology: The Future and the Historical Present

In recent years the eschatological dimension of revelation—and consequently of Christian existence—has been rediscovered.

According to traditional dogmatic theology, the treatise on the "last things" (death, judgment, heaven, hell, the end of the world, the resurrection of the dead) was a kind of appendix not too closely related to the central themes. This treatise began to be referred to as eschatology.[44] Its etymology suggested its appropriateness: *escatos*, "last," and *logos*, "treatise."[45]

Toward the end of the nineteenth century, the eschatological theme appeared in liberal Protestant theological studies (Johannes Weiss, Albert Schweitzer) on the message of Jesus and the faith of the primitive Christian community. Moltmann points out the impact of the rise of this line of thinking, but recalls also the pointlessness of these first efforts.[46] "Dialectical theology" came onto this scene from another vantage point and made eschatology the center of its thinking. The "first" Barth is its best representative. Under the influence of Kant, Barthian eschatology is what Urs von Balthasar calls "transcendental eschatology": eternity is the form of true being; time is nothing but appearance and shadow; the ultimate realities are the first principle of everything[47] and therefore the limit of all time.[48] It was this viewpoint, according to Moltmann, "which prevented the break-through of eschatological dimensions in dogmatics."[49]

But the eschatological theme has continued to gain in importance.[50] The term is controversial;[51] the notion much debated.[52] One idea, however, has emerged: the Bible presents eschatology as the driving force of salvific history radically oriented toward the future. Eschatology is thus not just one more element of Christianity, but the very key to understanding the Christian faith.

Basing his study on a rigorous exegesis of the Old Testament, Von Rad has completed an important attempt at clarification in this area. He believes it is inaccurate to think of the eschatological sphere as a "consistent body of ideas, made up of complex cosmic and mythological expectations about the future, from which the prophets drew what they wanted."[53] To reserve the term *eschatological* to designate the end of time, the fulfillment of history, that is to say, extrahistorical events, he thinks is not enough.[54] For Von Rad, the prophets have "eschatologized" Israel's conceptions of time and history. However, what is characteristic of the prophets is, on the one hand, their orientation toward the *future* and, on the other, their concern with the *present*.

It is due to their posture toward the *future* that the prophets are the typical representatives of the Yahwist religion. What is characteristic of the prophets' message is that the situation they announce "cannot be understood as the continuation of what went before."[55] Their starting point is an awareness of a break with the past; the sins of Israel have rendered it unacceptable; the guarantees given by Yahweh are no longer in force. Salvation can come only from a new historical action of Yahweh which will renew in unknown ways the earlier interventions in favor of the people; the signs announcing this action come to be dimly seen by the prophets' rereading those earlier events. The Exodus is a favorite theme of the prophets; what they retain of it is fundamentally the break with the past and the projection toward the future.[56] This causes Von Rad to conclude that "the message of the prophets has to be termed eschatological whenever it regards the old historical bases of salvation as null and void," and he notes that "we ought then to go on and limit the term. It should not be applied to cases where Israel gave a general expression of her faith in the future, or . . . in the future of one of her sacred institutions." Von Rad ends by saying that "the prophetic teaching is only eschatological when the prophets expelled Israel from the safety of the old saving actions and suddenly shifted the basis of salvation to a future action of God.[57] The core of eschatological thought is in this tension towards that which is to come, towards a new action of God. Hope in new acts of God is based on Yahweh's "fidelity," on the strength of his love for his people which was manifested in the past initiatives on their behalf. These new actions lead to and are nourished by an act to take place at the end of history.[58]

But there is another facet of the prophetic message which we have already considered and which will help us—despite its apparent opposition to the orientation toward the future which we have just mentioned—to pinpoint the notion of eschatology. We refer to the prophets' concern for the present, for the historical vicissitudes which they witness. Because of this concern the object of their hope is very proximate. But, this "closeness" does not exclude an action of Yahweh at the end of history. Indeed, the prophetic message proclaims and is realized in a proximate historical event; at the same time, it is projected beyond this event. This has been perceptively and clearly explained by Steinmann with respect to messianism in his comments on Isaiah's oracle of the "soul." The author distinguishes two meanings in this prophecy: the first, the only one comprehensible to his contemporaries, points to something "immediately offered by Yahweh to remedy the tragic situation created in Jerusalem by the onslaught of the Syro-Ephraimitic League";[59] this is the birth of a new heir to the crown. The second sense is but dimly perceived by the prophet: "It is through the gift of a child that Yahweh will save the world."[60] The eschatological prophecy refers, therefore, to a concrete event, and *in* it to another fuller and more comprehensive one to which history must be open.[61] What is especially important for an accurate understanding of eschatology is the relationship between these events. The relationship is found in the projection towards the future included in the present event. From a similar point of view, Von Rad interprets Deuteronomy, the book which contains the theology of the Covenant: "It is certain, literally, that Deuteronomy comes from the time after the conquest, for it speaks of the people on Mt. Horeb; thus it functions as fiction; because they had been living on the land for a long time. But here we see a clearly eschatological feature which permeates the whole. All the salvific benefits which it mentions, including a life of 'rest,' are proposed to the community again, now that it is called to decide for Yahweh. We are faced with one of the most interesting problems of Old Testament theology: the promises which have already been realized historically are not invalidated, but continue to be true in a new context and somewhat different form. The promise of the land was preached again without interruption as a future good, even after it had been achieved."[62] This interpretation allows him to speak of the eschatological scope of Deuteronomy, an opening to the future which is not only not suppressed by the implementations in the present, but is rather affirmed and dynamized by them.

The historical implementations of promises in the *present* are—insofar as they are ordered toward what is to come—as characteristic of eschatology as the opening to the *future*. More precisely, this tension toward the future lends meaning to and is expressed in the present, while simultaneously being nourished by it. It is thus that the attraction of "what is to come" is the driving force of history. The action of Yahweh in history and at the end of history are inseparable. It has been said often in recent years that the expression used in Exod. 3:14 (*'Ehyeh asher 'ehyeh*) is correctly translated not as "I am who am," which can be interpreted within our categories in the sense of a vigorous but static assertion of God's transcendence, but rather as "I will be who will be." A new kind of transcendence is emphasized: God is revealed as a force in our future and not as an ahistorical being.[63] Grammatically both translations are valid. It would be better perhaps to use an expression which emphasizes the characteristic of permanence: "I am he who is being." But the use of similar expressions (thirty-one times throughout the Bible) and the context of the Covenant in which the above passage is found, lead us rather to stress the active sense of the terminology employed. "To be" in Hebrew means "to become," "to be present," "to occupy a place." "I am" would mean "I am with you," "I am here ready to act" ("When I put forth my power against the Egyptians and bring the Israelites out from them, then Egypt will know that I am the Lord" [Exod. 7:5]). "I am the Lord, I will release you. . . . I will rescue you. . . . I will adopt you as my people. . . . I will lead you to the land. . . . I will give it to you for your possession" (Exod. 6:6-9; cf. also 3:10, 17; 8:18).[64]

The full significance of God's action in history is understood only when it is put in its eschatological perspective; similarly, the revelation of the final meaning of history gives value to the present. The self-communication of God points towards the future, and at the same time this Promise and Good News reveal humanity to itself and widen the perspective of its historical commitment here and now.

### Eschatological Promises: Historical Promises

What has been said will help us to frame better a classic question regarding the interpretation of Old Testament texts. We refer to the so-called spiritualizing influence which the New Testament has on them.[65]

According to this hypothesis, what the Old Testament announces and promises on the "temporal" and "earthly" level has to be translated to a "spiritual" level. A "carnal" viewpoint kept the Jewish people from seeing the hidden, figurative sense of these announcements and promises, which is revealed clearly only in the New Testament. This hermeneutical principle is strongly held in Christian circles. And it is not new. A famous text of Pascal's echoes this ancient tradition: "The prophecies have a hidden and spiritual meaning to which this people were hostile, under the carnal meaning which they loved. If the spiritual meaning had been revealed, they would not have loved it."[66]

Let us take as a recent and representative example of this line of interpretation the opinion of a well-known exegete. Regarding the prophetic promises,

Grelot asserts with his usual precision that there is a fundamental misunderstanding of the object of these promises. "On the one hand," he writes "they seem to refer to the *temporal redemption* of Israel, freed from secular oppression and reestablished in its past status in such a way that all nations participate in its privileges and enjoy with it the earthly goods promised at the time of the first Covenant. But on the other hand, they also seem to refer to the *spiritual* redemption of all men, as can be inferred from some of the brightest pages, not the longest but the purest."[67] In order to clarify this ambiguity, it is necessary to argue from the principle that the true object of the promises is veiled by the figurative language used by the prophets. The problem at hand, therefore, is to discover "what has to be taken literally and what is to be understood figuratively."[68] The answer is clear: the object of these promises is the "permanent *spiritual* drama of humanity which touches directly on the mystery of sin, suffering, and salvation, which constitutes the substance of its destiny"; the texts which transmit these promises to us, however, have only an "accidental relationship with *political* history."[69] The true sense is therefore the "spiritual" one. The New Testament will make this sense perfectly clear.[70]

But is this really a true dilemma: either spiritual redemption or temporal redemption? Is there not in all this an "excessive spiritualization" which Congar advises us to distrust?[71] All indications seem to point in this direction. But there is, perhaps, something deeper and more difficult to overcome. The impression does indeed exist that in this statement of the problem there is an assumption which should be brought to the surface, namely a certain idea of the spiritual characterized by a kind of Western dualistic thought (matter-spirit), foreign to the Biblical mentality.[72] And it is becoming more foreign also to the contemporary mentality.[73] This is a disincarnate "spiritual," scornfully superior to all earthly realities. The proper way to pose the question does not seem to us to be in terms of "temporal promise or spiritual promise." Rather, as we have mentioned above, it is a matter of partial fulfillments through liberating historical events, which are in turn new promises marking the road towards total fulfillment. Christ does not "spiritualize" the eschatological promises; he gives them meaning and fulfillment today (cf. Luke 4:21);[74] but at the same time he opens new perspectives by catapulting history forward, forward towards total reconciliation.[75] The hidden sense is not the "Spiritual" one, which devalues and even eliminates temporal and earthly realities as obstacles; rather it is the sense of a fullness which takes on and transforms historical reality.[76] Moreover, it is only in the temporal, earthly, historical event that we can open up to the future of complete fulfillment.

It is not sufficient, therefore, to acknowledge that eschatology is valid in the future as well as in the present. Indeed, this can be asserted even on the level of "spiritual" realities, present and future. We can say that eschatology does not lessen the value of the present life and yet expresses this in words which might be misleading. If by "present life" one understands only "present *spiritual* life," one does not have an accurate understanding of eschatology. Its presence is an intrahistorical reality. The grace-sin conflict, the coming of the Kingdom, and the expectation of the parousia are also necessarily and inevitably histori-cal, temporal, earthly, social, and material realities.

The prophets announce a kingdom of peace. But peace presupposes the establishment of justice: "Righteousness shall yield peace and its fruit [shall] be quietness and confidence forever" (Isa. 32:17; cf. also Ps. 85).[77] It presup-poses the defense of the rights of the poor, punishment of the oppressors, a life free from the fear of being enslaved by others, the liberation of the oppressed. Peace, justice, love, and freedom are not private realities; they are not only internal attitudes. They are social realities, implying a historical liberation. A poorly understood spiritualization has often made us forget the human conse-quences of the eschatological promises and the power to transform unjust social structures which they imply. The elimination of misery and exploitation is a sign of the coming of the Kingdom. It will become a reality, according to the Book of Isaiah, when there is happiness and rejoicing among the people because "men shall build houses and live to inhabit them, plant vineyards and eat their fruit; they shall not build for others to inhabit nor plant for others to eat. . . . My chosen shall enjoy the fruit of their labor" (65:21-22) because the fruit of their labor will not be taken from them. The struggle for a just world in which there is no oppression, servitude, or alienated work will signify the coming of the Kingdom. The Kingdom and social injustice are incompatible (cf. Isa. 29:18-19 and Matt. 11:5; Lev. 25:10ff. and Luke 4:16-21). "The struggle for justice," rightly asserts Dom Antonio Fragoso, "is also the strug-gle for the Kingdom of God."[78]

The eschatological promises are being fulfilled throughout history, but this does not mean that they can be identified clearly and completely with one or another social reality; their liberating effect goes far beyond the foreseeable and opens up new and unsuspected possibilities. The complete encounter with the Lord will mark an end to history, but it will take place in history. Thus we must acknowledge historical events in all their concreteness and significance, but we are also led to a permanent detachment. The encounter is present even now, dynamizing humanity's process of becoming and projecting it beyond its hopes (1 Cor. 2:6-9); it will not be planned or predesigned.[79] This "ignorance" accounts for the active and committed hope for the gift: Christ is "the Yes pronounced upon God's promises, every one of them" (2 Cor. 1:20).

## CHRIST AND INTEGRAL LIBERATION

The conclusion to be drawn from all the above is clear: salvation embraces all persons and the whole person; the liberating action of Christ—made human in this history and not in a history marginal to real human life—is at the heart of the historical current of humanity; the struggle for a just society is in its own right very much a part of salvation history.

It is fitting, nevertheless, to reconsider the question, reviewing how it has been posed and examining other aspects of it. This will allow us, furthermore, to summarize the ideas presented in this chapter.

## Temporal Progress and the Growth of the Kingdom

Chapter 3 of the first part of *Gaudium et spes* begins by asking about the meaning and value of human activity (no. 33) and ends by recalling, in an often-quoted text, that "earthly progress must be carefully distinguished from the growth of Christ's kingdom. Nevertheless, to the extent that the former can contribute to the better ordering of human society, it is of vital concern to the kingdom of God" (no. 39). The terms used are intentionally general, making different interpretations possible. The history of this text can help both our exegetical efforts and—what is of special interest to us—clarification of the question it poses.

The so-called Schema 13 became the most awaited document of the Council, after the interventions of Cardinals Montini and Suenens towards the end of the first session of the Council. Its principal task was to show the attitude of the Church towards the world.[80] A preliminary text, the so-called "Schema of Zurich," was presented at the third session of the Council; it was heavily attacked both inside and outside the conciliar chambers due to what was considered a "dualistic" approach to the natural and supernatural orders.[81] Its recasting produced what became known as the "Schema of Ariccia," which formed the basis for the present Constitution.

The tone of the Schema of Ariccia was very different from the former document. It vigorously stresses the unity of the human vocation (see Part 1, Chapter 4) and recalls what its principal drafter calls "this elemental but very forgotten truth that redemption embraces the totality of creation." And he adds, "This profound unity of the divine plan for humankind, creation, and the Kingdom is a leitmotiv of Schema 13."[82] Indeed, the Schema asserts that human "history and the history of salvation are closely implicated with each other; in the present, definitive economy of salvation the order of redemption includes the order of creation" (no. 50).[83] Two consequences flow from this statement. The first concerns the mission of the Church: "Since redemption includes the order of creation, the ministry of the Church necessarily encompasses—from its particular point of view—the whole complexus of human realities and problems" (no. 51). The phrase "from its particular point of view" seeks to establish the angle from which the scope of the mission of the Church ought to be considered. But this restriction does not detract from the strength and even the boldness of the text. The second consequence also results from "the inclusion of all creation in the order of redemption"; it refers to the unity of the Christian life: "All human activities, even the most humble, must be vivified for Christians by the Spirit of God and ordered to the Kingdom of God" (no. 52).[84] The text is based on the attitude of the prophets who "saw in injustice not a social disorder or an offense to the poor, but a violation of the divine law and an insult to the holiness of God." It emphasizes the fact that Christ not only did "not soften this doctrine; he perfected it" (no. 52). In this connection it refers to 1 John 3:14 and Matt. 25:31-46, texts which emphasize the oneness of the human attitude toward God and one's neighbor;

these texts have disappeared from the final version of the Constitution.

These texts make it very clear that the Schema of Ariccia adopts the "one history" approach. It defines, helps us to understand, and even corrects the formulation of the distinction which constitutes the immediate antecedent of no. 39 of *Gaudium et spes*: "It is clear that the perfection of the social state is of an order completely different from that of the growth of the Kingdom of God, and they cannot be identified" (no. 43). The text continues, "In all, the form of organization and government adopted by society has a great impact on the human and moral behavior of its citizens, making their entrance into the Kingdom easier or more difficult." Despite the intentions, the choice of words here is unfortunate and gives the impression of a static, extrinsicist, and even moralistic treatment of the question. In comparison, the present text, despite its general character, is better, but it lacks the context of the unified vision which the Schema of Ariccia presented.

The Schema of Ariccia was discussed at the beginning of the fourth session of the Council. At this time it was asked that the distinction between the natural and supernatural orders be clarified and that the confusion between temporal progress and salvation be avoided. This was supported, both by the "minority" as well as some representatives of the conciliar "majority" (Cardinals Doepfner and Frings). There was also objection to an excessive optimism. It was asked that more stress be laid on the meaning of sin and it was feared that the autonomy of the temporal sphere was not sufficiently emphasized. The text was watered down. The present Chapter 4 of the first part of *Gaudium et spes* does not emphasize as strongly as did the Schema of Ariccia the concrete and historical unity of these two orders.[85] With this background, the distinction established in *Gaudium et spes*, no. 39, can be seen in a different light.[86]

The Council refrained from delving into debatable theological questions. It did not oppose the position adopted in the Schema of Ariccia, but fell back on only those assertions which enjoyed a large consensus. This approach had been the intention of the drafters at Ariccia when they presented the text. Because these were "extremely serious questions deeply affecting the spirit of our contemporaries and at the same time referring to very difficult and unclarified problems of Christian revelation," the Mixed Commission did "not wish to espouse specific opinions; rather it preferred to limit itself to transmitting the common doctrine of the Church."[87] However, in the judgment of many persons the Ariccia text went beyond this moderate and prudent approach, and therefore its expressions had to be softened. The final text is limited to two general affirmations: there is a close relationship between temporal progress and the growth of the Kingdom, but these two processes are distinct. Those engaged in the latter not only cannot be indifferent to the former; they must show a genuine interest in and value it. However, the growth of the Kingdom goes beyond temporal progress. In short, there is close relationship but no identification. The conciliar text does not go beyond this. The field is open, within this framework, for different theological postures.[88] The dialogue among them will allow a penetration of this question and will gradually lead to a new consensus, as has happened so often in the history of the Church.

*Populorum progressio* goes a step further. Integral development is regarded as the change from less human to more human living conditions: "Less human conditions first affect those who are so poor as to lack the minimum essentials for life; . . . then they affect those who are oppressed by social structures which have been created by abuses of ownership or by abuses of power, by the exploitation of the workers or by unfair business deals." This subhuman condition is characterized by sin and injustice. It is necessary to rise gradually from this position toward a more human state of things: "More human conditions of life clearly imply passage from want to the possession of necessities, overcoming social evils, increase of knowledge and acquisition of culture. Other more human conditions are increased esteem for the dignity of others, a turning toward the spirit of poverty, cooperation for the common good, and the will for peace. Then comes the human acknowledgment of supreme values and of God, their source and finality." Then comes the most important text, expressed in new terms: "Finally, and above all, are faith, a gift of God accepted by man's good-will, and unity in the charity of Christ, who calls us all to share as sons in the life of the living God, the Father of all men" (no. 21). "More human . . . finally, and above all"—not superhuman or supernatural. This is a fuller idea of what is human, the reaffirmation of the single vocation to the grace of communion with God. This is why there is no solution based on a continuity between what is "natural" and grace; rather there is a profound integration and an ordering toward the fullness of all that is human in the free gift of the self-communication of God. This text is rich in implications and has a freshness absent from other parts of the encyclical dealing with social and economic questions. These ideas are not, however, treated in depth or outlined with great detail and their ramifications are not elaborated. That is a task which still would have to be undertaken.

### The Horizon of Political Liberation

The texts of the magisterium of the Church to which we have referred (with the exception of some points in *Populorum progressio*) are typical of the way contemporary theology treats this question. The approach seems to preclude the question regarding the ultimate meaning of human action in history or, to express it in the terms of *Gaudium et spes*, of the relationship between temporal progress and the growth of the Kingdom. Temporal progress is seen preferably in the dominion of nature by science and technology and in some of the repercussions on the development of human society; there is no radical challenge to the unjust system on which it is based. The conflictual aspects of the political sphere are absent; or rather they have been avoided.

Theologically, therefore, we will consider temporal progress as a continuation of the work of creation and explore its connection with redemptive action. Redemption implies a direct relation to sin, and sin—the breach of friendship with God and others—is a human, social, and historical reality which originates in a socially and historically situated freedom.

"Creation," the cosmos, suffers from the consequences of sin. To cite Rom. 8 in this regard is interesting and does broaden our perspective, but this passage is not directly related to the question at hand. The immediate relationship between creation and redemption easily leads to a juxtaposition or to an artificial inclusion of the former into the latter, in which creation is granted autonomy and yet struggles to escape from the straitjacket it is thus put into. It will be necessary to look at the question from a greater distance, or in other terms, to penetrate it more deeply, in order to capture in a single view or to establish on a single principle the creation-redemption relationship. In the way the problem has previously been stated, there is a curious omission of the liberating and protagonistic role of humankind, the lord of creation and co-participant in its own salvation.[89] As we have already pointed out in this chapter, only the concept of the mediation of human self-creation in history can lead us to an accurate and fruitful understanding of the relationship between creation and redemption. This line of interpretation is suggested by the outstanding fact of the Exodus; because of it, creation is regarded as the first salvific act and salvation as a new creation. Without the perspective of political liberation we cannot go beyond a relationship between two separate "orders," that of creation and that of redemption.[90] The liberation approach subverts also the very "order" involved in the posing of the question.

The human work, the transformation of nature, continues creation only if it is a human act, that is to say, if it is not alienated by unjust socio-economic structures. A whole theology of work, despite its evident insights, appears naive from a political point of view. Teilhard de Chardin is among those who contributed most to a search for a unity between faith and the "religion of the world," but he does so from a scientific point of view. He values the dominion over nature that humankind has achieved and speaks of it as the penetration point of evolution, enabling humankind to control it. Politically his vision is, on the whole, neutral.[91] This focus has had a definite impact, as could be expected, on the views of theologians of the developed world. The faith-science conflict and the application of science to the transformation of the world have sapped most of their energy. This is why concern for human society is translated into terms of development and progress.[92] In other areas the problems are different. The concerns of the so-called Third World countries revolve around the social injustice-justice axis, or, in concrete terms, the oppression-liberation axis.[93] Thus there is a great challenge to the faith of Christians in these countries. In contradistinction to a pessimistic approach to this world which is so frequent in traditional Christian groups and which encourages escapism, there is proposed in these other countries an optimistic vision which seeks to reconcile faith and the world and to facilitate commitment. But this optimism must be based on facts. Otherwise, this posture can be deceitful and treacherous and can even lead to a justification of the present order of things. In the underdeveloped countries one starts with a rejection of the existing situation, considered as fundamentally unjust and dehumanizing. Although this is a negative vision, it is nevertheless the only one which allows us to go to the root of the problems and to create without compromises a new social order, based on justice and fellowship. This rejection does not produce an escapist attitude, but rather a will to revolution.

The concept of political liberation—with economic roots—recalls the conflictual aspects of the historical current of humanity. In this current there is not only an effort to know and dominate nature. There is also a situation—which both affects and is affected by this current—of misery and despoliation of the fruit of human work, the result of the exploitation of human beings; there is a confrontation between social classes and, therefore, a struggle for liberation from oppressive structures which hinder persons from living with dignity and assuming their own destiny. This struggle is the human activity whose ultimate goal must in the first place be enlightened by faith. Once this has been achieved, other facets will likewise be illuminated. The horizon of political liberation allows for a new approach to the problem, it throws new light on it, and it enables us to see aspects which had been but dimly perceived; it permits us also to get away from an alleged apolitical science and provides a different context for the crucial role of scientific knowledge in the historical human praxis. Other religions think in terms of cosmos and nature; Christianity, rooted in Biblical sources, thinks in terms of history. And in this history, injustice and oppression, divisions and confrontations exist. But the hope of liberation is also present.

### Christ the Liberator[94]

The approach we have been considering opens up for us—and this is of utmost importance—unforeseen vistas on the problem of sin. An unjust situation does not happen by chance; it is not something branded by a fatal destiny: there is human responsibility behind it. The prophets said it clearly and energetically and we are rediscovering their words now. This is the reason why the Medellín Conference refers to the state of things in Latin America as a "sinful situation," as a "rejection of the Lord."[95] This characterization, in all its breadth and depth, not only criticizes the individual abuses on the part of those who enjoy great power in this social order; it challenges all their practices, that is to say, it is a repudiation of the whole existing system—to which the Church itself belongs.

In this approach we are far, therefore, from that naive optimism which denies the role of sin in the historical development of humanity. This was the criticism, one will remember, of the Schema of Ariccia and it is frequently made in connection with Teilhard de Chardin and all those theologies enthusiastic about human progress. But in the liberation approach sin is not considered as an individual, private, or merely interior reality—asserted just enough to necessitate "spiritual" redemption which does not challenge the order in which we live. Sin is regarded as a social, historical fact, the absence of fellowship and love in relationships among persons, the breach of friendship with God and with other persons, and, therefore, an interior, personal fracture. When it is considered in this way, the collective dimensions of sin are rediscovered. This is the Biblical notion that José María González Ruiz calls the "hamartiosphere," the sphere of sin: "a kind of parameter or structure which objectively conditions the progress of human history itself."[96] Moreover, sin does not appear as an afterthought, something which one has to mention so as not to stray from tradition or leave oneself open to attack. Nor is this a matter of escape into a fleshless spiritualism. Sin is evident in oppressive structures, in the exploitation of humans by humans, in the domination and slavery of peoples, races, and social classes. Sin appears, therefore, as the fundamental alienation, the root of a situation of injustice and exploitation.[97] It cannot be encountered in itself, but only in concrete instances, in particular alienations.[98] It is impossible to understand the concrete manifestations without understanding the underlying basis and vice versa. Sin demands a radical liberation, which in turn necessarily implies a political liberation.[99] Only by participating in the historical process of liberation will it be possible to show the fundamental alienation present in every partial alienation.

This radical liberation is the gift which Christ offers us. By his death and resurrection he redeems us from sin and all its consequences, as has been well said in a text we quote again: "It is the same God who, in the fullness of time, sends his Son in the flesh, so that he might come to liberate all men from all slavery to which sin has subjected them: hunger, misery, oppression, and ignorance, in a word, that injustice and hatred which have their origin in human selfishness."[100] This is why the Christian life is a passover, a transition from sin to grace, from death to life, from injustice to justice, from the subhuman to the human. Christ introduces us by the gift of his Spirit into communion with God and with all human beings. More precisely, it is because he introduces us into this communion, into a continuous search for its fullness, that he conquers sin—which is the negation of love—and all its consequences.[101]

In dealing with the notion of liberation in Chapter 2, we distinguished three levels of meaning: political liberation, human liberation throughout history, liberation from sin and admission to communion with God. In the light of the present chapter, we can now study this question again. These three levels mutually affect each other, but they are not the same. One is not present without the others, but they are distinct: they are all part of a single, all-encompassing salvific process, but they are to be found at different levels.[102] Not only is the growth of the Kingdom not reduced to temporal progress; because of the Word accepted in faith, we see that the fundamental obstacle to the Kingdom, which is sin, is also the root of all misery and injustice; we see that the very meaning of the growth of the Kingdom is also the ultimate precondition for a just society and a new humanity. One reaches this root and this ultimate precondition only through the acceptance of the liberating gift of Christ, which surpasses all expectations. But, inversely, all struggle against exploitation and alienation, in a history which is fundamentally one, is an attempt to vanquish selfishness, the negation of love. This is the reason why any effort to build a just society is liberating. And it has an indirect but effective impact on the fundamental alienation. It is a salvific work, although it is not all of salvation. As a human work it is not exempt from ambiguities, any more than what is considered to be strictly "religious" work. But this does not weaken its basic orientation or its objective results.

Temporal progress—or, to avoid this aseptic term, human liberation—and the growth of the Kingdom both are directed toward complete communion of human beings with God and among themselves. They have the same goal, but they do not follow parallel roads, not even convergent ones. The growth of the Kingdom is a process which occurs historically *in* liberation, insofar as liberation means a greater human fulfillment. Liberation is a precondition for the new society, but this is not all it is. While liberation is implemented in liberating historical events, it also denounces their limitations and ambiguities, proclaims their fulfillment, and impels them effectively towards total communion. This is not an identification.[103] Without liberating historical events, there would be no growth of the Kingdom. But the process of liberation will not have conquered the very roots of human oppression and exploitation without the coming of the Kingdom, which is above all a gift. Moreover, we can say that the historical, political liberating event *is* the growth of the Kingdom and *is* a salvific event; but it is not *the* coming of the Kingdom, not *all* of salvation. It is the historical realization of the Kingdom and, therefore, it also proclaims its fullness. This is where the difference lies. It is a distinction made from a dynamic viewpoint, which has nothing to do with the one which holds for the existence of two juxtaposed "orders," closely connected or convergent, but deep down different from each other.

The very radicalness and totality of the salvific process require this relationship. Nothing escapes this process, nothing is outside the pale of the action of Christ and the gift of the Spirit. This gives human history its profound unity. Those who reduce the work of salvation are indeed those who limit it to the strictly "religious" sphere and are not aware of the universality of the process. It is those who think that the work of Christ touches the social order in which we live only indirectly or tangentially, and not in its roots and basic structure. It is those who in order to protect salvation (or to protect their interests) lift salvation from the midst of history, where individuals and social classes struggle to liberate themselves from the slavery and oppression to which other individuals and social classes have subjected them. It is those who refuse to see that the salvation of Christ is a radical liberation from all misery, all despoliation, all alienation. It is those who by trying to "save" the work of Christ will "lose" it.

In Christ the all-comprehensiveness of the liberating process reaches its fullest sense. His work encompasses the three levels of meaning which we mentioned above. A Latin American text on the missions seems to us to summarize this assertion accurately: "All the dynamism of the cosmos and of human history, the movement towards the creation of a more just and fraternal world, the overcoming of social inequalities among persons, the efforts, so urgently needed on our continent, to liberate humankind from all that depersonalizes it—physical and moral misery, ignorance and hunger—as well as the awareness of human dignity (*Gaudium et spes*, no. 22)—all these originate, are transformed, and reach their perfection in the saving work of Christ. In him and through him salvation is present at the heart of human history, and there is no human act which, in the last instance, is not defined in terms of it."[104]

*Chapter Ten*

# ENCOUNTERING GOD
# IN HISTORY

As was mentioned above, the purpose of those who participate in the process of liberation is to "create a new humanity." We have attempted to answer our first question, namely, what is the meaning of this struggle, this creation, in the light of the Word accepted in faith? We can now ask ourselves what does this option mean for *humankind*?

In their political commitments, people today are particularly sensitive to the fact that the vast majority of humankind is not able to satisfy its most elementary needs; often they seek to make the service of those who suffer from oppression or injustice the guiding principle of their lives. Moreover, even Christians evaluate "religious" things in terms of their human meaning. This approach is not without ambiguities, but many prefer, in the words of José María González Ruiz, "to err on the side of the human."

We mentioned earlier that theology is tending more and more to reflect on the anthropological aspects of revelation.[1] But the Word is not only a Word about God and *about* human nature: the Word is *made* human. If all that is human is illuminated by the Word, it is precisely because the Word reaches us through human history; Von Rad comments that "it is in history that God reveals the secret of his person."[2] Human history, then, is the location of our encounter with God, in Christ.[3] Recalling the evolution of the revelation regarding the presence of God in the midst of the people will aid us in clarifying the form this encounter in history takes. Both God's presence and our encounter with God lead humanity forward, but we celebrate them in the present in eschatological joy.

## HUMANITY: TEMPLE OF GOD

The Biblical God is close to human beings, a God of communion with and commitment to human beings. The active presence of God in the midst of the people is a part of the oldest and most enduring Biblical promises. In connection with the first Covenant, God said: "I shall dwell in the midst of the Israelites, I shall become their God, and by my dwelling among them they will know that I am the Lord their God who brought them out of Egypt. I am the Lord their God" (Exod. 29:45-46; cf. 26:11-12). And in the proclamation of the new Covenant, God said: "They shall live under the shelter of my dwelling; I will become their God, and they shall become my people. The nations shall know that I the Lord am keeping Israel sacred to myself, because my sanctuary is in the midst of them forever" (Ezek. 37:27-28). This presence, often with the connotation of a dwelling, that is to say, a presence in a particular place (*shekinah*),[4] characterizes the type of relationship established between God and human beings. Thus, Congar can write: "The story of God's relations with his creation and especially with man is none other than the story of his ever more generous, ever deeper Presence among his creatures."[5]

The promise of that presence was fulfilled in different ways throughout history until it reached its fullness in a manner which surpassed all expectations: God became human. Henceforth God's presence became both more universal and more complete.

At the outset of the history of the chosen people, God's self-revelation took place especially on the *mountain*. Sinai was a privileged place for meeting God and for God's manifestations (Exod. 19). Yahweh ordered Moses, "Come up to me on the mountain" (Exod. 24:12; Deut. 10:1), because on the mountain rested the glory of the Lord (Exod. 24:16-17). The God of Israel was known for a long time as "a god of the hills and not a god of the valleys" (1 Kings 20:28). The presence of Yahweh came closer when it was linked to the *tent* which accompanied the Israelites in their pilgrimage through the desert. This was a place of encounter with Yahweh which Moses placed outside the camp and here spoke with Yahweh whenever Israel needed detailed instructions (Exod. 33:7-11; Num. 11:16, 24-26; Deut. 31:14).[6] The same was true of the *Ark of the Covenant,* which also in a sense implied a dwelling place of Yahweh;[7] in it Moses spoke with Yahweh (Num. 1:1). The idea of a dwelling was stressed to the point that there was even a curious identification between Yahweh and the Ark: "Whenever the Ark began to move, Moses said, 'Up, Lord and may thy enemies be scattered and those that hate thee flee before thee.' When it halted, he said, 'Rest, Lord of the countless thousands of Israel' " (Num. 10:35-36; cf. also Josh. 4:5, 13; 1 Sam. 4:17).

The tent, the Ark (and even the mountain) underscore the mobility of the presence of the Lord, who shared the historical vicissitudes of the people (2 Sam. 7:6-7). In a certain way, they precluded any precise, physical location. The situation changed with the temple.[8] The land of Canaan was initially designated as Yahweh's dwelling place. It was the land promised by Yahweh, who was not to be found outside it. David feared exile because he did not wish to be far from Yahweh (1 Sam. 26:19-20). After the prophet Elisha cured his leprosy, Naaman took a handful of the soil of Canaan to be able to offer sacrifices beyond its borders (2 Kings 5:15-19).

Certain places in the land of Canaan were privileged: these were the sanctuaries, generally located in high places. But very soon, especially after the Deuteronomic reform, there was but one official sanctuary in Jerusalem: Solomon's temple. The different traditions converged there: the obscurity of the Holy of Holies recalled the darkness through which Moses climbed Mt. Sinai; the Ark was placed in the temple; the temple is the heart of Jerusalem, and Jerusalem is the center of the land of Canaan—hence the importance of the temple in the life of the Israelites.[9] The connotation of house, dwelling, was greater than in the previous cases (2 Sam. 7:5; 1 Kings 3:1-3; Amos 1:2; and Isa. 2:2; 37:14; Ps. 27:4).

But at the same time—and to keep the balance—it was proclaimed that no temple could contain Yahweh. This idea was expressed forcefully in the famous prophecy of Nathan, motivated by David's desire to erect a temple for Yahweh (2 Sam. 7).[10] Moreover, at the very moment that the temple was consecrated, Solomon admitted that heaven is Yahweh's dwelling place: "Hear the supplication of thy servant and of thy people Israel when they pray towards this place. Hear thou in heaven thy dwelling and, when thou hearest, forgive" (1 Kings 8:30). The theme of the dwelling place of God in the heavens was old (cf. Gen. 11:5; 18:21; 28:12; Exod. 19:11; Deut. 4:36; Ps. 2:4), but it emerged clearly—and with the full strength of its transcendence and universality—at the very moment when the Israelites erected a dwelling, a fixed place, for the privileged encounter with Yahweh. The idea of a heavenly abode gathered strength gradually, especially after the exile. In the temple itself, the Holy of Holies was an empty space: God dwells everywhere.[11]

While these notions of transcendence and universality were taking shape and becoming established, the prophets were harsh in their criticism of purely external worship. Their censure extended to places of worship; God's presence is not bound to a material structure, to a building of stone and gold. "Men shall speak no more of the Ark of the Covenant of the Lord," writes Jeremiah. "They shall not think of it nor remember it nor resort to it; it will be needed no more" (Jer. 3:16). And regarding the temple: "These are the words of the Lord: heaven is my throne and earth my footstool. Where will you build a house for me, where shall my resting place be? All these are of my own making and these are mine. . . . The man I will look to is a man downtrodden and is humble and distressed, one who reveres my words" (Isa. 66:1-2). The last phrase indicates the essence of the criticism: Yahweh's preference is for a profound, interior attitude. To this effect, in proclaiming the new Covenant, Yahweh says: "I will take the heart of stone from your body and give you a heart of flesh. I will put my spirit into you and make you conform to my statutes, keep my laws and live by them" (Ezek. 36:26-27; cf. Jer. 31:33). God will be present in the very heart of every human being.

This proclamation was completely fulfilled with the *Incarnation* of the Son of God: "So the Word became flesh; he came to dwell [pitch his tent] among us" (John 1:14). Nathan's prophecy was accomplished in a most unexpected way. Christ not only announces a prayer "in spirit and in truth" which will have no need for a material temple (John 4:21-23), but he presents himself as the temple of God: "Destroy this temple . . . and in three days I will raise it again." And John specifies: "The temple he was speaking of was his body" (2:19, 20). And Paul tells us: "It is in Christ that the complete being of the Godhead dwells embodied" (Col. 2:9; cf. Eph. 2:20-22; 1 Pet. 2:4-8). God is manifested visibly in the humanity of Christ, the God-Man, irreversibly committed to human history.

Christ is the temple of God. This explains Paul's insistence that the Christian community is a temple of living stones, and that each Christian, a member of this community, is a *temple of the Holy Spirit*: "Surely you know that you are God's temple, where the Spirit of God dwells. Anyone who destroys God's temple will himself be destroyed by God, because the temple of God is holy; and that temple you are" (1 Cor. 3:16-17). "Do you not know that your body is a shrine of the indwelling Holy Spirit, and the Spirit is God's gift to you?" (1 Cor. 6:19).[12] The Spirit sent by the Father and the Son to carry the work of salvation to its fulfillment dwells in every human being—in persons who form part of a very specific fabric of human relationships, in persons who are in concrete historical situations.

Furthermore, not only is the Christian a temple of God; every human being is. The episode with Cornelius shows that the Jews "were astonished that the gift of the Holy Spirit should have been poured out even on Gentiles." Peter draws the conclusion. "Is anyone prepared to withhold the water for baptism from these persons, who have received the Holy Spirit just as we did ourselves?" (Acts 10:45, 47; cf. 11:16-18 and 15:8). For this reason the words of Christ apply to everyone: "Anyone who loves me will heed what I say; then my Father will love him, and we will come to him and make our dwelling with him" (John 14:23). "Many constitute the temple, but invisibly," says Congar referring to the well-known expression of Augustine of Hippo: "Many seem to be within who are in reality without and others seem to be without who are in reality within."[13] In the last instance, only the Lord "knows his own" (2 Tim. 2:19).

What we have here, therefore, is a twofold process. On the one hand, there is a universalization of the presence of God: from being localized and linked to a particular people, it gradually extends to all the peoples of the earth (Amos 9:7; Isa. 41:1-7; 45:20-25; 51:4; and the entire Book of Jonah). On the other hand, there is an internalization, or rather, an integration of this presence: from dwelling in places of worship, this presence is transferred to the heart of human history; it is a presence which embraces the whole person. Christ is the point of convergence of both processes. In him, in his personal uniqueness, the particular is transcended and the universal becomes concrete. In him, in his Incarnation, what is personal and internal becomes visible. Henceforth, this will be true, in one way or another, of every human being.

Finally, let us emphasize that here there is no "spiritualization" involved. The God made flesh, the God present in each and every person, is no more "spiritual" than the God present on the mountain and in the temple. God is even more "material." God is no less involved in human history. On the contrary, God has a greater commitment to the implementation of peace and justice among humankind. God is not more "spiritual," but is closer and, at the same time, more universal; God is more visible and, simultaneously, more internal.

Since the Incarnation, humanity, every human being, history, is the living temple of God. The "pro-fane," that which is located outside the temple, no longer exists.

## CONVERSION TO THE NEIGHBOR

The modes of God's presence determine the forms of our encounter with God. If humanity, each person, is the living temple of God, we meet God in our encounter with others; we encounter God in the commitment to the historical process of humankind.

### *To Know God Is to Do Justice*

The Old Testament is clear regarding the close relationship between God and the neighbor. This relationship is a distinguishing characteristic of the God of the Bible. To despise one's neighbor (Prov. 14:21), to exploit the humble and poor worker, and to delay the payment of wages, is to offend God: "You shall not keep back the wages of a man who is poor and needy, whether a fellow-countryman or an alien living in your country in one of your settlements. Pay him his wages on the same day before sunset, for he is poor and his heart is set on them: he may appeal to the Lord against you, and you will be guilty of sin" (Deut. 24:14-15; cf. Exod. 22:21-23). This explains why "a man who sneers at the poor insults his maker" (Prov. 17:5).

Inversely, to know, that is to say, to love Yahweh is to do justice to the poor and oppressed. When Jeremiah proclaimed the New Covenant, after asserting that Yahweh would inscribe the law in the hearts of human beings, Jeremiah said: "No longer need they teach one another to know the Lord; all of them, high and low alike, shall know me" (31:34). But Jeremiah advises us exactly on what knowing God entails: "Shame on the man who builds his house by unjust means, and completes its roof-chambers by fraud, making his countrymen work without payment, giving them no wage for their labor! Shame on the man who says, 'I will build a spacious house with airy roof-chambers, set windows in it, panel it with cedar, and paint it with vermilion'! If your cedar is more splendid, does that prove you are a king? Think of your father: he ate and drank, dealt justly and fairly; all went well with him. He dispensed justice to the cause of the lowly and poor; did this not show he knew me? says the Lord" (22:13-16). Where there is justice and righteousness, there is knowledge of Yahweh; when these are lacking, it is absent: "There is no good faith or mutual trust, no knowledge of God in the land, oaths are imposed and broken, they kill and rob; there is nothing but adultery and license, one deed of blood after another" (Hos. 4:1-2; cf. Isa. 1). To know Yahweh, which in Biblical language is equivalent to saying to love Yahweh, is to establish just relationships among persons, it is to recognize the rights of the poor. The God of Biblical revelation is known through interhuman justice. When justice does not exist, God is not known; God is absent. "God is everywhere," says the priest to the sacristan in José María Arguedas's novel *Todas las sangres*. And the sacristan, who knows no metaphysics, but is well acquainted with injustice and oppression, replies with accurate Biblical intuition: "Was God in the heart of those who broke the body of the innocent teacher Bellido? Is God in the bodies of the engineers who are killing 'La Esmeralda'? In the official who took the corn fields away from their owners. . . ?" Likewise, Medellín asserts: "Where this social peace does not exist there will we find social, political, economic, and cultural inequalities, there will we find the rejection of the peace of the Lord, and a rejection of the Lord himself" ("Peace," no. 14).

On the other hand, if justice is done, if the alien, the orphan, and the widow are not oppressed, "Then I will let you live in this place, in the land which I gave long ago to your forefathers for all time" (Jer. 7:7). This presence of Yahweh is active; Yahweh "deals out justice to the oppressed. The Lord feeds the hungry and sets the prisoner free. The Lord restores sight to the blind and straightens backs which are bent; the Lord loves the righteous and watches over the stranger; the Lord gives heart to the orphan and widow but turns the course of the wicked to their ruin." So "the Lord shall reign forever" (Ps. 146:7-10).[14]

This encounter with God in concrete actions towards others, especially the poor, is so profound and enriching that by basing themselves on it the prophets can criticize—always validly—all purely external worship. This criticism is but another aspect of the concern for asserting the transcendence and universality of Yahweh. "Your countless sacrifices, what are they to me? says the Lord; I am sated with whole offerings of rams. . . . The offer of your gifts is useless, the reek of sacrifice is abhorrent to me. . . . Though you offer countless prayers, I will not listen. There is blood on your hands. . . . Cease to do evil and learn to do right, pursue justice and champion the oppressed; give the orphan his rights, plead the widow's cause" (Isa. 1:10-17). We love God by loving our neighbor: "Is not this what I require of you as a fast: to loose the fetters of injustice, to untie the knots of the yoke, to snap every yoke and set free those who have been crushed? Is it not sharing your food with the hungry, taking the homeless poor into your house, clothing the naked when you meet them and never evading a duty to your kinsfolk?" (Isa. 58:6-7). Only then will God be with us, only then will God hear our prayer and will we be pleasing to God (Isa. 58:9-11). God wants justice, not sacrifices. Emphasizing the bond between the knowledge of God and interhuman justice, Hosea tells us that Yahweh wishes knowledge and not holocausts: "O Ephraim, how shall I deal with you? How shall I deal with you, Judah? Your loyalty to me is like the morning mist, like dew that vanishes early. Therefore have I lashed you through the prophets and torn you to shreds with my words; loyalty is my desire, not sacrifice, not whole-offerings but the knowledge of God" (Hos. 6:4-6).

Although it is true that in the texts cited the neighbor is essentially a member of the Jewish community, the references to aliens, who together with widows and orphans form a classic trilogy, indicate an effort to transcend these limitations.[15] Nevertheless, the bond between the neighbor and God is changed, deepened, and universalized by the Incarnation of the Word. The famous text so often quoted in recent years, Matt. 25:31-45, is a very good illustration of this twofold process.

### Christ in the Neighbor

The parable of the final judgment,[16] which concludes Matthew's eschatological discourse, seems to many to summarize the essence of the gospel message.[17] Exegetes are alarmed by the way that many theologians use this text and by the consequences which have been deduced for Christian life. Various recent studies have attempted to deal with these new questions; they have not, however, delved into the basic problems.[18] There are many factors involved in the reevaluation of the text. It is fertile soil for research by exegetes and theologians.

Jean-Claude Ingelaere, author of the most extensive and detailed of the studies made along these lines, observes that this pericope poses two fundamental questions: who are the nations judged by the Son of God and who are "the least of the brethren" of the Son of Man? In relation to these two questions, Ingelaere distinguishes three lines of interpretation of this text which have developed to date: some believe that this is a judgment of all persons—Christians and non-Christians—according to their love of neighbor, and particularly of the needy; others see in this a judgment of Christians with regard to their behavior towards the disadvantaged members of the Christian community itself (Origen, Luther); and finally, a minority believe it refers to the judgment of pagans based on their attitude towards Christians. The author obviously opts for the third interpretation. Although the work is thorough and well documented, it is less than convincing. The two restrictions involved in this third exegesis—although they do easily resolve various minor questions (for example, the failure to recognize Christ implied in the question, "When did we see you hungry," etc.)—go against the obvious sense of the text and the context, which stress the universality of the judgment and the central and universal character of charity.[19] This is actually an attempt to revive an old thesis of H. J. Holtzmann,[20] hardly mentioned by Ingelaere, which M. J. Lagrange, based on Loisy, Wiss, and Wellhausen, characterized as "strangely illogical."[21] The majority of the exegetes opt for what Ingelaere considers the first interpretation. The henotheistic expression "all nations" (v. 32) is considered to have a "clearly universal sense."[22] According to Mühlen, it includes "not the pagans as distinguished from the Jews and the Christians, but in fact all persons: pagans, Jews, and Christians."[23] On the other hand, there is also a general consensus regarding the universality of the content of the expression: "the least of my brethen" (v. 40). This term designates "all the needy, whoever they may be, and not only Christians."[24]

This is the line of thinking we will follow. The passage is rich in teachings. Basing our study on it and in line with the subject which interests us, we wish to emphasize three points: the stress on communion and fellowship as the ultimate meaning of human life; the insistence on a love which is manifested in concrete actions, with "doing" being favored over simple "knowing";[25] and the revelation of the human mediation necessary to reach the Lord.

The human person is destined to total communion with God and to the fullest fellowship with all other persons. "Dear friends, let us love one another, because love is from God. Everyone who loves is a child of God and knows God, but the unloving know nothing of God. For God is love" (1 John 4:7-8). This was Christ's revelation. To be saved is to reach the fullness of love; it is to enter into the circle of charity which unites the three Persons of the Trinity; it is to love as God loves. The way to this fullness of love can be no other than love itself, the way of participation in this charity, the way of accepting, explicitly or implicitly, to say with the Spirit: "Abba, Father" (Gal. 4:6). Acceptance is the foundation of all communion among human persons. To sin is to refuse to love, to reject communion and fellowship, to reject even now the very meaning of human existence. Matthew's text is demanding: "Anything you did not do for one of these, however humble, you did not do for me" (25:45). To abstain from serving is to refuse to love; to fail to act for another is as culpable as expressly refusing to do it. This same idea is found later in John: "The man who does not love is still in the realm of death" (1 John 3:14). The parable of the Good Samaritan ends with the famous inversion which Christ makes of the original question. They asked him, "Who is my neighbor?" and when everything seemed to point to the wounded man in the ditch on the side of the road, Christ asked, "Which of these three do you think was neighbor to the man who fell into the hands of the robbers?" (Luke 10:29, 36). The neighbor was the Samaritan who *approached* the wounded man and *made him his neighbor.* The neighbor, as has been said, is not the one whom I find in my path, but rather the one in whose path I place myself, the one whom I approach and actively seek. The other aspects of the Christian life become meaningful if they are animated by charity; otherwise, in Paul's words, they simply are empty actions (cf. 1 Cor. 13). This is why Matthew's text says we will be definitively judged by our love for others, by our capacity to create comradely conditions of life. From a prophetic viewpoint, the judgment ("crisis") will be based, according to Matthew, on the new ethic arising from this universal principle of love.[26]

But this charity exists only in concrete actions (feeding the hungry, giving drink to the thirsty, etc.);[27] it occurs of necessity in the fabric of relationships among persons. "Faith divorced from deeds is barren" (James 2:20). To know God is to do justice: "If you know that he is righteous, you must recognize that every man who does right is his child"(1 John 2:29). But charity does not exist alongside or above human loves; it is not "the most sublime" human achievement like a grace superimposed upon human love. Charity is God's love in us and does not exist outside our human capabilities to love and to build a just and friendly world, to "establish ties" as Saint-Exupéry says. "But if a man has enough to live on, and yet when he sees his brother in need shuts up his heart against him, how can it be said that the divine love dwells in him? My children, love must not be a matter of words or talk; it must be genuine and show itself in action" (1 John 3:17-18). Loving us as a human, Christ reveals to us the Father's love. Charity, the love of God for human beings, is found incarnated in human love—of parents, spouses, children, friends—and it leads to its fullness. The Samaritan approached the injured man on the side of the road not because of some cold religious obligation, but because "his heart was melting" (this is literally what the verb *splankhnizein* means in Luke 10:33; cf. Luke 1:7, 8; 7:13; 15:20), because his love for that man was made flesh in him.[28]

Luis Buñuel's film *Nazarín* is an excellent illustration of the idea we are attempting to convey. A first reading (which generally coincides with a first viewing) invites us to identify with Nazarín, an evangelical priest, poor and unhappy with the ecclesiastical establishment. Completely committed to doing good for the love of God, Nazarín appears gradually to discover the uselessness and failure of charity. And then he understands: the love of God is an illusion; only the love of human beings is important. The enigmatic final sequence emphasizes this revelation of humanity free from deceiving religious mediation. The outline is clear and so has been cited as an example of the "horizontalist" tendency of our times.[29] However, a second reading will reveal that, in fact, Nazarín's charity never existed. He did everything "out of duty." He never really loved with a human love as a person of flesh and blood. His heart never melted. He was more interested in the charitable action *he* was performing than in the concrete *person* for whom it was done. Buñuel cruelly enjoys showing the disastrous consequences of these charitable acts as well as Nazarín's indifference toward them. Nazarín goes through this world as if he were not in it. (The actor evidences this attitude by mechanically reciting his lines.) Buñuel subtly but persistently opposes the "charity" of Nazarín to the vital human love of other characters and shows that all Nazarín is capable of doing for the love of God, others can do for the love of humanity (for example, in the sequence of the town besieged by cholera). This indifference and this contrast are revealing. Nazarín's charity is foreign to human love. It is a fleshless charity and, therefore, nonexistent. Does "simple" human love displace God's love? No. Rather, what is discredited is a so-called charity which really has nothing to do with true love for human beings. This is the reason that, whether intentionally or not, Nazarín is on the right path: he will find the authentic love of God only by means of a real, concrete approach to human persons.[30] The painful complaint of César Vallejo's poem is addressed to the God of "Christians" like Nazarín: "My God, if you had been a man, you would know how to be God."[31] The lesson of Buñuel (that "atheist by the grace of God," as he himself once said) is paradoxical but fruitful: there is nothing more "horizontalist" than charity with no color or human flavor.

We turn to the third idea we wished to consider in connection with this text of Matthew: human mediation to reach God.[32] It is not enough to say that love of God is inseparable from the love of one's neighbor. It must be added that love for God is unavoidably expressed *through* love of one's neighbor.[33] Moreover, God is loved in the neighbor: "But if a man says, 'I love God,' while hating his brother, he is a liar. If he does not love the brother whom he has seen, it cannot be that he loves God whom he has not seen" (1 John 4:20). To love one's brother, to love all persons, is a necessary and indispensable mediation of the love of God; it is to love God: "You did it for me, . . . you did not do it for me." In his perceptive homily at the closing of the Council, Paul VI commented on Matthew's text saying that "a knowledge of humankind is a prerequisite for a knowledge of God"; and he summarized the objective of the Council as "a pressing and friendly invitation to humankind of today to rediscover in fraternal love the God 'to turn away from Whom is to fall, to turn to Whom is to rise again, to remain in Whom is to be secure, to return to Whom is to be born again, in Whom to dwell is to live' (St. Augustine, *Solil.* I, i, 3; P. L. 32, 870)."[34]

Ingelaere examines the different explanations regarding the identification of Christ and the neighbor. One of these he characterizes as being of a mystical order and "limited to establishing and contemplating this mysterious link between Christ and the poor" (A. Durand, T. H. Robinson); another sees in the Son of Man the ideal human being, the archetype of the new humanity "already present in each individual" (J. Héring); a third says that the Son of Man identifies with the human race "by an act of substitution" (T. Preiss); another sees in the Son of Man a "collective reality" (T. W. Manson); and finally there are those who believe that they see in this identification simply an expression which dramatizes the "Christological meaning" of love of the neighbor (G. Gross). Ingelaere discards each one of these explanations, and in line with his theory which restricts "the least" to Christians, he considers that the Lord is represented on earth by his followers (cf. Matt. 18:20). "This relationship," concludes the author, "is so intimate that every act directed towards his followers is an act done for the Son of Man present in their midst: this is 'sympathy' in the strongest sense of the word."[35]

But really this conclusion is valid not only for Christians, but for all persons who, in one way or another, welcome the Word of the Lord into their heart. God's presence in humanity, in each person, which is expressed, for example, in the idea of the temple mentioned above, seems to us more fruitful and richer in ramifications.[36] It is in the temple that we find God, but in a temple of living stones, of closely related persons, who together make history and fashion themselves. God is revealed in history, and it is likewise in history that persons encounter the Word made flesh. Christ is not a private individual; the bond which links him to all persons gives him a unique historical role.[37] God's temple is human history; the "sacred" transcends the narrow limits of the places of worship.[38] We find the Lord in our encounters with others, especially the poor, marginated, and exploited ones. An act of love towards them is an act of love towards God. This is why Congar speaks of "the sacrament of our neighbor," who as a visible reality reveals to us and allows us to welcome the Lord: "But there is one thing that is privileged to be a paradoxical sign of God, in relation to which men are able to manifest their deepest commitment—our Neighbor. The sacrament of our Neighbor!"[39]

"The lottery vendor who hawks tickets 'for the big one,' " wrote Vallejo in another poem, "somehow deep down represents God."[40] But every person is a lottery vendor who offers us "the big one": our encounter with that God who is deep down in the heart of each person.[41]

Nevertheless, the neighbor is not an occasion, an instrument, for becoming closer to God.[42] We are dealing with a real love of persons for their own sake and not "for the love of God," as the well-intended but ambiguous and ill-used cliché would have it—ambiguous and ill-used because many seem to interpret it in a sense which forgets that the love for God is expressed in a true love for persons themselves. This is the only way to have a true encounter with God. That my action towards another is at the same time an action towards God does not detract from its truth and concreteness, but rather gives it even greater meaning and import.

It is also necessary to avoid the pitfalls of an individualistic charity. As it has been insisted in recent years, the neighbor is not only a person viewed individually. The term refers also to a person considered in the fabric of social relationships, to a person situated in economic, social, cultural, and racial coordinates. It likewise refers to the exploited social class, the dominated people, the marginated. The masses are also our neighbor, as Chenu asserts.[43] This point of view leads us far beyond the individualistic language of the I-Thou relationship. Charity is today a "political charity," according to the phrase of Pius XII. Indeed, to offer food or drink in our day is a political action; it means the transformation of a society structured to benefit a few who appropriate to themselves the value of the work of others. This transformation ought to be directed toward a radical change in the foundation of society, that is, the private ownership of the means of production.

Our encounter with the Lord occurs in our encounter with others, especially in the encounter with those whose human features have been disfigured by oppression, despoliation, and alienation and who have "no beauty, no majesty" but are the things "from which men turn away their eyes" (Isa. 53:2-3). These are the marginal groups, who have fashioned a true culture for themselves and whose values one must understand if one wishes to reach them.[44] The salvation of humanity passes through them; they are the bearers of the meaning of history and "inherit the Kingdom" (James 2:5). Our attitude towards them, or rather our commitment to them, will indicate whether or not we are directing our existence in conformity with the will of the Father. This is what Christ reveals to us by identifying himself with the poor in the text of Matthew.[45] A theology of the neighbor, which has yet to be worked out, would have to be structured on this basis.[46]

## A SPIRITUALITY OF LIBERATION

To place oneself in the perspective of the Kingdom means to participate in the struggle for the liberation of those oppressed by others. This is what many

Christians who have committed themselves to the Latin American revolutionary process have begun to experience. If this option seems to separate them from the Christian community, it is because many Christians, intent on domesticating the Good News, see them as wayward and perhaps even dangerous. If they are not always able to express in appropriate terms the profound reasons for their commitment, it is because the theology in which they were formed—and which they share with other Christians—has not produced the categories necessary to express this option, which seeks to respond creatively to the new demands of the Gospel and of the oppressed and exploited peoples of this continent. But in their commitments, and even in their attempts to explain them, there is a greater understanding of the faith, greater faith, greater fidelity to the Lord than in the "orthodox" doctrine (some prefer to call it by this name) of reputable Christian circles.[47] This doctrine is supported by authority and much publicized because of access to social communications media, but it is so static and devitalized that it is not even strong enough to abandon the Gospel. It is the Gospel which is disowning it.

But theological categories are not enough. We need a vital attitude, all-embracing and synthesizing, informing the totality as well as every detail of our lives; we need a "spirituality."[48] Spirituality, in the strict and profound sense of the word is the dominion of the Spirit. If "the truth will set you free" (John 8:32), the Spirit "will guide you into all the truth" (John 16:13) and will lead us to complete freedom, the freedom from everything that hinders us from fulfilling ourselves as human beings and offspring of God and the freedom to love and to enter into communion with God and with others. It will lead us along the path of liberation because "where the Spirit of the Lord is, there is liberty" (2 Cor. 3:17).

A spirituality is a concrete manner, inspired by the Spirit, of living the Gospel; it is a definite way of living "before the Lord," in solidarity with all human beings, "with the Lord," and before human beings. It arises from an intense spiritual experience, which is later explicated and witnessed to. Some Christians are beginning to live this experience as a result of their commitment to the process of liberation. The experiences of previous generations are there to support it, but above all, to remind them that they must discover their own way. Not only is there a contemporary history and a contemporary Gospel; there is also a contemporary spiritual experience which cannot be overlooked. A spirituality means a reordering of the great axes of the Christian life in terms of this contemporary experience. What is new is the synthesis that this reordering brings about, in stimulating a deepened understanding of various ideas, in bringing to the surface unknown or forgotten aspects of the Christian life, and above all, in the way in which these things are converted into life, prayer, commitment, and action.

The truth is that a Christianity lived in commitment to the process of liberation presents its own problems which cannot be ignored and meets obstacles which must be overcome. For many, the encounter with the Lord under these conditions can disappear by giving way to what he himself brings forth and nourishes: love for humankind. This love, however, does not know the fullness of its potential. This is a real difficulty, but the solution must come from the heart of the problem itself. Otherwise, it would be just one more patchwork remedy, a new impasse. This is the challenge confronting a spirituality of liberation. Where oppression and human liberation seem to make God irrelevant—a God filtered by our longtime indifference to these problems—there must blossom faith and hope in him who came to root out injustice and to offer, in an unforeseen way, total liberation. This is a spirituality which dares to sink roots in the soil of oppression-liberation.

A spirituality of liberation will center on a *conversion* to the neighbor, the oppressed person, the exploited social class, the despised ethnic group, the dominated country. Our conversion to the Lord implies this conversion to the neighbor. Evangelical conversion is indeed the touchstone of all spirituality. Conversion means a radical transformation of ourselves; it means thinking, feeling, and living as Christ—present in exploited and alienated persons. To be converted is to commit oneself to the process of the liberation of the poor and oppressed, to commit oneself lucidly, realistically, and concretely. It means to commit oneself not only generously, but also with an analysis of the situation and a strategy of action. To be converted is to know and experience the fact that, contrary to the laws of physics, we can stand straight, according to the Gospel, only when our center of gravity is outside ourselves.

Conversion is a permanent process in which very often the obstacles we meet make us lose all we had gained and start anew. The fruitfulness of our conversion depends on our openness to doing this, our spiritual childhood. All conversion implies a break. To wish to accomplish it without conflict is to deceive oneself and others: "No one is worthy of me who cares more for father or mother than for me." But it is not a question of a withdrawn and pious attitude. Our conversion process is affected by the socio-economic, political, cultural, and human environment in which it occurs. Without a change in these structures, there is no authentic conversion. We have to break with our mental categories, with the way we relate to others, with our way of identifying with the Lord, with our cultural milieu, with our social class, in other words, with all that can stand in the way of a real, profound solidarity with those who suffer, in the first place, from misery and injustice. Only thus, and not through purely interior and spiritual attitudes, will the "new person" arise from the ashes of the "old."

Christians have not done enough in this area of conversion to the neighbor, to social justice, to history. They have not perceived clearly enough yet that to know God *is* to do justice. They still do not live *in one sole action* with both God and all humans. They still do not situate themselves in Christ without attempting to avoid concrete human history. They have yet to tread the path which will lead them to seek effectively the peace of the Lord in the heart of social struggle.

A spirituality of liberation must be filled with a living sense of *gratuitousness*. Communion with the Lord and with all humans is more than anything else a gift. Hence the universality and the radicalness of the liberation which it affords. This gift, far from being a call to passivity, demands a vigilant attitude. This is one of the most constant Biblical themes: the encounter with the Lord presupposes attention, active disposition, work, fidelity to God's will, the good use of talents received. But the knowledge that at the root of our personal and community existence lies the gift of the self-communication of God, the grace of God's friendship, fills our life with gratitude. It allows us to see our encounters with others, our loves, everything that happens in our life as a gift. There is a real love only when there is free giving—without conditions or coercion. Only gratuitous love goes to our very roots and elicits true love.

Prayer is an experience of gratuitousness. This "leisure" action, this "wasted" time, reminds us that the Lord is beyond the categories of useful and useless.[49] God is not of this world. The gratuitousness of God's gift, creating profound needs, frees us from all religious alienation and, in the last instance, from all alienation. The Christian committed to the Latin American revolutionary process has to find the way to real prayer, not evasion. It cannot be denied that a crisis exists in this area and that we can easily slide into dead ends.[50] There are many who—nostalgically and in "exile," recalling earlier years of their life—can say with the psalmist: "As I pour out my soul in distress, I call to mind how I marched in the ranks of the great to the house of God, among exultant shouts of praise, the clamor of the pilgrims" (Ps. 42:4). But the point is not to backtrack; new experiences, new demands have made heretofore familiar and comfortable paths impassable and have made us undertake new itineraries on which we hope it might be possible to say with Job to the Lord, "I knew of thee then only by report, but now I see thee with my own eyes" (42:5). Bonhoeffer was right when he said that the only credible God is the God of the mystics. But this is not a God unrelated to human history. On the contrary, if it is true, as we recalled above, that one must go through humankind to reach God, it is equally certain that the "passing through" to that gratuitous God strips me, leaves me naked, universalizes my love for others, and makes it gratuitous. Both movements need each other dialectically and move toward a synthesis. This synthesis is found in Christ; in the God-Man we encounter God and humankind. In Christ humankind gives God a human countenance and God gives it a divine countenance.[51] Only in this perspective will we be able to understand that the "union with the Lord," which all spirituality proclaims, is not a separation from others; to attain this union, I must go through others, and the union, in turn, enables me to encounter others more fully. Our purpose here is not to "balance" what has been said before, but rather to deepen it and see it in all its meaning.

The conversion to one's neighbors, and in them to the Lord, the gratuitousness which allows me to encounter others fully, the unique encounter which is the foundation of communion of persons among themselves and of human beings, with God, these are the source of Christian *joy.* This joy is born of the gift already received yet still awaited and is expressed in the present despite the difficulties and tensions of the struggle for the construction of a just society. Every prophetic proclamation of total liberation is accompanied by an invitation to participate in eschatological joy: "I will take delight in Jerusalem and rejoice in my people" (Isa. 65:19). This joy ought to fill our entire existence, making us attentive both to the gift of integral human liberation and history as well as to the detail of our life and the lives of others. This joy ought not to lessen our commitment to those who live in an unjust world, nor should it lead us to a facile, low-cost conciliation. On the contrary, our joy is paschal, guaranteed by the Spirit (Gal. 5:22; 1 Tim. 1:6; Rom. 14:17); it passes through the conflict with the great ones of this world and through the cross in order to enter into life. This is why we celebrate our joy in the present by recalling the passover of the Lord. To recall Christ is to believe in him. And this celebration is a feast (Apoc. 19:7),[52] a feast of the Christian community, those who explicitly confess Christ to be the Lord of history, the liberator of the oppressed. This community has been referred to as the small temple in contradistinction to the large temple of human history.[53] Without community support neither the emergence nor the continued existence of a new spirituality is possible.

The Magnificat expresses well this spirituality of liberation. A song of thanksgiving for the gifts of the Lord, it expresses humbly the joy of being loved by him: "Rejoice, my spirit, in God my Savior; so tenderly has he looked upon his servant, humble as she is. . . . So wonderfully has he dealt with me, the Lord, the Mighty One" (Luke 1:47–49). But at the same time it is one of the New Testament texts which contains great implications both as regards liberation and the political sphere. This thanksgiving and joy are closely linked to the action of God who liberates the oppressed and humbles the powerful. "The hungry he has satisfied with good things, the rich sent empty away" (vv. 52-53). The future of history belongs to the poor and exploited. True liberation will be the work of the oppressed themselves; in them, the Lord saves history. The spirituality of liberation will have as its basis the spirituality of the *anawim*.[54]

Living witnesses rather than theological speculation will point out, are already pointing out, the direction of a spirituality of liberation.[55] This is the task which has been undertaken in Latin America by those referred to above as a "first Christian generation."

*Chapter Eleven*

# ESCHATOLOGY AND POLITICS

The commitment to the creation of a just society and, ultimately, to a new humanity, presupposes confidence in the future. This commitment is an act open to whatever comes. What is the meaning of this *new* reality in the light of faith? It has often been noted that a characteristic of contemporary persons is that they live in terms of tomorrow, oriented towards the future, fascinated by what does not yet exist. The spiritual condition of today's person is more and more determined by the model of the person of tomorrow. Human self-awareness is heavily affected by the knowledge that humanity is outgrowing its present condition and entering a new era,[1] a world "to the second power," fashioned by human hands.[2] We live on the verge of human epiphany, "anthropophany." History is no longer, as it was for the Greeks, an *anamnesis*, a remembrance. It is rather a thrust into the future. The contemporary world is full of latent possibilities and expectations. History seems to have quickened its pace. The confrontation of the present with the future makes contemporaries impatient.

But are we not painting an idealized picture, valid perhaps for other places, but not for Latin America? It is, indeed, inaccurate to regard this sketch as a complete description of the contemporary life-experience of this continent. Large numbers of Latin Americans suffer from a fixation which leads them to overvalue the past. This problem has been correctly interpreted by Paulo Freire. It is one of the elements of what he has called a precritical consciousness, that is, the consciousness of one who has not taken hold of the reins of one's own destiny. Nevertheless, it is necessary to recall that the revolutionary process now under way is generating the kind of person who critically analyzes the present, controls personal destiny, and is oriented towards the future. This kind of person, whose actions are directed toward a new society yet to be built, is in Latin America more of a motivating ideal than a reality already realized and generalized. But things are moving in this direction. A profound aspiration for the creation of a new humanity underlies the process of liberation which the continent is undergoing.[3] This is a difficult creation which will have to overcome conflicts and antagonisms. Rightly does Medellín comment that "we are on the threshold of a new epoch in the history of our continent. It appears to be a time full of zeal for full emancipation, of liberation from every form of servitude, of personal maturity and of collective integration. In these signs we perceive the first indications of the painful birth of a new civilization."[4]

Latin America faces a complex situation which does not allow for a simple acceptance or rejection of this orientation toward the future which we noted as characteristic of contemporary humankind. But this situation does lead us to recognize the existence of other realities, of a transitional situation, and to specify that this thrust toward the future occurs *above all* when one participates in the building up of a just society, qualitatively different from the one which exists today. Moreover, one gets the impression that many in the developed countries do not have an intense experience, in political matters, of this typical characteristic of today's person, because they are so attached—in both the East and the West—not to the past, but rather to an affluent present which they are prepared to uphold and defend under any circumstances.

Here we have the same two approaches which we have already considered. For some, especially in the developed countries, the openness towards the future is an openness to the control of nature by science and technology with no questioning of the social order in which they live. For others, especially in dependent and dominated areas, the future promises conflicts and confrontations, a struggle to become free from the powers which enslave individuals and exploit social classes. For these persons the development of productive forces, in which scientific and technological advances do indeed play an important part, dialectically demands however that the established order be questioned. Without such a challenge, there is no true thrust into the future.

Be that as it may, the intensification of revolutionary ferment, which is to be found in varying degrees in the modern world, is accentuating and accelerating this thrust towards what is to come.[5] All this creates a complex reality which challenges the Christian faith. The idea of eschatology as the driving force of a future-oriented history attempts to provide a response.[6] But, as we have noted before, this opening of eschatology to the future is inseparably joined with its historical contemporaneity and urgency. This notion of eschatology is diametrically opposed to that which "eschatologist" theologians upheld some twenty years ago in opposition to the "Incarnationalists."[7] For them the eschatological tendency expressed the wish for a disengagement of the Christian faith from the powers of this world; the basis for this was a lack of interest in terrestrial realities and a historical pessimism which discouraged any attempt at great tasks. This school was also easy prey of all kinds of conciliatory juxtapositions.[8]

The current eschatological perspective has overcome these obstacles. Not only is it not an escape from history, but also it has clear and strong implications for the political sphere, for social praxis.[9] This is what recent reflections on hope, on the political impact of the evangelical message, and on the relationship between faith and historical utopia are convincingly demonstrating.

## TO ACCOUNT FOR THE HOPE

This new approach to eschatological problems has led to a renewal of the theology of hope. Before, this was very much forgotten or relegated to a modest place in the middle of the treatise "on the virtues," in which the theology of faith enjoyed the lion's share. "Saved in hope" (Rom. 8:24) we have in us the promised Spirit (Gal. 3:14), which makes us "overflow with hope" (Rom. 15:13; Acts 26:6). Christians must account for the hope that is in them (1 Pet. 3:15).

Some years ago Gabriel Marcel made a valuable contribution to the rediscovery of the role hope plays in reflecting on the Christian life and on the existence of all persons. But his approach was personal and conversational and did not stress the implications that hope has in historical and political reality.[10]

Ernst Bloch's focus is different. His most important work is entitled: "The Hope Principle" (*Das Prinzip Hoffnung*). For Bloch the human being hopes for and dreams of the future; but it is an active hope which subverts the existing order. He accepts Marx's assertion "philosophers have only *interpreted the world*, in various ways; the point, however, is to *change it*." He uses as his point of departure what Marx himself, in his first thesis on Feuerbach, asserted had been left out of all materialistic theories: "The chief defect of all hitherto existing materialism—that of Feuerbach included—is that the thing [*Gegenstand*], reality, sensuousness, is conceived only in the form of the *object* [*Objekt*] or of *contemplation* [*Anschauung*], but not as *human sensuous activity*, *practice*, not subjectively."[11] Bloch attempts to clarify in his work the meaning of these aspects of revolutionary activity, that is to say, of practico-critical activity.[12]

For Bloch there are two kinds of affections: those of society (envy, avarice) and those of expectation (anguish, fear, hope). The latter anticipate the future. Of these hope is the most important as well as the most positive and most liberating. Hope is "the most human of all emotions and only humans can experience it. It is related to the broadest and most luminous horizon."[13] Hope is a "daydream" projected into the future; it is "not-yet-conscious" (*Noch-Nicht-Bewusst*), the psychic representation of that which "is not yet" (*Noch-Nicht-Sein*). But this hope seeks to be clear and conscious, a *docta spes*. When that which is "yet-not-conscious" becomes a conscious act, it is no longer a state of mind; it assumes a concrete utopic function, mobilizing human action in history. Hope thus emerges as the key to human existence oriented towards the future, because it transforms the present. This ontology of what "is not yet" is dynamic, in contrast to the static ontology of being, which is incapable of planning history.[14] For Bloch what is real is an open-ended process. On one occasion he asserted that the formula "S is not yet P" summarizes his thought.[15] Bloch brings us into the area of the possibilities of potential being; this allows us to plan history in revolutionary terms.

The contemporary theology of hope is passing through the breach unexpectedly opened by Bloch.[16] Moltmann[17] and Pannenberg[18] have found in Bloch's analyses the categories which allow them to think through some of the important Biblical themes: Eschatology, Promise, Hope. In this, they are only following an indication of Bloch himself who said: "Where there is hope, there is also religion."[19]

For Moltmann, the Biblical revelation of God is not, as it was for the Greek mind, the "epiphany of the eternal present," which limits itself to explaining what exists.[20] On the contrary, revelation speaks to us about a God who comes to meet us and whom we can only await "in active hope."[21] The present order of things, that which is, is profoundly challenged by the Promise;[22] because of one's hope in the resurrected Christ, one is liberated from the narrow limits of the present and can think and act completely in terms of what is to come. For Moltmann, a theology of hope is simultaneously a theology of resurrection.[23] The resurrected Christ is humankind's future. The statements of the Promise "do not seek to illuminate the reality which exists, but the reality which is coming,"[24] and therefore establish the conditions for the possibility of "new experiences."[25] Thus there is maintained "a specific *inadaequatio rei et intellectus*" regarding "the existing and given reality,"[26] inaugurating a promising and productive "open stage for history."[27]

But as Alves has noted, for Moltmann the challenge to the present is derived from the Promise. The present is denied because of the Promise and not because of a human, concrete, historical experience. For Moltmann "there is one transcendental hope (because not related to any specific situation) that makes man aware of the pain of his present . . . . The event of promise, therefore, is the beginning of the criticism of everything that is."[28] God would resemble the Aristotelian *primum movens*, "pulling history to its future, but without being involved in history."[29] Hence the danger of "docetism" which Alves thinks he perceives in Moltmann's thought: "It is not the incarnation which is the mother of the future, but rather the transcendental future which makes man aware of the incarnation."[30]

It cannot be denied that despite all his efforts, Moltmann has difficulty finding a vocabulary both sufficiently rooted in human concrete historical experience, in an oppressed and exploited present, and yet abounding in potentialities—a vocabulary rooted in the possibilities of self-liberation.[31] Hence perhaps his idea of theological concepts mentioned above,[32] which "anticipate future being" and "do not limp after reality." But we are dealing with a human, historical, concrete, present reality, which we must do to prevent failure in our encounter with humanity—and with the God who is to come. The death and resurrection of Jesus are our future, because they are our perilous and hopeful present. The hope which overcomes death must be rooted in the heart of historical praxis; if this hope does not take shape in the present to lead it forward, it will be only an evasion, a futuristic illusion. One must be extremely careful not to replace a Christianity of the Beyond with a Christianity of the Future; if the former tended to forget the world, the latter runs the risk of neglecting a miserable and unjust present and the struggle for liberation.[33]

Despite these critical observations, Moltmann's work is undoubtedly one of the most important in contemporary theology.[34] It offers a new approach to the theology of hope and has injected new life into reflection on various aspects of Christian existence. Among other things, it helps us overcome the association between faith and fear of the future which Moltmann rightly considers characteristic of many Christians.[35]

To hope does not mean to know the future, but rather to be open, in an attitude of spiritual childhood, to accepting it as a gift. But this gift is accepted in the negation of injustice, in the protest against trampled human rights, and in the struggle for peace and fellowship. Thus hope fulfills a mobilizing and liberating function in history. Its function is not very obvious, but it is real and deep. Péguy has written that hope, which seemed to be led by her two older sisters, faith and charity, actually leads them. But this will be true only if hope in the future seeks roots in the present, if it takes shape in daily events with their joys to experience but also with their injustices to eliminate and their enslavements from which to be liberated. Camus was right when in another context he said "true generosity towards the future consists in giving everything to the present."

The somewhat overwhelming emergence of reflection both on eschatology and on its implications on the level of social praxis has put the theology of hope in the forefront. In former years, one had the impression that a theology centered on the love of God and neighbor had replaced a theology concerned especially with faith and the corresponding orthodoxy. The primacy of faith was followed by the "primacy of charity." This permitted the notion of love of neighbor to be recovered as an essential element of Christian life. But paradoxically, at the same time this was also partially responsible for the fact that for some the relationship with God was obscured and became difficult to live out and understand.[36] Today, due partly perhaps to such impasses, the perspective of a new primacy seems to be emerging—that of hope, which liberates history because of its openness to the God who is to come. If faith was reinterpreted by charity, both are now being reevaluated in terms of hope. All this is very sketchily drawn; we are also, of course, confronted here with a question of emphasis. Christian life and theological reflection must integrate these various dimensions into a profound unity. But the history of the Christian community continuously demonstrates how certain aspects of Christian experience are stressed at different times. New syntheses follow. It is possible that the evolution which we have recalled is leading us to one of these syntheses.

Be this as it may, it might be interesting to trace a parallel between this evolution of theology and that which we find in the thought of three very influential men of our times who have had a great impact on theology: Hegel, Feuerbach, and Marx. We will do this briefly, and only suggestively, but with the belief that a deeper study of this parallel would illuminate our theological reflection.

Feuerbach strongly contrasted love with faith: "Faith is the opposite of love."[37] For him faith was a way of opposing humankind to God. Indeed, the essence of humankind is the human race and this essence is concretely realized by love, the expression of the need one human being has for another.[38] God for him is this essence projected outside the individual, outside reality. "Knowledge of God is self-knowledge."[39] To find itself again, humankind must abandon faith in this nonexistent being. Human love is "the truth" (in the Hegelian sense of the word) of Christianity. Faith is based on the affirmation of God; love is based on the affirmation of humankind. Faith separates; love unites. Faith particularizes; love universalizes. Faith divides the person within; love unifies the person. Faith oppresses; love liberates.[40] For Feuerbach, the Hegelian system was based on faith, hence its strongly Christian character, its rigidity, its authoritarian and repressive characteristics.[41] Attempting to place himself in opposition to Hegelian thought, Feuerbach seeks to center his doctrine on love, going so far as to formulate it as a "religion of love."[42]

Marx, who accepts many of Feuerbach's criticisms of Hegel—especially those directed against religion—comments ironically on the religion of love of the so-called "true socialists," who find their inspiration in Feuerbach.[43] Moreover, he takes Feuerbach to task for overlooking the need for a revolution, due to his erroneous way of relating theory and praxis. In a well-turned phrase, Marx said: "As far as Feuerbach is a materialist he does not deal with history, and as far as he deals with history he is not a materialist." [44] Marx's idea of praxis is different; it is based on a dialectical conception of history— necessarily advancing, with eyes fixed on the future and with real action in the present, towards a classless society based on new relationships of production.

The theology of hope, on which Marxian thought exercises a certain amount of influence through the work of Bloch, is a response to the "death of God" approach, in which the presence of Feuerbach's thought is evident.[45]

## THE POLITICAL DIMENSION OF THE GOSPEL

The relationship between Gospel and politics is an old question; but it has also become very contemporary, having recently taken on a new dimension. The above chapters have touched on this. In this context we will study two ideas which are currently the subject of lively controversy: the so-called new political theology and the public character of the witness and message of Jesus.

### The "New Political Theology"

The eschatological vision becomes operative, the theology of hope becomes creative, when it comes in contact with the social realities of today's world and gives rise to what has been called "political theology."[46] Following the line of thought proposed by Bloch and Moltmann (and also by Pannenberg), Metz attempts to show the implications of eschatology and hope for political life.[47] He does not mean to suggest the creation of "a new theological discipline"; his intention is "to lay bare . . . a basic feature within theological awareness at large."[48] The approach is, therefore, that of fundamental theology.[49]

*Political theology* is an ambiguous expression. Metz has acknowledged this from the beginning.[50] Because of criticism, he has had to repeat and deepen his reasons for using such a controversial term.[51] This will be better understood if we study the content of his approach.

Metz's point of departure is what he considers a new way of thinking about the *political sphere*. He refers to the process of emancipation and autonomy of the political sphere which reached maturity with the Enlightenment (*Aufklärung*).[52] Since the Enlightenment, the political order is an order of freedom. Political structures are no longer given, previous to human freedom, but are rather realities based on freedom, taken on and modified by human-kind. Political history is, from that time forward, the history of freedom. This new definition of politics carefully distinguishes between state and society. The distinction, which "has an essentially anti-totalitarian thrust,"[53] allows us to differentiate between the public sphere of the state or the Church (or the combination of them) as powers from the public sphere "in which the interests of all persons as a social group are expressed."[54] Because in some cases this distinction was not made, we have had authoritarian and repressive "political theologies" which sought to restore a "Christian state" (Bonald, Donoso Cortés, and others). Metz's position not only does not "abandon the distinc-tion and the emancipation of politics from the "religious order," as some of his critics mistakenly assert, "rather it *presupposes* it."[55] He goes even further and asserts that what is important above all is to perceive the political sphere as the proper area of freedom. Without this focus one cannot understand what Metz means by his approach in political theology. For him all thought (and therefore all theology) which does not take into account the challenge born of the Enlightenment is precritical (or of the first degree); and inversely, all reflection which is aware of it is postcritical (or of the second degree). On this basis, Metz says that his political theology is opposed to "all forms of theology which politicize directly" and conditionally rejects "the mistaken notions of the neo-politicization of the faith or the neo-clericalization of politics, which seem to be associated with the idea of political theology, due to its historical ballast."[56] This is why he prefers to call his own approach "*new* political theology."

The shattering of the unity between religious and social life which began in modern times made the Christian religion appear as "a particular phenomenon within a pluralistic milieu. Thus its absolute claim to universality seemed to be historically conditioned."[57] The Enlightenment, and later Marx, criticized reli-gion, considering it an ideology emanating from specific social and historical structures. Theology, according to Metz, reacted by placing the social dimen-sion of the Christian message on a secondary and accidental level and insisting upon its essentially private aspect. The life of faith was thus reduced to a personal option and was abstracted from the social world in which it lived. This kind of theology "sought to solve its problem, a problem born of the Enlight-enment, by eliminating it. . . . The religious consciousness formed by this theology attributes but a shadowy existence to the social and political reality."[58]

This private, interior version of Christianity is proper to transcendentalist, existentialist, and personalist theologies. Faced with such an attitude which avoids the problem, the first task of political theology is the *de-privatization* which allows for criticism of "the understanding of the datum of our theology."[59]

The definition of the political sphere will keep the new political theology from mixing "politics and religion, the way the old political theology did." But at the same time, the deprivatization of the message will prevent religion from becoming uninterested in politics "and concerning itself with its proper sphere, that is, speaking about God, as the critics of the new political theology recommend."[60] Having rejected this alternative, the new political theology can advance positively towards the determination of a new kind of relationship "between religion and society, between Church and societal 'publicness,' between eschatological faith and societal life,"[61] between *theory and practice*.[62] This determination cannot be carried out by means of a precritical method condemned to identifying these realities anew, but by means of a reflection of the second degree, postcritical. The new type of relationship thus achieved will be based on the "critical, liberating force in regard to the social world and its historical process"[63] possessed by the saving message proclaimed by Jesus. This message becomes present and active because of what Metz calls the *memoria Christi*: "commemorating the advent of the Kingdom of God in the love of Jesus towards marginated persons."[64] The proclamation of the saving message is translated into promises of freedom, justice, and peace which make up the "eschatological proviso" and whose role is to stress the "provisional" character of "every historically real status of society."[65]

All this will lead the Church to become an "*institution of social criticism*."[66] Its critical mission will be defined as a service to the history of freedom, or more precisely, as a service to human liberation. The Church and not the individual Christian would then be the subject of the praxis of liberation, enlivened by the evangelical message. But in order for this to be true, the Church will have to become a nonrepressive institution, a "second-degree institution," critical and liberating. The current situation of the Church, a legacy of its past, seems to negate this possibility. Nevertheless Metz thinks it is possible, because the very existence of the Church as institution is under the sign of the eschatological proviso. The Church does not exist for itself. Preaching hope in the Kingdom of God, it lives "on the proclamation of [its] own proviso."[67] Metz is aware that this is an ideal concept of the Church and that for the Church to be an institution of freedom a new praxis is needed. Is this new praxis possible? He responds that his political theology lives in the hope that by exercising its critical function toward society the Church will find a new awareness of itself.[68]

The ideas advanced tentatively by Metz created great interest, but they also were severely criticized on various counts. He has been faulted for not taking the political domain seriously enough,[69] for using ambiguous philosophical notions,[70] for simplifying history and not respecting the pluralism of the political options of Christians,[71] for falling into neoclericalism,[72] for not having clearly determined what he means by political theology,[73] for neglecting the area proper to political ethics,[74] for painting too ideal a picture of the role the Church can play as a critical agent,[75] and for limiting the role of the Church to a function of negative criticism.[76]

Metz has tried to respond to these criticisms by expressing his thought more precisely. In formulating these responses he has had to enter into his critics' point of view and so he has perhaps lost some of his initial aggressiveness. In any case, many points need to be clarified and many questions remain open. We will consider only two.

Reading the works of Metz one gets the impression of a certain inadequacy in his analyses of the contemporary political situation. On the one hand, because the climate in which his reflections develop is far from the revolutionary ferment of the Third World countries, he cannot penetrate the situation of dependency, injustice, and exploition in which most of humankind finds itself. His conception of the political sphere lacks what could be acquired both by the experience of the confrontations and conflicts stemming from the rejection of this oppression of some persons by others and of some countries by others, as well as by the experience of the aspiration to liberation which emerges from the heart of these conditions.[77] Moreover, as a result there is a need for a critique of certain assumptions in Metz's thought. Indeed, the situation of the dominated countries explains more than one characteristic of the affluent societies, which are the immediate context for the new political theology. This explains the rather abstract level on which the political sphere is at times treated in Metz's writings. The analyses of political theology would have much to gain from the contribution of the social sciences; some of his supporters as well as Metz himself seem now to be turning to them. The analyses would also have much to gain from the contribution of certain aspects of Marxism, which, despite (or because of?) the mediation of Bloch's thought, do not seem to be sufficiently present.

However, Metz reacts, and rightly so, to a theology of secularization which advocates ultimately a peaceful coexistence of (privatized) faith with a secularized world; that is to say, he reacts to a conformist theology, which tends to become an ideology of advanced industrial society. Hence the critical character of Metz's thought when he stresses the public and political dimension of faith. Despite all this, he does not seem to have completely shaken off the theology of secularization. His analyses will have to be continued and deepened. This has been the purpose of Metz himself and of some of his former students who are now working energetically and intelligently in this direction.[78] Moreover, the universal existence of a secularized world and the privatization of the faith seem to have been taken for granted by political theology without further critical examination. Nevertheless, in places like Latin America, things are different.[79] The process here does not have the characteristics it exhibits in Europe. Faith, the Gospel, the Church, have in Latin America a complex public dimension which has played (and still plays) an important role in support of the established order, although currently it seems to be withdrawing its support—with unforeseeable consequences. To speak in this instance of "privatization" of the faith would be to oversimplify the problem. It is understandable that Metz did not take these realities into account; but it is a serious and dangerous error for those who wish to transplant his ideas without qualification to ignore them. Besides, does no "privatization" of the faith in fact hide other forms of politicization of the faith and of the Church? It is urgent that these questions be analyzed, but this cannot be done from a purely intraecclesiastical perspective.[80]

The new political theology represents, nevertheless, a fertile effort to think the faith through. It takes into consideration the political dimension of the faith and is indeed aware of the most pervasive and acute problems which persons encounter today. It also represents an original recasting of the question of the function of the Church in the world today. This has been a breath of fresh air for European theology. It has contrasted with other contemporary theological trends more tied to "tradition" but less related to living and urgent issues. But the approach of the new political theology must avoid the pitfalls both of "naiveté" regarding the influences of advanced capitalist society as well as of a narrow ecclesiastical framework, if it wishes to reach the arena where the future of society and the Church is being decided.[81]

### Jesus and the Political World

The current concern about the liberation of the oppressed, about the social revolution which is to transform the present order, about the counterviolence opposed to the violence which the existing order produces—and with which it defends itself—have all led many Christians to ask themselves about the attitude of Jesus regarding the political situation of his time. The question may surprise us. If so, it is because we take it for granted that Jesus was not interested in political life: his mission was purely religious. Indeed we have witnessed a process which Comblin terms the "iconization" of the life of Jesus: "This is a Jesus of hieratic, stereotyped gestures, all representing theological themes. To explain an action of Jesus is to find in it several theological meanings. In this way, the life of Jesus is no longer a human life, submerged in history, but a theological life—an icon. As happens with icons, his actions lose their human context and are stylized, becoming transformed into signs of the transcendent and invisible world."[82] The life of Jesus is thus placed outside history, unrelated to the real forces at play. Jesus and those whom he befriended, or whom he confronted and whose hostility he earned, are deprived of all human content. They are there reciting a script. It is impossible not to experience a sensation of unreality when presented with such a life of Jesus.

To approach the man, Jesus of Nazareth, in whom God was made flesh, to penetrate not only his teaching, but also his life, what it is that gives his word an immediate, concrete context, is a task which more and more needs to be undertaken. One aspect of this work will be to examine the alleged apolitical attitude of Jesus, which would not coincide with what we mentioned earlier regarding the Biblical message and Jesus' own teaching. Hence, a serious reconsideration of this presupposition is necessary. But it has to be undertaken with a respect for the historical Jesus, not forcing the facts in terms of our current concerns. If we wished to discover in Jesus the least characteristic of a contemporary political militant we would not only misrepresent his life and witness and demonstrate a lack of understanding on our part of politics in the present world; we would also deprive ourselves of what his life and witness have that is deep and universal and, therefore, valid and concrete for today.

The more recent studies on the life of Jesus related to the political problems of his time, although they have not reached a consensus on all matters, have highlighted some aspects of the question which had been somewhat neglected until now. We will concentrate on three of them which we consider indisputable: the complex relationship between Jesus and the Zealots, his attitude toward the leaders of the Jewish people, and his death at the hands of the political authorities.

It is becoming clearer that the *Zealot movement* is very important for an understanding of the New Testament and especially of the life and death of Jesus.[83] To situate Jesus in his time implies an examination of his connection with this movement of religious and political resistance to the Roman oppressors. Some of Jesus' close associates were Zealots (from the Greek *zelos*, "zeal"). He exercised a great attraction over these people who loved the Law, who were strong nationalists, who fiercely opposed Roman domination, and who ardently awaited the impending arrival of the Kingdom which was to end this situation. Cullmann has proved that some of the direct disciples of Jesus were Zealots or had some connection with them; he concludes his study with this assertion: "One of the Twelve—Simon the Zealot—*certainly* belonged to the Zealots; others *probably* did, like Judas Iscariot, Peter, and *possibly* the sons of Zebedee."[84] But there is more. We find many points of agreement between the Zealots and the attitudes and teachings of Jesus, for example, his preaching of the coming of the Kingdom and the role he himself plays in its advent, the assertion—which has been variously interpreted—that "the Kingdom of Heaven has been subjected to violence and violent men are seizing it" (Matt. 11:12), his attitude toward the Jews who worked for the Romans, his action of purifying the temple,[85] his power over the people who wanted to make him king.[86] For these reasons, Jesus and his disciples were often related to the Zealots (cf. Acts 5:37; 21:38; cf. also Luke 13:1).[87]

But at the same time, Jesus kept his distance from the Zealot movement. The awareness of the universality of his mission did not conform with the somewhat narrow nationalism of the Zealots. Because they disdainfully rejected the Samaritans and pagans, the Zealots must have objected to the behavior of Jesus towards them. The message of Jesus is addressed to all persons. The justice and peace he advocated know no national boundaries.[88] In this he was even more revolutionary than the Zealots, who were fierce defenders of literal obedience to the Law; Jesus taught an attitude of spiritual freedom toward it.

Moreover, for Jesus the Kingdom was, in the first place, a gift. Only on this basis can we understand the meaning of the active human participation in its coming; the Zealots tended to see it rather as the fruit of their own efforts. For Jesus, oppression and injustice were not limited to a specific historical situation; their causes go deeper and cannot be truly eliminated without going to the very roots of the problem: the disintegration of fellowship and communion. Besides, and this will have enormous consequences, Jesus is opposed to all politico-religious messianism which does not respect either the depth of the religious realm or the autonomy of political action. Messianism can be efficacious in the short run but the ambiguities and confusions which it entails frustrate the ends it attempts to accomplish. This idea was considered as a temptation by Jesus; as such, he rejected it.[89] The liberation which Jesus offers is universal and integral; it transcends national boundaries, attacks the foundation of injustice and exploitation, and eliminates politico-religious confusions, without therefore being limited to a purely "spiritual" plane.

It is not enough, however, to say that Jesus was not a Zealot. There are those who seek, in good faith but uncritically, to cleanse Jesus from anything which can give even an inkling of a political attitude on his part. But Jesus' posture precludes all oversimplification. To close one's eyes to this complexity amounts to letting the richness of his testimony on this score escape.

During all his public life, Jesus confronted the *groups in power* over the Jewish people. Herod, a man employed by the Roman oppressor, was called "the Fox" (Luke 13:32). The publicans, whom the people considered as collaborators with the dominant political power, were placed among the sinners (Matt. 9:10; 21:31; Luke 5:30; 7:34). The Sadducees were conscious that Jesus threatened their official and privileged position. Jesus' preaching strongly challenged their skepticism in religious matters; they were in the majority in the Great Sanhedrin which condemned him. His criticism of a religion made up of purely external laws and observances also brought him into violent confrontation with the Pharisees. Jesus turned to the great prophetic tradition and taught that worship is authentic only when it is based on profound personal dispositions, on the creation of true fellowship, and on real commitment to others, especially the most needy (cf., for example, Matt. 5:23-24; 25:31-45). Jesus accompanied this criticism with a head-on opposition to the rich and powerful and a radical option for the poor; one's attitude towards them determines the validity of all religious behavior; it is above all for them that the Son of Man has come. The Pharisees rejected Roman domination, but they had structured a complex world of religious precepts and norms of behavior which allowed them to live on the margin of that domination. They certainly accepted coexistence. The Zealots were well aware of this, thus their opposition to the Pharisees despite many other points of agreement with them. When Jesus struck against the very foundation of their machinations, he unmasked the falsity of their position and appeared in the eyes of the Pharisees as a dangerous traitor.

Jesus *died at the hands of the political authorities*, the oppressors of the

Jewish people. According to the Roman custom, the title on the cross indicated the reason for the sentence; in the case of Jesus this title denoted political guilt: King of the Jews.[90] Cullmann can therefore say that Jesus was executed by the Romans as a Zealot leader;[91] and he finds an additional proof of this affirmation in the episode of Barabbas who was undoubtedly a Zealot: "When he is set alongside Jesus it is quite clear that for the Romans both cases involved the same crime and the same verdict. Jesus, like Barabbas, was condemned by the Romans and not by the Jews, and in fact *as a Zealot*."[92] The Sanhedrin had religious reasons for condemning a man who claimed to be the Son of God, but it also had political reasons: the teachings of Jesus and his influence over the people challenged the privilege and power of the Jewish leaders. These political considerations were related to another which affected the Roman authority itself: the claim to be Messiah and King of the Jews. His trial closely combined these different reasons.[93] Crespy can therefore state: "If we attempt to conclude our investigation we see clearly that the trial of Jesus was a *political* trial and that he was condemned for being a Zealot, although the accusation was not solidly established."[94] From the moment he started preaching, Jesus' fate was sealed: "I have spoken openly to all the world" (John 18:20), he tells the High Priest. For this reason John's Gospel presents the story of Jesus as a case "brought, or intended to be brought, against Jesus by the world, represented by the Jews. This action reached its public, judicial decision before Pontius Pilate, the representative of the Roman state and holder of political power."[95]

What conclusions can we draw from these facts about the life of Jesus? For Cullmann—one of the authors who has studied this problem most seriously and carefully—the key to the behavior of Jesus in political matters is what he calls "eschatological radicalism,"[96] which is based on the hope of an impending advent of the Kingdom. Hence it follows that "for Jesus, all the realities of this world were necessarily *relativized* and that his allegiance, therefore, had to lie beyond the alternatives of 'existing order' or 'revolution.' "[97] Jesus was not uninterested in action in this world, but because he was waiting for an imminent end of history, he "was concerned *only* with the conversion of the individual and was not interested in a reform of the social structures." According to Cullmann, the attitude of Jesus cannot therefore be transposed to our times without qualification. From the moment that the development of history shows us that the end of the world is not imminent, it becomes clear that "more just social structures also promote the individual change of character required by Jesus." Henceforward, "a reciprocal action is therefore required between the conversion of the individual and the reform of the structures."[98]

In interpreting the behavior of Jesus in political matters, Cullmann gives the hope of the imminent end of time a definitive role. What has been called "consequent eschatology," in the perspective opened by Schweitzer, already held that Jesus had erroneously announced and awaited the imminent coming of the Kingdom.[99] This is a difficult and controversial exegetical point.[100] This approach does not provide a sufficiently sound basis for an understanding of the attitude of Jesus regarding political life. The interpretation is based on

Jesus' words but tends to diffuse or debilitate the tension between the present and the future which characterizes his preaching of the Kingdom.

Moreover, Cullmann uses this belief of Jesus to support his insistence on personal conversion as opposed, in a certain sense, to the need for the transformation of structures; the latter would appear only when the waiting draws long. But, in fact, when he preached personal conversion, Jesus pointed to a fundamental, permanent attitude which was primarily opposed not to a concern for social structures, but to purely formal worship, devoid of religious authenticity and human content.[101] In this, Jesus was only turning to the great prophetic line which required "mercy and not sacrifice," "contrite hearts and not holocausts." For the prophets this demand was inseparable from the denunciation of social injustice and from the vigorous assertion that God is known only by doing justice.[102] To neglect this aspect is to separate the call to personal conversion from its social, vital, and concrete context. To attribute the concern for social structures—except with the qualifications operative today—to the prolongation of the waiting period impoverishes and definitely distorts this dimension.

What then are we to think of Jesus' attitude in these matters?[103] The facts we have recalled vigorously ratify what we know of the universality and totality of his work. This universality and totality touch the very heart of political behavior, giving it its true dimension and depth. Misery and social injustice reveal "a sinful situation," a disintegration of fellowship and communion; by freeing us from sin, Jesus attacks the roots of an unjust order. For Jesus, the liberation of the Jewish people was only one aspect of a universal, permanent revolution. Far from showing no interest in this liberation, Jesus rather placed it on a deeper level, with far-reaching consequences.

The Zealots were not mistaken in feeling that Jesus was simultaneously near and far away. Neither were the leaders of the Jewish people mistaken in thinking that their position was imperiled by the preaching of Jesus, nor the oppressive political authorities when they sentenced him to die as a traitor. They were mistaken (and their followers have continued to be mistaken) only in thinking that it was all accidental and transitory, in thinking that with the death of Jesus the matter was closed, in supposing that no one would remember it. The deep human impact and the social transformation that the Gospel entails is permanent and essential because it transcends the narrow limits of specific historical situations and goes to the very root of human existence: relationship with God in solidarity with other persons. The Gospel does not get its political dimension from one or another particular option, but from the very nucleus of its message. If this message is subversive, it is because it takes on Israel's hope: the Kingdom as "the end of domination of person over person; it is a Kingdom of contradiction to the established powers and on behalf of humankind."[104] And the Gospel gives Israel's hope its deepest meaning; indeed it calls for a "new creation."[105] The life and preaching of Jesus postulate the unceasing search for a new kind of humanity in a qualitatively different society. Although the Kingdom must not be confused with the establishment of a just society, this does not mean that it is indifferent to this society. Nor does it mean that this just society constitutes a "necessary condition" for the arrival of the Kingdom nor that they are closely linked, nor that they converge. More profoundly, the announcement of the Kingdom reveals to society itself the aspiration for a just society and leads it to discover unsuspected dimensions and unexplored paths. The Kingdom is realized in a society of fellowship and justice; and, in turn, this realization opens up the promise and hope of complete communion of all persons with God. The political is grafted into the eternal.

This does not detract from the Gospel news; rather it enriches the political sphere. Moreover, the life and death of Jesus are no less evangelical because of their political connotations. His testimony and his message acquire this political dimension precisely because of the radicalness of their salvific character: to preach the universal love of the Father is inevitably to go against all injustice, privilege, oppression, or narrow nationalism.

## FAITH, UTOPIA, AND POLITICAL ACTION

The term *utopia* has been revived within the last few decades to refer to a historical plan for a qualitatively different society and to express the aspiration to establish new social relations among human beings.[106] Numerous studies have been and continue to be made on utopian thought as a dynamic element in the historical becoming of humanity. We must not forget, however, that what really makes this utopian thought viable and highlights its wealth of possibilities is the revolutionary experience of our times. Without the support of the life—and death—of many persons who, rejecting an unjust and alienating social order, throw themselves into the struggle for a new society, the idea of a utopia would never have left the realm of academic discussion.

The guidelines for utopian thought were essentially established by Thomas More's famous *Utopia*. Later, the term degenerated until it became in common language synonymous with illusion, lack of realism, irrationality.[107] But because today there is emerging a profound aspiration for liberation—or at least there is a clearer consciousness of it—the original meaning of the expression is again gaining currency.[108] Utopian thought is taking on, in line with the initial intention, its quality of being subversive to and a driving force of history. Three elements characterize the notion of utopia as we shall develop it in the following pages: its relationship to historical reality, its verification in praxis, and its rational nature.

Utopia, contrary to what current usage suggests, is characterized by its *relationship to present historical reality*. The literary style and fine sarcasm exhibited by More have deceived some and distracted others toward accidentals, but it has been demonstrated that the background of his work was the England of his time. The fiction of a utopia in which the common good prevails, where there is no private property, no money or privileges, was the opposite of his own country, in whose politics he was involved. More's utopia is a city of the future, something to be achieved, not a return to a lost paradise.[109]

This is the characteristic feature of utopian thought in the perspective from which we are speaking here. But this relationship to historical reality is neither simple nor static. It appears under two aspects which are mutually necessary and make for a complex and dynamic relationship. These two aspects, in Freire's words, are denunciation and annunciation."[110]

Utopia necessarily means a denunciation of the existing order. Its deficiencies are to a large extent the reason for the emergence of a utopia. The repudiation of a dehumanizing situation is an unavoidable aspect of utopia. It is a matter of a complete rejection which attempts to strike at the roots of the evil. This is why utopia is revolutionary and not reformist. As Eric Weil says, "Revolutions erupt when man is discontent with his discontent" (discontent with his reformism?). This denunciation of an intolerable state of affairs is what Marcuse has called—in the context of the affluent societies in which his thought moves—the "Great Refusal."[111] This is the retrospective character of utopia.

But utopia is also an annunciation, an annunciation of what is not yet, but will be; it is the forecast of a different order of things, a new society.[112] It is the field of creative imagination which proposes the alternative values to those rejected.[113] The denunciation is to a large extent made with regard to the annunciation. But the annunciation, in its turn, presupposes this rejection, which clearly delimits it retrospectively. It defines what is not desired. Otherwise, although it might seem to be an advancement, this utopia could be a subtle retrogression. Utopia moves forward; it is a pro-jection into the future, a dynamic and mobilizing factor in history. This is the prospective character of utopia.

According to Freire, between the denunciation and the annunciation is the time for building, the historical *praxis*. Moreover, denunciation and annunciation can be achieved only *in* praxis. This is what we mean when we talk about a utopia which is the driving force of history and subversive of the existing order. If utopia does not lead to action in the present, it is an evasion of reality. The utopian thesis, writes Ricoeur, is efficacious only "in the measure in which it gradually transforms historical experience," and he asserts, "Utopia is deceiving when it is not concretely related to the possibilities offered to each era."[114] A rejection will be authentic and profound only if it is made within the very act of creating more human living conditions—with the risks that this commitment implies today, particularly for dominated peoples. Utopia must necessarily lead to a commitment to support the emergence of a new social consciousness and new relationships among persons. Otherwise, the denunciation will remain at a purely verbal level and the annunciation will be only an illusion. Authentic utopian thought postulates, enriches, and supplies new goals for political action, while at the same time it is verified by this action. Its fruitfulness depends upon this relationship.

In the third place, utopia, as we understand it, belongs to the rational order. This viewpoint has been vigorously defended by Blanquart, who notes perceptively that utopia "is not irrational except as it relates to a transcended state of reason (the reason of conservatives), since in reality it takes the place of true reason."[115] Utopias emerge with renewed energy at times of transition and crisis, when science has reached its limits in its explanation of social reality, and when new paths open up for historical praxis.[116] Utopia, so understood, is neither opposed to nor outside of science. On the contrary, it constitutes the essence of its creativity and dynamism. It is the prelude of science, its annunciation. The theoretical construct which allows us to know social reality and which makes political action efficacious demands the mediation of the creative imagination: "The transition from the empirical to the theoretical presupposes a jump, a break: the intervention of the imagination."[117] And Blanquart points out that imagination in politics is called utopia.[118]

This is the difference between utopia and ideology. The term *ideology* has a long and varied history and has been understood in very different ways.[119] But we can basically agree that ideology does not offer adequate and scientific knowledge of reality; rather, it masks it. Ideology does not rise above the empirical, irrational level.[120] Therefore, it spontaneously fulfills a function of preservation of the established order. Therefore, also, ideology tends to dogmatize all that has not succeeded in separating itself from it or has fallen under its influence. Political action, science, and faith do not escape this danger. Utopia, however, leads to an authentic and scientific knowledge of reality and to a praxis which transforms what exists.[121] Utopia is different from science but does not thereby stop being its dynamic, internal element.[122]

Because of its relationship to reality, its implications for praxis, and its rational character, utopia is a factor of historical dynamism and radical transformation. Utopia, indeed, is on the level of the cultural revolution which attempts to forge a new kind of humanity. Freire is right when he says that in today's world only the oppressed person, only the oppressed class, only oppressed peoples, can denounce and announce.[123] Only they are capable of working out revolutionary utopias and not conservative or reformist ideologies. The oppressive system's only future is to maintain its present of affluence.

The relationship between faith and political action could, perhaps, be clarified by recalling the comments we have made above regarding the historical plan designated by the term *utopia*. When we discussed the notion of liberation, we said that we were dealing with a single process; but it is a complex, differentiated unity, which has within itself various levels of meaning which are not to be confused: economic, social, and political liberation; liberation which leads to the creation of a new humanity in a new society of solidarity; and liberation from sin and entrance into communion with God and with all persons.[124] The first corresponds to the level of scientific rationality which supports real and effective transforming political action; the second stands at the level of utopia, of historical projections, with the characteristics we have just considered; the third is on the level of faith. These different levels are profoundly linked; one does not occur without the others. On the basis of the clarifications we have just made, we can perhaps go one step further towards understanding the bond which unites them. It is not our intention to reduce to an oversimplified schematization what we have said regarding the complex relationship which exists between the Kingdom and historical events, between eschatology and politics. However, to shed light on the subject from another point of view may be helpful.

To assert that there is a direct, immediate relationship between faith and political action encourages one to seek from faith norms and criteria for particular political options. To be really effective, these options ought to be based on rational analyses of reality. Thus confusions are created which can result in a dangerous politico-religious messianism which does not sufficiently respect either the autonomy of the political arena or that which belongs to an authentic faith, liberated from religious baggage. As Blanquart has pointed out, politico-religious messianism is a backward-looking reaction to a new situation which the messianists are not capable of confronting with the appropriate attitude and means. This is an "infrapolitical movement" which "is not in accord with the Christian faith either."[125]

On the other hand, to assert that faith and political action have nothing to say to each other is to imply that they move on juxtaposed and unrelated planes. If one accepts this assertion, either he will have to engage in verbal gymnastics to show—without succeeding—how faith should express itself in a commitment to a more just society; or the result is that faith comes to coexist, in a most opportunistic manner, with any political option.

Faith and political action will not enter into a correct and fruitful relationship except through the effort to create a new type of person in a different society, that is, except through utopia, to use the term we have attempted to clarify in the preceding paragraphs.[126] This plan provides the basis for the struggle for better living conditions. Political liberation appears as a path toward the utopia of a freer, more human humankind, the protagonist of its own history.[127] Che Guevara has said: "Socialism currently, in this stage of the construction of socialism and communism, has not as its only purpose to have shining factories; it is intended to help the whole person; human beings must be transformed as production increases, and we would not be doing our job well if we produced only things and not at the same time persons." It follows that for him the important thing for the building up of a new society is simultaneously "a daily increase in both productivity and awareness."[128]

Utopia so understood, far from making political strugglers dreamers, radicalizes their commitment and helps them keep their work from betraying their purpose—which is to achieve a real encounter among persons in the midst of a free society without social inequalities. "Only utopia," comments Ricoeur, "can give economic, social, and political action a human focus."[129] The loss of utopia is responsible for humankind's falling into bureaucratism and sectarianism, into new structures which oppress humanity. The process, apart from understandable ups and downs and deficiencies, is not liberating if the plan for a new humankind in a freer society is not held to and concretized. This plan is not for later, when political liberation will have been attained. It ought to go side by side with the struggle for a more just society at all times. Without this critical and rational element of historical dynamism and creative imagination, science and political action see a changing reality slip out of their hands and easily fall into dogmatism. And political dogmatism is as worthless as religious dogmatism; both represent a step backward towards ideology. But for utopia validly to fulfill this role, it must be verified in social praxis; it must become effective commitment, without intellectual purisms, without inordinate claims; it must be revised and concretized constantly.

The historical plan, the utopia of liberation as the creation of a new social consciousness and as a social appropriation not only of the means of production, but also of the political process, and, definitively, of freedom, is the proper arena for the cultural revolution. That is to say, it is the arena of the permanent creation of a new humanity in a different society characterized by solidarity. Therefore, that creation is the place of encounter between political liberation and the communion of all persons with God. This communion implies liberation from sin, the ultimate root of all injustice, all exploitation, all dissidence among persons. Faith proclaims that the fellowship which is sought through the abolition of exploitation is something possible, that efforts to bring it about are not in vain, that God calls us to it and assures us of its complete fulfillment, and that the definitive reality is being built on what is transitory. Faith reveals to us the deep meaning of the history which we fashion with our own hands: it teaches us that every human act which is oriented towards the construction of a more just society has value in terms of communion with God—in terms of salvation; inversely it teaches that all injustice is a breach with God.

In human love there is a depth which the human mind does not suspect: it is through it that persons encounter God. If utopia humanizes economic, social, and political liberation, this humanness—in the light of the Gospel—reveals God. If doing justice leads us to a knowledge of God, to find God is in turn a necessary consequence. The mediation of the historical task of the creation of a new humanity assures that liberation from sin and communion with God in solidarity with all persons—manifested in political liberation and enriched by its contributions—does not fall into idealism and evasion. But, at the same time, this mediation prevents these manifestations from becoming translated into any kind of Christian ideology of political action or a politico-religious messianism. Christian hope opens us, in an attitude of spiritual childhood, to the gift of the future promised by God. It keeps us from any confusion of the Kingdom with any one historical stage, from any idolatry toward unavoidably ambiguous human achievement, from any absolutizing of revolution. In this way hope makes us radically free to commit ourselves to social praxis, motivated by a liberating utopia and with the means which the scientific analysis of reality provides for us. And our hope not only frees us for this commitment; it simultaneously demands and judges it.

The Gospel does not provide a utopia for us; this is a human work.[130] The Word is a free gift of the Lord. But the Gospel is not alien to the historical plan; on the contrary, the human plan and the gift of God imply each other. The

Word is the foundation and the meaning of all human existence; this foundation is attested to and this meaning is concretized through human actions. For whoever lives by them, faith, charity, and hope are a radical factor in spiritual freedom and historical creativity and initiative.

In this way, the claim that "the victory which has conquered death is our faith" will be lived, inescapably, at the very heart of history, in the midst of a single process of liberation which leads that history to its fulfillment in the definitive encounter with God. To hope in Christ is at the same time to believe in the adventure of history, which opens infinite vistas to the love and action of the Christian.

## Section Two

# THE CHRISTIAN COMMUNITY
# AND THE NEW SOCIETY

We have already attempted to see the relationship between faith, love, and hope on the one hand and the preoccupations of contemporary humankind on the other. What we have said concerning the meaning of the Gospel message lays the groundwork for an understanding of the meaning and mission of the Church in the world. The Church as a visible community is often being challenged in our times. Going beyond the achievements, the transformations, and the hopes of a postconciliar reformism, many Christians are asking themselves how they can be Church today. In this a determining role is played by the awareness of the comprehensiveness of the political sphere. The implications of the Gospel in this area have been perceived, as well as the role the Church has played up to now in relation to the existing social order. The roots of this approach thus go beyond the borders of the institutional Church; they are to be found in the contemporary task of building a new society. All this has an effect on the mission of the Church and leads to a deepening of what it means to belong to the Church.[1] The problem cannot be permanently resolved by the expediency of making a distinction between institution and community. The existence of a necessary and fruitful tension between these two is one thing; it is quite another to have a situation of the moral failure of an institution which seems to be on the verge of bankruptcy.

A radical revision of what the Church has been and what it now is has become necessary. The initial impulse for this has perhaps already been given by the Council—especially for the great majority of Christians. But now the movement has a dynamism all its own and is to a certain extent autonomous. For there have converged in this movement other currents which the Council seemed to have assimilated and channeled; but these currents did not lose their energy and are now seen in their full light. The attempt at *aggiornamento* of the Church has provided better conditions for entering into fruitful contact with these forces, but it has not suppressed the challenges that they bring with them. Rather it has strengthened and deepened them. So much the better. Not only do we gain nothing by trying to avoid them, but we lose much by not facing them straight on. To confront these challenges, moreover, is nothing more than a posture of humility before the facts.

The issue has caused alarm and concern.[2] For many there has even been a kind of evaporation of any meaning of the Church. And there are those who believe that this is the Church's inevitable destiny.[3] At the same time, however, we are witnessing both a rediscovery of the communitarian dimension of the faith as well as new ways of living it. The search—at times painful or wavering—has begun.[4] There is more than one indication that "that community called Church"—to use the expression of Juan Luis Segundo—has a persistent life. But this will be so only if there is a substantial transformation. If this does not happen with the hoped for rhythm and authenticity, it is not only because of bad or insufficient will, as some would have it. Also, and perhaps more than anything, it is because the path to be followed is not clearly discerned and because there is not a complete understanding of the historical and social factors which are obstacles to this transformation. What the Church needs today goes beyond authoritarian or desperate attitudes, beyond mutual accusations, and beyond personal disputes, all of which are only an expression of an inviable situation and an attitude of personal insecurity; what it needs is a courageous and serene analysis of the reasons for these situations and attitudes. This courage and serenity will be the opposite of a facile emotionalism which leads to arbitrary measures, superficial solutions, or evasions, but avoids the search for radical changes and untrodden paths. At stake in all this is the Church's faithfulness to its Lord.

The task is beyond us in this work and with our possibilities. This is what always happens: it is easier to point out what must be done than to do it. Two points, however, might help us to situate these questions. The first has to do with certain aspects of the very meaning of the Church and its mission in the world; the second with a primordial and inescapable condition for fulfilling that mission.

*Chapter Twelve*

# THE CHURCH:
# SACRAMENT OF HISTORY

Because the Church has inherited its structures and its lifestyle from the past, it finds itself today somewhat out of step with the history which confronts it. But what is called for is not simply a renewal and adaptation of pastoral methods. It is rather a question of a new ecclesial consciousness and a redefinition of the task of the Church in a world in which it is not only *present,* but of which it *forms a part* more than it suspected in the past. In this new consciousness and redefinition, intraecclesial problems take a second place.

## UNIVERSAL SACRAMENT OF SALVATION

The unqualified affirmation of the universal will of salvation has radically changed the way of conceiving the mission of the Church in the world. It seems clear today that the purpose of the Church is not to save in the sense of "guaranteeing heaven."[1] The work of salvation is a reality which occurs in history. This work gives to the historical becoming of humankind its profound unity and its deepest meaning.[2] It is only by starting from this unity and meaning that we can establish the distinctions and clarifications which can lead us to a new understanding of the mission of the Church. The Lord is the Sower who arises at dawn to sow the field of historical reality before we establish our distinctions. Distinctions can be useful for what Liégé calls "the new initiatives of God in the history of men," but as he himself says, "Too great a use of them, however, threatens to destroy the sense of a vocation to a single fulfillment toward which God has not ceased to lead the world, whose source he is."[3] The meaning and the fruitfulness of the ecclesial task will be clear only when they are situated within the context of the plan of salvation. In doing this we must avoid reducing the salvific work to the action of the Church. All our ecclesiology will depend on the kind of relationship that we establish between the two.

### A New Ecclesiological Perspective

The perspective we have indicated presupposes an "uncentering" of the Church, for the Church must cease considering itself as the exclusive place of

*143*

salvation and orient itself towards a new and radical service of people. It also presupposes a new awareness that the action of Christ and his Spirit is the true hinge of the plan of salvation.

Indeed, the Church of the *first centuries* lived spontaneously in this way. Its minority status in society and the consequent pressure that the proximity of the non-Christian world exercised on it made it quite sensitive to the action of Christ beyond its frontiers,[4] that is, to the totality of his redemptive work. This explains why, for example, the great Christian authors of that time affirmed without qualification human liberty in religious matters as a natural and human right and declared that the state is incompetent to intervene in this area. Because they had confidence in the possibility of salvation at work in everyone, they saw liberty not so much as a risk of wandering from the path as the necessary condition for finding the path and arriving at a genuine encounter with the Lord.[5]

The situation of the Christian community changed in *the fourth century.* Instead of being marginated and attacked, Christianity was now tolerated (Edict of Milan, A.D. 313) and quickly became the religion of the Roman state (Decree of Thessalonica, A.D. 381). The proclamation of the gospel message was then protected by the support of political authority, and the Christianization of the world of that time received a powerful impulse. This rapid advance of Christianity brought about a change in the manner of conceiving the relationship of humankind to salvation. It began to be thought that there were only two kinds of people: those who have accepted faith in Christ and those who have culpably rejected it. The Fathers continued to teach the doctrine of the universal will of salvation and held that this could not occur without free acceptance on the part of human beings. But they asserted that there was no longer any excuse for ignorance of the Savior, for thanks to the ministry of the Church, the voice of the Gospel had come in one way or another to all humans.[6] Neither Jews nor gentiles had any excuse. These ideas, which were presented with hesitation and even anguish in the fourth and fifth centuries, gradually gained ground. By the Middle Ages, when the Church was coextensive with the known world of that time and deeply pervaded it, Christians had the vital experience of security and tranquility that "outside the Church there is no salvation." *To be for or against Christ came to be fully identified with being for or against the Church.* Therefore it is not strange that there was no longer any mention of bits of truth which could be found beyond the frontiers of the Church; there was no longer any world outside the Church. The Church was regarded as the sole repository of religious truth. In a spontaneous and inevitable fashion there arose an ecclesiocentric perspective which centered more and more on the life and reflection of the Church—and continues to do so even up to the present time.

From that time on, therefore, there was a subtle displacement of religious liberty as "a human and natural right" of all humans by "the liberty of the act of faith"; henceforth, the right of liberty in religious matters would be synonymous with the right not to be coerced by the forced imposition of the Christian faith.[7] In a parallel fashion there occurred another important displacement: no longer was it a question of the "incompetence" of political power in religious matters; rather it was a question of the state's "tolerance"—which presupposed an "option" for the truth—toward religious error. The reason for these two displacements is the same: the position of strength of a Church which had begun to focus on itself, to ally itself with civil power, and to consider itself as the exclusive repository of salvific truth.

This condition of the Church began to change in the *modern period,* with the internal rupture of Christendom and the discovery of new peoples. But at the beginning of this period the ecclesiocentric perspective persisted, with a few exceptions. In the matter of religious liberty, which we have focused on here, it was the period of "religious tolerance": what Thomas Aquinas considered valid for the Jews was extended to the descendants of Christians who had "culpably" separated themselves from the Church. In the nineteenth century religious toleration gave rise to the by-product of the theory of the thesis and the hypothesis; this theory sought to respond to the ideas born in the French Revolution by giving a new impulse to the development of toleration. But fundamentally the condition continued being the same: salvific truth could be found only in the Church. It is for this reason that "modern freedoms" endangered the eternal destiny of humankind.[8]

The effects of the new historical situation in which the Church found itself began to be felt more strongly in the nineteenth century and even more so in recent decades. Vatican II did not hesitate to place itself in the line of a full affirmation of the universal will of salvation and to put an end to the anachronistic theological and pastoral consequences deduced from the ecclesiocentrism which we have already mentioned.[9] This explains the change of attitude regarding religious liberty. The declaration dedicated to this subject tried to achieve a consensus by placing itself simply on the level of the dignity of the human person. But this position implies a change of position with regard to deep theological questions having to do with the role of the Church in the encounter between God and humankind.[10]

We might speak here of a return to the posture of the Church in the first centuries.[11] Without being inexact, however, this affirmation tends to schematize the process. There is never a pure and simple regression. The process which began in the fourth century was not simply an "accident." It was a long and laborious learning experience. And that experience forms part of the contemporary ecclesial consciousness; it is a factor which explains many phenomena today. It also cautions us against what might happen again. What was spontaneously and intuitively expressed in the first centuries must manifest itself today in a more reflective and critical fashion.

### Sacrament and Sign

Thanks to the process which we have just reviewed, Vatican II was able to set forth the outlines of a new ecclesiological perspective. And it did this almost surprisingly by speaking of the Church as a sacrament.[12] This is undoubtedly one of the most important and permanent contributions of the Council.[13] The notion of sacrament enables us to think of the Church within the horizon of salvific work and in terms radically different from those of the ecclesiocentric emphasis. The Council itself did not place itself totally in this line of thinking. Many of the texts still reveal the burden of a heavy heritage; they timidly point to a way out from this turning in of the Church on itself, without always accomplishing this. But what must be emphasized is that in the midst of the Council itself, over which hovered an ecclesiocentric perspective, new elements arose which allowed for a reflection which broke with this perspective and was more in accord with the real challenges to the Christian faith of today.[14]

In theology the term *sacramentum* has two closely related meanings. Initially it was used to translate the Greek work *misterion*. According to Paul, *mystery* means *the fulfillment and the manifestation of the salvific plan*: "the secret hidden for long ages and through many generations, but now disclosed" (Col. 1:26). The Gospel is, therefore, "that divine secret kept in silence for long ages but now disclosed . . . made known to all nations, to bring them to faith and obedience" (Rom. 16:25-26).[15] This mystery is the love of the Father, who "loved the world so much that he gave his only Son" (John 3:16) in order to call all humans, in the Spirit, to communion with God. Human beings are called together, as a community and not as separate individuals, to participate in the life of the Trinitarian community, to enter into the circuit of love that unites the persons of the Trinity.[16] This is a love which "builds up human society in history."[17] The fulfillment and the manifestation of the will of the Father occur in a privileged fashion in Christ, who is called therefore the "mystery of God" (Col. 2:22; see also Col. 1:27; 4:3; Eph. 3:3; 1 Tim. 3:16).[18] For the same reason Sacred Scripture, the Church, and the liturgical rites were designated by the first Christian generations by the term *mystery,* and by its Latin translation, *sacrament.* In the sacrament the salvific plan is fulfilled and revealed; that is, it is made present among humans and for humans. But at the same time, it is through the sacrament that humans encounter God. This is an encounter *in* history, not because God comes *from* history, but because history comes from God. The sacrament is thus the efficacious revelation of the call to communion with God and to the unity of all humankind.

This is the primordial meaning of the term *sacrament* and it is in this way that it is used in the first centuries of the Church. At the beginning of the third century, however, Tertullian introduced a nuance which gradually gave rise to a second meaning derived from the first. This African Father began to use the term *sacrament* to designate the rites of Baptism and the Eucharist. Gradually the two terms, *mystery* and *sacrament,* became distinct. The first referred more to the doctrinal mysteries; the second designated what we commonly call sacraments today. The theology of the Middle Ages recovered the meaning of sacrament, in the strict sense, in the formula *efficacious sign of grace.* The sign marks the character of visibility of the sacrament, by means of which there occurs an effective personal encounter of God and the human person. But the sign transmits a reality from beyond itself, in this case the grace of communion, which is the reason for and the result of this encounter.[19] This communion is also an intrahistorical reality.

To call the Church the "visible sacrament of this saving unity" (*Lumen gentium,* no. 9) is to define it in relation to the plan of salvation, whose fulfillment in history the Church reveals and signifies to the human race. A visible sign, the Church imparts to reality "union with God" and "the unity of all humankind" (*Lumen gentium,* no. 1). The Church can be understood only in relation to the reality which it announces to humankind. Its existence is not "for itself," but rather "for others." Its center is outside itself, it is in the work of Christ and his Spirit. It is constituted by the Spirit as "the universal sacrament of salvation" (*Lumen gentium,* no. 48); outside of the action of the Spirit which leads the universe and history towards its fullness in Christ, the Church is nothing. Even more, the Church does not authentically attain consciousness of itself except in the perception of this total presence of Christ and his Spirit in humanity. The mediation of the consciousness of the "other"—of the world in which this presence occurs—is the indispensable precondition of its own consciousness as community-sign. Any attempt to avoid this mediation can only lead the Church to a false perception of itself—to an ecclesiocentric consciousness.

Through the persons who explicitly accept his Word, the Lord reveals the world to itself. He rescues it from anonymity and enables it to know the ultimate meaning of its historical future and the value of every human act.[20] But by the same token the Church must turn to the world, in which Christ and his Spirit are present and active; the Church must allow itself to be inhabited and evangelized by the world. It has been said for this reason that a theology of the Church in the world should be complemented by "a theology of the world in the Church."[21] This dialectical relationship is implied in the emphasis on the Church as sacrament. This puts us on the track of a new way of conceiving the relationship between the historical Church and the world. The Church is not a non-world; it is humanity itself attentive to the Word. It is the People of God which lives in history and is orientated toward the future promised by the Lord. It is, as Teilhard de Chardin said, the "reflectively Christified portion of the world." The Church-world relationship thus should be seen not in spacial terms, but rather in dynamic and temporal ones.[22]

As a sacramental community, the Church should signify in its own internal structure the salvation whose fulfillment it announces. Its organization ought to serve this task. As a sign of the liberation of humankind and history, the Church itself in its concrete existence ought to be a place of liberation. A sign should be clear and understandable. If we conceive of the Church as a sacrament of the salvation of the world, then it has all the more obligation to manifest in its visible structures the message that it bears. Since the Church is not an end in itself, it finds its meaning in its capacity to signify the reality in function of which it exists. Outside of this reality the Church is nothing; because of it the Church is always provisional; and it is towards the fulfillment of this reality that the Church is oriented: this reality is the Kingdom of God which has already begun in history.[23] The break with an unjust social order and the search for new ecclesial structures—in which the most dynamic sectors of the Christian community are engaged—have their basis in this ecclesiological perspective. We are moving towards forms of presence and structure of the Church the radical newness of which can barely be discerned on the basis of our present experience. This trend, at its best and healthiest, is not a fad; nor is it due to professional nonconformists. Rather it has its roots in a profound fidelity to the Church as sacrament of the unity and salvation of humankind and in the conviction that its only support should be the Word which liberates.

We must recognize, nevertheless, that the ecclesiocentric point of view is abandoned more rapidly in the realm of a certain theological reflection than in the concrete attitudes of the majority of the Christian community. This presents not a few difficulties, for what is most important is what happens at this second level. To dedicate oneself to intraecclesial problems—as is often done in certain forms of protest in the Church, especially in the developed countries—is to miss the point regarding a true renewal of the Church. For this renewal cannot be achieved in any deep sense except on the basis of an effective awareness of the world and a real commitment to it. Changes in the Church will be made on the basis of such awareness and commitment. To seek anxiously after changes themselves is to pose the question in terms of survival. But this is not the question. The point is not to survive, but to serve. The rest will be given.

In Latin America the world in which the Christian community must live and celebrate its eschatological hope is the world of social revolution; the Church's task must be defined in relation to this. Its fidelity to the Gospel leaves it no alternative: the Church must be the visible sign of the presence of the Lord within the aspiration for liberation and the struggle for a more human and just society. Only in this way will the message of love which the Church bears be made credible and efficacious.

## EUCHARIST AND HUMAN FELLOWSHIP

The place of the mission of the Church is where the celebration of the Lord's supper and the creation of human fellowship are indissolubly joined. This is what it means in an active and concrete way to be the sacrament of the salvation of the world.

### "In Memory of Me"

The first task of the Church is to celebrate with joy the gift of the salvific action of God in humanity, accomplished through the death and resurrection of Christ. This is the Eucharist: a memorial and a thanksgiving. It is a memorial of Christ which presupposes an ever-renewed acceptance of the meaning of his life—a total giving to others. It is a thanksgiving for the love of God which is revealed in these events. The Eucharist is a feast, a celebration of the joy that the Church desires and seeks to share. The Eucharist is done within the Church, and simultaneously the Church is built up by the Eucharist. In the Church "we celebrate," writes Schillebeeckx, "that which is achieved outside the Church edifice, in human history."[24] This Work, which creates a profound human fellowship, gives the Church its reason for being.

In the Eucharist we celebrate the cross and the resurrection of Christ, his Passover from death to life, and our passing from sin to grace. In the Gospel the Last Supper is presented against the background of the Jewish Passover, which celebrated the liberation from Egypt and the Sinai Covenant.[25] The Christian Passover takes on and reveals the full meaning of the Jewish Passover.[26] Liberation from sin is at the very root of political liberation. The former reveals what is really involved in the latter. But on the other hand, communion with God and others presupposes the abolition of all injustice and exploitation. This is expressed by the very fact that the Eucharist was instituted during a meal. For the Jews a meal in common was a sign of fellowship. It united the diners in a kind of sacred pact. Moreover, the bread and the wine are signs of fellowship which at the same time suggest the gift of creation. The objects used in the Eucharist themselves recall that fellowship is rooted in God's will to give the goods of this earth to all persons so that they might build a more human world.[27] The Gospel of John, which does not contain the story of the Eucharistic institution, reinforces this idea, for it substitutes the episode of the washing of the feet—a gesture of service, love, and fellowship. This substitution is significant: John seems to see in this episode the profound meaning of the Eucharistic celebration, the institution of which he does not relate.[28] Thus the Eucharist appears inseparably united to creation and to the building up of a real human fellowship. "The reference to community," writes Tillard, "does not therefore represent a simple consequence, an accidental dimension, a second level of a rite that is in the first place and above all individual—as the simple act of eating is. From the beginning it is seen in the human context of the meal as it was conceived in Israel. The Eucharistic rite in its essential elements is communitarian and orientated toward the constitution of human fellowship."[29]

A text in Matthew is very clear regarding the relationship between worship and human fellowship: "If, when you are bringing your gift to the altar, you suddenly remember that your brother has a grievance against you, leave your gift where it is before the altar. First go and make your peace with your brother, and only then come back and offer your gift" (Matt. 5:23-24).[30] This is not a question of a scrupulous conscience, but rather of living according to the demands placed on us by the other: "If . . . you suddenly remember that your brother has a grievance against you." To be the cause of a fracture of fellowship disqualifies one from participation in that worship which celebrates the action of the Lord which establishes a profound community among persons. "The Christian community," said Camilo Torres, "cannot offer the sacrifice in an authentic form if it has not first fulfilled in an effective manner the precept of 'love of thy neighbor.' "[31] The separation of sacrifice from the love of neighbor is the reason for the harsh criticism which Jesus—speaking from a strong prophetic tradition—addressed to all purely external worship. For if "our relationship of service to our neighbor in the world (a relationship profoundly expressed in prayer and the liturgy) were in fact absent, then in this case the prayer and the whole liturgy, as well as our speaking of God . . . would fall into a vacuum and degenerate into a false and useless superstructure."[32] This is how Paul understood it. Before recounting the institution of the Eucharist he indicated the necessary precondition for participation in it when he reproached the Corinthians for their lack of interpersonal charity in their gatherings to celebrate the Lord's Supper (1 Cor. 11:17-24; cf. James 2:14).

The profound unity among the different meanings of the term *koinonia* in the New Testament both expresses and summarizes these ideas. Congar has pointed out that *koinonia* simultaneously designates three realities.[33] First it signifies the common ownership of the goods necessary for earthly existence: "Never forget to show kindness and to share what you have with others, for such are the sacrifices which God approves" (Heb. 13:16; cf. Acts 2:44; 4:32). *Koinonia* is a concrete gesture of human charity. Thus Paul uses this word to designate the collection organized on behalf of the Christians in Jerusalem; the Corinthians glorify God because of their "liberal contribution to their need and to the general good" (2 Cor. 9:13; cf. 2 Cor. 8:34; Rom. 15:26-27). Second, *koinonia* designates the union of the faithful with Christ through the Eucharist: "When we bless 'the cup of blessing,' is it not a means of sharing in the blood of Christ? When we break the bread, is it not a means of sharing in the body of Christ?" (1 Cor. 10:16). And third, *koinonia* means the union of Christians with the Father—"If we claim to be sharing in his life while we walk in the dark, our words and our lives are a lie" (1 John 1:6; cf. 1:3 )—with the Son—"It is God himself who calls you to share in the life of his Son" (1 Cor. 1:9; cf. 1 John 1:3)—and with the Spirit—"The grace of the Lord Jesus Christ, and the love of God, and fellowship in the Holy Spirit, be with you all" (2 Cor. 13:14; cf. Phil. 2:1).

The basis for fellowship is full communion with the persons of the Trinity. The bond which unites God and humanity is celebrated—that is, effectively recalled and proclaimed—in the Eucharist. Without a real commitment against exploitation and alienation and for a society of solidarity and justice, the Eucharistic celebration is an empty action, lacking any genuine endorsement by those who participate in it. This is something that many Latin American Christians are feeling more and more deeply, and they are thus more demanding both of themselves and of the whole Church.[34] "To make a remembrance" of Christ is more than the performance of an act of worship; it is to accept living under the sign of the cross and in the hope of the resurrection. It is to accept the meaning of a life that was given over to death—at the hands of the powerful of this world—for love of others.

### Denunciation and Annunciation

The primary task of the Church, as we have said, is to celebrate with joy the salvific action of the Lord in history. In the creation of fellowship implied and signified by this celebration, the Church—taken as a whole—plays a role which is unique, but varies according to historical circumstances.

In Latin America to be Church today means to take a clear position regarding both the present state of social injustice and the revolutionary process which is attempting to abolish that injustice and build a more human order. The first step is to recognize that in reality a stand has already been taken: the Church is tied to the prevailing social system. In many places the Church contributes to creating "a Christian order" and to giving a kind of sacred character to a situation which is not only alienating but is the worst kind of violence—a situation which pits the powerful against the weak. The protection which the Church receives from the social class which is the beneficiary and the defender of the prevailing capitalist society in Latin America has made the institutional Church into a part of the system and the Christian message into a part of the dominant ideology.[35] Any claim to noninvolvement in politics—a banner recently hoisted by conservative sectors—is nothing but a subterfuge to keep things as they are.[36] The mission of the Church cannot be defined in the abstract. Its historical and social coordinates, its here and now, have a bearing not only on the adequacy of its pastoral methods. They also should be at the very heart of theological reflection.

The Church—with variations according to different countries—has an obvious social influence in Latin America.[37] Without overestimating it, we must recognize that numerous facts have demonstrated this influence, even up to the present day. This influence has contributed, and continues to contribute to supporting the established order. But this is no longer the entire picture. The situation has begun to change. The change is slow and still very fragile, but in this change are involved growing and active minorities of the Latin American Christian community. The process is not irreversible, but it is gradually gaining strength. It is still afflicted with many ambiguities, but the initial experiences are beginning to provide the criteria by which these ambiguities can be resolved. Within these groups—as might have been expected—there has arisen a question; on its answer will depend to a large degree the concrete path to be followed. The question is: Should the change consist in the Church's using its social influence to effect the necessary transformations? Some fear a kind of "Constantinianism of the Left," and believe that the Church should divest itself of every vestige of political power.[38] This fear is opportune because it points out a genuine risk which we must keep in mind. But we believe that the best way to achieve this divestment of power is precisely by resolutely casting our lot with the oppressed and the exploited in the struggle for a more just society. The groups that control economic and political power will not forgive the Church for this. They will withdraw their support, which is the principal source of the ambiguous social prestige which the Church enjoys in Latin America today. Indeed, this has already begun. Moreover, formulated in this way the question is somewhat artificial. How can the Church preach the Word, incarnated where the pulse of Latin American history throbs, without putting this social influence at stake? How can it perform a disappearing act with the situation which—with all its ambiguities—is the Church's own? How can it denounce the unjust order of the continent and announce the Gospel outside of the concrete position which it has today in Latin American society? Indeed, it is not a question of whether the Church should or should not use its influence in the Latin American revolutionary process. Rather, the question is in what direction and for what purpose is it going to use its influence: for or against the established order, to preserve the social prestige which comes with its ties to the groups in power or to free itself from that prestige with a break from these groups and with genuine service to the oppressed?[39] It is a question of social realism, of becoming aware of an already given situation, to start from it, and to modify it; it is not a question of creating that situation. The situation is already there and is the concrete, historical framework for the task of the Latin American Church.

Within this framework the Latin American Church must make the prophetic *denunciation* of every dehumanizing situation, which is contrary to fellowship, justice, and liberty. At the same time it must criticize every sacralization of oppressive structures to which the Church itself might have contributed. Its denunciation must be public, for its position in Latin American society is public. This denunciation may be one of the few voices—and at times the only one—which can be raised in the midst of a country submitted to repression. In this critical and creative confrontation of its faith with historical realities—a task whose roots must be in the hope in the future promised by God—the Church must go to the very causes of the situation and not be content with pointing out and attending to certain of its consequences. Indeed, one of the most subtle dangers threatening a "renewed" Church in Latin America is to allow itself to be assimilated into a society which seeks certain reforms without a comprehensive critique. It is the danger of becoming functional to the system all over again, only this time to a system which tries to modernize and to suppress the most outrageous injustices without effecting any deep changes.[40] In Latin America this denunciation must represent a radical critique of the present order, which means that the Church must also criticize itself as an integral part of this order. This horizon will allow the Church to break out of its narrow enclosure of intraecclesial problems by placing these problems in their true context—the total society and the broad perspective of commitment in a world of revolutionary turmoil.

It has been pointed out, and rightly so, that this critical function of the Church runs the risk of remaining on a purely verbal and external level and that it should be backed up with clear actions and commitments. Prophetic denunciation can be made validly and truly only from within the heart of the struggle for a more human world. The truth of the Gospel, it has been said, is a truth which must be done. This observation is correct and necessary. This presupposes, we should recall, that given the concrete conditions in which the Church finds itself in Latin American society, a precise and opportune denunciation on the part of the Church is not only a "word" or a "text"; it is an action, a stand.

Because of its very social influence, its words—if they are clear and incisive—will not be hollow. When the Church speaks, it can cause the old underpinnings of the established order to fall, and it can mobilize new energies. This is so much the case that simply because of their "speaking" or "making statements," certain organisms of the Church and many Christians have undergone severe attacks and serious difficulties at the hands of the representatives of the established order—including the loss of liberty and even the loss of life. It is not at all our purpose to overestimate the word and so to diminish the value of concrete actions; but simply to be realistic we should remember that at times the word is also an important gesture of commitment. In this regard, the critical function of the Church in Latin America—given its historical and social coordinates—has preconditions for its exercise and possibilities for action in relation to the process of liberation which are not found elsewhere. Therefore, its responsibility is all the greater.

The denunciation, however, is achieved by confronting a given situation with the reality which is *announced*: the love of the Father which calls all persons in Christ and through the action of the Spirit to union among themselves and communion with him. To announce the Gospel is to proclaim that the love of God is present in the historical becoming of humankind. It is to make known that there is no human act which cannot in the last instance be defined in relation to Christ. To preach the Good News is for the Church to be a sacrament of history, to fulfill its role as community—a sign of the convocation of all humankind by God. It is to announce the coming of the Kingdom. The Gospel message reveals, without any evasions, what is at the root of social injustice: the rupture of the fellowship based on our being offspring of the Father; the Gospel reveals the fundamental alienation which lies below every other human alienation. In this way, evangelization is a powerful factor in personalization.[41] Because of it persons become aware of the profound meaning of their historical existence and live an active and creative hope in the fulfillment of the fellowship that they seek with all their strength.

Moreover, the personalization stimulated by the annunciation of the Gospel can take on—in cases like Latin America—very particular and demanding forms. If a situation of injustice and exploitation is incompatible with the coming of the Kingdom, the Word which announces this coming ought normally to point out this incompatibility. This means that the people who hear this message and live in these conditions by the mere fact of hearing it should perceive themselves as oppressed and feel impelled to seek their own liberation. Very concretely, they should "feel their hunger" and become aware that this hunger is due to a situation which the Gospel repudiates. The annunciation of the Gospel thus has a conscienticizing function, or in other words, a politicizing function. But this is made real and meaningful only by living and announcing the Gospel from within a commitment to liberation, only in concrete, effective solidarity with people and exploited social classes. Only by participating in their struggles can we understand the implications of the gospel message and make it have an impact on history. The preaching of the Word will be empty and ahistorical if it tries to avoid this dimension.[42] It will not be the message of the God who liberates, of "Him who restores," as José María Arguedas says.

Some years ago, a pope who is beyond any suspicion of "horizontalism," Pius XII, then Cardinal Pacelli, said that the Church civilizes by evangelizing. And this assertion was accepted without opposition. In the contemporary Latin American context it would be necessary to say that the Church should politicize by evangelizing. Will this expression receive the same acceptance? Probably not. To many it will seem offensive; they will perhaps accuse it of "humanizing" the Gospel message or of falling into a deceitful and dangerous "temporalism." This reaction can be explained in part by the fact that there are still many who—lacking a realistic and contemporary conception of the political sphere—do not wish to see the Gospel "brought down" to a level which they believe is nothing more than partisan conflict. But the more severe attacks will doubtless come from those who fear the upsurge of a true political consciousness in the Latin American masses and can discern what the contribution of the Gospel to this process might be. When it was a question of "civilizing," they had no objection, because this term was translated as the promotion of ethical, cultural, and artistic values and at the most as a very general and uncommitted defense of the dignity of the human person. But "to politicize," "to conscienticize"—these terms have today in Latin America a deeply subversive meaning. Can we say that the struggle against the "institutionalized violence" endured by the weak and the struggle for social justice are therefore less human, less ethical, less "civilizing" than the promotion of moral, cultural, and esthetic values which are bound to a given social system? Girardi is correct when he says that "institutionalized violence generally goes along with institutionalized hypocrisy."[43]

When we affirm that the Church politicizes by evangelizing, we do not claim that the Gospel is thus reduced to creating a political consciousness in persons or that the revelation of the Father—which takes on, transforms, and fulfills in an unsuspected way every human aspiration—is thereby nullified. We mean that the annunciation of the Gospel, precisely insofar as it is a message of total love, has an inescapable political dimension, because it is addressed to people who live within a fabric of social relationships, which, in our case, keeps them in a subhuman condition. But did those who think in this way believe that Pius XII was reducing the Gospel to a civilizing work? If they did not believe it before, why do they think so now? Let us speak openly: to "civilize" does not seem to challenge their privileged situation in *this* world; to conscienticize, to politicize, to make the oppressed become aware that they are human beings—do challenge that privilege.

This conscienticizing dimension of the preaching of the Gospel, which rejects any aseptic presentation of the message, should lead to a profound revision of the pastoral activity of the Church. Thus this activity should be addressed effectively and primarily to those who are oppressed in the oppressed nations and not—as is presently the case—to the beneficiaries of a system designed for their own benefit. Or still better, the oppressed themselves should be the agents of their own pastoral activity. The marginated and the dispossessed still do not have their own voice in the Church of him who came to the world especially for them.[44] The issue is not accidental. Their real presence in the Church would work a profound transformation in its structures, its values, and its actions. The owners of the goods of this world would no longer be the "owners" of the Gospel.

It would be naive, nevertheless, to claim that the revolutionary exigencies in Latin America do not bring with them the danger of oversimplifying the Gospel message and making it a "revolutionary ideology"—which would definitively obscure reality. But we believe that the danger is not averted simply by noting its presence. It is not evaporated by a climate of alarm. It is necessary to look at it face to face and lucidly to analyze its causes as well as the factors which make it important for Christians committed to the social struggle. Are we not in this position because we have tried to hide the real political implications of the Gospel? Those who—without stating so—neutralized these implications or oriented them for their own benefit are those who now have the least authority for giving lessons in evangelical "purity." We cannot expect the true and opportune counsel today to come from those who are "verticalists" in theory and "horizontalists" in practice. The problem exists, but the solution can come only from the very roots of the problem. It is where the annunciation of the Gospel seems to border on submersion into the purely historical realm that there must be born the reflection, the spirituality, and the new preaching of a Christian message which is incarnated—not lost—in our here and now.[45] To evangelize, Chenu has said, is to incarnate the Gospel in time. This time today is sinister and difficult only for those who ultimately do not know how or hesitate to believe that the Lord is present in it.

The concrete measures for effecting the denunciation and the annunciation will be discerned little by little. It will be necessary to study carefully in a *permanent* fashion the signs of the times (*Gaudium et spes*, no. 4), responding to specific situations without claiming to adopt at every step positions valid for all eternity. There are moments in which we will advance only by trial and error.[46] It is difficult to establish ahead of time—as we have perhaps tried to do for a long time—the specific guidelines which ought to determine the behavior of the Church, taken as a whole, in these questions. The Church should rise to the demands of the moment with whatever lights it has at that moment and with the will to be faithful to the Gospel. Some chapters of theology can be written only afterwards.

But the incertitude and apprenticeship involved in this task should not lead us to disregard the urgency and necessity of taking stands or to forget what is permanent—that the Gospel annunciation opens human history to the future promised by God and reveals God's present work. On the one hand, this annunciation will indicate that in every achievement of fellowship and justice among humans there is a step toward total communion. By the same token, it will indicate the incomplete and provisional character of any and every human achievement. The Gospel will fulfill this function based on a comprehensive vision of humankind and history and not on partial focuses, which have their own proper and effective instruments of criticism. The prophetic character of the Christian message "always works from an eschatological option and affirmation. According to it, history—as long as it has not achieved its eschatological end—will not achieve its total maturity. Therefore every historical period always has new possibilities before it."[47] On the other hand, by affirming that human fellowship is possible and that it will indeed be achieved, the annunciation of the Gospel will inspire and radicalize the commitment of the Christian in history. In history and only in history is the gift of the love of God believed, loved, and hoped for.[48] Every attempt to evade the struggle against alienation and the violence of the powerful and for a more just and more human world is the greatest infidelity to God. To know God is to work for justice. There is no other path to reach God.

## Faith and Social Conflict *

The council led us onto a new path on which there is no turning back: openness to the world. The history in which the Christian community, the church, plays a part today is marked by various kinds of opposition among individuals, human groups, social classes, racial groupings, and nations. In addition, the situation gives rise to confrontations that lead to various kinds of violence. Meanwhile, a choice was made at Medellín that has been a decisive one for the church during the years since then: the preferential option for the poor.[49] By "the poor" I mean here those whose social and economic condition is the result of a particular political order and the concrete histories of countries and social groups.[50]

At this point challenging questions arise: How are we to live evangelical charity in the midst of this situation? How can we reconcile the universality of charity and a preferential solidarity with the poor who belong to marginalized cultures, exploited social classes, and despised racial groups? Furthermore, unity is one of the essential notes of the church. How, then, are we to live this unity in a history stamped by social conflict? These are questions we cannot avoid. They hammer at the Christian conscience everywhere but are especially acute in Latin America, the only part of the world in which the majority is both poor and Christian. The problem is especially urgent in the pastoral sphere in which the church lives its everyday life; it is therefore a challenge to any theology that endeavors to serve the proclamation of the gospel.

If we are to face these challenges in the right way, we must first see the real world without evasion, and we must be determined to change it. Let me say

---

*The section entitled "Christian Fellowship and Class Struggle" in the first edition of this book gave rise to misunderstandings that I want to clear up. I have rewritten the text in the light of new documents of the magisterium and by taking other aspects of the subject into account.

at the very outset that none of us can accept with unconcern, much less with satisfaction, a situation in which human beings live in confrontation with one another. This is not acceptable to us either as human beings or as Christians. This state of affairs is doubtless one of the most painful aspects of human life. We would like things to be different and must therefore try to overcome the oppositions at work. But we must not fail to see the situation as it is and to understand the causes that produce it. Social conflict—including one of its most acute forms: the struggle between social classes—is a painful historical fact.[51] We may not decide not to look at it in light of faith and the demands of the kingdom. Faith in the God who is love is the source of light and energy for Christian commitment in this situation.

1. The claim that conflict is *a social fact* does not imply an unqualified acceptance of it as something beyond discussion.[52] On the contrary, the claim is subject to scientific analysis, and science is in principle always critical of its own claims. The various social sciences, to say nothing of simple empirical observation, tell us that we are faced today with an unjust social situation in which racial groupings are discriminated against, classes exploited, cultures despised, and women, especially poor women, are "doubly oppressed and marginalized."

Situations such as the one in South Africa display a cruel and inhuman racism and an extreme form of conflictual confrontation that is also to be found, even if in less obvious forms, in other parts of the world. It raises difficult questions for Christians living in these countries. These and other situations, such as those in Northern Ireland, Poland, Guatemala, and Korea, show us that in addition to economic factors others of a different character play a part in oppositions between social groups.

Acknowledgment of the facts of social conflict, and concretely of the class struggle, is to be seen in various documents of the church's magisterium. There are passages in the writings of Pius XI that are clear in this regard. He says, for example, in *Quadragesimo Anno*: "In fact, human society now, because it is founded on classes with divergent aims and hence opposed to one another and therefore inclined to enmity and strife, continues to be in a violent condition and is unstable and uncertain" (no. 82). A few lines later, he speaks of how far the struggle can go: "As the situation now stands, hiring and offering for hire in the so-called labor market separate persons into two divisions, as into battle lines, and the contest between these divisions turns the labor market itself almost into a battlefield where, face to face, the opposing lines struggle bitterly" (no. 83). The class struggle is a fact that Christians cannot dodge and in the face of which the demands of the gospel must be clearly stated.[53]

In 1968 the French episcopal commission on the working classes issued a statement that said, among other things:

Oppression of the workers is a form of class struggle to the extent that it is carried on by those managing the economy. For the fact of class struggle must not be confused with the Marxist interpretation of this struggle. *The class struggle is a fact* that no one can deny. If we look for those responsible for the class struggle, the first are those who deliberately keep the working class in an unjust situation, oppose its collective advancement, and combat its efforts at self-liberation. Its actions do not indeed justify hatred of it or violence directed against it; it must nevertheless be said that the "struggle for justice" (to use Pius XII's expression), which is what the struggle of the working class is, is in itself conformed to the will of God.[54]

This statement is still primarily concerned with saying that the class struggle is a fact. At the same time, however, it points to those chiefly responsible for it, while also rejecting "hatred of them or violence directed against them."[55]

In his encyclical on human work John Paul II has dealt extensively and in depth with this difficult point. In the section "Conflict between Labor and Capital in the Present Phase of History" the pope writes:

Throughout this period, which is by no means yet over, the issue of work has of course been posed on the basis of the *great conflict* that in the age of, and together with, industrial development emerged between "capital" and "labor"—that is to say, between the *small* but highly influential *group* of entrepreneurs, owners or holders of the means of production, and the *broader multitude* of persons who lacked these means and who shared in the process of production solely by their labor [*Laborem Exercens*, 11; emphasis added].

The conflict has its origin in exploitation of workers by "the entrepreneurs . . . following the principle of maximum profit" (ibid.). A few pages later, the pope repeats his point that behind a seemingly abstract opposition there are concrete persons:

It is obvious that, when we speak of opposition between labor and capital, we are not dealing only with abstract concepts or "impersonal forces" operating in economic production. Behind both concepts there are persons, *living, actual persons:* on the one side are those who do the work *without being the owners* of the means of production, and on the other side those who act as entrepreneurs and *who own these means* or represent the owners. [ibid., 14; emphasis added].

This fact enables him to conclude: "Thus *the issue of ownership or property* enters from the beginning into the whole of this historical process" (ibid.). What we have, then, is an opposition of *persons* and not a conflict between abstract concepts or impersonal forces. This is what makes the whole matter so thorny and challenging to a Christian conscience.

2. This harsh and painful situation cannot be ignored.[56] Only if we acknowledge its existence can we give a *Christian evaluation* of it and find ways of resolving it. This second step should of course be the most important thing

for us. These situations are caused, after all, by profound injustices that we cannot accept. Any real resolution requires, however, that we get to the causes that bring about these social conflicts and that we do away with the factors that produce a world divided into the privileged and dispossessed, into superior and inferior racial groupings. The creation of a fraternal society of equals, in which there are no oppressors and no oppressed, requires that we not mislead others or ourselves about the real state of affairs.

Earlier in this book I said that awareness of the conflict going on in history does not mean acceptance of it and that the important thing is to struggle "for the establishment of peace and justice amid all humankind."[57] The connection of peace with justice is an important theme in the Bible. Peace is promised along with the gift of the kingdom, and it requires the establishment of just social relationships. Drawing inspiration from some words of Paul VI, which it cites, Medellín begins its document on peace by saying. " 'If development is the new name for peace,' Latin American underdevelopment, with its own characteristics in its different countries, is an unjust situation promoting tensions that conspire against peace" ("Peace," 1).

These tensions, which can develop into very sharp conflicts, are part of everyday life in Latin America. Moreover, they often place us in disconcerting situations in which theological reflection can advance only gropingly and in an exploratory way.[58] But the trickiness of the subject does not justify an approach that forgets the universalist demands of Christian love and ecclesial communion. On the other hand, these demands must be shown to have a necessary connection with the concrete situations mentioned above if we are to give adequate and effective answers to the Christians who face them.

The gospel proclaims God's love for every human being and calls us to love as God loves. Yet recognition of the fact of class struggle means taking a position, opposing certain groups of persons, rejecting certain activities, and facing hostilities. For if we are convinced that peace indeed supposes the establishment of justice, we cannot remain passive or indifferent when the most basic human rights are at risk. That kind of behavior would not be ethical or Christian. Conversely, our active participation on the side of justice and in defense of the weakest members of society does not mean that we are encouraging conflict; it means rather that we are trying to eliminate its deepest root, which is the absence of love.[59]

When we thus assert the universality of Christian love, we are not taking a stand at an abstract level, for this universality must become a vital energy at work in the concrete institutions within which we live. The social realities to which I have been referring in this section are difficult and much debated, but this does not dispense us from taking sides. It is not possible to remain neutral in the face of poverty and the resulting just claims of the poor; a posture of neutrality would, moreover, mean siding with the injustice and oppression in our midst.[60] The position we take under the inspiration of the gospel must be real and effective.

In his encyclical on work John Paul II acknowledges that the reaction of workers in the nineteenth century to the exploitation from which they suffered "was justified from the point of view of social morality." He goes on to mention the validity of the solidarity movements now being formed in the world of work, and he says that "the church is firmly committed to this cause, for it considers it its mission, its service, a proof of its fidelity to Christ, so that it can truly be the 'church of the poor' " (no. 8).[61]

Given the experience of Latin America, it is not difficult to see the importance of this solidarity with worker movements and with those who suffer "the scourge of unemployment" (*Laborem Exercens*, 8). We know the price that many Christians have had to pay for this solidarity. We know, too, that in it "our fidelity to Christ is proved." I am obviously not identifying the preferential option for the poor with any ideology or specific political program. Even if they represent legitimate options for the Christian laity, they do not at all satisfy fully the demands of the gospel.

The universality of Christian love is, I repeat, incompatible with the exclusion of any persons, but it is not incompatible with a preferential option for the poorest and most oppressed. When I speak of taking into account social conflict, including the existence of the class struggle, I am not denying that God's love embraces all without exception. Nor is anyone excluded from our love, for the gospel requires that we love even our enemies; a situation that causes us to regard others as our adversaries does not excuse us from loving them. There are oppositions and social conflicts between diverse factions, classes, cultures, and racial groupings, but they do not exclude respect for persons,[62] for as human beings they are loved by God and are constantly being called to conversion.

The conflict present in society cannot fail to have repercussions in the church, especially when, as is the case in Latin America, the church is, for all practical purposes, coextensive with society. Social tensions have effects within the church itself, which I understand here as the totality of its members—that is, as the people of God.

These tensions are reflected in statements the Latin American episcopate has been addressing with some frequency to Christians who occupy positions of economic or political power. The bishops reproach these individuals for using their position to marginalize and exploit their brothers and sisters. The censure has in some cases taken the form of excommunications issued by episcopal conferences and individual bishops (for example, in Paraguay, Brazil, and Chile) against Christians who deliberately ignore the demands of ethics and the gospel concerning respect for the life, physical integrity, and freedom of others. These may seem to be extreme cases, but they demonstrate the seriousness of the situation. Without going as far as excommunication, other bishops have issued calls to order that, though less severe, are of a similar kind. The sternness shown in these statements and in the actions taken does not, however, prevent our also seeing in them the love that the bishops have for brothers and sisters who have strayed from the right path.

If the church is really present in the world, it cannot but reflect in its own life the events disturbing the world. But in the face of social divisions in which even Christians are involved, the affirmation of unity as the fundamental vocation of the church is increasingly necessary. Even within the church's own precincts it is important and even absolutely necessary that we see things as they really are, for otherwise we distort the Lord's summons to unity. The fact that there are oppositions among members of the Christian community does not negate the principle of the church's essential unity, but they are indeed an obstacle on the church's historical journey toward this unity, an obstacle that must be overcome with lucidity and courage.

The promise of unity is at the heart of Christ's work; in him human beings are sons and daughters of the Father and brothers and sisters to one another. The church, the community of those who confess Christ as their Lord, is a sign of unity within history (*Constitution on the Church*, 1). For this reason, the church must help the world to achieve unity, while knowing that "unity among human beings is possible only if there is real justice for all."[63] In a divided world the role of the ecclesial community is to struggle against the radical causes of social division. If it does so, it will be an authentic and effective sign of unity under the universal love of God.

Jesus does not ask the Father to take us from a world in which the forces of evil seek to divide his disciples. He asks only that we may be one as he and the Father are one. This prayer of Jesus springs from the conviction that grace is stronger than sin; he does not deny the presence of sin in the world, but believes that it will not conquer love (see John 17).

One important and pressing task of the church in Latin America is to strengthen this unity—a unity that does not conceal real problems but brings them to light and evaluates them in the light of faith. The deeper unity of a community that is on pilgrimage in history is a unity that is never fully achieved.[64] The unity of the church is first and foremost a gift of the Lord, an expression of his unmerited love; but it is also something built up, something freely accepted within time; it is our task and a victory we win in history.

This call to unity certainly reaches beyond the boundaries of the Catholic Church. It extends to all Christians and is the wellspring of the ecumenism to which Vatican II gave such an important stimulus. The paths of ecumenism may not be quite the same in Latin America as in Europe. Among us, as experience has shown, the commitment to proclaiming the love of God for all in the person of the poorest is a fruitful meeting ground for Christians from the various confessions. At the same time, we are all trying to follow Jesus on the path leading to the universal Father.

## Chapter Thirteen

# POVERTY:
# SOLIDARITY AND PROTEST

For some years now we have seen in the Church a recovery of a more authentic and radical witness of poverty.[1] At first this occurred within various recently founded religious communities. It quickly went beyond the narrow limits of "religious poverty," however, raising challenges and questions in other sectors of the Church. Poverty has become one of the central themes of contemporary Christian spirituality and indeed has become a controversial question. From the concern to imitate more faithfully the poor Christ, there has spontaneously emerged a critical and militant attitude regarding the countersign that the Church as a whole presents in the matter of poverty.

Those who showed this concern—with John XXIII at the head—knocked insistently at the doors of Vatican II. In an important message in preparation for the opening of the Council, John opened up a fertile perspective saying, "In dealing with the underdeveloped countries, the Church presents herself as she is and as she wants to be—as the Church of all men and especially the Church of the poor."[2] Indeed, from the first session of the Council the theme of poverty was very much in the air.[3] Later there was even a "Schema 14," which on the issue of poverty went beyond "Schema 13" (the draft for *Gaudium et spes*). The final results of the Council, however, did not correspond to the expectations. The documents allude several times to poverty, but it is not one of the major thrusts.[4]

Later, *Populorum progressio* is somewhat more concrete and clear with regard to various questions related to poverty. But it will remain for the Church on a continent of misery and injustice to give the theme of poverty its proper importance: *the authenticity of the preaching of the Gospel message depends on this witness.*[5]

The theme of poverty has been dealt with in recent years, especially in the field of spirituality.[6] In the contemporary world, fascinated by a wealth and power established upon the plunder and exploitation of the great majorities, poverty appeared as an inescapable precondition to sanctity. Therefore the greatest efforts were to meditate on the Biblical texts which recall the poverty of Christ and thus to identify with Christ in this witness.

More recently a properly theological reflection on poverty has been undertaken, based on ever richer and more precise exegetical studies. From these first attempts there stands out clearly one rather surprising result: poverty is a notion which has received very little theological treatment and in spite of everything is still quite unclear.[7] Lines of interpretation overlap; various exegeses still carry weight today, even though they were developed in very different contexts which no longer exist; certain aspects of the theme function as static compartments which prevent a grasp of its overall meaning. All this has led us onto slippery terrain on which we have tried to maneuver more by intuition than by clear and well-formulated ideas.

## AMBIGUITIES IN THE TERM "POVERTY"

*Poverty* is an equivocal term. But the ambiguity of the term does nothing more than express the ambiguity of the notions themselves which are involved. To try to clarify what we understand by *poverty*, we must clear the path and examine some of the sources of the ambiguity. This will also permit us to indicate the meaning we will give to various expressions which we will use later.

The term *poverty* designates in the first place *material poverty*, that is, the lack of economic goods necessary for a human life worthy of the name. In this sense poverty is considered degrading and is rejected by the conscience of contemporary persons. Even those who are not—or do not wish to be—aware of the root causes of this poverty believe that it should be struggled against. Christians, however, often have a tendency to give material poverty a positive value, considering it almost a human and religious ideal. It is seen as austerity and indifference to the things of this world and a precondition for a life in conformity with the Gospel. This interpretation would mean that the demands of Christianity are at cross purposes to the great aspirations of persons today who want to free themselves from subjection to nature, to eliminate the exploitation of some persons by others, and to create prosperity for everyone.[8] The double and contradictory meaning of *poverty* implied here gives rise to the imposition of one language on another and is a frequent source of ambiguities. The matter becomes even more complex if we take into consideration that the concept of material poverty is in constant evolution. Not having access to certain cultural, social, and political values, for example, is today part of the poverty that persons hope to abolish. Would material poverty as an "ideal" of Christian life also include lacking these things?

On the other hand, poverty has often been thought of and experienced by Christians as part of the condition—seen with a certain fatalism—of marginated peoples, "the poor," who are an object of our mercy. But things are no longer like this. Social classes, nations, and entire continents are becoming aware of their poverty, and when they see its root causes, they rebel against it. The contemporary phenomenon is a collective poverty that leads those who suffer from it to forge bonds of solidarity among themselves and to organize in the struggle against the conditions they are in and against those who benefit from these conditions.

What we mean by material poverty is a subhuman situation. As we shall see later, the Bible also considers it this way. Concretely, to be poor means to die of hunger, to be illiterate, to be exploited by others, not to know that you are being exploited, not to know that you are a person. It is in relation to this poverty—material and cultural, collective and militant—that evangelical poverty will have to define itself.

The notion of *spiritual poverty* is even less clear. Often it is seen simply as an interior attitude of unattachment to the goods of this world. The poor, therefore, are not so much the ones who have no material goods; rather it is they who are not attached to them—even if they do possess them. This point of view allows for the case of the rich person who is spiritually poor as well as for the poor person who is rich at heart. These are extreme cases that distract attention toward the exceptional and the accessory. Claiming to be based on the Beatitude of Matthew concerning "the poor in spirit," this approach in the long run leads to comforting and tranquilizing conclusions.

This spiritualistic perspective rapidly leads to dead ends and to affirmations that the interior attitude must necessarily be incarnated in a testimony of material poverty. But if this is so, questions arise: What poverty is being spoken of? The poverty that the contemporary conscience considers subhuman? Is it in this way that spiritual poverty should be incarnated? Some answer that it is not necessary to go to such extremes, and they attempt to distinguish between destitution and poverty. The witness involves living poverty, not destitution. But then, as we have said, we are not referring to poverty as it is lived and perceived today, but rather to a different kind of poverty, abstract and made according to the specifications of our spiritual poverty. This is to play with words—and with persons.

The distinction between evangelical counsels and precepts creates other ambiguities. According to it, evangelical poverty would be a counsel appropriate to a particular vocation and not a precept obligatory for all Christians. This distinction kept evangelical poverty confined incommunicado for a long time within the narrow limits of religious life, which focuses on "the evangelical counsels."[9] Today the distinction is only another source of misunderstandings.[10]

Because of all these ambiguities and uncertainties we have been unable to proceed on solid ground; we have wandered along an unsure path where it is difficult to advance and easy to wander. We have also fallen into very vague terminology and a kind of sentimentalism which in the last analysis justifies the status quo. In situations like the present one in Latin America this is especially serious. We see the danger, for example, in various commentaries on the writings of Bossuet regarding "the eminent dignity of the poor in the Church"; or in symbolism like that which considers the hunger of the poor as "the image of the human soul hungering for God"; or even in the expression "the Church of the poor," which—in spite of the indisputable purity of intention of John XXIII—is susceptible to an interpretation smacking of paternalism.

Clarification is needed. In the following pages we will attempt to sketch at least the broad outlines. We will try to keep in mind that—as one spiritual writer has said—the first form of poverty is to renounce the idea we have of poverty.

## BIBLICAL MEANING OF POVERTY

Poverty is a central theme both in the Old and the New Testaments. It is treated both briefly and profoundly; it describes social situations and expresses spiritual experiences communicated only with difficulty; it defines personal attitudes, a whole people's attitude before God, and the relationships of persons with each other. It is possible, nevertheless, to try to unravel the knots and to clear the horizon by following the two major lines of thought that seem to stand out: poverty as a scandalous condition and poverty as spiritual childhood.[11] The notion of evangelical poverty will be illuminated by a comparison of these two perspectives.[12]

### *Poverty: A Scandalous Condition*

In the Bible poverty is a scandalous condition inimical to human dignity and therefore contrary to the will of God.

This rejection of poverty is seen very clearly in the vocabulary used.[13] In the Old Testament the term which is used least to speak of the poor is *rash*, which has a rather neutral meaning.[14] As Gelin says, the prophets preferred terms which are "photographic" of real, living persons.[15] The poor person is, therefore, *ébyôn*, the one who desires, the beggar, the one who is lacking something and who awaits it from another.[16] He is also *dal*, the weak one, the frail one; the expression *the poor of the land* (the rural proletariat) is found very frequently.[17] The poor person is also *ani*, the bent over one, the one laboring under a weight, the one not in possession of his whole strength and vigor, the humiliated one.[18] And finally he is *anaw*, from the same root as the previous term but having a more religious connotation—"humble before God."[19] In the New Testament the Greek term *ptokós* is used to speak of the poor person. *Ptokós* means one who does not have what is necessary to subsist, the wretched one driven into begging.[20]

*Indigent, weak, bent over, wretched* are terms which well express a degrading human situation. These terms already insinuate a protest. They are not limited to description; they take a stand.[21] This stand is made explicit in the vigorous rejection of poverty. The climate in which poverty is described is one of indignation. And it is with the same indignation that the cause of poverty is indicated: the injustice of oppressors. The cause is well expressed in a text from Job:

> Wicked men move boundary-stones
>     and carry away flocks and their shepherds.
> In the field they reap what is not theirs,
>     and filch the late grapes from the rich man's
>         vineyard.
> They drive off the orphan's ass
>     and lead away the widow's ox with a rope.
> They snatch the fatherless infant from the breast
>     and take the poor man's child in pledge.
> They jostle the poor out of the way;
>     the destitute huddle together, hiding from them.
> The poor rise early like the wild ass,
>     when it scours the wilderness for food;
> But though they work till nightfall,
>     their children go hungry.
> Naked and bare they pass the night;
>     in the cold they have nothing to cover them.
> They are drenched by rain-storms from the hills
>     and hug the rock, their only shelter.
> Naked and bare they go about their work,
>     and hungry they carry the sheaves;
> They press the oil in the shade where two walls meet,
>     they tread the winepress but themselves go thirsty.
> Far from the city, they groan like dying men,
>     and like wounded men they cry out; . . .
> The murderer rises before daylight
>     to kill some miserable wretch [Job 24:2-12, 14].

Poverty is not caused by fate; it is caused by the actions of those whom the prophet condemns:

> These are the words of the Lord:
>     For crime after crime of Israel
>     I will grant them no reprieve
> because they sell the innocent for silver
>     and the destitute for a pair of shoes.
> They grind the heads of the poor into the earth
>     and thrust the humble out of their way
>                         [Amos 2:6-7].

There are poor because some are victims of others. "Shame on you," it says in Isaiah,

> you who make unjust laws
> and publish burdensome decrees,

     depriving the poor of justice,
     robbing the weakest of my people of their rights,
     despoiling the widow and plundering the orphan
          [10:1-2].[22]

The prophets condemn every kind of abuse, every form of keeping the poor in poverty or of creating new poor. They are not merely allusions to situations; the finger is pointed at those who are to blame. Fraudulent commerce and exploitation are condemned (Hos. 12:8; Amos 8:5; Mic. 6:10-11; Isa. 3:14; Jer. 5:27; 6:12), as well as the hoarding of lands (Mic. 2:1-3; Ezek. 22:29; Hab. 2:5-6), dishonest courts (Amos 5:7; Jer. 22:13-17; Mic. 3:9-11; Isa. 5:23, 10:1-2), the violence of the ruling classes (2 Kings 23:30, 35; Amos 4:1; Mic. 3:1-2; 6:12; Jer. 22:13-17), slavery (Neh. 5:1-5; Amos 2:6; 8:6), unjust taxes (Amos 4:1; 5:11-12), and unjust functionaries (Amos 5:7; Jer. 5:28).[23] In the New Testament oppression by the rich is also condemned, especially in Luke (6:24-25; 12:13-21; 16:19-31; 18:18-26) and in the Letter of James (2:5-9; 4:13-17; 5:16).

But it is not simply a matter of denouncing poverty. The Bible speaks of positive and concrete measures to prevent poverty from becoming established among the People of God. In Leviticus and Deuteronomy there is very detailed legislation designed to prevent the accumulation of wealth and the consequent exploitation. It is said, for example, that what remains in the fields after the harvest and the gathering of olives and grapes should not be collected; it is for the alien, the orphan, and the widow (Deut. 24:19-21; Lev. 19:9-10). Even more, the fields should not be harvested to the very edge so that something remains for the poor and the aliens (Lev. 23:22). The Sabbath, the day of the Lord, has a social significance; it is a day of rest for the slave and the alien (Exod. 23:12; Deut. 5:14). The triennial tithe is not to be carried to the temple; rather it is for the alien, the orphan, and the widow (Deut. 14:28-29; 26:12). Interest on loans is forbidden (Exod. 22:25; Lev. 25:35-37; Deut. 23:20). Other important measures include the Sabbath year and the jubilee year. Every seven years the fields will be left to lie fallow "to provide food for the poor of your people" (Exod. 23:11; Lev. 25:2-7), although it is recognized that this duty is not always fulfilled (Lev. 26:34-35). After seven years the slaves were to regain their freedom (Exod. 21:2-6) and debts were to be pardoned (Deut. 15:1-18). This is also the meaning of the jubilee year of Lev. 25:10ff.[24] "It was," writes de Vaux, "a general emancipation . . . of all the inhabitants of the land. The fields lay fallow: every man re-entered his ancestral property, i.e. the fields and houses which had been alienated returned to their original owners."[25]

Behind these texts we can see three principal reasons for this vigorous repudiation of poverty. In the first place, poverty contradicts the very meaning of *the Mosaic religion*. Moses led his people out of the slavery, exploitation, and alienation of Egypt[26] so that they might inhabit a land where they could live with human dignity. In Moses' mission of liberation there was a close relationship between the religion of Yahweh and the elimination of servitude:

Moses and Aaron then said to all the Israelites, "In the evening you will know that it was the Lord who brought you out of Egypt, and in the morning you will see the glory of the Lord, because he has heeded your complaints against him; it is not against us that you bring your complaints; we are nothing." "You shall know this," Moses said, "when the Lord, in answer to your complaints, gives you flesh to eat in the evening, and in the morning bread in plenty. What are we? It is against the Lord that you bring your complaints, and not against us" [Exod. 16:6-8].

The worship of Yahweh and the possession of the land are both included in the same promise. The rejection of the exploitation of some by others is found in the very roots of the people of Israel. God is the only owner of the land given to people (Lev. 25:23, 38); God is the one Lord who saves the people from servitude and will not allow them to be subjected to it again (Deut. 5:15; 16:22; Lev. 25:42; 26:13). And thus Deuteronomy speaks of "the ideal of a brotherhood where there was no poverty."[27] In their rejection of poverty, the prophets, who were heirs to the Mosaic ideal, referred to the past, to the origins of the people; there they sought the inspiration for the construction of a just society. To accept poverty and injustice is to fall back into the conditions of servitude which existed before the liberation from Egypt. It is to retrogress.

The second reason for the repudiation of the state of slavery and exploitation of the Jewish people in Egypt is that it goes against *the mandate of Genesis* (1:26; 2:15). Humankind is created in the image and likeness of God and is destined to dominate the earth.[28] Humankind fulfills itself only by transforming nature and thus entering into relationships with other persons. Only in this way do persons come to a full consciousness of themselves as subjects of creative freedom which is realized through work. The exploitation and injustice implicit in poverty make work into something servile and dehumanizing. Alienated work, instead of liberating persons, enslaves them even more.[29] And so it is that when just treatment is asked for the poor, the slaves, and the aliens, it is recalled that Israel also was alien and enslaved in Egypt (Exod. 22:21-23; 23:9; Deut. 10:19; Lev. 19:34).

And finally, humankind not only has been made in the image and likeness of God; it is also *the sacrament of God.* We have already recalled this profound and challenging Biblical theme.[30] The other reasons for the Biblical rejection of poverty have their roots here: to oppress the poor is to offend God; to know God is to work justice among human beings. We meet God in our encounter with other persons; what is done for others is done for the Lord.

In a word, the existence of poverty represents a sundering both of solidarity among persons and also of communion with God. Poverty is an expression of a sin, that is, of a negation of love. It is therefore incompatible with the coming of the Kingdom of God, a Kingdom of love and justice.

Poverty is an evil, a scandalous condition,[31] which in our times has taken on enormous proportions.[32] To eliminate it is to bring closer the moment of seeing God face to face, in union with other persons.[33]

## Poverty: Spiritual Childhood

There is a second line of thinking concerning poverty in the Bible. The poor person is the "client" of Yahweh; poverty is "the ability to welcome God, an openness to God, a willingness to be used by God, a humility before God."[34]

The vocabulary which is used here is the same as that used to speak of poverty as an evil. But the terms used to designate the poor person receive an ever more demanding and precise religious meaning.[35] This is the case especially with the term *anaw*, which in the plural (*anawim*) is the privileged designation of the spiritually poor.

Repeated infidelity to the Covenant of the people of Israel led the prophets to elaborate the theme of the "tiny remnant" (Isa. 4:3; 6:13). Made up of those who remained faithful to Yahweh, the remnant would be the Israel of the future. From its midst there would emerge the Messiah and consequently the first fruits of the New Covenant (Jer. 31:31-34; Ezek. 36:26-28). From the time of Zephaniah (seventh century B.C.), those who awaited the liberating work of the Messiah were "poor": "But I will leave in you a people afflicted and poor, the survivors in Israel shall find refuge in the name of the Lord" (Zeph. 3:12-13). In this way the term acquired a spiritual meaning. From then on poverty was presented as an ideal: "Seek the Lord, all in the land who live humbly by his laws, seek righteousness, seek a humble heart" (Zeph. 2:3). Understood in this way poverty is opposed to pride, to an attitude of self-sufficiency; on the other hand, it is synonymous with faith, with abandonment and trust in the Lord.[36] This spiritual meaning will be accentuated during the historical experiences of Israel after the time of Zephaniah. Jeremiah calls himself poor (*ébyôn*) when he sings his thanksgiving to God (20:13). Spiritual poverty is a precondition for approaching God. "All these are of my own making and all these are mine. This is the very word of the Lord. The man I look to is a man down-trodden and distressed, one who reveres my words" (Isa. 66:2).

The Psalms can help us to understand more precisely this religious attitude. To know Yahweh is to seek him (9:11; 34-11), to abandon and entrust oneself to him (10:14; 34:9, 37:40), to hope in him (25:3-5, 21; 37:9), to fear the Lord (25:12, 14; 34:8, 10), to observe his commandments (25:10); the poor are the just ones, the whole ones (34:20, 22; 37:17-18), the faithful ones (37:28; 149:1). The opposite of the poor are the proud, who are the enemy of Yahweh and of the helpless (10:2; 18:28; 37:10; 86:14).

Spiritual poverty finds its highest expression in the Beatitudes of the New Testament. The version in *Matthew*—thanks to solid exegetical studies—no longer seems to present any great difficulties in interpretation. The poverty which is called "blessed" in Matt. 5:1 ("Blessed are the poor in spirit") is spiritual poverty as understood since the time of Zephaniah: to be totally at the disposition of the Lord. This is the precondition for being able to receive the Word of God.[37] It has, therefore, the same meaning as the gospel theme of spiritual childhood. God's communication with us is a gift of love; to receive this gift it is necessary to be poor, a spiritual child. This poverty has no direct relationship to wealth; in the first instance it is not a question of indifference to the goods of this world. It goes deeper than that; it means to have no other sustenance than the will of God. This is the attitude of Christ. Indeed, it is to him that all the Beatitudes fundamentally refer.[38]

In *Luke's* version ("Blessed are you poor" [6:20]) we are faced with greater problems of interpretation.[39] Attempts to resolve these difficulties follow two different lines of thinking. Luke is the evangelist who is most sensitive to social realities. In his Gospel as well as in Acts the themes of material poverty, of goods held in common, and of the condemnation of the rich are frequently treated. This has naturally led to thinking that the poor whom he blesses are the opposite of the rich whom he condemns; the poor would be those who lack what they need. In this case the poverty that he speaks of in the first Beatitude would be *material poverty.*

But this interpretation presents a twofold difficulty. It would lead to the canonization of a social class. The poor would be the privileged of the Kingdom, even to the point of having their access to it assured, not by any choice on their part but by a socio-economic situation which had been imposed on them. Some commentators insist that this would not be evangelical and would be contrary to the intentions of Luke.[40] On the opposite extreme within this interpretation are those who claim to avoid this difficulty and yet preserve the concrete sociological meaning of poverty in Luke. Situating themselves in the perspective of wisdom literature, they say that the first Beatitude opposes the present world to the world beyond; the sufferings of today will be compensated for in the future life.[41] Extraterrestrial salvation is the absolute value which makes the present life insignificant. But this point of view implies purely and simply that Luke is sacralizing misery and injustice and is therefore preaching resignation to it.

Because of these impasses, an explanation is sought from another perspective: Matthew's. Like Matthew, Luke would be referring to *spiritual poverty,* or to openness to God. As a concession to the social context of Luke there is in this interpretation an emphasis on real poverty insofar as it is "a privileged path towards poverty of soul."[42]

This second line of interpretation seems to us to minimize the sense of Luke's text. Indeed, it is impossible to avoid the concrete and "material" meaning which the term *poor* has for this evangelist. It refers first of all to those who live in a social situation characterized by a lack of the goods of this world and even by misery and indigence. Even further, it refers to a marginated social group, with connotations of oppression and lack of liberty.[43]

All this leads us to retrace our steps and to reconsider the difficulties—which we have recalled above—in explaining the text of Luke as referring to the materially poor.

"Blessed are you poor for yours is the Kingdom of God" does not mean, it seems to us: "Accept your poverty because later this injustice will be compensated for in the Kingdom of God." If we believe that the Kingdom of God is a gift which is received in history, and if we believe, as the eschatological promises—so charged with human and historical content—indicate to us, that the Kingdom of God necessarily implies the reestablishment of justice in this world,[44] then we must believe that Christ says that the poor are blessed *because* the Kingdom of God has begun: "The time has come; the Kingdom of God is upon you" (Mark 1:15). In other words, the elimination of the exploitation and poverty that prevent the poor from being fully human has begun; a Kingdom of justice which goes even beyond what they could have hoped for has begun. They are blessed because the coming of the Kingdom will put an end to their poverty by creating a world of fellowship. They are blessed because the Messiah will open the eyes of the blind and will give bread to the hungry. Situated in a prophetic perspective, the text in Luke uses the term *poor* in the tradition of the first major line of thought we have studied: poverty is an evil and therefore incompatible with the Kingdom of God, which has come in its fullness into history and embraces the totality of human existence.[45]

## AN ATTEMPT AT SYNTHESIS: SOLIDARITY AND PROTEST

Material poverty is a scandalous condition. Spiritual poverty is an attitude of openness to God and spiritual childhood. Having clarified these two meanings of the term *poverty* we have cleared the path and can now move forward towards a better understanding of the Christian witness of poverty. We turn now to a third meaning of the term: poverty as a commitment of solidarity and protest.

We have laid aside the first two meanings. The first is subtly deceptive; the second partial and insufficient. In the first place, if *material poverty* is something to be rejected, as the Bible vigorously insists, then a witness of poverty cannot make of it a Christian ideal. This would be to aspire to a condition which is recognized as degrading to persons. It would be, moreover, to move against the current of history. It would be to oppose any idea of the domination of nature by humans and the consequent and progressive creation of better conditions of life. And finally, but not least seriously, it would be to justify, even if involuntarily, the injustice and exploitation which is the cause of poverty.

On the other hand, our analysis of the Biblical texts concerning *spiritual poverty* has helped us to see that it is not directly or in the first instance an interior detachment from the goods of this world, a spiritual attitude which becomes authentic by incarnating itself in material poverty. Spiritual poverty is something more complete and profound. It is above all total availability to the Lord. Its relationship to the use or ownership of economic goods is inescapable, but secondary and partial. Spiritual childhood—an ability to receive, not a passive acceptance—defines the total posture of human existence before God, persons, and things.

How are we therefore to understand the evangelical meaning of the witness of a real, material, concrete poverty? *Lumen gentium* invites us to look for the deepest meaning of Christian poverty *in Christ*: "Just as Christ carried out the work of redemption in poverty and under oppression, so the Church is called to follow the same path in communicating to others the fruits of salvation. Christ Jesus, though He was by nature God . . . emptied himself, taking the nature of a slave (Phil. 2:6), and being rich, he became poor (2 Cor. 8:9) for our sakes. Thus, although the Church needs human resources to carry out her mission, she is not set up to seek earthly glory, but to proclaim humility and self-sacrifice, even by her own example" (no. 8). The Incarnation is an act of love. Christ became human, died, and rose from the dead to set us free so that we might enjoy freedom (Gal. 5:1). To die and to rise again with Christ is to vanquish death and to enter into a new life (cf. Rom. 6:1-11). The cross and the resurrection are the seal of our liberty.

The taking on of the servile and sinful human condition, as foretold in Second Isaiah, is presented by Paul as an act of voluntary impoverishment: "For you know how generous our Lord Jesus Christ has been: He was rich, yet for your sake he became poor, so that through his poverty you might become rich" (2 Cor. 8:9). This is the humiliation of Christ, his *kenosis* (Phil. 2:6-11). But he does not take on the human sinful condition and its consequences to idealize it. It is rather because of love for and solidarity with others who suffer in it. It is to redeem them from their sin and to enrich them with his poverty. It is to struggle against human selfishness and everything that divides persons and allows that there be rich and poor, possessors and dispossessed, oppressors and oppressed.

Poverty is an act of love and liberation. It has a redemptive value. If the ultimate cause of human exploitation and alienation is selfishness, the deepest reason for voluntary poverty is love of neighbor. Christian poverty has meaning only as a commitment of solidarity with the poor, with those who suffer misery and injustice. The commitment is to witness to the evil which has resulted from sin and is a breach of communion. It is not a question of idealizing poverty, but rather of taking it on as it is—an evil—to protest against it and to struggle to abolish it. As Ricoeur says, you cannot really be with the poor unless you are struggling against poverty. Because of this solidarity— which must manifest itself in specific action, a style of life, a break with one's social class—one can also help the poor and exploited to become aware of their exploitation and seek liberation from it. Christian poverty, an expression of love, is solidarity *with the poor* and is a protest *against poverty*.[46] This is the concrete, contemporary meaning of the witness of poverty. It is a poverty lived not for its own sake, but rather as an authentic imitation of Christ; it is a poverty which means taking on the sinful human condition to liberate human-kind from sin and all its consequences.[47]

Luke presents the community of goods in the early Church as an ideal. "All whose faith had drawn them together held everything in common" (Acts 2:44); "not a man of them claimed any of his possessions as his own, but everything was held in common" (Acts 4:33). They did this with a profound unity, one "in heart and soul" (ibid.). But as J. Dupont correctly points out, this was not a question of erecting poverty as an ideal, but rather of seeing to it that there were no poor: "They had never a needy person among them, because all who had property in land or houses sold it, brought the proceeds of the sale, and laid the money at the feet of the apostles; it was then distributed to any who stood in need" (Acts 4:34-35). The meaning of the community of goods is clear: to eliminate poverty because of love of the poor person. Dupont rightly concludes, "If goods are held in common, it is not therefore in order to become poor for love of an ideal of poverty; rather it is so that there will be no poor. The ideal pursued is, once again, charity, a true love for the poor."[48]

We must pay special attention to the words we use. The term *poor* might seem not only vague and churchy, but also somewhat sentimental and aseptic. The "poor" person today is the oppressed one, the one marginated from society, the member of the proletariat struggling for the most basic rights; the exploited and plundered social class, the country struggling for its liberation. In today's world the solidarity and protest of which we are speaking have an evident and inevitable "political" character insofar as they imply liberation. To be with the oppressed is to be against the oppressor. In our times and on our continent to be in solidarity with the "poor," understood in this way, means to run personal risks—even to put one's life in danger. Many Christians—and non-Christians—who are committed to the Latin American revolutionary process are running these risks. And so there are emerging new ways of living poverty which are different from the classic "renunciation of the goods of this world."

Only by rejecting poverty and by making itself poor in order to protest against it can the Church preach something that is uniquely its own: "spiritual poverty," that is, the openness of humankind and history to the future promised by God.[49] Only in this way will the Church be able to fulfill authentically—and with any possibility of being listened to—its prophetic function of denouncing every human injustice. And only in this way will it be able to preach the word which liberates, the word of genuine fellowship.[50]

Only authentic solidarity with the poor and a real protest against the poverty of our time can provide the concrete, vital context necessary for a theological discussion of poverty. The absence of a sufficient commitment to the poor, the marginated, and the exploited is perhaps the fundamental reason why we have no solid contemporary reflection on the witness of poverty.

For the Latin American Church especially, this witness is an inescapable and much-needed sign of the authenticity of its mission.

# CONCLUSION

The theology of liberation attempts to reflect on the experience and meaning of the faith based on the commitment to abolish injustice and to build a new society; this theology must be verified by the practice of that commitment, by active, effective participation in the struggle which the exploited social classes have undertaken against their oppressors. Liberation from every form of exploitation, the possibility of a more human and dignified life, the creation of a new humankind—all pass through this struggle.

But in the last instance we will have an authentic theology of liberation only when the oppressed themselves can freely raise their voice and express themselves directly and creatively in society and in the heart of the People of God, when they themselves "account for the hope," which they bear, when they are the protagonists of their own liberation. For now we must limit ourselves to efforts which ought to deepen and support that process, which has barely begun. If theological reflection does not vitalize the action of the Christian community in the world by making its commitment to charity fuller and more radical, if—more concretely—in Latin America it does not lead the Church to be on the side of the oppressed classes and dominated peoples, clearly and without qualifications, then this theological reflection will have been of little value. Worse yet, it will have served only to justify half-measures and ineffective approaches and to rationalize a departure from the Gospel.

We must be careful not to fall into intellectual self-satisfaction, into a kind of triumphalism of erudite and advanced "new" visions of Christianity. The only thing that is really new is to accept day by day the gift of the Spirit, who makes us love—in our concrete options to build a true human fellowship, in our historical initiatives to subvert an order of injustice—with the fullness with which Christ loved us. To paraphrase a well-known text of Pascal, we can say that all the political theologies, the theologies of hope, of revolution, and of liberation, are not worth one act of genuine solidarity with exploited social classes. They are not worth one act of faith, love, and hope, committed—in one way or another—in active participation to liberate humankind from everthing that dehumanizes it and prevents it from living according to the will of the Father.

174

# NOTES

## INTRODUCTION TO THE ORIGINAL EDITION

1. The point being made here at the very beginning of the book is essential if we are to understand the approach taken in the theology of liberation. This theology represents a reflection that starts with an acceptance of the challenge contained in the word of the Lord; it is a theological judgment on faith, hope, and love as they are lived out in a commitment to liberation. It is not possible, however, to deduce from the gospel a single political course that all Christians must follow; as soon as we enter the political sphere we are in the area of free choices in which factors of another order (social analysis; the concrete histories of nations) have a role to play. The faith does indeed set down certain ethical requirements in making these choices, but the requirements do not entail a specific political program. John Paul II reminded us of this when he wrote: "The church's social doctrine is not a 'third way' between liberal capitalism and Marxist collectivism, or even a possible alternative to other solutions less radically opposed to one another. Rather it constitutes a category of its own" (*Sollicitudo Rei Socialis*, 41, in *Origins*, 17 [1987–88] 655). The social doctrine of the church "belongs to the field . . . of theology and particularly of moral theology" (ibid., p. 656).

## INTRODUCTION TO THE REVISED EDITION

1. My lecture entitled "A Theology of Liberation," which had been delivered to a national meeting of lay persons, religious, and priests, was published first in Lima and then, a few months later, in Montevideo (MIEC, Pax Romana, 1969). It was expanded and delivered again at a meeting of Sodepax (Cartigny, Switzerland, 1969).

2. I have endeavored to meet this obligation by reassessing my original insights in various forums. I have done so in books—*Beber en su propio pozo* (1983; English translation, *We Drink From Our Own Wells,* Orbis, 1984); *Hablar de Dios desde el sufrimiento del inocente* (1986; English translation, *On Job. God-Talk and the Suffering of the Innocent,* Orbis, 1987); *El Dios de la Vida* (1988)—and in numerous interviews for newspapers and periodicals. I have also taken account of recent discussions in my book, *La verdad los hará libres* (1986).

3. I have in mind especially the two Instructions of the Congregation for the Doctrine of the Faith—*Libertatis Nuntius,* 1984, translated in *Origins,* 14 (1984–85) 193–204, and *Libertatis Conscientia,* 1986, translated in *Origins,* 15 (1985–86) 713–28—and the important letter of John Paul II to the bishops of Brazil (April 1986), translated in *Origins,* 16 (1986–87) 12–15.

4. See M. H. Ellis, *Toward a Jewish Theology of Liberation* (Orbis, 1987).

5. I have added to the body of the book a few notes that aim at revising and completing, as far as possible, aspects discussed in this Introduction. The section "Faith

and Social Conflict," in chapter 12, is a reformulation of the section "Christian Fellowship and Class Struggle" found at the same point in the first edition.

6. I sought to highlight this connection by dedicating *A Theology of Liberation* to two dear friends: José María Arguedas, a Peruvian writer on Indian culture, and Henrique Pereira Neto, a black priest in Brazil. That same intention was in my mind when I wrote the opening lines of the original introduction: "This book is an attempt at reflection, based on the gospel and the experiences of men and *women* committed to the process of liberation, in the oppressed and exploited land of Latin America."

7. Some aspects of this world have been discussed at length in my *We Drink From Our Own Wells* (Orbis, 1984).

8. At the beginning of a year dedicated to calling attention to the plight of the black population, the Brazilian bishops wrote as follows: "The Campaign of Fellowship 1988 is one more summons to the preferential option for the poor for which the gospel calls. The black community is suffering the consequences of its past enslavement. But awareness of this also makes us aware of other social sectors in Brazil that are not given sufficient attention by the liberating fellowship of Christians and by Brazilians generally in their solidarity with one another" (*Ouvi o clamor desto povo. Texto base,* 1987).

9. On this subject, see the encyclical *Sollicitudo Rei Socialis,* 20–22.

10. On the subject of Marxist analysis, *Octogesima Adveniens* of Paul VI (1971) and the letter of Father Arrupe (December 1980) provide important distinctions and guidelines for this work of discernment.

11. I have dealt at length with these themes in "Teología y ciencias sociales," *Páginas,* 63–64 (September 1984), and in *La verdad los hará libres,* pp. 77–112.

12. For example, in the encyclical *Redemptoris Mater* (March 1987), 37, and in his address at Ars, France (May 1987).

13. Final Report II, in *Origins,* 15 (1985–86) 450.

14. See, e.g., *On Job; La verdad los hará libres,* pp. 222–34; and *El Dios de la Vida.*

15. "Carta al Consejo de Indias" (1531), in *Obras escogidas* (Madrid: BAE, 1958), p. 44.

16. See *We Drink From Our Own Wells,* pp. 124–26.

17. "Towards an Asian Theology of Liberation: Some Religio-Cultural Guidelines," in *Asia's Struggle for Full Humanity,* V. Fabella, ed. (Orbis, 1980), pp. 75–95.

18. See the Final Statement of the Fifth EATWOT Conference (New Delhi, August 1981) in *Irruption of the Third World,* V. Fabella and S. Torres, eds. (Orbis, 1983), p. 201: "It is well known that liberation (*mukti*) has been a perennial quest of the world religions. Although the emphasis has been on internal and spiritual liberation, their search also includes dimensions with social relevance: the stress on freedom from greed as well as from overattachment to material or mental possessions and to one's private self. Voluntary poverty, so central to Asiatic religious ideals, and the simplicity of lifestyle it implies, are powerful antidotes to capitalist consumerism and to the worship of mammon."

19. J. Cone, *The Spirituals and the Blues. An Interpretation* (New York: Seabury, 1972).

20. All this is clear for Latin America, but it is also valid for other perspectives adopted in the area of liberation theology, as South African theologian Allan Boesak wisely says in his *Farewell to Innocence* (Orbis, 1977), p. 7: "While we acknowledge that all expressions of liberation theology are not identical, we must protest very strongly against the total division (and contrast) some make between Black Theology in South Africa and Black Theology in the United States; between Black Theology and African

theology; between Black Theology and the Latin American theology of liberation. As a matter of principle, we have therefore treated all these different expressions within the framework where they belong: the framework of the theology of liberation."

21. As the Peruvian bishops said in dealing with this subject, "for Christians the supreme norms of truth in ethical and religious matters are to be found in revelation as interpreted by those who have legitimate authority to do so. Every theology must be based on revelation as contained in the deposit of faith. With that as its starting point it can reflect on anything and everything, including praxis, which is always subordinate to revelation" (*Documento sobre teología de la liberación* [October 1984], 44).

22. See *La verdad los hará libres,* pp. 140–47.

23. See *We Drink From Our Own Wells,* pp. 45–51.

24. These are questions I have asked in my book *On Job.* (Ayacucho, a city in Peru that has been buffeted by poverty and violence, is a Quechuan name meaning "the corner of the dead.")

25. On undertakings in this area in Latin America, see *El rostro femenino de la teología* (San José, Costa Rica: DEI, 1986), which is a collection of the position papers read by various women theologians at the "Reunión Latinoamericana de Teología de la Liberación desde la perspectiva de la mujer" (Buenos Aires, 1985).

26. Translated in J. Gremillion, ed., *The Gospel of Peace and Justice. Catholic Social Teaching Since Pope John* (Orbis, 1976), p. 393.

27. On this point, see my *La verdad los hará libres,* pp. 180–202.

28. *The Pope Speaks,* 21 (1976) 19.

29. Still echoing Medellín, Puebla would say at a later point: "We opt for . . . a church that is a sacrament of communion . . . a servant church . . . a missionary church . . . that commits itself to the liberation of the whole human being and all human beings" (1301-4).

30. Address of December 7, 1965: "It might be said that all this and everything else we might say about the human values of the Council have diverted the attention of the Church in Council to the trend of modern culture, centered on humanity. We would say rather not diverted but *directed*. . . . If we remember, venerable brothers, and all of you, our children, gathered here, how in everyone we can and must recognize the countenance of Christ (Matt. 25:40), the Son of Man, especially when tears and sorrows make it plain to see, and if we can and must recognize in Christ's countenance the countenance of our heavenly Father—'He who sees me,' Our Lord said 'sees also the Father' (John 14:9)—then our humanism becomes Christianity, our Christianity becomes centered on God. To put it differently, a knowledge of the human person is, of necessity, a prerequisite for a knowledge of God" (in *Catholic Mind* 64, no. 1202 [April 1966] 62–63).

31. Words dictated to Cardinal Cigognani on May 24, 1963, shortly before the pope's death. The passage is cited in Peter Hebblethwaite, *Pope John XXIII: Shepherd of the Modern World* (Garden City, N.Y.: Doubleday, 1985), pp. 498–99 (emphasis added).

## 1. THEOLOGY: A CRITICAL REFLECTION

1. What Antonio Gramsci said of philosophy is also true of theology: "It is necessary to destroy the widely-held prejudice that philosophy is something extremely difficult because it is the intellectual activity proper to a certain category of scientific specialists or professional and systematic philosophers. It is necessary, therefore, to demonstrate first that all persons are 'philosophers,' establishing the parameters and characteristics

of this 'spontaneous philosophy' proper to 'everyman' " ("Avviamemento allo studio della filosofia e del materialismo storico, Saggio introduttivo" in *La formazione dell'uomo* [Rome: Editori Riuniti, 1969], p. 217).

2. "Théologie et mission de l'Église" in *Lumière et Vie* 14, no. 71 (January-February 1965), p. 55. See the well-known article of Congar, "Théologie" in *Dictionnaire de Théologie Catholique* (written in 1939, published in 1943); in English see Congar's *A History of Theology*, trans. and ed. Hunter Guthrie (Garden City, N.Y.: Doubleday, 1968), based on the *DTC* article. See also Congar's *La foi et la théologie* (Tournai: Desclée, 1962) and the thought-provoking study by José Comblin, *História da teologia católica* (São Paulo: Editôra Herder, 1969).

3. *Situation et tâches présentes de la théologie* (Paris: Les Éditions du Cerf, 1967), p. 11; see also Gustave Thils, *Orientations de la théologie* (Louvain: Éditions Ceuterick, 1958); Adolf Kolping, *Katholische Theologie gestern und heute; Thematik und Entfaltung deutscher katholischer Theologie vom 1. Vaticanum bis zur Gegenwart* (Bremen: Carl Schuenemann, 1964); Walter Kasper, *The Methods of Dogmatic Theology*, trans. John Drury (New York: Paulist Press, Deus Books, 1969); P. Touilleux, *Introduction à une théologie critique* (Paris: Lethielleux, 1967).

4. The terms *learned* and *saintly* were interchangeable to a certain point. See Congar, "Théologie," *Foi et théologie, Situation et tâches*, and Louis Bouyer, *The Spirituality of the New Testament and the Fathers* (New York: Desclée Company, 1960).

5. Hence the term *sacra pagina* or *sacra eruditio*. See Joseph de Ghellinck, "*Pagina et Sacra Pagina*, Histoire d'un mot et transformation de l'objet primitivement désigné" in *Mélanges Auguste Pelzer* (Louvain: Éditions de l'Institut Supérieur de Philosophie, 1947), pp. 23-59.

6. See Henri de Lubac, *Exégèse médiévale: Les quatre sens de l'Écriture*, 4 vols. (Paris: Aubier, 1959-64).

7. See the works of R. Bultot on "contempt for the world"; a good overall view of the controversy they stirred is found in L.J. Bataillon and J.P. Jossua, "Le mépris du monde," *Revue des Sciences Philosophiques et Théologiques* 51, no. 1 (January 1967): 23-28.

8. See *Dictionnaire de Théologie Catholique*, s.v. "Platonisme des Pères."

9. The works of Guardini, Congar, Voillume, Evely, Paoli, Régamey, and many others are examples of this effort.

10. Hans Urs von Balthasar pointed this out years ago: "Théologie et sainteté," *Dieu Vivant*, no. 12, pp. 15-31; see also by the same author, "Spirituality," in *Word and Redemption: Essays in Theology II* (New York: Herder and Herder, 1965), pp. 87-108.

11. See Congar, *Foi et théologie*, p. 238.

12. *Summa Theologica*, I, q. 1; see also Congar, "Théologie," *Foi et théologie*, and *Situations et tâches*; Comblin, *Teologia católica*; and M.D. Chenu, O.P., *Is Theology a Science?*, trans. A.H.N. Green Armytage (New York: Hawthorn Books, 1959).

13. See in this regard the strong commentary on *Summa Theologica*, I, q. 1, of Michel Corbin, "La fonction et les principes de la théologie selon la Somme Théologique de saint Thomas d'Aquin," *Recherches de Science Religieuse* 55, no. 3 (July-September 1967): 321-66.

14. A point well developed by C. Dumont, S.J., in "La réflexion sur la méthode théologique," *Nouvelle Revue Théologique* 83, no. 10 (December 1961): 1034-50, and 84, no. 1 (January 1962): 17-35.

15. See also ibid.

16. "According to classic scholastic theology, the scientific character of theology

consists in its systematization. . . . The role of reason is confined to clarity of exposition" (Comblin, *Teología católica*, p. 71).

17. Ibid., p. 10. Because of this the theological centers close to the magisterium, especially the Roman universities, were invested with greater authority.

18. See also among others Gérard Gilleman, *The Primacy of Charity in Moral Theology*, trans. William F. Ryan and André Vachen (Westminster, Md.: The Newman Press, 1959); Jean Mouroux, *I Believe, The Personal Structure of Faith*, trans. Michael Turner (New York: Sheed and Ward, 1959); Bernard Häring, C.Ss.R., *The Law of Christ*, trans. Edwin G. Kaiser, C.Pp.S., 3 vols. (Westminster, Md.: The Newman Press, 1966); Pierre-André Liégé, O.P., *Consider Christian Maturity*, trans. and intr. Thomas C. Donlan, O.P. (Chicago: The Priory Press, 1965); Joseph Ratzinger, *The Open Circle, The Meaning of Brotherhood*, trans. W. A. Glen-Doeple (New York: Sheed and Ward, 1966); C. Spicq, O.P., *Théologie morale du nouveau testament*, 2 vols. (Paris: J. Gabalda et Cie, Éditeurs, 1965).

19. See also Iohannes Alfarot, S.I., "Fides in terminologia biblica," *Gregorianum* 42, no. 3 (1961): 463-505.

20. See *Summa Theologica*, II-II, q. 188.

21. It is common knowledge that the phrase is Nadal's, but it expresses well the intuition of Ignatius of Loyola. See Maurice Giuliani, S.J., "Trouver Dieu en toutes choses," *Christus*, no. 6 (April 1955): 172-94, and G. Fessard, *La Dialectique des "Exercises Spirituels" de s. Ignace de Loyola* (Paris: Aubier, 1958).

22. See Yves M.J. Congar, O.P., *Lay People in the Church*, trans. Donald Attwater (Westminster, Md.: The Newman Press, 1965), especially Chapter 9, "In the World and Not of the World"; Olivier A. Rabut, *Valeur spirituelle du profane* (Paris: Les Éditions du Cerf, 1963); P. Roqueplo, *Expérience du monde: expérience de Dieu?* (Paris: Les Éditions du Cerf, 1968).

23. Karl Rahner writes, "Dogmatic theology today has to be theological anthropology, and . . . such an anthropocentric orientation of theology is both necessary and fruitful" ("Theology and Anthropology," in *The Word in History*, ed. T. Patrick Burke [New York: Sheed and Ward, 1966, p. 1]). See also J.B. Metz, *Christliche Anthropozentrik: Ueber die Denkform des Thomas von Aquin* (Munich: Kösel Verlag, 1962); C. Dumont, S.J., "Pour une conversion 'anthropocentrique' dans la formation des clercs," *Nouvelle Revue Théologique* 87, no. 5 (May 1965): 449-65; L. Malevez, S.J., "Présence de la théologie à Dieu et à l'homme, *Nouvelle Revue Théologique* 90, no. 8 (October 1968), 785-800.

24. *Christengemeinde und Bürgergemeinde* (Zollikon-Zurich: Evangelischer Verlag, 1946), p. 36; English version: *Against the Stream: Shorter Post-War Writings, 1946-52* (New York: Philosophical Library, 1954).

25. *Situation et tâches*, p. 27.

26. See the debate between Congar (ibid., pp. 62-67) and the periodical *Frères du Monde*, nos. 46-47 and 49-50 (1967); for an overall view of this subject see Jean-Pierre Jossua, "Christianisme horizontal ou vertical?" *Parole et Mission* 11, no. 41 (April 1968): 245-55.

27. See below Chapter 10.

28. M.D. Chenu, O.P., "La théologie au Saulchoir" (1937 text), *La Parole de Dieu*, vol. 1, *La foi dans l'intelligence* (Paris: Les Éditions du Cerf, 1964), p. 259. René Laurentin has rightly recalled this character of *locus theologicus* proper to the Church in *Liberation, Development and Salvation*, trans. Charles Underhill Quinn (Maryknoll, New York: Orbis Books, 1972), pp. 7-8.

29. Despite its great interest, the notion of the signs of the times is far from being a clear and well-defined area. *Gaudium et spes* does not attempt to define it; it only provides a description and some consequences for the life of faith. See M.D. Chenu, "Les signes des temps: Réflexion théologique," *L'Église dans le monde de ce temps*, ed. Y.M.J. Congar, O.P., and M. Peuchmaurd, O.P., 3 vols. (Paris: Les Éditions du Cerf, 1967), 2:205-25; see also the documentation of the "Signs of the Times" in *Understanding the Signs of the Times*, ed. Franz Böckle, *Concilium* 25 (New York: Paulist Press, 1967), pp. 143-52; from a more Latin American viewpoint see Marcos McGrath, "The Signs of the Times in Latin America Today" and Eduardo F. Pironio, "Christian Interpretation of the Signs of the Times in Latin America Today," *The Church in the Present-day Transformation of Latin America in the Light of the Council*, vol. 1, Position Papers of the Second General Conference of Latin American Bishops, Medellín, Colombia,1968 (Bogotá: General Secretariat of CELAM, 1970), pp. 79-106 and 107-28.

30. See Maurice Blondel, *L'Action* (Paris: Alcan, 1893); for a good treatment of Blondelian methodology, see Henry Duméry, *Critique et religion* (Paris: SEDES, 1957) and by the same author, *Raison et religion dans la philosophie de l'action* (Paris: Les Éditions du Seuil, 1963); in English see James M. Somerville, ed., *Total Commitment: Blondel's L'Action* (Washington, D.C.: Corpus Books, 1968).

31. The Marxian text is well known: "The philosophers have only *interpreted* the world, in various ways; the point, however, is to *change* it" ("Theses on Feuerbach," no.11, in Karl Marx and Friedrich Engels, *On Religion* [New York: Schocken Books, 1964], p. 72). The exact role of the idea of praxis in Marxian thought is a controversial subject; for a quick review of the different positions see Adolfo Sánchez Vázquez, *Filosofía de la praxis* (Mexico, D.F.: Grijalbo, 1967), pp. 43-45.

32. "Marxisme et philosophie de l'existence," a letter quoted in Roger Garaudy, *Perspectives de l'homme,* 3rd ed. (Paris: Presses Universitaires de France, 1961), p. 112.

33. See the collective work *Christentum und Marxismus-heute*, ed. Erich Kellner (Vienna: Europa Verlag, 1966); *Marxism and Christianity*, trans. Kevin Traynor (New York: The Macmillan Company, 1968); Georges M.-M. Cottier, *Chrétiens et marxistes* (Tours: Maison Mame, 1967); Roger Garaudy, *From Anathema to Dialogue*, trans. Luke O'Neill (New York: Herder and Herder, 1966). A high-level theoretical and practical confrontation is needed, however, to get away from the well-trodden paths of "dialogue" and explore the possibilities for creative innovation. To this end, grassroots experiences in social praxis are fundamental. Experiments up to this point have not been of sufficient duration or number. For this purpose what is happening in all of Latin America—and not only in Cuba and Chile—can be regarded as laboratory experiments.

34. Nowadays the same need of maintaining a balance requires that we criticize no less sharply the tendency to a quasi-exclusive emphasis on orthopraxis. This was not the case in 1968. This much is certain: orthodoxy and orthopraxis are related each to the other; each feeds the other. If we limit ourselves to one, we reject both. It is also clear that we are doing theology when we reflect "in the light of faith," to use the traditional formula so often repeated in the theology of liberation. It would be meaningless, on the other hand, to say that we analyze praxis "in the light of praxis." The ultimate criteria for judgment come from revelation, not from praxis itself. See *Libertatis Nuntius* (= "Instruction of the Congregation for the Doctrine of the Faith on Certain Aspects of the 'Theology of Liberation' ") VIII, 4-5; X, 3-5; XI, 13; and the *Documento de los Obispos Peruanos* (October 1984), no. 44. On the whole subject, see my *La verdad los hará libres* (Lima: CEP, 1986), pp. 135-47.

35. "La teología," in *Los catôlicos holandeses* (Bilbao: Desclée de Brouwer, 1970). See also the interesting article of Michel de Certeau, "La rupture instauratrice ou le christianisme dans la culture," *Ésprit* 39, no. 6 (June 1971): 1177-1214.

36. *Lettre aux anglais* (Paris: Gallimard, 1948), p. 245; English version: *Plea for Liberty: Letters to the English, the Americans, the Europeans* (New York: Pantheon Books, Inc., 1944). Regarding the—in a certain sense—traditional character of the importance of praxis, see the observations of C. Dumont, "De trois dimensions retrouvées en théologie," *Nouvelle Revue Théologique* 92, no. 6 (June-July 1970): 570-80.

37. What José Carlos Mariátegui wrote in another context is definitely valid for a theology so conceived: "The ability to think history and the ability to make it or create it become one" (*Peruanicemos al Perú* [Lima: Empresa Editora Amauta, 1970], p.119). This approach of theology as critical reflection is found in our work, *La pastoral de la Iglesia en América Latina* (Montevideo: Ediciones del Centro de Documentación MIEC-JECI, 1968), p. 15.

38. See the relevant remarks of Rudolf Schnackenburg on expressions such as "building up the Kingdom of God" or "spreading the Kingdom of God on earth" (*God's Rule and Kingdom* [New York: Herder and Herder, 1963], p. 354). Criticism on this subject has been gathered by Hans Küng, *The Church* (New York: Sheed and Ward, 1967), pp. 90-92.

39. "All bodies together, and all minds together, and all their products, are not equal to the least feeling of charity . . . . From all bodies and minds, we cannot produce a feeling of true charity" (Blaise Pascal, "Pensées," no. 793, in *Pascal*, Great Books of the Western World, vol. 33 [Chicago: William Benton, Publishers; Encyclopaedia Britannica, Inc., 1952], p. 327).

40. Theological reflection takes place within the ecclesial community and is at the service of its task of evangelization. In theology primacy belongs to the revealed word, and the work of theology is always guided by the faith of the church, which possesses the charisms of governing, prophecy, and teaching. The church is "a privileged *locus theologicus* for understanding the faith"; in other words, it is in the church that we find the "deposit of faith." For these several reasons, theological methodology and spirituality are, in my view, closely connected: the path of theological activity lies within the path by which we become Christians. I have attempted to develop these points in *We Drink From Our Own Wells* and *On Job*. See above, the Introduction to the Revised Edition.

41. "Theology," wrote Karl Barth in another context, "follows the language of the Church, so far as, in its question as to the correctness of the Church's procedure therein, it measures it, not by a standard foreign to her, but by her very own source and object" (*Church Dogmatics*, vol. 1, part 1, *The Doctrine of the Word of God* [Edinburgh: T. & T. Clark, 1936], p. 2).

42. *Situation et tâches*, p. 72.

43. Henri Bouillard, *Conversion et grace chez S. Thomas d'Aquin* (Paris: Aubier, 1944), p. 219.

44. Oscar Cullmann, *The Christology of the New Testament,* rev. ed., trans. Shirley C. Guthrie and Charles A.M. Hall (Philadelphia: The Westminster Press, 1963), p.14.

45. See "La formazione degli intellettuali," *Scritti politici* (Rome: Editori Riunti, 1967), pp. 830-40.

46. *Católicos holandeses*, p. 29. Just previously the author acknowledges that the hermeneutics of the Kingdom of God also presupposes a reinterpretation of the Bible.

47. See Jürgen Moltmann's interesting article entitled "Towards a Political Hermeneutics of the Gospel," in *Union Seminary Quarterly Review* 23, no. 4 (Summer 1968):
303–23, and in a slightly different form in Moltmann's *Religion, Revolution, and the
Future,* trans. M. Douglas Meeks (New York: Charles Scribner's Sons, 1969), pp. 83–
107.

48. This effort at concretization is being made in the several Third World theologies
that adopt the perspective of the minorities in various countries or the feminist perspective. The work being produced is extensive and diversified. Readers may consult the
volumes containing the papers of the meetings organized by the Ecumenical Association
of Third World Theologians: S. Torres and V. Fabella, eds., *The Emergent Gospel*
(Orbis, 1979); K. Appiah-Kubi and S. Torres, eds., *African Theology en Route* (Orbis,
1979); V. Fabella, ed., *Asia's Struggle for Full Humanity* (Orbis, 1980); S. Torres and J.
Eagleson, eds., *The Challenge of Basic Christian Communities* (Orbis, 1981); V. Fabella
and S. Torres, eds., *Irruption of the Third World* (Orbis, 1983); V. Fabella and S. Torres,
eds., *Doing Theology in a Divided World* (Orbis, 1985). There is a good description of
these various theologies in Phillip Berryman, *Liberation Theology* (New York: Pantheon, 1987); Deane Ferm, *Third World Liberation Theologies* (Orbis, 1986); Roger
Haight, *An Alternative Vision* (New York: Paulist, 1985). For the course taken by black
theology and a comparison of this type of theology with other similar theologies, see
G. Wilmore and J. Cone, *Black Theology: A Documentary History, 1966–1979*
(Orbis, 1979). The bibliography on feminist theology is vast; see R. Ruether, *Sexism
and God-Talk: Toward a Feminist Theology* (Boston: Beacon Press, 1984); and
B. Harrison, *Making Connections: Essays in Feminist Social Ethics* (Boston: Beacon
Press, 1986).

49. *On Not Leaving It to the Snake* (New York: The Macmillan Company, 1967),
p.12.

50. *Theology of Hope* (New York: Harper & Row, Publishers, 1967), p. 36.

## 2. LIBERATION AND DEVELOPMENT

1. See Thomas Suavet, "Développement," in *Dictionnaire économique et social*, 2nd
ed. (Paris: Économie et Humanisme, Les Éditions Ouvrières, 1962). For L.J. Lebret,
"the idea of development originates in 1945" (*Dynamique concrète du développement*
[Paris: Les Editions Ouvrières, 1967], p. 38), but he does not indicate the source of this
information. See also the systematic study of Jacques Freyssinet, *Le concept du
sousdèveloppement* (Paris: Mouton, 1966).

2. See *Theorie der Wirtschaftlichen Entwicklung* (Leipzig: Dunker & Humblot,
1912); English edition: *The Theory of Economic Development: An Inquiry into Profits,
Capital, Credit, Interest, and the Business Cycle*, trans. Redvers Opie (Cambridge:
Harvard University Press, 1934).

3. *Théorie de l'évolution économique* [French translation] (Paris: Dalloz, 1935).

4. *Teoría del desenvolvimiento económico* [Spanish translation] (Mexico, D.F.:
Fondo de Cultura Económica, 1944).

5. *The Conditions of Economic Progress* (London: Macmillan and Co., 1940).

6. See in this regard Odette Guitard, *Bandoeng et le réveil des anciens peuples
colonisés* (Paris: Presses Universitaires de France, 1961).

7. "The word *development* has not been in use long enough for its meaning to have
become absolutely determined" (Suavet, "Développement").

8. Among them is a work which due to special circumstances and carefully planned
methods of distribution became widely known in the underdeveloped countries: Walt W.

Rostow's *The Stages of Economic Growth: A Non-Communist Manifesto* (New York: Cambridge University Press, 1960).

9. "Development is a total social process, and only for methodological convenience or in a partial sense can one speak of economic, political, cultural, and social development" (Helio Jaguaribe, *Economic & Political Development: A Theoretical Approach & a Brazilian Case Study* [Cambridge: Harvard University Press, 1968], p. 4). See also Giorgio Ceriani Sebregondi, *Sullo sviluppo della società italiana* (Turin: Boringhieri, 1965); Raymond Barre, *Le développement économique: Analyse et politique* (Paris: Cahiers de l'Institut de Science Economique Appliquée, 1958).

10. See below Chapter 6.

11. "La notion de développement," in *L'économie de XXe siècle*, 2nd ed., enl., (Paris: Presses Universitaires de France, 1964), pp. 155 and 171. Perroux had already addressed himself to this perspective in "From the Avarice of Nations to an Economy for Mankind," *Cross Currents* 3, no. 3 (Spring 1953): 193-207. "Development for us," writes Lebret, "is *the object itself of human economics.* . . . This is the discipline of the transition . . . from a less human to a more human condition as fast and as cheaply as possible, bearing in mind the solidarity among subpopulations and populations . . . " (*Dynamique concrète*, p. 28). The same idea is expressed in another definition of development by the same author: "To have more in order to be more." As is well known, both of these expressions were used in the encyclical *Populorum progressio*. See also Luis Velaochaga, *Concepción integral del desarrollo*, pamphlet (Lima: Universidad Católica, 1967).

12. See the themes of the "new man" and the "whole man" of communist society. In it, according to an early text of Karl Marx, man will be defined not by what he has but by what he is: " . . . The positive transcendence of private property . . . should not be conceived merely in the sense of *immediate, one-sided gratification*—merely in the sense of *possession*, of *having*. Man appropriates his total essence in a total manner, that is to say, as a whole man" (*Economic and Philosophic Manuscripts of 1844*, ed. Dirk J. Struik, trans. Martin Milligan [New York: International Publishers, 1964], p. 138; the final italics are ours). See also Garaudy, *Perspectives*, pp. 347-51; Henri Lefebvre, *Dialectical Materialism*, trans. John Sturrock (London: Jonathan Cape, 1968), pp. 148-66; Karel Kosik, *Dialéctica de lo concreto* (Mexico, D.F.: Grijalbo, 1963, translated from the Czech), especially pp. 235-69.

13. An example of this inevitable progression to a wider context is the following paragraph of Vincent Cosmao: "We are therefore led beyond the integration of social development with economic development, or in other words of the noneconomic factors with economic development, to a vision of history in which mankind collectively takes hold of its collective destiny, humanizing it for the benefit of the whole man and of all men" ("Les exigences du développement au service de l'homme," *Parole et Mission* 10, no. 39 [October 15, 1967]: 581).

14. See the anthology *Del desarrollo al desarrollismo* (Buenos Aires: Galerna, 1969), especially the article by Juan Pablo Franco, "Reflexiones críticas en torno al desarrollismo."

15. See Chapter 6 below.

16. As regards Latin America, the International Monetary Fund (IMF), the Inter-American Development Bank (IDB), the Alliance for Progress, and on another level the Economic Commission for Latin America (ECLA), especially in its first period.

17. Related aspects of this problem as they apply specifically to Latin America will be dealt with in Chapter 6 below.

18. The term "development" points to a specific technical aspect that still retains its

urgency. But the perspective of liberation (which is opposed to developmentalism but not to development) undoubtedly brings greater depth and dynamism to the process in which the poor countries are involved. John Paul II alludes to this process that has matured in Latin America when he says, "In the period following the publication of the encyclical *Populorum Progressio,* a new way of confronting the problems of poverty and underdevelopment has spread in some areas of the world, especially in Latin America. This approach makes liberation the fundamental category and the first principle of action. The positive values as well as the deviations and risks of deviation, which are damaging to the faith and are connected with this form of theological reflection and method, have been appropriately pointed out by the church's magisterium" (*Sollicitudo Rei Socialis,* 46; *Origins,* p. 657).

19. In connection with the events in France of May 1968, Marcuse has said, "The students have not rebelled against a poor and badly organized society, but against a quite wealthy one; it is well organized in its luxury and its wastefulness, although 25% of the population of the country live in poverty-ridden ghettos. The rebellion does not oppose the grief caused by this society, but its benefits. It is a new phenomenon, peculiar to what is called the affluent society." (Quoted in J. M. Palmier, *Sur Marcuse* [Paris: Union Générale d'Éditions, 1968], p. 167). In a similar vein Paul Ricoeur writes, "This revolution attacks capitalism, not only because of its failure to achieve social justice, but also because of its success in seducing people into its inhuman design for quantitative well-being. . . . In the face of this meaningless society, the revolution hopes to give more importance to the creation of well-being, of ideas, of values, rather than to their consumption" ("Réforme et révolution dans l'Université," *Esprit* 36, no. 372 [June-July 1968]: 987).

20. On the dependence of our self-understanding on the humankind-nature relationship, see Edward Schillebeeckx, "L'immagine di Dio in un mondo secolarizzato," *Ricerca* (Rome), March 31, 1969; reproduced in *Processo alla religione* (Rome: IDOC, 1968). This point has been heavily emphasized by Marx.

21. "For philosophy to be born or reborn it is necessary that the sciences be. This is perhaps why philosophy in the strict sense did not come into being until Plato's time, stimulated by the existence of Greek mathematics; it was transformed by Descartes, its modern revolution having been provoked by the physics of Galileo; Kant made it over under the influence of the Newtonian discovery; it was remodeled by Husserl, prompted by the first axiomatics, etc." (Louis Althusser, *Lénine et la philosophie* [Paris: François Maspero, 1969], p. 27). For a severe critique of the historical aspects of the relationship between science and philosophy according to Althusser, see André Regnier, "Les surprises de l'idéologie: Heisenberg et Althusser," *L'Homme et la Société*, no. 15 (January-March 1970) pp. 247-50.

22. According to J.B. Metz, St. Thomas Aquinas initiated the anthropological viewpoint in opposition to the cosmological vision of the ancient world; see *Christliche Anthropozentrik: Üeber die Denkform des Thomas von Aquin* (Munich: Kösel, 1962).

23. "The Critique of Pure Reason," Preface to the second edition, 1787, in *Kant*, Great Books of the Western World, vol. 24, p. 7.

24. The point of view of a philosophy of history is already present in Kant (orientation toward the realm of ends) and even before him. But the systematic organization of the subject was done by Hegel. After Hegel, modern awareness will be a "historical awareness." See Henrique de Lima Vaz, *Cristianismo e conciencia histórica* (São Paulo, 1963), p. 20, reproduced in a collection of articles by the same author, *Ontologia e história* (São Paulo: Duas Cidades, 1968).

25. *The Phenomenology of Mind*, trans. J. B. Baillie (New York: The Humanities Press, Inc., 1964), pp. 229, 232-33.

26. This view has been especially stressed by Alexandre Kojève, *Introduction to the Reading of Hegel*, ed. Allan Bloom, trans. James H. Nichols, Jr. (New York: Basic Books, Inc., 1969).

27. Hegel, *Phenomenology*, pp. 238-39. See Kojève's commentary on this passage in *Introduction*, pp. 48ff. Karl Marx in an early work praised this Hegelian intuition: "The outstanding achievement of Hegel's *Phenomenology* . . . is . . . that Hegel conceives the self-creation of man as a process. . . . He thus grasps the essence of *labor* and comprehends objective man—true, because real man—as the outcome of man's *own labor*" *(Manuscripts of 1844*, p. 177).

28. *Reason in History*, trans. Robert S. Hartman (New York: Liberal Arts Press, 1953), p. 25. "Universal history . . . shows the development of the consciousness of freedom . . . " ("The Philosophy of History" in *Hegel*, Great Books, p. 182).

29. This matter is studied by Marcuse from the perspective of a history of ideas and in a personal fashion (Herbert Marcuse, *Reason and Revolution: Hegel and the Rise of Social Theory* [Boston: Beacon Press, 1941]).

30. We are not implying that Marx's work is but a socio-economic presentation of Hegelian thought. His originality is indisputable, although it has given rise to a variety of interpretations. See for example the different positions of Louis Althusser, *For Marx*, trans. Ben Brewster (New York: Pantheon Books, 1969); Ernest Mandel, *The Formation of the Economic Thought of Karl Marx*, trans. Brian Pearce (New York: Monthly Review Press, 1971); Kosik, *Dialéctica*.

31. It is common knowledge that Hegel did not deal with economics, especially in his youth. See György Lukács, *Der junge Hegel und die Probleme der kapitalistischen Gesselschaft* (Berlin: Aufbau-Verlag, 1954). See also Jean Hyppolite, *Studies on Marx and Hegel*, trans. John O'Neill (New York: Basic Books, Inc., 1969). At no time is this part of his work as rigorous as Marx's; furthermore, it can be stated that it is thanks to the latter that the works of Hegel's youth have been reevaluated.

32. This is the kind of evasion Georges Politzer referred to in his polemical essay on Bergson's philosophy: "In a word, the slave is freer insofar as he is more a slave, that is to say, the more interior and profound in his submission. It is not by escaping that the prisoner recovers his freedom, but by becoming a voluntary prisoner. It is not by preaching rebellion that one propagandizes freedom, but by preaching total submission. Freedom will reign only when slaves have the souls of slaves" *(Le Bergsonisme: Une mystification philosophique* [Paris: Éditions Sociales, 1949], p. 77).

33. The idea of psychic conflict is sketched for the first time by Freud in 1892 (J. M. Charcot, *Poliklinische Vorträge*, trans., intr., and notes by Sigmund Freud [Leipzig and Vienna: Deuticke, 1892-94], p. 137, translator's note; included in *The Standard Edition of the Complete Psychological Works of Sigmund Freud*, ed. James Strachey, vol. 1, *Pre-Psycho-Analytic Publications and Unpublished Drafts* [London: The Hogarth Press and the Institute of Psycho-Analysis, 1966], p. 138). The idea grew and gained precision in the years immediately following. It was an important and definitive gain. The forces involved in this confrontation were initially described in terms of instinctive drives and social pressures; later, after much correction, they were expressed in the statements of the pleasure principle and the reality principle.

34. See in this connection the observations of Harvey Cox in "Political Theology for the United States," in *Projections: Shaping an American Theology for the Future*, ed.

Thomas F. O'Meara and Donald M. Weisser (Garden City, N.Y.: Doubleday & Company, Inc., 1970), pp. 41-49.

35. "Introduction" in the anthology (Stokely Carmichael, John Gerassi, Paul Sweezy, Herbert Marcuse, Lucien Goldmann et al.) *To Free a Generation: The Dialectics of Liberation*, ed. David Cooper (London: Collier Books, 1968), pp. 9-10.

36. The life and work of Frantz Fanon were generously and creatively dedicated to this problem; see *The Wretched of the Earth*, trans. Constance Farrington (New York: Grove Press, 1963) and *Studies in a Dying Colonialism*, trans. Haakon Chevalier (New York: Monthly Review Press, 1965). For a study of Fanon, see Renate Zahar, *Colonialismo y enajenación: Contribución a la teoría política de Frantz Fanon* (Mexico, D.F.: Siglo Veintiuno, 1970).

37. In the political and ideological sphere, the difficult subject of democracy and participation within the framework of socialist societies is very much on the agenda today, as can be seen in the discussion of "real socialism" or in the events taking place in the Soviet Union. Freedom and democratic participation are inalienable rights of the human person; these matters are therefore of primordial importance for those in Latin America who are thinking of the construction of a new society.

38. See Freud's letter of July 28, 1929, included in Ernst Jones, M.D., *The Life and Work of Sigmund Freud,* 3 vols. (New York: Basic Books, Inc., 1957), 3: 448.

39. *Eros and Civilization* (Boston: Beacon Press, 1955).

40. *One-Dimensional Man* (Boston: Beacon Press, 1964).

41. *An Essay on Liberation* (Boston: Beacon Press, 1969), pp. ix-x.

42. See the inspiring studies of Ernst Bloch, *Das Prinzip Hoffnung* (Frankfurt: Suhrkamp Verlag, 1959); in English see his *Man on his Own* (New York: Herder and Herder, 1970), and *On Karl Marx*, trans. John Maxwell (New York: Herder and Herder, 1971). See also Jürgen Moltmann, *Theology of Hope*, referred to below in Chapter 11.

43. See Chapter 9.

44. The work of Jean-Yves Calvez, S.J., and Jacques Perrin, S.J., *The Church and Social Justice: The Social Teaching of the Popes from Leo XIII to Pius XII (1878-1958)* (Chicago: Regnery Company, 1961), contains no reference to this idea.

45. See René Laurentin, *Liberation, Development, and Salvation*, pp. 102-03.

46. There is an entire chapter devoted to it in the sequel to the work cited in note 42—first published four years later and dedicated to John XXIII: Jean-Yves Calvez, S.J., *The Social Thought of John XXIII: Mater et Magistra*, trans. George J. M. McKenzie, S.M. (Chicago: Henry Regnery Company, 1964).

47. In the texts quoted here the italics are ours.

48. In a less important statement of two years before, there is an interesting text of Paul VI regarding the consequences of technological progress on work styles: "No one foresaw that new work styles would awaken in the worker the awareness of his *alienation*, that is to say, the will no longer to work for others, with instruments belonging to others, not alone but with others. Did no one think that the desire for an economic and social liberation would arise, hindering his appreciation of the moral and spiritual redemption offered through faith in Christ?" (Allocution of May 1, 1965, in *L'Osservatore Romano*, May 3, 1965; the italics are ours).

49. See the analyses of René Dumont in "Populorum Progressio: Un pas en avant, trop timide," *Esprit* 35, no. 361 (June 1967): 1092-96; Raymundo Ozanam de Andrade, " 'Populorum Progressio': Neocapitalismo ou revolução," *Paz e Terra* (Rio de Janeiro), no. 4 (August 1967), pp. 209-21; François Perroux, " 'Populorum Progressio': L'encyclique de la Résurrection," *L'Église dans le monde de ce temps*, 3:201-12; Herné

Chaigne, "Force et faiblesse de l'encyclique," *Frères du Monde*, nos. 46-47 (1967), pp. 58-74, which proposes "to radicalize the encyclical."

50. It is not our intention to negate the values of *Populorum progressio*, highlighted for example by Ricardo Cetrulo, S.J., " 'Populorum progressio': De la 'animación' de la sociedad al análisis de situación," *Víspera* (Montevideo), no. 3 (October 1967), pp. 5-10. The author comments perceptively on the change of style and perspective in relation to preceding encyclicals. Regarding the encyclical's step forward in the doctrine of the ownership of means of production, see *Comentarios de cuademos para el diálogo a la Populorum progressio* (Madrid: Ed. Cuadernos para el Diálogo, 1967), especially the observations of Joaquín Ruiz-Giménez (pp. 16-20) and Eduardo Ciereo (pp. 31-49). See also the thought-provoking and warm commentary of the Italian Marxist Lucio Lombardo Radice, *Socialismo e libertà* (Rome: Editori Riuniti, 1968), pp. 136-48. Pope Paul VI has taken up these subjects in his recent and in many ways innovative letter to Cardinal Roy, *Octogesima adveniens*. There he says that "today men yearn to *free* themselves from need and dependence" (no. 45; our italics).

51. Reprinted, among others, in *Between Honesty and Hope: Documents from and about the Church in Latin America. Issued at Lima by the Peruvian Bishops' Commission for Social Action*, trans. John Drury (Maryknoll, New York: Maryknoll Publications, 1970), pp. 3-12.

52. We will study these texts in greater detail in Chapter 7.

53. *Creation and Fall, Temptation* (New York: The Macmillan Company, 1966), p. 37. Paul VI suggestively points out that freedom "will develop in its deepest human reality: to involve itself and to spend itself in building up active and lived solidarity." And he adds, "It is by losing himself in God who sets him free that man finds true freedom, renewed in the death and resurrection of the Lord" (*Octogesima adveniens*, no. 47).

54. See Laurentin, *Liberation, Development, and Salvation*, p. 63 and also p. 39.

55. Liberation in Christ reaches to the very root of all enslavement—namely, sin—and thus gives unity to the entire process. The concern is for a total liberation that receives its unity, in the final analysis, from communion with God and with other human beings. At the same time, however, it is necessary to distinguish and not confuse three dimensions or levels within this total liberation. We must distinguish in order to unite, for unity is not simply a sum of parts but implies a normative focus and directing center that gives meaning to the whole; this center is the saving love of God that is revealed in Jesus. There is no question, therefore, of giving an immanentist interpretation of the focal center. From the viewpoint of faith, history is the place where human beings freely and definitively decide the meaning of their lives by answering with a yes or no to the call of God's unmerited love.

56. An old comparison unexpectedly presented by St. Augustine of Hippo in his own inimitable style is related to the intimate relationship of the different levels of meaning of the term *liberation*: the soul under the control of sin, he says, resembles a country subdued by the enemy. See his commentary on Psalm 9, no. 8, quoted by Congar in "Christianisme et libération de l'homme," *Masses Ouvrières* (Paris), no. 258, (December, 1969), p. 3.

## 3. THE PROBLEM

1. See Gustave Thils, *Théologie des réalités terrestres*, vol. 1, *Préludes* (Paris: Desclée de Brouwer, 1947). For Congar this remains an open question: "There are some chapters of theology which still need to be worked out: together with the one on the relationship

between creation and redemption, there is the problem of the so-called theology of temporal realities" (*Situation et tâches*, p. 79).

2. For a statement of this question and some bibliographical comments, see Joseph Comblin, *Vers une théologie de l'action*, Études Religieuses, no. 767 (Brussels: La Pensée Catholique, 1964), pp. 87–108.

3. For a presentation of the scope of this effort see Vincent Cosmao, "Towards a Theology of Development," *IDOC International, North American Edition*, no. 5 (June 13, 1970), pp. 86–96. See also the abundant bibliography on this and related subjects prepared by Gerhard Bauer and published by the Committee on Society, Development and Peace (SODEPAX), *Towards a Theology of Development: An Annotated Bibliography* (Geneva, 1970).

4. The position of J. B. Metz will be studied in Chapter 11.

5. Writing on this subject is increasing, but quality varies. See Hugo Assmann, "Caracterização de una Teologia de Revolução," *Ponto Homem*, no. 4 (September–October 1968), pp. 6–45; Richard Shaull, "Hacia una perspectiva cristiana de la revolución social," *Cristianismo y Sociedad* 3, no. 7, pp. 6–16; in English, see Shaull's "Revolutionary Change in Theological Perspective," *Christian Social Ethics in a Changing World*, ed. J. C. Bennett (New York: Association Press, 1966), pp. 23–43. See also Richard A. McCormick, S.J., "The Theology of Revolution," *Theological Studies* 29, no. 4 (December 1968): 685–97; Joseph Smolik and Concilium General Secretariat, "Revolution and Desacralization," *Sacralization and Secularization*, ed. Roger Aubert, *Concilium* 47 (New York: Paulist Press, 1969), pp. 163–79; on the impasses implicit in a theology of revolution, see the interesting articles of Paul Blanquart, "Foi chrétienne et révolution," *A la recherche d'une théologie de la violence* (Paris: Les Éditions du Cerf, 1968), pp. 138–55; see also the anthology *Christianisme et révolution*, a colloquium organized by "Lettre" and IDOC International (Paris: Éditions La Lettre, 1968); *When All Else Fails: Christian Arguments on Violent Revolution*, ed. IDOC (Philadelphia: Pilgrim Press, 1970), includes several of these articles; see also Ernst Feil and Rudolf Weth, *Diskussion zur Theologie der Revolution* (Munich-Mainz: Kaiser-Grünewald, 1969). A related topic is theological reflection on violence; see *Recherche* mentioned above and another anthology, *La violenza dei cristiani* (Assisi: Cittadella, 1969), especially Giulio Girardi's article, "Amore cristiano e violenza rivoluzionaria."

6. Johannes B. Metz, *Theology of the World*, trans. William Glen-Doepel (New York: Herder and Herder, 1969), p. 93. Christian Duquoc, O.P., wrote in the same vein some years ago: "The question of the Church and the world is irritatingly complex" ("L'Église et le Monde," *Lumière et Vie* 14, no. 73 [May-July 1955]:49).

7. *La risposta dei teologi* (Brescia: Queriniana, 1969), p. 61.

8. See for example nos. 39 and 43.

9. Moreover, this approach will be truer to the spirit of the Council: "Conciliar renewal," said Paul VI, "is not measured so much by changes in exterior practices, regulations, and customs as by changes in habitual behavior and by the rejection of a kind of inertia, a kind of heartfelt resistance to a truly Christian spirit. We must think *in a new way*: this is the beginning of reform and *aggiornamento*" (Allocution at a general audience in January 1966; italics are ours).

10. See below Chapter 8.

11. The political sphere, however, remains ambiguous. Although universal in its significance, its empirical reality cannot be entirely separated from particular instances.

12. "The *Socius* and the Neighbor," *History and Truth*, trans. Charles A. Kelbley (Evanston, Ill.: Northwestern University Press, 1965), pp. 98–109. We should clarify

that to affirm that all human reality has a political dimension in no way means, as the term itself indicates, to reduce everything to this dimension.

13. "Les masses pauvres," in G. Cottier et al., *Église et pauvreté* (Paris: Les Éditions du Cerf, 1965), p. 174. See also the interesting observations concerning the political sphere in Pierre Eyt, "Pour une réflexion en matière politique," *Nouvelle Revue Théologique* 93, no. 10 [December 1971]: 1055-75).

14. Many Christians have sought answers to these questions in relatively novel ways. This search has produced many experiences, sometimes confused. See in this connection René Laurentin's *Enjeu du IIe Synode et contestation dans l'Église* (Paris: Éditions du Seuil, 1969); see also *A la recherche d'une Église*, special issue of *Parole et Mission* 12, no. 46 (July 15, 1969); *Le due chiese* (Rome: IDOC, 1969); and the collection edited by Malcolm Boyd, *The Underground Church* (New York: Sheed and Ward, 1968).

15. In this context the starting point would be what P.-A. Liégé called some time ago "the human credibility of Christianity" ("Bulletin d'Apologétique," *Revue des Sciences Philosophiques et Théologiques* 33 [1949]: 67).

## 4. DIFFERENT RESPONSES

1. We express here some ideas we have had an opportunity to develop more fully in Gustavo Gutiérrez, *La pastoral en la Iglesia en América Latina* (Montevideo: Ediciones del Centro de Documentacion MIEC-JECI, 1968), re-edited as *Líneas pastorales de la Iglesia en América Latina, Análisis Teológico* (Lima: Centro de Estudios y Publicaciones, and Santiago de Chile: Instituto Catequístico Latinoamericano, 1970). This work is a series of talks to university students and is an attempt to present a typology of pastoral thinking in the Latin American Church, subject of course to further study and more precise delineations.

2. See the historical study of H.-X Arquillère, *L'Augustinisme politique,* 2nd ed. rev. and enl. (Paris: Librairie Philosophique J. Vrin, 1955); see also, regarding this work, the critical observations and clarifications proposed by Henri de Lubac, S.J., in *Augustinianism and Modern Theology*, trans. Lancelot Sheppard (New York: Herder and Herder, 1969).

3. "The Church did not face an autonomous world, since society was ordered towards serving the ends of eternal salvation according to rules determined by the Church" (Yves Congar, "Église et Monde," *Le Concile au jour le jour, troisième session* (Paris: Éditions du Cerf, 1965), p. 143.

4. This point of view was evident in a classic work of another period by Luigi Civardi, *A Manual of Catholic Action,* trans. C.C. Martindale, S.J. (New York: Sheed and Ward, 1943); see especially Chapters 6 and 8.

5. It was only with Vatican II that the Church began to abandon in any real sense the mentality of Christendom, a historical period which had already ended—four centuries before.

6. See for example the case of the most widely discussed schema of the Council: Religious Freedom. In this regard see our study "Libertad religiosa y diálogo salvador" in *Salvación y construcción del mundo* (Barcelona: Nova Terra, 1968), pp. 11-43.

7. This idea is explained fully in his well-known work *True Humanism* (New York: Charles Scribner's Sons, 1938).

8. Maritain's thought was very influential in certain Christian sectors of Latin America. Argentina was one of the most significant examples. See Fernando Martínez Paz, *Maritain, política e ideología: Revolución cristiana en la Argentina* (Buenos Aires:

Editorial Nahuel, 1966). Furthermore, Maritain's ideas provoked strong controversies in which Maritain himself took part; see Luis Arturo Pérez, *Estudio de filiosofía político-social*(Santiago de Chile, 1948), and the response by Julio Jiménez, *La ortodoxia de Maritain: Ante un ataque reciente* (Talca, Chile: Editiones Cervantes, 1948). See also the texts—including a letter by Maritain—compiled in *Una polémica sensacional: Jacques Maritain* (Santiago de Chile, 1944). All this, however, amounts only to a simple repetition of Maritain's ideas and a fruitless discussion of his "orthodoxy." A more personal approach is to be found in Brazil in the work of Tristão de Athayde (Alceu Amoroso Lima), who spread Maritain's thought beginning in the '30s.

9. This was keenly felt by those Latin American Christians who began to awaken to their political commitment. See Juan Luis Segundo, *Función de la Iglesia en la realidad rioplatense* (Montevideo: Barreiro y Ramos, 1962), p. 41.

10. Maritain, *Humanism,* p. 291. This distinction will gain wide acceptance; see for example Alfred de Soras, *Action catholique et action temporelle* (Paris: Spes, 1938).

11. See Maritain, *Humanism,* pp. 264-67. This gave rise to the modern parties of socio-Christian inspiration.

12. In spite of efforts to the contrary, this position still has traces of the ecclesiocentric ideology of which we have made note. For example, Maritain asks how a non-Christian can participate in a political party inspired by Christian principles; but he does not consider the more relevant question in today's world: Under what conditions can a Christian participate in a political party which is alien and perhaps even hostile to a Christian viewpoint?

13. The experiences and thinking of the French Church—source of inspiration for the vanguard in Latin America during recent years—has had a great impact in this regard. (See in this connection, for example, the comments of Hector Borrat, "¿La Iglesia para qué?," *Cristianismo y Sociedad* no. 22 [1970], pp. 7-29). The distinction of planes was in fact the central point of the more advanced movements of the lay apostolate in Latin America. The works of Congar are most representative of this position; see *Lay People* and the articles in *A Gospel Priesthood,* trans. P. J. Hepburne-Scott (New York: Herder and Herder, 1967) and *Christians Active in the World,* trans. P.J. Hepburne-Scott (New York: Herder and Herder, 1968). See also A. Chavasse et al., *Église et Apostolat,* 2nd ed. (Paris: Casterman, 1955); Gerard Philips, *The Role of the Laity in the Church,* trans. John R. Gilbert and James W. Moudry (Cork: The Mercier Press, Limited, 1956); Jerome Hamer, O.P., *The Church is a Communion* (New York: Sheed and Ward, 1964).

14. See for example *Civilisation et évanigélisation: Note Doctrinale du comité théologique de Lyon* (Lyons: Emmanuel Vilte, 1957).

15. This idea appears in writings of the French bishops and is a result of the experience of the specialized apostolic movements. See *Directoire pastoral en matière sociale,* no. 32 (Paris: Bonne Presse, 1954); *Gaudium et spes,* no. 43, echoes this point of view.

16. According to M. D. Chenu, this distinction is a result of French "Social Christianity" ("Misión de la Iglesia en el mundo contemporáneo," *La Iglesia en el mundo de hoy,* ed. Guillermo Barauna [Madrid: Studium, 1967], pp. 390-91).

17. *Christians Active,* p. 71. See also the works mentioned in note 13. Congar has reaffirmed his opinion regarding the existence of these two missions of the Church in "Le rôle de l'Église dans le monde de ce temps," *L'Église dans le monde de ce temps,* 2:305.

18. P.A. Liégé distinguishes between temporal Christian institutions that are "power-bearing" (*potestatives*) and those that are "educational" (*éducatives*) in "La mission contre les institutions chrétiennes?" in *Parole et Mission* 4, no. 15 (October 15, 1961):

501-02. The same author distinguishes between "heavy" institutions (*lourdes*), which endow the Church with power, and "light" ones (*légères*), which "come under the heading of service," in "La pauvreté, compagne de la mission," in *Église et Pauvreté,* pp. 167-68.

19. See the well-known and pertinent comments of Emmanuel Mounier, for example, "Feu la Chrétienté," *Oeuvres de Mounier,* 4 vols. (Paris: Éditions du Seuil, 1961-63), 3:686-714.

20. See the famous Chapter 3 on "Kingdom, Church and World," and "Hierarchy and Faithful People" in *Lay People.*

21. This is the position taken by Congar, A. Chavasse, G. Philips, and others. Karl Rahner, in an article which provoked heated controversy, affirmed that the lay person's only concern should be the building up of the world ("L'apostolat des laïcs," *Nouvelle Revue Théologique* 78, no. 1 (January 1956): 3-32. See also Charles Baumgartner, "Formes diverses de l'apostolat des laïcs," *Christus,* no.13 (January 1957), pp. 9-33, which deals with the same ideas in different terms. Congar explicitly rejected this opinion (*Christians Active,* pp. 78-79). See also the comments of the moderators of the specialized Catholic Action groups for French workers in "A propos de l'apostolat des laïcs," *Masses Ouvrières,* no. 130 (May 1957), pp. 1-29.

22. See for example Chavasse, *Église et apostolat,* p. 18. This work inspired the 1962 pastoral plan of the Chilean bishops, who at that time were at the vanguard of the Latin American Church (The text is reproduced in *Recent Church Documents from Latin America* [Cuernavaca, Mexico: CIF, 1962-63], pp. 1-12).

23. See *Lay People,* Chapter 8, which deals with Catholic Action and the temporal commitment of the laity.

24. See Jourdain Bonduelle, *La révision de vie* (Paris: Les Éditions du Cerf, 1964), and in a more recent perspective C. Perani, *La revisione di vita strumento de evangelizzazione, alla luce del Vaticano II* (Turin, 1968).

25. "Le rôle de l'Église," p. 306.

26. However, this distinction is clearly expressed in the decree on the apostolate of the laity, *Apostolicum actuositatem* (see, for example, no. 5).

## 5. CRISIS OF THE DISTINCTION OF PLANES MODEL

1. André Manaranche recalls and criticizes these distinctions in "Foi d'aujourd'hui et distinctions d'hier," *Projet* 16 (June 1967): 641-56.

2. Regarding one of the first manifestations of this crisis, see *Association catholique de la jeunesse française: Signification d'une crise, Analyse et documents* (Paris: Éditions de l'Épi, 1964).

3. "It is an illusion to believe that young people can be given a living spiritual formation detached from temporal problems . . . . A religious and human education is supposed to enable the militants in our movement to work out in the light of the Gospel a concrete solution to the problems they face in life. They cannot do this except within the movements" (Reports of a leader in the French *Jeunesse Étudiantine Chrétienne* [JEC] in 1950, ibid., p. 59).

4. On the current state of the French JEC see Louis de Vaucelles's article "Les mutations de la J.E.C.," *Études* 333 (August-September 1970): 278-86. The author's "Critical Reflection" seems somewhat harsh to us. Below in Chapter 7 we will treat this question with respect to the Latin American Church.

5. See José A. Diáz, *La crisis permanente de la acción católica* (Barcelona: Nova

Terra, 1966). In Latin America, particularly in Brazil, this problem has taken on serious proportions. See Chapter 7 below.

6. Joseph Comblin was questioning this some time ago: *Échec de l'action catholique?* (Paris: Éditions Universitaires, 1961). But the solution he proposed seemed to be in direct opposition to the movement which had provoked the crisis.

7. Hugo Assmann analyzes well "La función legitimadora de la religión para la dictadura brasilera," *Perspectivas para el Diálogo* (Montevideo), no. 46 (August 1970), pp. 171-81.

8. See for example *Las tareas de la Iglesia en América Latina* (Bogotá: FERES, 1964), and Francois Houtart and Emile Pin, *The Church in the Latin American Revolution*, trans. Gilbert Barth (New York: Sheed and Ward, 1965), pp. 222-23.

9. *Secularization* is a term which has actually been in circulation for a long time. At first it referred to a return to the world of something which had acquired a certain sacred character, for example Church property. For a history of this idea see Hermann Lübbe, *Säkularisierung. Geschichte eines ideenpolitischen Begriffs* (Freiburg: Alber, 1965). Regarding the different meanings of the term, see Thomas E. Clarke, S.J.,"What is Secular Christianity?" in *Proceedings of the Twenty-first Convention of the Catholic Theological Society of America, Providence, Rhode Island, June 20-23, 1966* (Yonkers, New York, 1967), pp. 201-21.

10. *The Secular City* (New York: The Macmillan Company, 1965), p. 17.

11. See Antoine Vergote, "Il realismo della fede di fronte alla desacralizzazione del mondo," in the anthology *Il cristianesimo nella società di domani*, ed. Pietro Prini (Rome: Abete, 1968), pp. 101-13. The author suggests renewing the theology of creation by means of anthropology (pp. 108-12).

12. Carlos Alvarez Calderón in *Pastoral y liberación humana* (Quito: Colección IPLA; Lima: Centro de Estudios y Publicaciones, 1970) shows the consequences for pastoral action of this shift in perspective.

13. See Chapter 2 above.

14. See the excellent comments by Schillebeeckx on "the new image of God" in a secularized world in "La vie religieuse dans un monde sécularisé," *Approches théologiques IV, La mission de l'Église* (Brussels: Éditions du CEP, 1969), pp. 285-89.

15. The first person to point out the potential meaning of secularization for the faith was Friedrich Gogarten in his *Verhängnis und Hoffnung der Neuzeit. Die Säkularisierung als theologisches Problem* (Stuttgart: Friedrich Vorwerk Verlag, 1953), pp. 11ff. English version: *Despair and Hope for Our Time*, trans. Thomas Wieser (Philadelphia: Pilgrim, 1970). See also Juan Ochagavía, "El proceso de secularización: luces y sombras," *Teología y Vida* (Santiago de Chile) 8, no. 4 (1967): 275-90; Heinz Robert Schlette, "Valutazione teologica della secolarizzazione" in *Processo alla religione* (Rome: IDOC Documenti Nuovi, 1968), pp. 39-61; and Karl Rahner, "Theological Reflections on the Problem of Secularization" in L. K. Shook, ed., *Theology of Renewal* (New York: Herder and Herder, 1968), 1:346-357. For a confrontation, handled with an open and understanding attitude, of the idea of secularization with the texts of Vatican II, see Buenaventura Kloppenburg, O.F.M., *El cristiano secularizado* (Bogotá: Instituo de Liturgia de Medellín, Ediciones Paulinas, and Indo-American Press Service, 1971). Regarding the relationship between the theology of secularization and acceptance of the norms of industrialized society, see the critical analyses in the anthology *Les deux visages de la théologie de la sécularisation* (Tournai: Casterman, 1970), especially the article of Marcel Xhaufflaire, "La théologie après la théologie de la sécularisation" (pp. 85-105).

16. It might be well to recall at this point the distinction initially made by Gogarten between secularization and secularism. The former refers to the historical process itself which we have described; the latter to an ideology which tends to contain this process within a framework which excludes all religious values (*Vërhangnis*).

17. See *Letters and Papers from Prison*, ed. Eberhard Bethge, trans. Reginald H. Fuller (London: SCM Press, 1953).

18. César Aguiar accurately refers to "Latin American forms of secularization: the revolutionary ideology, the political radicalization—but certainly not science, technique, and modern world that Europeans talk of so much, and above all not the urban civilization and social mobility that Cox sees as constitutive of the secular city" ("Currents and Tendencies in Contemporary Latin American Catholicism," *IDOC-NA*, no. 13 [November 14, 1970], p. 61).

19. Leon Trotsky proclaimed the laws of "uneven" and "combined" development, referring to a complex situation in which there coexisted different types of economies, different social and juridical structures, and different rhythms of growth and evolution; this enabled him to explain why the revolution of the proletariat had occurred in Russia, although this country had not attained the unilineal capitalist development of the major Western countries. The idea of an uneven and combined development emphasized the mutual influences among countries. In other words the situation in one country—and its revolutionary potential—must be seen from an international perspective. This notion will be the foundation of the theory of "permanent revolution" (See Trotsky's *The History of the Russian Revolution*, trans. Max Eastman, 3 vols. [New York: Simon and Schuster, 1934], especially 1:5-6; see also the same author's *The Permanent Revolution and Results and Prospects* [London: New Park Publications, 1962]). This expression is now common in the social sciences and is applied to the so-called underdeveloped countries.

20. The precise form this redefinition should take is a controversial point and it is being studied. The relationship between evangelization and popular religiosity is beginning to appear in a different light. See for example Segundo Galilea, *Introducción a la religiosidad latinoamericana*, pamphlet (Mexico, D.F., 1967), and "La religiosidad popular latinoamericana" in the same author's *Para una pastoral latinoamericana* (Mexico,D.F.: Ediciones Paulinas, S.A., 1968), pp. 94-146; José Comblin, "Reflexões sôbre a Condição Concreta de Evangelização Hoje," *Revista Brasileira* 27, no. 3 (September 1967): 590-97; Aldo J. Büntig, "Interpretación motivacional del catolicismo popular," *Víspera* (Montevideo), no. 10 (May 1969), pp. 13-20; Felipe Berryman, "Conscientización y religiosidad popular," *Víspera* no. 12 (September 1969), pp. 8-10; in English see Berryman's "Popular Catholicism in Latin America," *Cross Currents* 21, no. 3 (Summer 1971): 284-301; Lucio Gera and Guiermo Rodríguez Melgarejo, "Apuntes para una interpretación de la Iglesia argentina," *Víspera*, no. 15 (February 1970), pp. 59-88; and the critical comments on this last article by M. Kaplun, "Pueblo, fe y alienación" *Perspectivas para el Diálogo*, nos. 44-45 (June-July 1970), pp. 129-35.

21. The doctrine of pure nature has been completely abandoned in contemporary theology. See in this regard an attempt to place it in its context in the history of theology as well as a review of the most recent criticisms it has undergone in Henri de Lubac, *The Mystery of the Supernatural*, trans. Rosemary Sheed (New York: Herder and Herder, 1967), pp. 1-24.

22. In a solid historical work Juan Alfaro delineates the development of theology from Thomas Aquinas to Cajetan: *Lo natural y lo sobrenatural: Estudio histórico desde Santo Tomás hasta Cayetano (1274-1534)* (Madrid: Consejo Superior de Investiga-

ciones Científicas, 1952). See also de Lubac, *Mystery of Supernatural*.

23. See for example M.-D. Roland-Gosselin, O.P., "Béatitude et désir naturel d'après S. Thomas d'Aquin," *Revue des Sciences Philosophiques et Théologiques* 18 (1929): 193-222; and A.-R. Motte, O.P., "Désir naturel et béatitude surnaturelle," *Bulletin Thomiste* 3, nos. 3-4 (July-December 1932): 651-76.

24. See for example Joseph Maréchal, "De Naturali Perfectae Beatitudinis Deside-rio,"in *Mélanges Joseph Maréchal* (Paris: Desclée de Brouwer, 1950), 1:323-38. J. Alfaro, "Transcendencia e inmanencia de lo sobrenatural," *Gregorianum* 38, no. 1 (1957): 5-50.

25. "Introduction" in Maurice Blondel, *Pages Religieuses* (Paris: Aubier, Éditions Montaigne, 1945).

26. *Surnaturel* (Paris: Aubier, 1946).

27. Karl Rahner, "Concerning the Relationship between Nature and Grace," *Theological Investigations*, vol. 1 (Baltimore: Helicon, 1961), pp. 297-317. See also some later comments in "Nature and Grace," *Theological Investigations*, vol. 4 (Baltimore: Helicon, 1966), pp. 165-188.

28. Albert Valensin, S.J., in *Dictionnaire d'Apologétique de la Foi Catholique*, s.v."Immanence." See also Maurice Blondel's *History and Dogma* included in *The Letter on Apologetics and History and Dogma*, ed. and trans. Alexander Dru and Illtyd Trethowan (New York: Holt, Rinehart and Winston, 1965). For an integrated view of the discussions brought about by these ideas see the classic article by L. Malevez,"La gratuité du surnaturel," *Nouvelle Revue Théologique* 75, no. 6 (June 1953): 561-86, and 75, no. 7 (July-August 1953): 673-89.

29. This line of thinking appears discreetly in Vatican II. See for example *Gaudium et spes*, nos. 22, 24, and 29. See also Chapter 9 below.

30. See Anita Röper, *The Anonymous Christian*, trans. Joseph Donceel, S.J. (New York: Sheed and Ward, 1963), and the Afterword of the same work by Klaus Riesenhu-ber, S.J.,"The Anonymous Christian According to Karl Rahner."

31. Edward Schillebeeckx, *World and Church*, trans. N.D. Smith (New York: Sheed and Ward, 1971), pp. 115-39.

32. See Karl Rahner, *The Christian of the Future* (New York: Herder and Herder, 1967).

33. Misuse of both the term and the idea of anonymous Christianity has recently provoked numerous criticisms. See for example Michel de Certeau,"Apologie de la différence," *Études* 328 (January 1968): 99-101; Maurice Bellet, *Les sens actuels du christianisme: Un exercice initial* (Paris: Desclée de Brouwer, 1969), p. 59; André Manaranche, *Quel salut?* (Paris: Éditions du Seuil, 1969), p. 197. Also regarding implicit faith see P.-A. Liégé,"La foi implicite en procès," *Parole et Mission* 11, no. 41 (April 15, 1968): 203-13. Karl Rahner has answered these criticisms by distinguishing between the problem of terminology—which in the last resort "has no importance at all"—and content—"the thing intended by the terminology." For him the reality itself is indisputable if one wishes to be logical in asserting the universal will of salvation. "Anonymous Christianity and the Missionary Talk of the Church," *IDOC-NA*, no. 1 (April 4, 1970), pp. 70-96.

34. See Manuel Ossa's study "Cristianismo y sentido de la historia," *Mensaje* 15, no. 153 (October 1966): 539-51.

35. The writings of Teilhard de Chardin, among others, have greatly influenced the trend toward reaffirmation of Christ as Lord of history and the cosmos. This influence has not always been openly acknowledged; this is so, for example, in the conclusions of the first part of *Gaudium et spes*.

36. The term *supernatural*—which appeared late in theology—is scarcely used by Vatican II and is found almost exclusively in minor documents. It is not used in *Gaudium et spes* or in *Dei verbum; Lumen gentium* contains only two allusions.

37. Gustave Martelet, *Les idées Maîtresses de Vatican II* (Paris: Desclée de Brouwer, 1966), p. 137, n. 1.

38. We do not mean to imply that these terms express a totally coherent teaching of the ecclesiastical magisterium. There are ambiguities even in *Gaudium et spes*. Juan Luis Segundo has pointed them out in "Hacia una exégesis dinámica," *Víspera*, no. 3 (October 1967), pp. 77-84. "The great difficulty is that Vatican II juxtaposes assertions without working out a perfectly coherent position—but could it have done otherwise?" (Manaranche, "Foi d'aujourd'hui," p. 654).

39. "The Church and Mankind," *The Church and Mankind*, ed. Edward Schillebeeckx, *Concilium* 1 (Glen Rock, N.J.: Paulist Press, 1965), p. 90. Karl Rahner had included all humanity in the notion of "the People of God" years before; see his "Membership of the Church According to the Teaching of Pius XII's Encyclical 'Mystici Corporis Christi,' " *Theological Investigations*, vol. 2 (Baltimore: Helicon Press, 1963), pp. 1-88.

40. *Theology of the World*, p. 93. From a more eschatological viewpoint, the author later asserts that "the decisive relationship between the Church and the world is not spatial but temporal" (ibid., p. 94).

41. Chavasse supported a similar viewpoint when he asserted that the work of civilization is an "indirect apostolate of the Church" (*Église et Apostolate*, pp. 155-57). This idea was rejected by the more orthodox supporters of the distinction of planes model (see the comments of the French *Action Catholique Ouvrière* already mentioned).

42. See Chapter 9 below.

43. See Karl Rahner, "History of the World and Salvation-History," *Theological Investigations*, vol. 5 (Baltimore: Helicon Press, 1966), pp. 97-114. See also Heinz Robert Schlette, *Epiphanie als Geschichte* (Munich: Kösel, 1966).

44. Hans Urs von Balthasar comments ironically but perceptively, "Nowadays, in the same breath of conviction, we hear it announced that the world has been finally demythologized and has become purely secular; and yet that it must be perceived as a total eucharistic mystery, as the evolving mystical body of Christ: a mythologization and 'divinization' of the cosmos far beyond anything that the medieval realists provided for in their Christian philosophy of the universe. But (in these naive syntheses) the creation is—in its evolutionary aspect as well—conceived of directly as a theological and sacramental mystery; and, in spite of their previous demythologization, all secular and worldly processes are immediately transformed into spiritual processes. To all intents and purposes, this implies no more than that the processes of the world are subject only to man's technical mind and his way of perceiving them: the world that has been demythologized to the point of atheism is, as such, also the world made sacred to the point of divinizing it. But these are just empty phrases: a noisy chatter with which Christians deceive themselves in the contemporary world—a world which can get along very well without them while, in all innocence, they're doing no more than chucking sand in their own eyes. If you've already secretly cancelled the distinctions, it's absolutely pointless to pretend you can still maintain them; it's ludicrous to think you're saying something deeply meaningful in any Christian sense, when you call the secular 'spiritual,' and the spiritual 'secular' " (*Who is a Christian?* trans. John Cumming [Westminster, Md.: Newman Press, 1968], pp. 48-49; for a similar viewpoint see Manaranche, *Quel Salut?*).

## 6. THE PROCESS OF LIBERATION IN LATIN AMERICAN

1. *Dependencia y desarrollo en América Latina* (first published in mimeo, Santiago de Chile: ILPES, 1967; republished in Mexico, D.F.: Siglo Veintiuno, 1969), p. 4.

2. The Economic Commission for Latin America (ECLA), an organ of the United Nations, has played a prominent role in this. See the texts which appear in *América Latina: El pensamiento de la CEPAL* (Santiago de Chile: Tiempo Latinoaméricano, 1969).

3. United Nations, Organization of American States (OAS), International Monetary Fund (IMF), Inter-American Development Bank (IDB), Agency for International Development (AID), Alliance for Progress.

4. See Rostow, *Stages of Economic Growth,* Chapter 6. For a critique of this work see Fernando Henrique Cardoso, *Cuestiones de sociología del desarrollo en América Latina* (Santiago de Chile: Universitaria, 1968), pp. 10-16, and Antonio Garicía, "La estructura social y el desarrollo latinoamericano: Réplica a la teoría del nuevo contrato social de W.W. Rostow," *El Trimestre Económico* (Mexico, D.F.), no. 129 (January-March 1966), pp. 3-42.

5. Fernando Henrique Cardoso, "Desarrollo y dependencia: Perspectivas en el análisis sociológico," in the anthology *Sociología del desarrollo* (Buenos Aires, 1970), pp. 19-20. See also Fernando Henrique Cardoso and Francisco Weffort, "Consideraciones generales sobre el desarrollo," in *Ensayos de interpretación sociológico-política* (Santiago de Chile: Tiempo Latinoamericano, 1970), pp. 14-33.

6. See Cardoso and Faletto, *Dependencia y desarrollo,* and Theotonio Dos Santos, "La crisis de la teoría del desarrollo y las relaciones de dependencia en América Latina" in *La dependencia politico-económica de América Latina* (Mexico, D.F.: Siglo Veintiuno, 1969); initially published in *Boletín* (Santiago de Chile), CESO, no. 3, October 1968. On the same subject André Gunder Frank speaks of a "development of underdevelopment"; see his "The Development of Underdevelopment" in *Latin America: Underdevelopment or Revolution* (New York: Monthly Review Press, 1969).

7. Felipe Herrera, "Viabilidad de una comunidad latinoamáricana," *Estudios Internacionales* (Santiago de Chile), no. 1 (April 1967). Along the same lines is the testimony of another important figure during the decade of development, the economist Raúl Prebisch, *Hacia una dinámica del desarrollo latinoamáricano* (Mexico, D.F.: Fondo de Cultura Económica, 1963). See also ECLA's *Economic Study of Latin America, 1966,* especially the texts quoted from the Spanish version in Dos Santos, "Crisis," pp. 164-65. See also Celso Furtado, *Obstacles to Development in Latin America,* trans. Charles Ekker (Garden City, N.Y.: Anchor Books, 1970).

8. Cardoso and Faletto, *Dependencia y desarrollo,* p. 8.

9. Gonzalo Arroyo, S.J., offers a good synthesis of this new situation with ample bibliographical references up to 1968 in "Pensamiento latinoamericano sobre subdesarrollo y dependencia externa," *Mensaje* 17, no. 173 (October 1968): 516-20. This article has been revised and enlarged by the author in "Le sousdéveloppement et la dépendence externe au miroir de la littérature latinoaméricaine," *Cultures et Développement* 2, no. 1 (1969-70): 121-41.

10. "The exclusively economic explanations predominant in developmentalist ideologies slowly gave way to strictly political concerns" (Cardoso, "Desarrollo y dependencia," p. 22).

11. Dos Santos, "Crisis," p. 153.

12. Osvaldo Sunkel has studied the historical genesis of this in *El marco histórico del proceso de desarrollo y subdesarrollo* (Santiago de Chile: ILPES, 1967); this study has been republished in Osvaldo Sunkel and Pedro Paz, *El subdesarrollo latinoamericano y la teoría del desarrollo* (Mexico, D.F.: Siglo Veintiuno, 1970). See also the anthology *La dominación de América Latina* (Lima: Moncloa, 1968); Jorge Bravo Bresani, *Desarrollo y subdesarollo* (Lima: Moncloa, 1967); and Celso Furtado, *Economic Development of Latin America: A Survey from Colonial Times to the Cuban Revolution* (New York: Cambridge University Press, 1970).

13. Anibal Quijano, *El proceso de urbanización en Latinoamérica,* mimeo (Santiago de Chile: CEPAL, 1966), p. 14. See also the same author's *Dependencia, cambio social y urbanización de Latinoamérica,* mimeo (Santiago de Chile: CEPAL, 1967).

14. André Gunder Frank does not accept the traditional thesis concerning the feudalism of Latin American societies. He holds that Latin America has been capitalist (that is, subject to mercantilist capitalism) since its earliest days, or, even earlier, since its conception *(Capitalism and Underdevelopment in Latin America: Historical Studies of Chile and Brazil* (New York and London: Monthly Review Press, 1967). This thesis had already been upheld by Sergio Bagú, *Economía de la sociedad colonial: Ensayo de la historia comparada de América Latina* (Buenos Aires: El Ateneo, 1949). See also the criticism of Dos Santos regarding the methodology and conclusions of Frank; Dos Santos prefers to speak of "precapitalist" means of production in "Capitalismo colonial según A.G. Frank," *Monthly Review* (selected texts in Spanish), November 1968, pp. 17-27. Frank responds to this criticism in *Lumpenburgesía: Lumpendesarrollo* (Bogotá: Oveja Negra, 1970).

15. Francisco C. Weffort, *Clases populares e desenvolvimento social,* mimeo (Santiago de Chile: ILPES, 1968), p. 26.

16. "Desarrollo y dependencia," p. 24. Dos Santos proposes the following definition of dependence: "It is a situation in which the economy of one group of countries is conditioned by the development and expansion of another economy. The relationship of interdependence between two or more economies and between certain economies and world trade assumes the form of dependence when some countries (the dominant ones) are able to develop themselves while others (the dependent ones) can only reflect that expansion, which can have a positive or negative effect upon their immediate development. In any case the basic relationship of dependence leads to a world-wide situation which characterizes the dependent countries as backward and exploited by the dominant countries" ("Crisis," p. 180).

17. Cardoso, "Desarrollo y dependencia," p. 24. "It is not possible in our times to consider the influence of the United States as an external variable which affects the national economic structure merely by means of foreign trade and financing. On the contrary, our dependence is much deeper and more complex; it affects the very roots of the economic and social structure, forming—in the words of Bettelheim—a 'net' from which the backward countries must escape if they intend to actualize their potential. Imperialism must be thought of as structural, active in the core of our national structures, shaping the roots of an economic, technological, political, and cultural dependence. One of the elements basic to an understanding of this structural penetration is its relationship with the different social classes in Latin American countries. . . . Imperialism is then no longer a factor operating from 'outside' the dependent countries; it is a force active from 'inside,' tied to the national structures. Imperialism becomes 'nationalized' (not because of the interests it defends, but because of its geographic and social ties), while the ruling classes become 'denationalized' (insofar as they foreswear

autonomous development—which was still possible up to a certain point—and commit themselves to the defense of imperialist interests, whose profits they share)" (Juan Pablo Franco, *La influencia de los Estados Unidos en América Latina* [Montevideo: Ediciones Tauro, 1967]).

18. *Dependencia y desarrollo,* pp. 130-50.

19. José Nun, *Misión Rockefeller: ¿Porque y para que?,* mimeo, 1970, p. 3.

20. Regarding the idea of an enclave, see Cardoso and Faletto, *Dependencia y desarrollo,* pp. 48-53.

21. See in this regard, Theotonio Dos Santos, *El nuevo carácter de la dependencia* (Santiago de Chile: CESO, 1968). This work contains data regarding the areas affected by foreign investment, especially in Brazil. See also Nun, *Misión Rockefeller.*

22. "The image of foreign interests is even more offensive. They are imagined to be linked exclusively to an agricultural-export economy and opposed to industrialization. Moreover, the struggle for industrialization is depicted as anti-imperialistic and revolutionary. Despite the fact that in some countries this image may make some sense, for the developing countries it is completely anachronistic. In these countries industrialization and foreign capital join together and progressively become a single reality" (Dos Santos, *Nuevo carácter,* p. 9). Anibal Quijano believes that "the redefinition of the modalities of imperialistic domination in Latin America" provides a general framework within which to understand certain political changes occurring in Latin America (*Carácter y perspectiva del actual régimen militar en el Perú,* mimeo [Santiago de Chile: CESO, 1970]). His framework here is very broad and must be refined by taking into consideration specific national peculiarities.

23. Celso Furtado analyzes the concentration of economic power in large corporations in *La concentración del poder económico en los Estados Unidos y sus reflejos en América Latina* (Buenos Aires: Centro Editor de América Latina, 1969). On multinational corporations see also the study by Harry Magdoff and Paul M. Sweezy, "Notes on the Multinational Corporation," *Monthly Review* 21, no. 5 (October 1969): 1-13 and 21, no. 6 (November 1969): 1-13.

24. For a quick overall view of these authors' thought, see Piero Santi, "II dibattito sull'imperialismo nei classici marxismo," *Crítica Marxista* (Rome), 3rd year, no. 3 (May-June 1965), pp. 84-134; and Charles Pailloux, "La question de l'impérialisme chez V.I. Lenine et Rose Luxemburg," *L'Homme et la Societé,* no. 15 (January-March 1970), pp. 103-108.

25. "La teoría clásica del imperialismo, el subdesarrollo y la acumulación socialista," *Cuadernos de la realidad nacional* (Santiago de Chile), no. 4 (June 1970), pp. 137-60.

26. See the studies published in *Imperialismo y dependencia externa* (Santiago de Chile: CESO, 1968). Franz J. Hinkelammert has an interesting essay on this subject in this work. According to him the classical theory of imperialism presupposes "capitalist society is essentially developmentalist and industrializing." Capitalism, the theory says, if left to itself, would unleash totally new productive forces (p. 138); should this not happen, it would be due to obstacles which a bourgeois revolution is called upon to eliminate. Hinkelammert holds, on the other hand, that even if this was the case in the countries which developed first, in the underdeveloped countries—which are the other side of the coin of their progress—capitalism, under any of its forms, produces only stagnation. The only true solution would be then a socialist accumulation—from the beginning. See also Orlando Caputo and Roberto Pizzarro, *Imperialismo, dependencia y relaciones internacionales,* mimeo (Santiago de Chile: CESO, 1970).

27. Augusto Salazar Bondy, "La cultura de la dominación," in *Perú problema* (Lima: Moncloa, 1968), p. 75. From another ideological context, two Argentine intellectuals, J. Sabato and Natalio Botana, hold, however, that because the scientific technological revolution is in full swing, Latin America still has the potential to participate and "attain technical-scientific capabilities of its own by making science and technology an integral part of the process of development." The authors refer to the combination of these elements as an "innovation" and outline the strategy for accomplishing it ("La ciencia y la técnica en el desarrollo futuro de América Latina," mimeo, position paper presented at the World Order Models Conference, 1968 [Lima: Instituto de Estudios Peruanos, 1970]). See also the comments made by Manuel Sadosky, vice-dean of the School of Science of the University of Buenos Aires, who proposes an "inexpensive science . . . based on national needs . . . at the highest level . . . and allied to an aware and liberating political commitment" ("Construir nuestra ciencia," *Víspera,* no.18 (August 1970), pp. 16-17. See also the recent work of Orlando Fals Bordam, *Ciencia propia y colonialismo intelectual* (Mexico, D.F.: Editorial Nuestro Tiempo, 1970).

28. See in this regard the interesting comments of Pablo Gónzalez Casanova in "La sociología y la crisis de América Latina," *CIDOC,* no. 98 (Cuernavaca, Mexico: CIDOC, 1968), pp. 1-9. The author holds that "the new sociology has to face a moral reality. This fact poses a twofold problem: to use its tools both persuasively and also analytically so that popular movements in Latin America will succeed with the maximum of psychological security and the minimum of mistakes"; to this end "the first objective would be to express discoveries in clear and emphatic language to persuade others of the validity of the conclusions"; second, research "cannot follow the same pattern as in recent years, which was believed to be the scientific ideal; but neither can it be like the previous sociology, which was intuitive and rhetorical" (p. 5).

29. Cardoso,"Desarrollo y dependencia," p. 25. The author postulates, moreover, the need for "a kind of preliminary phenomenology of dependence to describe the relationship among the structures implied in the concepts *dependent* and *dominant*" (p. 24).

30. Regarding the factors which should be considered in a theory of dependence and in particular the tasks it is expected to perform, see Arroyo, "Pensamiento latinoamericano" and "Sousdéveloppement." Besides those mentioned by this author, an important task would be to differentiate in greater detail the position of the countries which were already on the road to economic development around 1930 and those which reached this level twenty or more years later. The differences create social and political circumstances which cannot be encompassed by the same categories.

31. The social sciences, like all forms of scientific knowledge, are evolving on all fronts. In its day, the theory of dependency was an important contribution to understanding the real situation in Latin America; at the present time, however, the theory is widely challenged, even if many elements of it remain valid. The international situation, as well as internal developments in many countries of the region, have changed in important ways. On these matters two critical studies give the state of the question: G. Palma, "Dependency: A Formal Theory of Underdevelopment or a Methodology for the Analysis of Concrete Situations of Underdevelopment?," *World Development,* 6 (1986) 881–924; K. Griffin and J. Gurley, "Radical Analysis of Imperialism, the Third World, and the Transition to Socialism: A Survey Article," *Journal of Economic Literature,* 23 (1985) 1089–1143. See also F. Cardoso (one of the major contributors to the theory of dependency), "A dependência revisitada," in *As ideias e seu lugar*

(Petrópolis: Vozes, 1980), pp. 57-87. A. McGovern, "Latin America and Dependency Theory," *This World* (Washington, D.C.) 14 (Spring-Summer 1986) 104-23, takes into account recent discussions of the subject in the United States.

32. The theory of dependence met a new pitfall a short time ago: the danger of being accepted—nominally at least—by representatives of the prevailing system. It is the old policy of domesticating terms and ideas, weakening them, and causing them to lose their subversive character with regard to the status quo. Nun comments that "it is indeed significant that in the past few years dependence has become a habitual topic for discussion in organizations, conferences, and documents approved by the system. This phenomenon can be explained in several ways. The first is tactical. In the face of such a massive and open penetration, it is advisable to reassure public opinion by acknowledging part of the problem and thus silencing the critics. Meanwhile nothing really effective is done to change the situation. Moreover, as in the case of agrarian reform, the purpose is to do away with certain forms of external domination, proper to the classical stage of the agricultural-export cycle, while at the same time restricting the eventual penetration of the area by other competitive powers" (*Misión Rockefeller,* p. 7). We have here the same subtle defense mechanisms employed by the dominant societies which have turned rebellion and protest into successful consumer items; see in this regard Hélan Jaworski, "The Integrated Structures of Dependence and Domination in the Americas," *Freedom and Unfreedom in the Americas: Toward a Theology of Liberation,* ed. Thomas E. Quigley (New York: IDOC, 1971), pp. 16-27.

33. According to his students' notes, Hegel asserted more than 140 years ago that "America is therefore the land of the future where in years to come world history will be forged *perhaps by the antagonism between North and South America (La raison dans l'histoire* [Paris: Union Générale d'Éditions, 1965], p. 242; the italics are ours).

34. The bibliography on this subject is extensive. We mention only a few works: James Petras and Maurice Zeitlan, ed., *Latin America: Reform or Revolution?* (New York: Fawcett Publications, Inc., 1968); Orlando Fals Borda, *Las revoluciones inconclusas en América Latina, 1809-1968* (Mexico, D.F.: Siglo Veintiuno, 1968); and an interesting analysis of the present situation by Theotonio Dos Santos, "Dependencia ecónomica y alternativas de cambio en América Latina, in *Lucha de clases y dependencia en América Latina* (Bogotá: Oveja Negra, 1970), pp. 239-305. For a critical study of the position of Dos Santos, see Ayton Fausto, "La nueva situación de dependencia y el análisis socio-político de Theotonio Dos Santos," *Revista Latinoamericana de Ciencias Sociales,* no. 1 (June-December 1971), pp. 198-211.

35. It is common knowledge that the relationship of the current Cuban regime with certain Latin American revolutionary groups has become very complex in the last few years.

36. For a bibliography on this subject, see Richard Gott, *Guerrilla Movements in Latin America* (Garden City, New York: Doubleday & Company, Inc., 1971), pp. 555-69. See also the summary presented by the same author in "La guerrilla en América Latina," *Mensaje* 17, no. 174 (November 1968): 557-66; see also the documents reproduced in *Primera Conferencia de la Organización Latinoamericana de Solidaridad* (Montevideo: Nativa Libros, 1967); Regis Debray, *Strategy for Revolution,* ed. Robin Blackburn (New York: Monthly Review Press, 1970); *Regis Debray and the Latin American Revolution,* ed. Leo Huberman and Paul M. Sweezy (New York: Monthly Review Press, 1968); and the studies collected, together with a reply by Debray, in *Debray y la revolución latinoamericana* (Mexico, D.F.: Nuestro Tiempo, 1969). See also two works with different viewpoints: Alberto Methol Ferré, "La Revolución verde

oliva: Debray y la OLAS," *Víspera*, no. 3 (October 1967), pp. 17-39; and Edgar Rodríguez, "La crise du mouvement révolutionnaire latino-américain et l'expérience du Venezuela," *Les Temps Modernes* (Paris), July 1970, pp. 74-99. See also Héctor Béjar, *Perú 1965: Apuntes sobre una experiencia guerrillera* (Lima: Campodónico Ediciones, 1969); and Roque Dalton, *¿Revolución en la revolución? y la crítica de derecha* (Havana, 1969). For an evaluation and explanation of the working hypothesis of the numerous studies on these questions being made in the United States, see Pablo González Casanova, "La violence latinoaméricaine dans les enquétes empiriques nord-américaines," *L'Homme et la Société,* no. 15 (January-March 1970), pp. 159-81.

37. Among recent examples of this reaction especially notorious is the current Brazilian regime. The torture of political prisoners has been denounced internationally. See the facts, eye-witness accounts, and condemnations in *Torturas en Brasil* (Lima: CEP, 1970).

38. *Spirale de la violence* (Paris: Desclée de Brouwer,1970). Dom Helder supports "a liberating moral pressure" to destroy the oppressive and unjust structures which prevail in Latin America. However, there are many who hold that this liberation will sooner or later take some form of counterviolence in response to the legalized violence. For an analysis of certain aspects of revolutionary violence, see the articles published in *Paz e Terra* (Rio de Janeiro), no. 7 (1968); and Francisco León, "La violencia revolucionaria," *Mensaje* 17, no. 175 (December 1968): 621-29.

39. "Aniversario y balance," in *Ideología y política* (Lima: Empresa Editora Amauta, 1969), p. 249.

40. "Mensaje al congreso obrero (1927)," ibid., p. 112.

41. *Defensa del marxismo* (Lima: Empresa Editora Amauta, 1959), p. 36. He also deals with the "canon of Marx." See also p. 63 and p. 105. Mariátegui borrowed this idea from Benedeto Croce for whom "historical materialism, so-called, is not a philosophy of history," but "simply a canon of interpretation" (*Materialismo storico ed economia marxista* [1900] [Bari: Laterza, 1968], pp. 2, xii; English version: *Historical Materialism and the Economics of Karl Marx* [New York: Russell & Russell, 1966]). In another context the current vogue of interpreting Marxism in Latin America according to Althusser has spread the idea of historical materialism as a "science of history" which tries to free itself from all ideological elements. See the studies of two Latin American authors regarding Althusser: Jose A. Giannotti, "Contra Althusser," *Teoría e Prática* (São Paulo), no. 3 (1968), pp. 66-82; and Saul Karsz, "Lectura de Althusser" in *Lectura de Althusser* (Buenos Aires: Galerna, 1970), pp. 13-230. The former is critical, the latter favorable. We hope to present soon a study of certain questions concerning the ambiguities in the use of the term *materialism* and the various interpretations of Marxism as a total conception of life or a science of history. We hope therefore to situate the vision of human nature and atheistic ideology in Marxism.

42. "True revolutionaries," wrote Mariátegui, "never act as if history began with them" (*Peruanicemos al Perú, p.* 117).

43. There still has not appeared a deep, critical, and comprehensive study of Mariátegui. See the work of Francisco Posada, *Los orígenes del pensamiento marxista en Latinoamérica* (Madrid: Editorial Ciencia Nueva, 1968); Augusto Salazar Bondy, "El pensamiento de Mariátegui y la filosofía marxista" in *Historia de las ideas en el Perú contemporáneo* (Lima: Moncloa, 1959), 2:311-42; Manfred Kossok "J.C. Mariátegui y el desarrollo del pensamiento marxista en el Perú," in *Documentos políticos* (Bogotá), no. 37 (1964). Antonio Melis, "Mariátegui: Primo marxista dell'America," *Crítica Marxista* (Rome) 5, no. 2 (March-April 1967): 732-57; Robert Paris, "El pensamiento

de Mariátegui," *Aportes* (July 1970), pp. 6-30; and the recent well-documented study by Yerko Moretic, *José Carlos Mariátegui* (Santiago de Chile: Universidad Técnica del Estado, 1970).

44. In these matters it is essential to maintain the critical attitude mentioned in the text. The criticism is motivated not by an aseptic view of history but by a desire for commitment that is effective. In recent years the debate on "real socialism" has brought a more penetrating study of the historical expressions of socialism to which I refer in the text. The question is important in the area of political options and necessary for an analysis of the socialist way. See R. Bahro, *La Alternativa. Contribución a la crítica del socialismo realmente existente* (Madrid: Alianza Editorial, 1980).

45. Fidel Castro has repeatedly called for support for this posture. In January 1968 he said, "Our country will deepen its revolutionary ideas and will carry its banners forward as far as it can; our country will maintain its distinctive character, a product of its experience and history; ideologically, its criterion is absolute independence, its own course, determined by our people and our experience"; and some months later, "We do not pretend to be the most perfect revolutionaries, . . . but we do have our own way of interpreting socialism, Marxist-Leninism, and communism" (quoted by Aldo Büntig, "La Iglesia en Cuba, Hacia una nueva frontera," *Revista del CIAS* [Buenos Aires], no. 193 [June 1970], p. 24).

46. See above Chapter 2.

47. "Man and Socialism in Cuba," in *Venceremos! The Speeches and Writings of Ernesto Che Guevara,* ed. John Gerassi (New York: The Macmillan Company, 1968), p. 396. "Let me say, with the risk of appearing ridiculous, that the true revolutionary is guided by strong feelings of love. It is impossible to think of an authentic revolutionary without this quality. . . . In these conditions the revolutionary leaders must have a large dose of humanity, a large dose of a sense of justice and truth, to avoid falling into dogmatic extremes, into cold scholasticism, into isolation from the masses. They must struggle every day so that their love of living humanity is transformed into concrete deeds, into acts that will serve as an example, as a mobilizing factor" (ibid., p. 398). See also the writings of the young Bolivian Néstor Paz: "I believe that the fight for liberation is rooted in the prophetic line of Salvation-History. . . . The oft-betrayed whip of justice will fall on the exploiter, that false Christian who forgets that the force of his love ought to drive him to liberate his neighbor from sin, that is to say, from every lack of love. We believe in a 'new man,' made free by the blood and resurrection of Jesus. We believe in a New Earth, where love will be the fundamental law. This will only come about, however, by breaking the old patterns based on egoism" ("Revolutionary Proclamation of Nestor Paz on Leaving to Join the Guerrilla Band of Teoponte" in "Nestor Paz: Mystic, Christian, Guerrilla," *IDOC-NA,* no. 23 (April 10, 1971), p. 45.

48. See Paulo Freire, *Pedagogy for the Oppressed* (New York: Herder and Herder, 1970).

49. See Paulo Freire, *La educación como práctica de la libertad* (Montevideo: Tierra Nueva, 1969), and the articles which appeared in *Contribución al proceso de concientización en América Latina,* a special supplement of *Cristianismo y Sociedad* (Montevideo: Junta Latinoamericana de Iglegia y Sociedad, 1968). See also Luis Alberto Gomes de Souza, "Problemática de la educación en América Latina," *Educación Latinoamericana* (Bogotá), no. 2 (October 1967), pp. 54-64; the contributions of Hiber Conteris, Julio Barreiro, Julio de Santa Ana, Ricardo Cetrulo, and Vincent Gilbert in the anthology *Conciencia y Revolución,* (Montevideo: Tierra Nueva, 1969); and Ernani

Fiori, "Education and Conscientization," *Conscientization for Liberation,* ed. Louis M. Colonnese (Washington, D.C.: Division for Latin America-USCC, 1971), pp. 123-44.

50. See the comments by Noel Olaya and Germán Zabala, "En la ruta de Golconda," *Víspera,* nos. 13-14 (November-December 1969), pp. 36-39.

## 7. THE CHURCH IN THE PROCESS OF LIBERATION

1. Ivan Vallier accurately points to the beginnings of this separation in "Religious Elites: Differentiations and Developments in Roman Catholicism," in *Elites in Latin America,* Seymour Martin Lipset and Aldo Solari, eds. (New York: Oxford University Press, 1967), pp. 190-232. I have some reservations about the typology he proposes, however.

2. Among the most recent projects, see for the Church in Argentina the excellent analysis by Luis Gera and Guillermo Rodríguez, "Apuntes para una interpretación de la Iglesia Argentina" in *Víspera,* no. 15 (February 1970), pp. 59-88. Regarding certain aspects of the Peruvian Church, see the study by Carlos Alberto Astiz, "The Catholic Church in Politics: the Peruvian Case" (position paper presented at the Eighth World Congress of the International Political Science Association, Munich, August 31-September 5, 1970). The Cuban Church is now living through a totally new experience, which can provide many lessons for all of Latin America. See on this point, Aldo Büntig, "Iglesia en Cuba," who traces the evolution of the posture of the Church toward the present Cuban regime and examines the situation. Regarding recent developments in the Brazilian Church, see the account by Henri Fresquet, "L'Église catholique au Brésil" in *Le Monde* (Paris), September 8-10, 1970. Regarding the Bolivian Church see the interesting report by Lorenzo Pérez, "Bolivia: la Iglesia y la política," *Spes,* no. 11 (October 1970), pp. 1-9. See also Jordan Bishop, "Christianisme et révolution en Amérique Latine," *Ésprit* 39, no. 1 (January 1971): 16-30; in English see Bishop's "The Church in Latin America," in *Shaping a New World: An Orientation to Latin America,* ed. Edward L. Cleary, O.P. (Maryknoll, New York: Orbis Books, 1971). Regarding other aspects of the life of the Latin American Church, see René Laurentin, *L'Amérique latine à l'heure de l'enfantement* (Paris: Editions du Seuil, 1969); Hector Borrat, "Le heurt de l'Église et des pouvoirs publics en Amérique Latine," *Terre Entière,* nos. 42-43 (July-October 1970), pp. 35-67. For another point of view, it might be interesting to see also the report commissioned by the U.S. State Department: Luigi Einaudi, Richard Maullin, Alfred Sepan, and Michael Fleet, *Latin American Institutional Development: The Changing Catholic Church* (Santa Monica, California: The Rand Corporation, 1969).

3. The Chilean instance was perhaps the most typical and also the most lasting. See G. Wayland-Smith, *The Christian Democratic Party in Chile,* Cuernavaca, Mexico, CI-DOC, Sondeo no. 39.

4. This period began around 1960-62 among university movements of various South American countries; see, for example, the change from the "historical ideal," reminiscent of Maritain (see JUC, *Boletim Nacional,* no. 4, 1960, Rio de Janeiro) to "historical awareness," obviously influenced by Henrique de Lima Vaz (see Equipo Nacional, "Reflexões sôbre o sentido do movimento" in JUC, *Boletim Nacional,* no. 1, 1963). See also Gustavo Gutiérrez, *Misión de la Iglesia y apostolado universitario,* pamphlet (Lima: UNEC, 1960); and Patricio Rodó, *Promoción del laicado,* pamphlet (Montevideo, 1963).

5. See for example the role of lay apostolic movements in the Brazilian revolutionary Left. In this regard see Candido Mendes, *Memento dos vivos* (Rio de Janeiro: Tempo Brasileiro, 1966), and Marcio Moeira Alves, *O Cristo do povo* (Rio de Janeiro: Ed. Sabía, 1968).

6. Literature on this problem is abundant but not easily accessible. See, however, a good panoramic view of university apostolic movements in Gilberto Giménez, *Introducción a una pedagogía de la pastoral universitaria*, MIEC-JECI, Servicio de Documentación (Montevideo), series 1, doc. 19, 1968. See also the report presented to Pope Paul VI by the Department of University Pastoral Planning of CELAM: "La realidad universitaria y sus implicaciones pastorales" in *Educación Latinoamericana* (Bogotá), October 1968. The problem is particularly acute in the Brazilian Church; see in this regard Michael Schooyans, *O desafío de secularização* (São Paulo: Ed. Herder, 1968).

7. Roqueplo has considered this problem well although in a slightly different context (*Expérience du monde*, pp. 41-44). "One of the reasons," he writes, "why I am writing this book is the experience of these crises and the lack of reflection there has been on them" (p. 42, n. 19). See also Alfonso Alvarez Bolado's excellent observations, within the framework of the Spanish situation, in "Compromiso terrestre y crisis de fe" in *Vida cristiana y compromiso terrestre* (Bilbao: Editorial Mensajero, 1970), pp. 151-218. This was partially published in *Víspera*, no. 22 (April 1971), pp. 9-17.

8. In this connection, Enrique López Oliva has published *Los católicos y la revolución latinoamericana* (Havana: Instituto del Libro, 1969). Its publication in Montevideo has been announced; see *Pensamiento Crítico* (Havana), no. 31 [August 1969], p. 190). Regarding collaboration and dialogue with Marxist groups, see Arturo Gaete, "El largo camino del diálogo cristiano-marxista," *Mensaje* 17, no. 169 (June 1968): 209-19; see also by the same author, "Socialismo y comunismo: historia de una problemática condenación," *Mensaje* 20, no. 200 (July 1971): 290-302.

9. Regarding attitudes in Christian circles, see Aguiar, "Currents and Tendencies."

10. Fidel Castro's statement regarding Camilo Torres is interesting in this regard: "Camilo Torres is the case of a priest who went to die for those struggling to liberate their people. This is why he has become a symbol of the revolutionary unity of the people of Latin America" (Speech delivered January 4, 1969, quoted in Büntig, "Iglesia en Cuba," p. 40).

11. In Evangelical churches, just as in some sectors of the Catholic Church, ties with the current unjust order are being rejected: "Our churches are not only an integral part of these structures which perpetuate the oppression, but they even reinforce this state of human alienation by claiming to operate by 'divine right,' if we may use this expression" (Christian Lalive D'Épinay, "La Iglesia evangélica y la revolución latinoamericana," in *CIDOC*, no. 78, 1968, p. 6). See also Waldo A. Cesar, Richard Shaull, Orlando Fals Borda, Beatriz Muniz de Souza, *Protestantismo e imperialismo na América Latina* (Petrópolis, Brazil: Vozes, 1968). ISAL (Iglesia y Sociedad para América Latina) is an important experiment in cooperation among Christians of different denominations who have made a clear option for liberation. See the statements made by Julio de Santa Ana, "ISAL: un movimiento anti-imperialista y antioligárquico," in *NADOC*, no. 95, October 15, 1969. See also the lucid analysis of Rubem Alves, "El protestantismo como una forma de colonialismo," *Perspectivas para el Diálogo*, no. 38 (November 1968), pp. 242-48.

12. This new emphasis is just beginning to be treated in writing. See for example, at the level of peasant movements, Silvio Sant'Anna's *Una experiencia de concientización: Con MIJARC en el Cono Sur*, MIEC-JECI series 2, doc. 7, 1969. Regarding labor, see

the conclusions of the Latin American Meeting of Coordinating Teams of JOC, held in Lima in 1970. The experiences and reflections of Buenaventura Pelegrí deal with university movements: *Introducción a la metodología de los movimientos apostólicos universitários*, MIEC-JECI, series 1, doc. 17-18, 1969, and *Pedagogía de la explicitación de la fe*, MIEC-JECI, series 1, doc. 20-21, 1970.

13. The symposia on the theology of liberation provide an interesting example. See Gustavo Pérez Ramírez, "Palabras introductorias" in *Aportes para la liberación* (Bogotá: Editorial Presencia, 1970), pp. 1-4; in English see "Theology of Liberation: Bogotá, 1970" in *IDOC-NA*, no. 14 (November 28, 1970), pp. 66-78.

14. For a good synoptic view see Michel de Certeau, "Problèmes actuels du sacerdoce en Amérique Latine," *Recherches de Sciences Religieuses* 56, no. 4 (October-December 1968): 591-601; also J. Comblin, "Problémes sacerdotaux d'Amérique Latine," *La Vie Spirituelle* 118, no. 547 (March 1968): 319-43. Regarding Brazilian problems, see the results of a recent study by José Marins, "Pesquisa sobre o clero do Brasil," in *Revista Eclesiástica Brasileira* 29, no. 1 (March 1969): 121-38. As regards religious, one ought to mention the active and interesting work carried on by the Latin American Conference for Religious (CLAR), as a result of its commitment to the process of liberation.

15. "Sacerdotes para el Tercer Mundo" (Argentina) and "Movimiento Sacerdotal ONIS (Oficina Nacional de Investigación Social; Peru) are at this point perhaps the most active and best organized. Until recently, although it moves within a different perspective, the "Golconda" group (Colombia) also qualified; this group has had a deep impact. Similar groups exist in Ecuador (Comisión Nacional de Presbíteros), Chile ("Los Ochenta"), Guatemala (Confederación de Sacerdotes de Guatemala [CODES-GUA]), and Mexico (Movimiento de Sacerdotes para el Pueblo). The "Declaración de la comisión permanente del episcopado argentino" is very critical of some of the theses of the "Sacerdotes para el Tercer Mundo" movement (see *NADOC*, no. 164, September 1970); see also in this regard the letter addressed by Bishop Jerónimo Podestá to the Argentinian Episcopal Conference (*NADOC*, no. 183, January 1971) and especially the extensive and well-documented reply of the Priests for the Third World: *Nuestra reflexión: Carta a los obispos argentinos* (Buenos Aires, 1970); for selected texts in English in this connection see "Argentina: Priests for the Third World," *IDOC-NA*, no. 15 (December 12, 1970), pp. 58-96. Concerning these groups, see also the short study of Gonzalo Arroyo, "Católicos de izquierda en América Latina, *Mensaje* 19, no. 191 (August 1970): 369-72.

16. These clashes have taken place in almost all Latin American countries, the most serious being perhaps in Brazil, Argentina, and Guatemala. In this regard see the documents reproduced by SEDOC (Petrópolis, Brazil), CIDOC (Cuernavaca, Mexico), and NADOC (Lima, Peru).

17. The instance of Camilo Torres is well known. See his collected works in *Camilo Torres por el P. Camilo Torres, 1956-1965* (Cuernavaca, Mexico: CIDOC, 1966); English version: *Camilo Torres, Revolutionary Writings* (New York: Herder and Herder, 1969); in English see also *Revolutionary Priest: The Complete Writings & Messages of Camilo Torres*, ed. John Gerassi (New York: Vintage Books, 1971); see also *Camilo Torres: liberación o muerte* (Havana: Instituto del Libro, 1967); and the most complete edition, *Camilo Torres, cristianismo y revolución* (Mexico, D.F.: Era, 1970). See also Germán Guzmán, *Camilo Torres*, trans. John D. Ring (New York: Sheed and Ward, 1969). This is a well-documented work, but some of its opinions are debatable; see the comments of Oscar Maldonado, "El Camilo Torres de Germán Guzmán," *CIDOC*, no. 48, 1967. See also José María González Ruiz, "Camilo Torres o el buen

samaritano," *Perspectivas para el Diálogo*, no. 25 (July 1968), pp. 139-41; see also an essay which situates Camilo Torres in Colombian political history: Orlando Fals Borda, *Subversion and Social Change in Colombia*, trans. Jacqueline D. Skiles (New York: Columbia University Press, 1969), pp. 160-69. See also Horacio Bogorje and others, *Retrato de Camilo Torres* (Mexico, D.F.: Grijalbo, 1969). On some of the repercussions of Camilo Torres, see Enrique López Oliva, *El camilismo en la América Latina* (Havana: Casa de las Américas, 1970); according to this author the impact of Torres demonstrates that the "Latin American revolutionary front" is gaining ground (p. 11). Torres is not at all a unique case. Political commitment is found in differing degrees among many priests in Latin America.

18. After recognizing certain similarities between the movements, Jorge Vernazza, in the name of the Permanent Secretariat of the "Sacerdotes para el Tercer Mundo" movement wrote as follows to a representative of the "Echanges et Dialogue" movement in France: "However, we believe that our focus is fundamentally different. Our main objective is not 'to put an end to our status as clergy': but rather to commit ourselves as priests to the Latin American revolutionary process. Undoubtedly our social and ecclesiastical conditioning is very different: Latin America demands above all a salvation which is verified in liberation from widespread injustice and oppression. It is the Church that must proclaim and support this liberation, and the Church is in the eyes of the people permanently linked to the image and function of the priest. It is for this reason that—although our actions and words may cause, in fact have already caused, opposition and suspicion on the part of much of the "official" Church—we are concerned that we do not appear to be separate from it. We do not want to detract from the efficacy of our action and we believe that the Church has a great conscienticizing impact upon the people. . . . It seems to us that for many sociological and historical reasons we Latin Americans regard the 'clerical status' differently from you. Perhaps less formality and efficiency and also more relaxed and 'democratic' social relationships in our ecclesiastical government have led us to feel less oppressed by it. . . . Therefore, we believe that our very commitments to humanity and the revolutionary process impel us to continue as clerics" (letter dated December 10, 1969, which appeared in *Enlace*, the bulletin of the Priests for the Third World movement [Buenos Aires], no. 10 [1970], pp. 22-23).

And in an open letter to the Dutch clergy regarding the problem of celibacy, the same group of Argentinian priests says: "Celibate or married, the important thing is that you make present in today's world the salvation of Jesus Christ. But this salvation in 1970 demands an end of the 'imperialism of money. . . . ' You, priests of Holland, you are witnesses of Jesus Christ and his salvation in a rich, imperialistic, and exploitive country. Allow us to address this call to you: While you were celibate you did not know how or were not able to be the voice of the exploited countries, those suffering the consequences of the unjust economic policy of the leaders of your countries. We hope that once you are married you can do this better. Indeed, if marriage does not help you to be more open to the world in general and especially to those who are being exploited by the 'laws' of international trade, you will have accomplished nothing more than becoming more bourgeois. Remember that while you seek the right to establish a home, many poor persons in the Third World are renouncing theirs to give themselves completely to the liberation of their brother" (in *Liberación* [Mexico, D.F.], March 1970).

19. A recent example of this is Henrique Pereira, a priest in Recife, Brazil. See the documentation reproduced in *SEDOC*, August 1969, pp. 143-49; also, "Ante el asesinato del P. Henrique Pereira," *Spes*, no. 1, September 1969. See also in this connection

the thoughts of Buenaventura Pelegrí, "Meditación ante el cadáver del Padre Henrique," *Víspera*, no. 12 (September 1969), pp. 3-7.

20. In this regard, after affirming that "Marxism needs to develop, to become less rigid, to interpret today's realities objectively and scientifically, to behave as a revolutionary force and not as a pseudo-revolutionary Church," Fidel Castro adds, "these are the paradoxes of history. When we see that sectors of the clergy are becoming revolutionary forces, how can we resign ourselves to sectors of Marxists becoming ecclesiastical forces?" (speech delivered at the concluding session of the Congress of Intellectuals, January 12, 1968, quoted in Fidel Castro, *Révolution Cubaine* [Paris: Maspero, 1969], 2:253).

21. See for example the writings of Dom Helder Câmara published in several volumes in *Pronunciamientos de Dom Helder*, Nordeste II, Secretariado Regional, CNBB, Recife, Brazil; *Revolution Through Peace*, ed. Ruth N. Anshen, trans. Amparo McLean (New York: Harper and Row, 1971); see also his *Church and Colonialism: The Betrayal of the Third World*, trans. William McSweeney (Denville, New Jersey: Dimension Books, 1969), and José de Broucker, *Dom Helder Camara: The Violence of a Peacemaker*, trans. Herma Briffault (Maryknoll, New York: Orbis Books, 1970); see also A. B. Fragoso, *Évangile et révolution sociale* (Paris: Les Éditions du Cerf, 1969).

22. See the outspoken analysis of the situation in Brazil presented by Dom Cándido Padim as a working paper for the Ninth General Assembly of the National Conference of Brazilian Bishops in 1968, "La doctrina de la seguridad nacional a la luz de la doctrina de la Iglesia" in Roberto Magni and Lirio Zanotti, *America Latina: La Chiesa si contesta* (Rome: Editori Riuniti, 1969), pp. 240-67. For an overview and the recent position of the Brazilian bishops in their difficult situation see Charles Antoine, "L'épiscopat brésilien face au pouvoir (1962-1969)," in *Études* 333 (July 1970): 84-103. The author ends his study asserting that "the year 1969 ends with the official position of the Brazilian bishops being considerably weaker. Undoubtedly their assertions are clearly stated, perhaps even aggressively so, but their impact is greatly reduced by the context." See also Charles Antoine, *L'Église et le pouvoir au Brésil: Naissance du militarisme* (Paris: Desclée de Brouwer, 1971), English translation, *Church and Power in Brazil* (Maryknoll, N.Y.: Orbis, 1973).

23. A well-known instance is the excommunication of three high officials of the Paraguayan government (a minister and two police chiefs) by the bishops of Paraguay. Excommunication is an unusual procedure today. But it is even more unusual that it should be used against persons in power who claim to defend "Western and Christian" civilization (see "Los sucesos de octubre en Asunción," *Spes*, no. 3 [November, 1969], pp. 6-9; and *Paraguay: conflicto Iglesia-estado, Informe especial*, mimeo [Montevideo: Centro de Documentación MIEC-JECI, 1969]).

24. Norman Gall recounts some of these instances in "La reforma católica," in *Mundo Nuevo*, June 1970, pp. 20-43; see also Norman Gall, "Latin America: The Church Militant," *Commentary*, April 1970, pp. 25-37.

25. Many of these texts have been published in *Between Honesty and Hope: Documents from and about the Church in Latin America, Issued at Lima by the Peruvian Bishops' Commission for Social Action*, trans. John Drury (Maryknoll, New York: Maryknoll Publications, 1970). See also the documents published in *Medellín, La Iglesia nueva* (Montevideo: Cuadernos de Marcha, 1968); and a more recent publication, *Iglesia latinoamericana, ¿ protesta o profecía?* (Avellaneda, Argentina: Ediciones Búsqueda, 1969); and also *Los católicos postconciliares en la Argentina* (Buenos Aires: Galerna, 1970). We will cite the texts only of the last three years.

26. "Closing Statement of the Thirty-sixth Peruvian Episcopal Conference," 1969, in *Between Honesty and Hope*, p. 230. The same idea is found in "Message to the People of Latin America," *The Church in the Present-Day Transformation of Latin America in the Light of the Council*, Documents of the Second General Conference of Latin American Bishops, Medellín, Colombia, August-September 1968, vol. 2, *Conclusions* (Bogotá: General Secretariat of CELAM, 1970), p. 39; hereafter this work is cited as *Medellín*; and also Dom Helder Câmara's speech at the tenth convention of CELAM, 1966, in *Between Honesty and Hope*, pp. 30-31. See also "Los cristianos y el poder," a statement of lay persons and priests from Sante Fe, Argentina, 1968, in *Iglesia latinoamericana*, pp. 121-22; "Carta de sacerdotes tucumanos al arzobispo de Buenos Aires," 1969, ibid., p. 137; "La Iglesia en el proceso de transformaciôn," a statement from a meeting of lay persons, priests, religious, and bishops in Cochabamba, Bolivia, 1968, ibid., p. 154; *Carta pastoral del episcopado mexicano sobre el desarrollo e integración del país*, Mexico, D.F., 1968, pp. 9, 12.

27. Conclusions of the first week of joint pastoral planning in El Salvador, June 1970, in *NADOC*, no. 174, p. 2. "The first thing that the Church must do is confess publicly its sin" (General Statement of the "Encuentro sobre el hombre nuevo," of the Cuban Christian Student Movement in *Spes*, no. 4 [December 1969], p. 3).

28. "Peace," no. 16, in *Medellín*. We must emphasize that this is not merely a phrase mentioned in passing; the whole document is constructed around this focus. See also "A Letter to the Peoples of the Third World," a message signed by eighteen Third World bishops in *Between Honesty and Hope*, pp. 10-11. In the "Declaración del II seminario de sacerdotes latinoamericanos," organized by ILADES in 1970, there is a denunciation of the fact that injustice "has put law and order at its service" (*NADOC*, no. 122, p. 3). "Let us recall the great amount of violence that this situation entails for those who suffer under it, especially if we consider that while their rights are theoretically recognized, in practice they are denied within the present economic and social order" ("Carta pastoral de Adviento de Monseñor Parteli y su presbitério," Montevideo, 1967, p. 11). For a commentary on the Medellín text concerning institutionalized violence, see Gonzalo Arroyo, "Violencia institucionalizada en América Latina," *Mensaje* 17, no. 175 (December 1968): 534-44. See also Pierre Bigo, "Ensenanza de la Iglesia sobre la violencia," *Mensaje* 17, no. 174 (November 1968): 574-78.

29. In "Carta al Presidente del Brasil," 1965, the bishop of San Andrés and his clergy denounce, among other things, the fact that unemployment "threatens with death, with slaughter, thousands of workers" (*Iglesia latinoamericana*, p. 174). See especially "Latin America: A Continent of Violence," a document signed by more than 900 Latin American priests, 1968, in *Between Honesty and Hope*, pp. 81-84. The same idea is expressed by an episcopate which is considered moderate, *Carta del episcopado mexicano*, pp. 10-21.

30. "Peace," no. 16, in *Medellín*.

31. "Continent of Violence," in *Between Honesty and Hope*, p. 84.

32. "Peace," no. 14, in *Medellín*; see also no. 1, "Justice," no. 2, and Dom Helder Câmara, in *Between Honesty and Hope*, p. 32; "Opresión social y silencio de los cristianos," a statement of priests of San Juan, Argentina, 1969, in *Iglesia latinoamericana*, p. 141.

33. "Brazilian Realities and the Church," a statement of 300 Brazilian priests, 1967, in *Between Honesty and Hope*, p. 138. See also "Carta de 120 sacerdotes de Bolivia a su conferencia episcopal," 1970, in *NADOC*, no. 148, p. 2. Concerning the rejection of God implied in injustice, see *Nordeste, Desenvolvimento sem justica* (Recife, Brazil:

Ação católica operária, Secretariado Regional do Nordeste, 1967), especially p. 78.

34. "Peace," nos. 2-10, in *Medellín*.

35. "Presence of the Church in Latin American Development," a document drawn up by presiding officers of various episcopal commissions for social action at Itapoán, Brazil, in May 1968, in *Between Honesty and Hope*, p. 21. See also *Populorum progressio* and Latin American Realities," a communiqué issued by participants in the first seminar for priests sponsored by the Social Department of CELAM in Chile, 1967, and signed by 38 priests, ibid., p. 71; "A Lay Critique of the Medellín Draft," a statement of leaders of various Latin American lay organizations, 1968, in *Between Honesty and Hope*, p. 194; "Underdevelopment in Colombia," a document issued by the priests who met at Golconda, Colombia, in 1968, in *Between Honesty and Hope*, pp. 85-86; "Los cristianos y el imperialismo," a statement of Bolivian Protestants and Catholics, 1969, in *Iglesia latinoamericana*, p. 167; "II Seminario de ILADES," pp. 2-3; "Conclusiones de la Comisión Ecuatoriana de Justicia y Paz," December 1970, in *NADOC*, no. 191.

36. "Orientaciones del Encuentro Regional Andino de Justicia y Paz" (Peru), 1970, in *NADOC*, no. 147, p. 2. (The whole document is of interest.) The political situation in Cuba is very different from that of the other Latin American countries. It is of interest to note what the Cuban bishops say in this area after several years of silence. Regarding difficulties for development, they assert, "There are internal difficulties stemming from the newness of the problems and technical complexity as well as from the deficiencies and sins of men. No less serious, however, are the external difficulties, which are connected to the complicated contemporary structures of relationships among nations. These structures are unjustly disadvantageous to the weak, small, and underdeveloped countries. Is this not the case of the economic blockade to which our country has been subjected, a blockade whose automatic prolongation has caused severe hardships to our country?" (communiqué of the Cuban Episcopal Conference, April 10, 1969, in *SEDOC*, September 1969, p. 350).

37. *Juventud y cristianismo en América Latina*, document of the Department of Education of CELAM (Bogotá: Indo American Press Service, 1969), p. 23.

38. *Presencia activa de la Iglesia en el desarrollo y la integración de América Latina*, Conclusions of the Episcopal Conference of CELAM, Mar de Plata, 1966, Documentos CELAM, no. 1 (Bogotá: CELAM, 1967).

39. This substitution has been very well treated by Hector Borrat in "El gran impulso," *Víspera*, no. 7 (October 1968), p. 9.

40. "Letter to Peoples of the Third World," in *Between Honesty and Hope*, p. 3.

41. "Carta de 120 sacerdotes de Bolivia a su Conferencia Episcopal," 1970, in *NADOC*, no. 148, p. 2. "For some time now, however, a new element has been taking shape in this panorama of poverty and injustice. It is the rapid and growing self-awareness of the exploited peoples, who see a real possibility for their own liberation. For many this liberation is impossible without a fundamental change in the socioeconomic structures of our continent. More than a few feel that the time is already past for accomplishing this by purely nonviolent means" ("Continent of Violence," in *Between Honesty and Hope*, p. 83).

42. "Education," no. 8, in *Medellín*.

43. "Justice," no. 3, in *Medellín*. The notion of liberation is found frequently in other documents from Medellín as well ("Message of the People of Latin America," "Introduction to the Final Documents," "Pastoral concern for the Elites," "Poverty of the Church," etc.). See also "Statement of Peruvian Episcopal Conference," in *Between*

*Honesty and Hope*, pp. 228-34; "*Populorum progressio* and Latin American Realities," ibid., pp. 70-73; "Underdevelopment in Colombia," ibid., pp. 85-92; and the ONIS statement of October 4, 1969, in *IDOC-NA*, no. 4 (May 23, 1970), pp. 37-41 (the original Spanish version is "Conclusiones del II Encuentro Nacional de ONIS" in *Movimiento Sacerdotal ONIS, Declaraciones* [Lima: Centro de Estudios y Publicaciones, 1970]). This idea is a constant theme in the documents of ONIS.

44. Cardinal Landázuri Ricketts, "Closing Address at Medellín Episcopal Conference," in *Between Honesty and Hope*, p. 223.

45. Cardinal Landázuri Ricketts, "Servants to Society," baccalaureate address at the University of Notre Dame, 1966, in *Between Honesty and Hope*, p. 60.

46. "Cristianos y poder," in *Iglesia latinoamericana*, p. 120; see also "The Socioeconomic Structures of Peru," a declaration by a group of priests in Peru, 1968, in *Between Honesty and Hope*, p. 79.

47. "Encuentro Regional Andino," p. 5.

48. "El presente de la transformación nacional," in *ONIS Declaraciones*, p. 42. See this entire document as well as the ONIS statement of January 22, 1970, in *IDOC-NA*, no. 4, pp. 41-43. (Original version: "Declaración ante problemas laborales," in *ONIS Declaraciones*, p. 36). Regarding the rejection of capitalism, see also "Carta pastoral de Adviento," pp. 7-8.

49. ONIS statement in *IDOC-NA*, no. 4, p. 43. See also "Evangelio y explotación," a statement of priests and lay persons of Chaco, Argentina, 1968, in *Iglesia latinoamericana*, p. 126; "Hacia una sociedad mas justa," a statement of lay persons and priests of Corrientes, Argentina, 1968, ibid., p. 116; "ISAL en Bolivia, Pronunciamiento ante las guerrillas de Teoponte," 1970, in *NADOC*, no. 157, pp. 6-7. See also "Manifesto of the Executive Committee, ISAL, Bolivia," in *IDOC-NA*, no. 17 (January 16, 1971), pp. 27-32.

50. "If the economic and social policies followed in the last fifteen years have not allowed for the resolution of the problem of poverty in Latin America, this is because of the very conception of development which has inspired them. The objective has been for each of the countries of this continent to pass from a kind of preindustrial society to a kind of modern capitalist society. But this limits the problem simply to its technical aspects. The human dimension is disregarded; the deep sources of injustice remain intact" (P. Muñoz Vega, archbishop of Quito, "Hora del cambio de estructuras y justicia social," September 1970, in *NADOC*, no. 171, p. 5). See also "II Seminario de ILADES," p. 5.

51. "Against a Reconstruction of Injustice," statement of ONIS in *IDOC-NA*, no. 16 (December 26, 1970), p. 93 (originally appearing in *Expreso* [Lima], July 27, 1970, p. 8). The document refers to the tenacity of domination and its recourse to modernization to preserve itself.

52. Landázuri Ricketts, in *Between Honesty and Hope*, p. 61; "Letter to Peoples of the Third World," ibid., p. 4; "Socioeconomic Structures of Peru," ibid., p. 78; "The Church in Bolivia," letter of eighty Bolivian priests to their bishops, in *Between Honesty and Hope*, p. 141. "Clearly this situation cannot be overcome without real revolution, one that will displace the present ruling classes in our country through whom foreign domination is exercised" ("Underdevelopment in Colombia," in *Between Honesty and Hope*, p. 86; see also the ONIS statement in *IDOC-NA*, no. 4, pp. 37-41).

53. "It is easy to hurl the charge of communism at all those who, lacking any ties with the party or the ideology, dare to point out the materialistic roots of capitalism; at all those who dare to point out that, strictly speaking, we do not yet have one uniform

socialism or capitalism, but a variety of socialisms and capitalisms" (Helder Câmara, in *Between Honesty and Hope*, p. 35). "In certain circles there arises the fear, the suspicion, or the accusation of 'communism.' It seems to us that this is no time for the luxury of fearing communism in Peru. Indeed, when social consciousness, or authentic national consciousness, is the patrimony of only a few, and when economic inequality, cultural disintegration, and exploitation affect the great majority, it is naive or immoral to accuse of communism certain efforts, certain achievements, or certain concurrences" ("El presente de la transformación nacional," in *ONIS Declaraciones*, p. 42; see this entire document).

54. "Underdevelopment in Colombia," in *Between Honesty and Hope*, p. 90.

55. "Coincidencias básicas," in *Sacerdotes para el Tercer Mundo* (Buenos Aires: Ed. del Movimiento, 1970), p. 69. This is also the option of ISAL in Bolivia; see *NADOC*, no. 147, pp. 5-8; and "Presentación de ISAL al ampliado de la COB," mimeo, May 1970, p. 1. "A new man and a new society will not be reached by capitalistic paths because the moving force of every type of a capitalism is private profit and private ownership for profit. The oppressed will not be liberated by becoming capitalist. A new man and a new society will not be possible unless labor comes to be understood as the only effective human principle, when the fundamental stimulus of the economic activity of man is social interest, when capital is subordinated to the work, and the means of production come under social ownership" ("Private Property and the New Society,") a statement of ONIS in *IDOC-NA*, no. 16 (December, 26, 1970), p. 96. See also "Letter to Peoples of the Third World," in *Between Honesty and Hope*, pp. 6-7. "The truly new persons are they who feel themselves called to the daily activity of creating a better present and future, who struggle for the elimination of poverty, injustice, discrimination, exploitation, and every act of oppression constituted by the elements characteristic of capitalist society" (statement of the Cuban MEC in *Spes*).

56. "Proyección y transformación de la Iglesia en Latinoamérica," an address delivered July 17, 1970, in "Confrontación de dos obispos mexicanos," *CIP Documenta* (Cuernavaca, Mexico), no. 7 (September 1970), p. 4. This same issue includes the reaction of the Archbishop of Puebla and the controversy caused by the address of the Bishop of Cuernavaca. See also the statements of Bishop Gerardo Valencia to CENOS (Mexico, D.F.), February 10, 1970: "With my companions of Golconda I definitively proclaim myself to be a revolutionary and a socialist, because we cannot remain indifferent before the capitalist structure which is leading the people of Colombia and Latin America into injustice and the greatest of frustrations."

57. In this regard see the position—which is qualified, but which opens the possibility of an interesting dialogue—of Jorge Manrique, Archbishop of La Paz, in "El socialismo y la Iglesia en Bolivia," a pastoral exhortation of October 1970, in *NADOC*, no. 175 (English text in *IDOC-NA*, no. 16 [December 26, 1970], pp. 54-64). In the conclusions of their third national meeting, ISAL-Bolivia clarifies what it understands by socialism and concludes, "There are not, therefore, any third paths to socialism which are not of the socialist government of the people" (February 23, 1971). It is well known that Paul VI initiated a new attitude of openness orientated toward a better understanding of socialism. He distinguishes among "the various levels of expression of socialism: a generous aspiration and a seeking for a more just society, historical movements with a political organization and aim, and an ideology which claims to give a complete and self-sufficient picture of the human being" (*Octogesima adveniens*, no. 31).

58. See, for example, "Letter to Peoples of the Third World," in *Between Honesty*

*and Hope*, pp. 6-7. The Archbishop of La Paz advocates a new Christian ethic which ought to "recognize that work is more important than property in the use of material goods. . . . Thus every system of property ought to be evaluated according to its ability to humanize life and the labor of workers." ("Enfoque de la nueva etica cristiana," pastoral letter, in *CIDOC*, no. 224, 1970, p. 4).

59. "Private Property," statement of ONIS, *IDOC-NA*, no. 16, pp. 94-95. See also the ONIS statement "La Iglesia ante la reforma agraria," in *Iglesia latinoamericana*, pp. 335-36; "Coincidencias," in *Sacerdotes para el Tercer Mundo*, p. 70. All this recasts the interpretation of the so-called social doctrine of the Church. See *Carta del episcopado mexicano*, p. 21. Regarding the meaning that that social doctrine might have today, see Manaranche, *Y a-t-il une éthique social-chrétienne?* and Luis Velaochaga, "La doctrina social de la Iglesia," in *Expreso* (Lima), August 16, 1970.

60. *El presente de Chile y el Evangelio*, mimeo (Santiago de Chile, 1970).

61. *CIDOC*, no. 254, 1970. See also the statement of Jorge Hourton, the Bishop of Puerto Montt, regarding the result of the presidential election, in *CIDOC*, no. 251, 1970, and the communiqué of the Rural Catholic Action in *CIDOC*, no. 255, 1970.

62. "Comunicado a la prensa de los sacerdotes participantes en las jornadas 'Participacion de los cristianos en la construcción del socialismo en Chile,' " in *El Mercurio* (Santiago de Chile), April 17, 1971.

63. *Justicia en el Mundo*, Lima, August 14,1971; English translation in *IDOC-NA*, no. 37 (December 11, 1971), p. 9. See also the articles by Ricardo Antoncich in the daily *Expreso* (Lima), September-October 1971.

64. See "Presence of the Church," in *Between Honesty and Hope*, p. 28.

65. "Letter to Peoples of the Third World," ibid., p. 9. "They must count on themselves and their own initiatives more than on the help of the rich" (ibid.); they must unite and defend their right to life (ibid., p. 11). See also "Statement of Peruvian Episcopal Conference," ibid., p. 257; "Declaración de ISAL," in *NADOC*, no. 147, p. 7; "Chile, voluntad de ser," Permanent Committee of the Chilean Bishops, 1968, p. 11c.

66. *IDOC-NA*, no. 4, p. 38. See also *ONIS Declaraciones*, p. 24, regarding the participation of the campesino in agrarian reform and the ONIS statement in *IDOC-NA*, no. 16, pp. 91-94. See also *Carta del episcopado mexicano*, pp. 22, 37, 49-50.

67. "Peace," no. 18, in *Medellín*; see also no. 7 and *ONIS Declaraciones*, pp. 29-37.

68. "Statement of Peruvian Episcopal Conference," in *Between Honesty and Hope*, pp. 229-30 and also p. 231; see for example "*Populorum progressio* and Latin American Realities," in *Between Honesty and Hope*, p. 71; and "Cristianos y poder," in *Iglesia latinoamericana*, p. 121. "The fact that they had to have recourse to such measures as the occupation of churches is also a reflection on the press and the other media of communication, property of those in economic power and hence the voice of their interests. These media play down the masses as of little importance, turn a deaf ear to their just claims, gloss over or make no mention of petitions, labor disputes, and other events which are a true echo of the life of these sectors of the population" (ONIS statement in *IDOC-NA*, no. 4, p. 42). See also *Carta del episcopado mexicano*, pp. 12-14, 25. Paternalism and margination of the poor have also been present in the Church; see the statement of the Argentinian laity, 1968, in *Iglesia latinoamericana*, p. 109.

69. "Hopefully the Church will now address herself as well to those who are the victims of the unjust structures and to the organizations that represent them" ("The Church's Shortcomings," a statement by Peruvian lay persons, in *Between Honesty and Hope*, p. 157). "To our brother peasants and workers we say that we will do all in our

power to 'encourage and support all the efforts of the people' " ("Statement of Peruvian Episcopal Conference," ibid., p. 231).

70. "Peace," no. 27, in *Medellín*.

71. Ibid., no. 20. See also "Lay Critique," in *Between Honesty and Hope*, p. 200.

72. "Poverty of the Church," no. 10, in *Medellín*.

73. "Carta del clero peruano a la Asemblea episcopal," in *Iglesia latinoamericana*, p. 321.

74. "Statement of Peruvian Episcopal Conference," in *Between Honesty and Hope*, p. 231.

75. "Poverty of the Church," no. 11, in *Medellín*.

76. *Carta del episcopado mexicano*, pp. 28-29.

77. "Letter to Peoples of the Third World," in *Between Honesty and Hope*, p. 5.

78. See, for example, the statement of the Argentinian Priests for the Third World on the consecration of Argentina to the Immaculate Heart of Mary by General Juan Carlos Onganía, president of the country, in 1969 (*NADOC*, no. 115, and *IDOC-NA*, no. 15, pp. 75-78); the document rejects both the utilization of religious sentiment to endorse an unjust situation as well as the attempt to make the Church seem to be in agreement with the existing policy.

79. See "Carta de los obispos paraguayos," 1969, addressed to the congress of the country, "in the face of the grave threat to the moral conscience and the dignity of the nation represented by the new bill on the 'Defense of Democracy and the Political and Social Order of the State' "; the Paraguayan Church vigorously rejected the bill (*NADOC*, no. 89, pp. 1-3). See also the "Carta pastoral de Monseñor de Jerónimo Pechillo, Prelado de Coronel Oviedo," Paraguay, 1970, which states that conflicts exist between the Church and the state because "the Church in Paraguay cannot remain blind and deaf to the continuous violation of the rights which God has given to human beings." (*NADOC*, no. 129, pp. 3-4).

80. "Clero peruano a la Asamblea episcopal," in *Iglesia latinoamerica*, pp. 314-15. "One of the clearest signs of the evangelical independence and liberty that our church is meant to give would be the relinquishing of every economic tie with political power and the renouncing of every type of legal protection and privilege, including all the various rights acquired in the course of our history" (ONIS statement in *IDOC-NA*, no. 4, p. 39); "The Church as institution must break off every concrete tie to any kind of public economic or social power, even at the risk of being persecuted and criticized or of losing economic resources or possibilities of support; it must do this in order to be always, like Christ, at the service of those who suffer, the poorest and most needy, and to witness to the poverty that all need in the service of justice and love" ("Carta pastoral de Adviento," p. 19).

81. Statement of the Cuban MEC in *Spes*.

82. "Peace," no. 20, in *Medellín*.

83. "Socioeconomic Structures of Peru," in *Between Honesty and Hope*, p. 74. "The absence of authentic evangelization often leads to a situation where the religious attitudes of our people act as a brake on personal initiative and integral development. So we must present the faith as a factor promoting change and a more just society" ("Underdevelopment in Colombia," in *Between Honesty and Hope*, p. 91); see also *Carta del episcopado mexicano*, pp. 16-17.

84. "Manifiesto de la Iglesia metodista de Bolivia," 1970, in *NADOC*, no. 140, p. 3; English version in *IDOC-NA*, no. 7, pp. 39-48. This same document points out the need for an effort at conscientization: "The formation of a critical awareness in the Bolivian

people . . . is part of the mission which God has entrusted to us" (ibid., p. 6). Within the process of liberation there are possibilities for an authentic ecumenism: "We believe that the Christian churches are able to give a common message in these decisive moments, thus indicating the love which comes from God to all, the dignity of the human being, as well as offering an invitation to join the struggle for a more just Peru" ("Llamado a las Iglesias," of the Ecumenical Committee of Churches of Lima, 1969, in *NADOC*, no. 59).

85. "Evangelio y subversión," manifesto of 21 priests from Buenos Aires, 1967, in *Iglesia latinoamericana*, p. 106.

86. Statement of the Pastoral Conference of the Diocese of Salto, Uruguay, 1968, in *Iglesia latinoamericana, p. 373*. "The Commission ought to contribute to awakening in the whole people of God an awareness of the seriousness and the urgency of the process of liberation in such a way that the action of the Church is orientated toward this change and their active participation in it" ("Encuentro Regional Andino," in *NADOC*, no. 147, p. 4).

87. *Juventud y cristianismo*, p. 35. See also *Pastoral indigenista en Mexico*, the final document of the first pastoral meeting on the mission of the Church in the aboriginal cultures (Bogotá: Department of Missons of CELAM, 19, pp. 40-42.

88. "Peace, no. 24, in *Medellín*.

89. "Pastoral Conference," Salto, Uruguay, in *Iglesia latinoamerica*, p. 374.

90. Ibid., p. 377. See also "Poverty," no. 9, in *Medellín*.

91. There are few serious studies regarding the wealth of the Church in Latin America. Some bishops are beginning to be concerned with the problem. See, for example, "Statement of Peruvian Episcopal Conference," in *Between Honesty and Hope*, p. 232; and "Resoluciones de la conferencia episcopal ecuatoriana," June 1969, in *NADOC*, no. 73.

92. "Church in Bolivia," in *Between Honesty and Hope*, p. 142; see also "Brazilian Realities," regarding commercialized faith and Church property, ibid., pp. 135-36. See also the clear, extensive statement of the Conferencia Latinoamericana de Religiosas (CLAR), *Pobreza y vida religiosa en América Latina* (Bogotá, 1970).

93. "Poverty of the Church," nos. 8-18, in *Medellín*.

94. "Church in Bolivia," in *Between Honesty and Hope*, pp. 141-42. See also "Formation of the Clergy," no. 1, in *Medellín*; "Joint Pastoral Planning," no. 5, ibid.; "Presence of the Church in Latin American Development," in *Between Honesty and Hope*, pp. 22-23; "Underdevelopment in Colombia," ibid., pp. 89-90; "Church's Shortcomings," ibid., pp. 156-57; the statement of the Argentinian lay persons in *Iglesia latinoamericana*, pp. 108-10.

95. "Lay Critique," in *Between Honesty and Hope*, p. 22. See also *Carta del episcopado mexicano*, p. 54. "What we propose is the rejuvenation of the structures of the Church. We consider this to be its greatest need so that they might capacitate it for its present task, to commit itself to society in the construction of the new human being" (statement of the Cuban MEC, in *Spes*).

96. See "Declaración de Sacerdotes para el Tercer Mundo," 1970, in *NADOC*, no. 147, p. 9. Regarding education in particular, see the controversial case of the closing of an important school in Mexico by the Jesuits in "Motivos principales de nuestra decisión sobre el Instituto Patria," in *NADOC*, no. 194.

97. "Priests," no. 1, in *Medellín*.

98. See for example *La pastoral en las misiones de América Latina* (Bogotá: Departamento de Misiones del CELAM, 1968), pp. 38-39.

99. "Carta de Sacerdotes tucumanos," in *Iglesia latinoamericana*, p. 137; see also "Sacerdotes bonaerenses responden a su obispo," 1969, ibid., pp. 130-31; "Underdevelopment in Colombia," in *Between Honesty and Hope*, pp. 87-89; "Socioeconomic Structures of Peru," ibid., p. 79.

100. "Clero peruano," in *Iglesia latinoamericana*, p. 318; see also ONIS statement, *IDOC-NA*, no. 4, pp. 37-41. After recalling that in general priests make their living from religious services, the Ecuadorian priests assert that "today this situation has become intolerable, not only in the eyes of society, but also in the eyes of the priest himself, both because of the impression of exploitation it gives as well as the necessity of depending on alms. It is for this reason that priests are thinking about taking up professions that will provide them with the income necessary to earn a living" ("Conclusiones de la primera convención nacional de presbíteros del Ecuador," January 1970, in *NADOC*, no. 141, p. 13).

101. See, for example, "Por qué los sacerdotes recurrimos a la opinión pública," letter of 57 priests to the Archbishop of Quito, December 1968, in *NADOC*, no. 30.

102. See the essay of Ricardo Cetrulo on the "level of depth" of these texts in "Conclusiones críticas," in *Iglesia latinoamericana*, pp. 403-24.

103. The change of tone—and origin—can be easily seen by consulting, for example, *Recent Church Documents from Latin America*, CIF Monograph (Cuernavaca, Mexico: CIF, 1963), where episcopal documents of 1962-63 are reproduced.

## 8. STATEMENT OF THE QUESTIONS

1. Thomas G. Sanders asserts, "The Roman Catholic Church has long been criticized for helping to maintain an anachronistic social system and economic underdevelopment. . . . Yet today no institution in Latin America is changing more rapidly than the Catholic Church" ("The Church in Latin America," *Foreign Affairs* 48, no. 2 [January 1970]1: 285).

2. *The Rockefeller Report on the Americas* (Chicago: Quadrangle Books, 1969), p. 31. "Today the most ancient monarchy seated on the rock of the first bishop of Rome is faced with a subversion of its sacred values. And it is not the silent and scandalized laity, but rather the clergy who are breaking through the rigid boundaries of their evangelical service to become on not a few occasions standard bearers for an openness to Marxism—with all the ferocity and incontinence in which converts traditionally have gloried" (Alberto Lleras Camargo, *Visión*, May 9, 1969, p. 17).

3. "La Igiesia perseguida: desafío latinoamericano," *Perspectivas para el Diálogo*, no. 35 (July 1969), p. 148.

4. In this regard see the observations of Michel de Certeau, "L'articulation du *dire* et du *faire*," *Études Théologiques et Religieuses* (Montpellier), 45, no. 1 (1970): 25–44.

5. In the process which has led to this posture, the Latin American Episcopal Council (CELAM) has played a decisive role. Even though when it began in 1955 it was something new among ecclesiastical structures of that time, its activity was confined to traditional models. The change occurred in 1963 under the orientation of Don Manuel Larraín, the Bishop of Talca, Chile. During his presidency there were created the various departments of CELAM, which assumed different pastoral areas. In these departments bishops and experts collaborated closely. Beginning in 1966, while Dom Avelar Brandão was president, meetings were organized which produced statements—at times quite surprising. These meetings likewise manifested an initial effort at reflection and commitment. They were also an effective preparation for Medellín: vocations (Lima, 1966);

education (on Catholic universities; Buga, 1967); missions (Melgar, 1968); social action (Itapoán, 1968); and the diaconate (Buenos Aires, 1968).

6. See the alarmed observations concerning the bishops' conference at Medellín which this caused: Alberto Lleras Camargo, "La Iglesia militante," *Visión*, September 29, 1968.

7. On this subject, see the section "Faith and Social Conflict" (pp. 156–61), below.

8. This is why there is now talk of the gradual creation of "two Churches." Regarding the Evangelical Churches, Christian Lalive d'Epinay writes, "Between these two forms of Churches there exists a qualitative break which makes any reformist transition impossible. The transformation of Latin American Protestantism implies a radical challenge to the first form. It implies creating breaches in that petrified structure so that it destructuralizes. Only in this way will a new restructuring be possible. Here—as in the socio-political field in Latin America—the reformist path is no longer feasible. And only radical challenge will enable the opening of new paths" (*CIDOC*, no. 78, p. 12).

9. See the perceptive analyses of Juan Luis Segundo, "¿Hacia una Iglesia de Izquierda?" *Perspectivas para el Diálogo*, no. 32 (April 1969), pp. 35-39, and Ricardo Cetrulo, "Utilización política de la Iglesia," ibid., pp. 40–44.

10. Hector Borrat observes that the hopes awakened for the role of the Church institution by Medellín are beginning to turn into frustration and uneasiness ("La Iglesia ¿para qué?" p. 14).

11. Cesar Aguiar speaks of the emergence in Latin America of a different kind of "Underground Church," underground in relation to the political establishment and not to ecclesiastical power (as is the case of the churches of the affluent countries). He also foresees the need to develop a theology of persecution, which might enable a rediscovery of the meaning of the cross, "which we had forgotten for some time" ("Currents and Tendencies," *IDOC-NA*, no. 13, p. 63). But this will not come simply from the radicalness of commitment. Borrat points out perceptively and satirically that "the Church is going to pay a very heavy price for the revolutionary novitiate of some of its members. . . . It is easy to foresee that during the '70s no other social group will be as vulnerable as the Church to the mechanisms of repression. There are few so naively stubborn as certain groups of the vanguard within the Church. They publicize their 'subversion,' they profess their violence before exercising it, they hand themselves over freely to their political adversaries" ("La Iglesia ¿para qué?," p. 12).

12. See Gustavo Gutiérrez, "De la Iglesia colonial a Medellín," *Víspera*, no. 16 (April 1970), pp. 3-8.

13. See Henrique de Lima Vaz, "Igreja-reflexo vs. Igreja-fonte," *Cadernos Brasileiros*, March-April 1968. What Hegel has already pointed out is indeed still valid: "Whatever happens in America is only the echo of the old world and the expression of a foreign life." He further asserted that "America should separate itself from the soil on which universal history has developed until now" (*Raison dans l'histoire*, p. 242).

14. Regarding theological reflection, it has been stated that "there is an urgent need for the Latin American hierarchy to urge its theologians to work up new aspects of theology that are in line with local needs. They cannot rest content with a theology that was elaborated, in large measure, by theologians living in other regions and under different historical conditions" ("Presence of the Church in Latin American Development," in *Between Honesty and Hope*, p. 22); see also "Working Draft of the Medellín Conference," ibid., pp. 191-92. "This is a critical moment . . . ," stated Cardinal Landázuri Ricketts in his closing address at the Medellín Episcopal Conference. "It

marks the end of several things: a stage of religious dependence, a long period of imitating alien ideologies and postures. We now propose to seek solutions from within our real situation and potential" (*Between Honesty and Hope*, p. 224).

15. Regarding the role of "Christian consciousness" in the growth of Latin American consciousness, see the fine study of Enrique Düssel, *América latina y conciencia cristiana* (Quito: IPLA, 1970).

## PART 4. PERSPECTIVES

1. To avoid repetition we will not explicitly mention the experiences—and the texts which outline a reflection on them—which we have already cited in the third part of this work. But it is clear that the reflections which follow do not add to these commitments to the process of liberation which is underway in Latin America. On the contrary, these commitments substantially and permanently nourish these reflections; moreover, they constitute their arena of verification.

2. *Risposta dei teologi*, p. 68.

## SECTION 1. FAITH AND THE NEW HUMANITY

1. Karl Rahner speaks of the not too distant possibility that the Church give an "univocal no" to certain tendencies or interpretations of Christianity (*Risposta dei teologi*, p. 71).

2. See above Chapter 6.

3. What Karl Marx wrote more than a hundred years ago is still valid: "The present generation is like the Jews whom Moses led through the desert. Not only does it have to conquer a new world, it also has to perish to give room to the men who are to live in the new world" (*Les luttes sociales en France 1848-1850* [Paris: Éditions Sociales, 1952], p. 90; English translation: *The Class Struggles in France (1848-50)* [New York: International Publishers, 1934]).

4. These recall in a certain way the celebrated programmatic questions of *Kant*: "What can I *know*? What ought I to *do*? What may I *hope*?" ("The Critique of Pure Reason," in *Kant,* Great Books of the Western World, Vol. 42, p. 236; the italics are ours). Regarding the meaning and evolution of these questions, see Jean Louis Bruch, *La philosophie religieuse de Kant* (Paris: Aubier, Éditions Montaigne, 1968), pp. 21-30.

## 9. LIBERATION AND SALVATION

1. This is clearly indicated by Piet Smulders, "La Iglesia como Sacramento de la salvación," in *La Iglesia del Vaticano II*, ed. Guillermo Baráuna (Madrid: Juan Flora, 1966), 1:379; French version: "L'Église sacrement du salut," *L'Église de Vatican II* (Paris: Les Éditions du Cerf, 1966), 2:313-38. More recently Yves Congar has written, "There is a question on which very little has been written: What does it mean, for the world and for humankind, to be saved? In what does salvation consist?" (*Situation et tâches*, p. 80; see also p. 68); and in another place he writes, "It is necessary to ask ourselves again very seriously about our idea of salvation. There is hardly any other theological notion implying immediate consequences—very concrete and very important—which has been left so vague and which calls in a most urgent way for an adequate elaboration" ("Christianisme et libération de l'homme," *Masses Ouvrières*, no. 258 [December 1969], p. 8).

2. Even including the very term *salvation*; with its connotation of evasion it would seem more and more inadequate to express the reality in question.

3. See Juan Luis Segundo, "Intelecto y salvación," *Salvación y construcción del mundo*, pp. 47-91; Manaranche, *Quel salut?*; Christian Duquoc, "Qu'est-ce que le salut?" in *L'Église vers l'avenir*, ed. M. D. Chenu (Paris: Les Éditions du Cerf,1969), pp. 99-102; and the interesting posing of the question in the recent article of Jean-Pierre Jossua, "L'enjeu de la recherche théologique actuelle sur le salut," *Revue des Sciences Philosophiques et Théologiques* 54, no. 1 (January 1970): 24-25. The old book of Congar, *The Wide World My Parish: Salvation and its Problems*, trans. Donald Attwater (Baltimore: Helicon Press, 1961) gathered together different studies on the notion of salvation and opened new paths which are still relevant. Moreover, we cannot forget in this regard the concerns and intuitions of Teilhard de Chardin.

4. For a historical study of this point, see the classic work of Louis Capéran, *Le problème du salut des infidèles*, 2 vols. (Toulouse: Grand Séminaire, 1934); see also Angel Santos Hernández, *Salvación y paganismo* (Santander: Editorial Sal Terrae, 1960).

5. See the solid study of Hendrik Nys, *Le salut sans l'Évangile* (Paris: Les Éditions du Cerf, 1966); see also the article of Joseph Ratzinger, "Salus extra ecclesiam nulla est," in *Naturaleza salvífica de la Iglesia* (Barcelona: DO-C, 1964); English mimeo published by DO-C (Rome), research paper no. 88.

6. In the first place, for a theology of the Church (see below Chapter 12) and therefore for a theology of missionary activity, see the study done by the missionary periodical *Spiritus*, no. 24 (August-September 1965), and the position papers of the Thirty-fifth Missiology Week gathered in *Repenser la mission* (Louvain: Desclée deBrouwer, 1965); these are revealing examples of the crisis caused by this revision which has led to the clear and simple affirmation of the universality of salvation. See the state of the question of this revision in Boniface Willems, "Who Belongs to the Church?" in *Concilium* 1, pp. 131-51.

7. "For the orthodox tradition, the profane does not exist, only the profaned" (Olivier Clement, "Un ensayo de lectura ortodoxa de la constitución," in *La Iglesia en el mundo de hoy* (Madrid: Studium, 1967), p. 673. The same idea is found in Charles Moeller, "Renewal of the Doctrine of Man," *Theology of Renewal* (Montreal: Palm, 1968), p. 458.

8. *La pastoral en las misiones de América Latina*, conclusions of the meeting at Melgar organized by the Department of Missions of CELAM (Bogotá, 1968), pp. 16-17. The same idea is found in another text which also presents an interesting theological reflection: "Men respond of their own free will to this salvation that is offered to them in Christ. They can respond to it somehow, even when they do not know Jesus Christ explicitly; they do so when, under the influence of grace, they try to move out of their egotism, to take on the task of constructing the world, and to enter into communion with their fellow men. . . . They fail to respond when they refuse to recognize this task of building the world and serving others in fellowship, thus committing sin" ("Working Draft of the Medellín Conference," in *Between Honesty and Hope*, p. 189).

9. Ibid., pp. 187-88.

10. Regarding the interpretation of the Beatitudes in Luke from this viewpoint, see below Chapter 13. In the interesting essay on the notion of salvation which we have already mentioned, Juan Luis Segundo notes a difference in focus between the thinking of Paul and the other authors of the New Testament, a difference parallel to the one we have just pointed out; Segundo concludes, "We can say then that Christi-

anity, although like the religions of extraterrestrial salvation because of its absolute salvation, differs from them because it introduced this absolute value into the midst of the historical and apparently profane reality of human existence" ("Intelecto y salvación," p. 87).

11. Some years ago Christian Duquoc compared these two positions from another viewpoint: "What mattered then to the theologian was the way persons worked in relation to their transcendent end; what matters to [the theologian] today is what they do" ("Eschatologie et réalités terrestres," *Lumière et Vie* 9, no. 50 [November-December 1960]: 5).

12. See above Chapter 5.

13. In this regard see the effort of Jossua, "L'enjeu."

14. We will cite the testimony of two theologians considered rather moderate in their views. From a Biblical perspective, Pierre Grelot writes, "Profane history and sacred history are not two separate realities. . . . They are intertwined in each other. Concretely there is *only one* human history which develops *at the same time* on these two levels. The grace of redemption, whose mysterious itinerary constitutes sacred history, is at work in the very heart of profane history. . . . Sacred history integrates all of profane history, on which it confers, in the last instance, its intelligible meaning." Having said this, the author adds, "In the midst of profane history, which runs down through the centuries, sacred history has its points of emergence which enable us to establish its reality and know its essential aspects" (*Sens chrétien de l'Ancien Testament* [Tournai: Desclée & Cie, Éditeurs, 1962], p. 111). Nevertheless, the notion of "points of emergence" does not seem very clear. Do these have their own history in the midst of the general history of humanity? Are they necessary to establish the reality of sacred history? Or are they nothing more than the interpretation of history in the light of the Word of God?

For his part, Emile Rideau believes that "if the vocation of the world and of humankind is supernatural, there does not exist, in fact and in the deepest sense, anything but a supernatural reality. The profane world is nothing but an abstraction in relation to the supernatural world of faith" ("Y a-t-il un monde profane?" *Nouvelle Revue Théologique* 88, no. 10 [December 1966]: 1080). This does not weaken for him the consistency of the temporal sphere, because we are before "a lively dialectic of the relationship between, on the one hand, a world that is profane only insofar as it is not perceived as divine and, on the other, a supernatural reality which seeks to assume it, to ransom it, to consecrate it, to divinize it" (ibid., p. 1082).

The position of Karl Rahner, on the other hand, seems more ambiguous; see "History of the World and Salvation-history," in *Theological Investigations*, 5:97-114. See also Ovidio Pérez Morales, who clearly affirms the existence of a single history: *Fe y desarollo* (Caracas: Ediciones Paulinas, 1971), p. 49.

15. See the comments of Heinrich Schlier, *Der Brief an die Epheser* (Dusseldorf: Patmos-Verlag, 1958), pp. 37–48.

16. See the reflections of Piet Schoonenberg concerning the mutual implications of creation and the Covenant in *Covenant and Creation* (London: Sheed and Ward, 1968), pp. 141-49.

17. Gerhard Von Rad, *Old Testament Theology*, trans. D. M. G. Stalker (New York: Harper and Brothers, 1962), 1:139; see also Von Rad's, *Genesis*, trans. John H. Marks (London: SCM Press Ltd., 1961).

18. "With the creation of the world (the six-day schema) the dimension of history opens up. Only by referring history to the creation of the world could the saving action

within Israel be brought into its appropriate theological frame of reference, because creation is part of Israel's etiology" (Von Rad, *Old Testament Theology* [New York: Harper & Row, Publishers, 1965], 2:341-42.

19. A. Jacob, *Théologie de l'Ancien Testament* (Neuchatel: Delachaux et Niestlé, 1953), p. 43. Regarding the message of Deutero-Isaiah, see the excellent article of A. Gamper, "Der Verkündigungsauftrag Israels nach Deutero-Jesaja," *Zeitschrift für Katholische Theologie* 91 (1969): 411-29.

20. "Die theologische Stellung des Schöpfungsglaubens bei Deuterojesaias," *Zeitschrift für Theologie und Kirche* 51 (1954): 10, cited by Walter Kern, "La creación como presupuesto de la Alianza," in *Mysterium Salutis* (Madrid: Cristiandad, 1969), I:503; original German: *Mysterium Salutis* (Einsiedeln, Zurich, Cologne: Benziger Verlag, 1967).

21. As is well known the accounts of the creation are strongly marked by the experience of the Exodus and the Covenant. This is the case especially in the so-called *Yahwistic* narrative; Gen. 2:4-16 follows the outline of the Covenant pact.

22. See Jean Steinmann, *Le prophète Isaïe* (Paris: Les Éditions du Cerf, 1950), p. 221.

23. See Kern, "Creación como presupuesto."

24. In this regard see Rubem Alves, *A Theology of Human Hope* (Washington, D.C.: Corpus Books, 1969), p. 129. See also Arnaldo Zenteno, *Liberación social y Cristo* (Mexico, D.F.: Secretariado Social Mexicano, 1971).

25. Albert Gelin, "Moïse dans l'Ancien Testament," in *Moïse, L'homme de l'Alliance* (Paris: Desclée & Cie, Éditeurs, 1955), p. 39.

26. Regarding the central characteristic of the theme of the Covenant, see the short but interesting note of Beltrán Villegas, "El tema de la Alianza y el vocabulario teológico del A. T.," *Teología y Vida* 2, no. 3 (July-September 1961): 178-82; and in a recent exegetical perspective, see the analysis of Paul Beauchamp, "Propositions sur l'Alliance de l'Ancien Testament comme structure centrale," *Recherches de Science Religieuse* 58, no. 2 (April-June 1970): 161-93.

27. Cited by Congar in "Christianisme et libération," p. 8.

28. *Moses and the Vocation of the Jewish People*, trans. Irene Marinoff (New York: Harper Torchbooks, 1959), pp. 136-37.

29. See the commentary on some of these texts in Franz Mussner, "Creación en Cristo," in *Mysterium Salutis*, 1:506-11.

30. See Charles Harold Dodd, *The Interpretation of the Fourth Gospel* (Cambridge [Eng.]: University Press, 1953), p. 269; Charles Kingsley Barrett, *The Gospel According to St. John* (London: S.P.C.K., 1955), pp. 125-32; and A. Feuillet, "Prologue du quatrième Évangile," *Supplément au Dictionnaire de la Bible*, fasc. 44,1969, col. 623-88.

31. "With a little arrangement," writes M. E. Boismard, "we might say that St. John meant to divide Christ's life into seven periods of seven days, in seven weeks. We should do wrong to see in this a mere puerile game on the part of the evangelist, or even a convenient or artificial frame in which to enclose the life of Christ. This structural scheme corresponds to the plan already indicated in the Prologue: to draw a parallel between the work of creation, and the work of the Messiah: the seven times seven days of Messianic ministry correspond to the seven days of creation" (*St. John's Prologue*, trans. Carisbrooke Dominicans [Westminster, Md.: Newman Press, 1957], p. 107).

32. See Severino Croatto, "La creación en la Kerygmática actual," in *Salvación y construcción del mundo*, pp. 95-104; A. Feuillet, *Le Christ sagesse de Dieu d'après les Épitres pauliennes* (Paris: J. Gabalda et Cie, 1966); regarding this work and this theme

in general, see the perceptive observations of Juan Alfaro, *Hacia una teología del progreso humano* (Barcelona: Herder, 1969), p. 22, no. 22.

33. This was pointed out very clearly by Harvey Cox in *The Secular City*. But it should be clarified that this "desacralization" refers to something different from the "sacred": it is not what is untouchable and separated from profane life, but rather something present and active in the heart of human history.

34. Fritz Fanon put it quite emphatically: "To educate the masses politically . . . means . . . to try, relentlessly and passionately, to teach the masses that everything depends on them; that if we stagnate it is their responsibility, and that if we go forward it is due to them too, that there is no such thing as a demiurge, that there is no famous man who will take the responsibility for everything, but that the demiurge is the people themselves and the magic hands are finally only the hands of the people" (*The Wretched of the Earth*, pp. 157-58).

35. In Hebrew there is no special term to signify *promise*. A combination of terms and expressions designate it: blessing, oath, inheritance, promised land. See Julius Schniewind and Gerhard Friedrich, "Epangelia," in *Theological Dictionary of the New Testament*, 2:576 ff.

36. *The Key Concepts of the Old Testament*, trans. George Lamb (New York: Sheed and Ward, 1955), pp. 36-37.

37. Jürgen Moltmann, *Theology of Hope*, pp. 139ff.

38. Joseph Ruby observes that "the object of the promise, 'to inherit the world,' is not found in this form in the passage from Genesis (15:1-7) to which Paul refers. 'This land' which God promised to Abraham was the land of Canaan. But in other texts (Gen. 12:3; 22:17-18) the promise was extended by the proclamation of blessings that would include all the families and nations of the earth. Therefore Jewish thought, according to certain of its representatives, was led to extend the boundaries of the land promised to Abraham until they were coterminous with the boundaries of the world" (*Saint Paul, Épitre aux Romains* [Paris: Beauchesne et ses Fils, 1957], p. 173).

39. In reality this is not an innovation. In the Old Testament the oath of God to the patriarchs is often recalled; see Deut. 1:8; 6:10, 18; 7:8; Ecclus. 44:19 23; Jcr. 11:5; Mic. 7:20; Ps. 105:6-9.

40. Gelin, *Key Concepts*, p. 37.

41. "What we call the New Testament is the realization of the promise, and the actual taking possession of the inheritance" (L. Cerfaux, *The Church in the Theology of St. Paul*, trans. Geoffrey Webb and Adrian Walker [New York: Herder and Herder, 1959], p. 35). Incipiently, we should say, to be exact. But what we are saying concerning the historical fulfillment of the promise should not make us forget the lesson of Exodus: the significance of human self-generation in the historical political struggle. On this point we are far from the position of Jürgen Moltmann (*Theology of Hope*) criticized perceptively by Rubem Alves (*Theology of Human Hope*, pp. 55-68); Moltmann would give the impression that he does not keep sufficiently in mind human participation in human liberation.

42. Karl Barth, *Kirchliche Dogmatik* 4/3, pp. 385 and 387, quoted by Moltmann, *Theology of Hope*, p. 87.

43. "The reason," Moltmann asserts, "for the overplus of promise and for the fact that it constantly overspills history lies in the inexhaustibility of the God of promise, who never exhausts himself in any historic reality but comes 'to rest' only in a reality that wholly corresponds to him" (*Theology of Hope*, p. 106).

44. The term is not very old. In 1924, E. Mangenot said that *eschatology* had been

"used, for some years now, especially in Germany and England, to designate the part of systematic theology which treats ultimate ends." He noted that this term "has still not received general acceptance in French theology" (*Dictionnaire de Théologie Catholique*, s.v., "Eschatologie").

45. In Ecclesiasticus the term *escata* is used to speak of death and judgment after this life (7:36; 28:6; 38:20).

46. *Theology of Hope*, pp. 37-39.

47. "In the Biblical sense, to speak of the last things is to speak of an end understood so radically, of a reality so transcendent to all things, that the existence of these things would be solely and integrally rooted in that reality, of an end, therefore, that in truth is also their source" (Karl Barth, *Die Auferstehung der Toten* [Zurich: Evangelischer Verlag, 1953], p. 61; the first edition is 1924; English translation: *The Resurrection of the Dead*, trans. H. J. Stenning [New York; Fleming H. Revell Co., 1933]).

48. "To speak of final history, of the last time, would be to speak only of an end so radically understood, of a reality so elevated over every event and temporality, that to refer to the end of history and time would really be to refer to that which establishes all time and everything that occurs in it. Final history would signify the same thing as original history. The limit of time would be the limit of all time, that is the origin of time" (ibid., p. 59). These texts are cited by Raúl Gabás Pallas, *Escatología protestante en la actualidad* (Vitoria: Editorial Eset, 1964), pp. 67-68; the author presents the thinking of the most important contemporary Protestant theologians on the question.

49. Moltmann, *Theology of Hope*, p. 40.

50. Karl Rahner describes well the evolution of the term *eschatology* in *Sacramentum Mundi* (New York: Herder and Herder, 1968), 2:242–46. See also Rahner's, "The Hermeneutics of Eschatological Assertions," in *Theological Investigations*, 4:323–46.

51. Moltmann notes that "the term 'eschato-*logy*' " is wrong. There can be no " 'doctrine' of the last things, if by 'doctrine' we mean a collection of theses which can be understood on the basis of experiences that constantly recur and are open to anyone" (*Theology of Hope*, p. 17).

52. See Von Rad, *Old Testament Theology*, 2:112ff.

53. Ibid., p. 113.

54. Ibid., p. 114.

55. Ibid., p. 115.

56. Rudolph Bultmann says that "radical openness for the future" is the characteristic and definitive trait of existence according to the Bible (*Primitive Christianity in Its Contemporary Setting*, trans. R. H. Fuller [New York: Meridian Books, 1956], pp. 180ff.).

57. Von Rad, *Old Testament Theology*, 2:118. See also Norbert Lohfink "Escatología en el Antiguo Testamento," *Exégesis bíblica y teología* (Salamanca: Ediciones Sígueme, 1969), pp. 163-87.

58. John A. T. Robinson notes that *parousia* is a term with no plural. The presence (or coming) of Christ is a unique event and is not repeated (*Jesus and His Coming* [New York: Abingdon Press, 1957], p. 185).

59. *Le prophète Isaïe*, p. 89.

60. Ibid., p. 92. An objection to this interpretation is posed in terms of this dilemma: Is Emmanuel the Messiah or is Ezekiel? Steinmann rightly answers, "Emmanuel is the Messiah in Ezekiel." He clarifies his position saying, "Emmanuel is incarnated in the time of Isaias, but the promises of which he is the object transcend him (like those made

to Abraham) and refer to Christ, the definitive Anointed One. Ezekiel has exercised his role of Savior without exhausting it" (ibid., p. 377).

61. This is why Gelin speaks of a "bivalence" of the concept of eschatology in the Old Testament: "It designates either the end of the world or an important event in human history like the beginning of a new era" (*Supplément au Dictionnaire de la Bible*, s.v. "Messianisme").

62. Cited in Lohfink, *Exégesis bíblica*, pp. 169-70.

63. See Wolfhart Pannenberg, "The God of Hope," in *Basic Questions in Theology*, trans. George H. Kehm (Philadelphia: Fortress Press, 1971), 2:235-49.

64. See George T. Montague, *The Biblical Theology of the Secular* (Milwaukee: Bruce Publishing Company, 1968); Georges Auzou, *De la servidumbre al servicio* (Madrid: Ediciones FAX, 1969]), pp. 114-26; French edition, *De la servitude au service* (Paris: Édition de l'Orante, 1961); and Michel Allard, "Note sur la formule ''Ehyeh aser 'ehyeh,' '' in *Recherches de Science Religieuse* 45, no. I (January-March 1957): 79-86. "The shade of meaning expressed by the verb *'ehyeh* is not so much the possession of being. Rather it should be understood as referring to a presence, an openness toward another subject" (ibid., p. 85).

65. This question is but a part of a broader one: the relationship between the two Testaments. As is well known the hiatus which Bultmann believed existed between the two contributed to a devaluation of the Old Testament texts. Today the attitude is changing. The present concerns of Christian life and theology are leading us—at times with a certain simplistic approach—to a recovery of the Old Testament. Von Rad, who dedicates several lucid pages to this point, believes that this is a "still debated question" in which there are two aspects: "that the Old Testament is to be understood in the light of Christ" and "that we also need the Old Testament to understand Christ." Regarding the first point it seems to him that we can speak of a general consensus. This is not so regarding the second point (*Old Testament Theology*, 2:386). To illuminate this second proposition, to clarify certain interpretive criteria, would avoid the impression of opportunism which at times is given by recourse to Old Testament texts. For this illumination there were perhaps necessary certain conditions which are beginning to be met: a critical attitude, for example, regarding our "Western" categories concerning time and history, or spirit and matter.

66. "Pensées," no. 571, in *Pascal*, Vol. 33 of Great Books of the Western World, p. 274.

67. *Le sens chrétien de l'Ancien Testament*, p. 392.

68. Ibid., p. 395.

69. Ibid., p. 396. In the quoted texts the italics are the author's.

70. Ibid., pp. 397-98. "The promises of temporal goods are substituted by purely spiritual ones" (M. García Cordero, "Promesas," in *Enciclopedia de la Biblia* (Barcelona: Ediciones Garriga, 1963), 5:1291. From a similar perspective see Leon Roy, "Libération, Liberté," *Vocabulaire de théologie biblique*, 2nd ed. (Paris: Les Éditions du Cerf, 1970), p. 661.

71. "Christianisme et libération," p. 7.

72. As has often been recalled, in the Bible the spiritual realm is not opposed to the corporal or to the material, but rather to the carnal—understood as a selfish turning in upon oneself. This is why Paul does not hesitate to speak of a "spiritual body" (I Cor. 15:44) and of a "carnal mind" (Col. 2:18). In this regard see Beltrán Villegas, "El Evangelio: una noticia siempre increíble," *Mensaje* 20, no. 196 (January-February

1971): 27, n. 7. See also the classic study of John A. T. Robinson, *The Body: A Study in Pauline Theology* (London: SCM Press, 1952).

73. On this point see the brief observations of Lohfink, *Exégesis bíblica*, p. 184.

74. Yves Congar, "Mystère de Jésus et Église des pauvres," in *L'Église aujourd'hui* (Paris: Desclée et Cie., 1967), p. 55.

75. "Christ wants the liberation of humankind and its total liberation, . . . and this is not limited to spiritual liberation" (Antonio Fragoso, *Évangile et révolution sociale* [Paris: Les Éditions du Cerf, 1969], p. 15).

76. To support his interpretation of the hidden and veiled meaning of the prophecies, Grelot asserts that we can speak of "a *spiritual* meaning hidden under the *letter* of the prophecies." The author immediately recognizes that the Pauline distinction between letter and spirit initially was applied to the Law, but he adds, "Its transposition to the problem of the prophecies is not therefore any less legitimate" (*Sens chrétien de l'Ancien Testament*, p. 394, n. 1). But is it just a question of a transposition from the Law to prophecy? Does the transposition not carry with it a transformation of the very sense of the distinction? The *letter* is not opposed to the spirit as the *terrestrial* is to the spiritual. Paul's distinction belongs to another order of ideas. Thomas Aquinas put it very well: "The letter denotes any writing that is external to the human being, even that of the moral precepts such as are contained in the Gospel" (*Summa Theologica*, I-II, q. 106, art. 2).

77. This text of Isaiah (added after the promulgation of the Constitution) is legitimately interpreted in *Gaudium et spes* (no. 78) as referring to social justice.

78. *Évangile et révolution sociale*, p. 15. The text continues, "It is impossible that the Gospel should not strike the conscience of Christians and stimulate an understanding among all persons of good will regarding the liberation of all, especially the poorest and most abandoned." "To struggle to establish justice among men," wrote the Peruvian bishops, "is to begin to be just before the Lord" ("Justice in the World," in *IDOC-NA*, no. 37 [December 11, 1971], p. 5).

79. "The mystery of the 'when' and 'where,' " comments Rudolf Schnackenburg, 'is reserved to the knowledge and decision of God. This fact gives us an important key to the understanding of Jesus' preaching about the future. The eschaton is reserved to the wisdom and command of God." Thus Jesus' "sayings do not emphasize the doctrine but rather the challenge and admonition. The prophetic style and form in which Jesus presents his preaching about the future manifests forcefully and solemnly that Jesus is concerned with the proper teaching of the eschatological disposition" (*Present and Future* [Notre Dame: University of Notre Dame Press, 1966], pp. 10, 16-17). "What a theologian," writes Karl Rahner, "must state in the first place regarding this future is, it seems to me, that it remains unknown not only for reasons of fact, but also for reasons of right" ("L'avenir de la théologie," *Nouvelle Revue Théologique* 93, no. 1 [January 1971]:4).

80. See the excellent history of the text in Philippe Delhaye, "Histoire des textes de la Constitution pastorale," *L'Église dans le monde de ce temps*, 1:215-77.

81. See the summary of the statements made in this regard in the Council in *Relationes particulares*, "Schema of Ariccia," p. 98. See also the address "Church and World" by Edward Schillebeeckx in September 1964 in the DO-C Center in Rome and reproduced in his *Le monde et l'Église* (Brussels: Éditions du CEP, 1967), pp. 149-67; English version in mimeo as a DO-C research paper, series 2, papers dealing with Schema 13.

82. Pierre Hauptmann, "Le schéma de la Constitution Pastorale, De ecclesia in

mundo huius temporis," *Études et documents*, publication of the conciliar secretariat of the French episcopate, August 25, 1965, p. 9.

83. The basis of this affirmation is the Incarnation. "The Word of the Father assumed through the Incarnation the entire man, body and soul; in him he sanctified all nature created by God, not excluding matter; thus everything that exists acclaims the Redeemer in its own way" (ibid.).

84. This number is the basis for *Gaudium et spes*, no. 43.

85. The relationship which Ariccia (no. 50) establishes between creation and redemption gave rise at this initial stage to a text modified in this way: "Although in the present economy the order of redemption includes in itself the order of creation, and human history is profoundly implicated in the history of salvation, this inclusion, nevertheless, in no way destroys the order of creation; rather it elevates it and preserves it in its dignity." After much reworking, there resulted the final version: "Though the same God is Savior and Creator, Lord of human history as well as of salvation history, in the divine arrangement itself the rightful autonomy of the creature, and particularly of man, is not withdrawn. Rather it is reestablished in its own dignity and strengthened in it" (*Gaudium et spes*, no. 41). Because of this same effort at moderation regarding the mission of the Church, the first lines of no. 51 of the Schema of Ariccia—already quoted—are reduced, or rather transformed, into "The union of the human family is greatly fortified and fulfilled by the unity, founded on Christ, of the family of God's sons" (*Gaudium et spes*, no. 42).

86. Thirty-seven bishops were opposed to the final version of no. 39. According to them it is impossible to distinguish adequately in the concrete between temporal progress and the growth of the Kingdom, for charity unites the two processes. They believed, moreover, that to assert that the first was of "importance" to the second is a very vague formula which says nothing ("Expensio modorum" in Chapter 3, Part 1, pp. 225-26). Schille-beeckx believes that this opposition was well founded ("Foi chrétienne et attente terrestre," *L'Église dans le monde de ce temps* [Tours: Mame, 1967], p. 135, no. 5.

87. Statement of G. Garrone, September 21, 1965, regarding Chapter 3 of the first part in "Relationes circa schema Constitutionis Pastoralis de Ecclesia in mundo huius temporis," p. 8.

88. In an excellent article, Juan Luis Segundo examines three possible interpretations of *Gaudium et spes*, no. 39: "The ends of temporal progress and those of the Kingdom are different"; "the ends of temporal progress and the ends of the progress of the Kingdom are the same" the difference being that the Christians "know"; the third is distinguished from the second only in the affirmation that the Church also contributes to history "the content of revelation" ("Evangelización y humanización," *Perspectivas para el Diálogo*, no. 41 [March 1970], pp. 9-17).

89. According to the famous text of St. Augustine of Hippo, quoted in the Schema of Ariccia but not found in the final version, "He who made you without you does not justify you without you. He created you without your knowing it: he will justify you if you will it."

90. The text of Ariccia does not escape these reproaches. In it there is a tendency to oversimplify by identifying the "order" of creation with the natural order and redemption with the supernatural order.

91. The well-documented work of P. L. Mathieu, *La pensée politique et économique de Teilhard de Chardin* (Paris: Éditions du Seuil, 1969), gathers and synthesizes the thinking of Teilhard in this regard. In spite of the effort of the author, the impression that one gets from this work is clear: questions of social justice, of human exploitation,

do not occupy an important place in the concerns of the illustrious Jesuit.

92. This is not the basis for certain works like the theologies of development, progress, etc. It is not a matter merely of the title, but also, especially, of the fashion of posing and resolving the question. The greater part of these authors recognize the influence of Teilhard in the posing of the problem.

93. As André Gunder Frank correctly points out, the term *dependence* is definitely nothing more than a euphemism for oppression, injustice, and alienation (*Lumpen-burgesía*, p. 18).

94. The Latin American theology of liberation and other theologies working along similar lines have reflected deeply on the theme of Christ the Liberator and made it one of their richest lodes. See the following important works: L. Boff, *Jesus Christ Liberator* (Orbis, 1978); J. Sobrino, *Christology at the Crossroads* (Orbis, 1978); H. Echegaray, *The Practice of Jesus* (Orbis, 1984); J. L. Segundo, *Jesus of Nazareth Yesterday and Today* (5 vols., Orbis, 1984-88).

95. See "Peace," nos. 1 and 14, in *Medellín*.

96. *Pobreza evangélica y promoción humana*, p. 29.

97. The religious resonances of Hegel's use of the term *alienation* (*Entäusserung* and *Entfremdung*) are well known. See George Cottier, *L'athéisme du jeune Marx* (Paris: Librairie Philosophique J. Vrin, 1959), pp. 34-43; and Albert Chapelle, *Hegel et la religion, Annexes, Les textes théologiques de Hegel* (Paris: Éditions Universitaires, 1967), pp. 99-125.

98. See Christian Duquoc, "Qu'est-ce que le salut?," pp. 101-2.

99. Without overestimating its importance, it is interesting to recall here the comparison that Marx establishes between sin and private ownership of the means of production. Because of this private ownership workers are separated, alienated, from the fruit of their work: "This primitive accumulation plays in political economy about the same part as original sin in theology. Adam bit the apple, and thereupon sin fell on the human race" ("Capital," Part 8, Chapter 26, in *Marx*, Great Books of the Western World, 50:354).

100. "Justice," no. 3, in *Medellín*. The italics are ours. See also the interesting reflections of Eduardo Pironio, *La Iglesia que nace entre nosotros* (Bogotá: Indo-American Press Service, 1970).

101. Sin is a rejection of friendship with God and, in consequence, with other human beings. It is a personal, free act by which we refuse to accept the gift of God's love (see *We Drink From Our Own Wells,* pp. 97-99). As seen in the light of faith, sin thus understood is the root of all social injustice, because sin, like every human act, necessarily has a social dimension. This accounts for the expressions "sinful situation" (Medellín, "Peace," 1) and "social sin" (John Paul II, encyclical *Reconciliatio et Paenitentia,* 16). In *Sollicitude Rei Socialis* the pope comes back to this point and says: " 'Sin' and 'structures of sin' are categories seldom applied to the situation of the contemporary world. However, one cannot easily gain a profound understanding of the reality that confronts us unless we give a name to the root of the evils that afflict us" (no. 36; *Origins,* p. 653). At the same time, he reminds us that these sinful structures "are rooted in personal sin and thus always linked to the concrete acts of individuals who introduce these structures, consolidate them, and make them difficult to remove" (ibid.). The grace of Christ alone can penetrate to this root. On these matters, see F. Moreno, *Teología moral desde los pobres* (Madrid: Instituto Superior de Ciencias Sociales, 1986), pp. 126-38.

102. This is what was implied, partially and in other terms, in the text of *Populorum progressio* which we have already quoted.

103. An accurate understanding of the relationship between the growth of the Kingdom and the process of liberation is of decisive importance in my theological approach. The Kingdom is at the heart of the message of Jesus; it is a gift of God but also requires certain behaviors from those who receive it. It is *already* present in history, *but* it does not reach its complete fulfillment therein. Its presence already produces effects, but these are "not *the* coming of the Kingdom, not *all* of salvation"; they are anticipations of a completion that will be realized only beyond history. (In part 2 of *El Dios de la vida* [1988] I deal at length with the subject of the kingdom of God.)

104. *La pastoral en las misiones de América Latina*, p. 16.

## 10. ENCOUNTERING GOD IN HISTORY

1. See above Chapter 1. See also Christian Duquoc, "Eschatologie et réalités terrestres," *Lumière et Vie* 9, no. 50 (November-December 1960): 4-22.

2. *Old Testament Theology*, 2:338. "The self-revelation of God in the Biblical witnesses is not of a direct type in the sense of a theophany, but is indirect and brought about by means of the historical acts of God" (Wolfhart Pannenburg, *Revelation as History*, ed. Wolfhart Pannenburg, trans. David Granskou [New York: The Macmillan Company, 1968], p. 125).

3. Following Bonhoeffer, André Dumas writes "The space of God is the world; the secret of the world is the hidden presence of God. Jesus Christ is the structuralization of this space and the name of this secret" (*Une théologie de la réalité* [Geneva: Éditions Labor et Fides, 1968], p. 182; English version: *Dietrich Bonhoeffer: Theologian of Reality*, trans. R. M. Brown [New York: Macmillan, 1971]).

4. "This Hebrew word (*Shekinah*) should be translated by *indwelling* rather than by *presence*. It indicates that God takes up his abode in some given place and dwells there. Whilst the word 'presence' does not imply any place, any attachment, any preference, 'indwelling' presupposes that there has been a choice of a place in which to remain" (M.-J. Lagrange, *Le judaïsme avant Jésus Christ* [Paris, 1931], p. 446, quoted in Yves M.-J. Congar, O.P., *The Mystery of the Temple* [Westminster, Md.: The Newman Press, 1962], p. 18, n. 9).

5. Congar, *Mystery of the Temple*, p. ix.

6. Von Rad points out the difference between the tent on the one hand and the Ark and its tabernacle on the other (*Old Testament Theology*, 1:234-39).

7. Some exegetes consider the Ark as a throne; see Frank Michaeli, *Dieu a l'image de l'homme* (Neuchatel: Delachaux & Niestlé S.A., 1950), p. 59.

8. Martin Buber is against the conceptions of God which conceal these localizations in the Ark and the temple and sees in this "a classic expression of the tensions between the free God of history and the fettered deity of natural things" (*The Prophetic Faith* [New York: Harper & Row, Publishers, 1960], p. 83).

9. "Since the Temple had thus exercised an attractive function which led to the crystallization of various traditions, it can be understood that piety was determined by it and became centered in its orbit" (Edmond Jacob, *Theology of the Old Testament*, trans. Arthur W. Heathcote and Philip J. Allcock [London: Hodder & Stoughton, 1958], p. 259).

10. See the commentary of Congar, *Mystery of the Temple*, pp. 20-53.

11. This has frequently been noted; see for example Montague, *Biblical Theology of the Secular*, p. 15.

12. The "body" (*soma*) in the Jewish apocalypse signifies the whole person insofar

as he or she has a corporeal existence in a historical world of interpersonal relationships. The body is the precondition for the possibility of these relationships. From that time on, true worship will be celebrated in this world (see Rom. 12:1). See Anton Grabner-Haider, "Zur Kultkritik im Neuen Testament," *Diakonia* 4 (1969): 138-46; and Heribert Mühlen, *L'Esprit dans l'Église* (Paris: Les Éditions du Cerf, 1969), 1:169-73.

13. Congar, *Mystery of the Temple,* pp. 197-98.

14. On this subject see the excellent study of Sigmund Mowinckel, *Die Erkenntnis Gottes bei den alttestamentlichen Propheten* (Oslo, 1941).

15. See K. Hruby, "L'amour du prochain dans la pensée juive," *Nouvelle Revue Théologique* 91, no. 5 (May 1969): 493-516.

16. We speak of "parable," following the standard usage; but as has been noted, the text in question is difficult to classify. A misunderstanding due especially to the context has resulted in the classification of this eschatological vision as a parable; see Théo Preiss, *Life in Christ,* trans. Harold Knight (Naperville, Ill.: Alec R. Allenson, Inc., 1957), p. 46.

17. According to Roger Mehl for certain theologians "the summary of the Gospel is Matt. 25:31-46" ("La catholicité de l'Église," *Revue d'Histoire et de Philosophie Religieuses* 48, no. 4 [1968]: 369). Indeed this is what an exegete like Wolfgang Trilling believes; he writes, "The passage is . . . a summary of the whole teaching of the Gospel and a restatement of its demands in the light of judgment" (*The Gospel According to St. Matthew* [New York: Herder and Herder, 1969], 2:216). The central position that this text holds in the thinking of John A. T. Robinson is well known; see *Honest to God* (Philadelphia: The Westminster Press, 1963), especially p. 61.

18. See J. Winandy, "La scène du Jugément dernier," *Sciences Ecclésiastiques,* 1966, pp. 170-86; Lamar Cope, "Matthew 25:31-46, 'The Sheep and the Goats' Reinterpreted," *Novum Testamentum* 11, fasc. 1/2 (January-April 1969): 32-44; Jean-Claude Ingelaere, "La 'parabole' du Jugément Dernier (Matthieu 25:31-46)," *Revue d'Histoire et de Philosophie Religieuses* 50, no. 1 (1970): 23-60.

19. Among other things if the interpretation of Ingelaere were exact, the love of which Matthew speaks could be practiced only by pagans in contact with Christians.

20. *Die Synoptiker,* 3rd ed. (Tübingen, 1901).

21. *Évangile selon Saint Matthieu,* 7th ed. (Paris: J. Gabalda et Cie, Éditeurs, 1948), p. 485. The position of Lagrange is rather complicated: the judgment is universal but the teaching is addressed in the first place to Christians: "Everyone appears together at the judgment, but from then on Christ is concerned only with his disciples" (ibid.).

22. Wolfgang Trilling, *Das wahre Israel: Studien zur Théologie des Matthäus Evangeliums* (Munich, 1964), p. 26. See also by the same author *Gospel According to St. Matthew,* 2:216.

23. Mühlen, *Esprit dans l'Église,* 1:149. See also Josef Schmid, *Das Evangelium des Matthäus* (Ratisbona, 1952), pp. 352ff., cited in ibid.; and Georg Strecker, *Der Weg der Gerechtigkeit: Untersuchung zur Theologie des Matthäus* (Göttingen: Vandenhoeck & Ruprecht, 1962), pp. 218-19.

24. Pierre Bonnard, *L'Évangile selon Saint Matthieu* (Neuchatel: Éditions Delachaux & Niestlé, 1963), p. 367. "The Son of Man has made himself one with all those who objectively need help, whatever be their subjective dispositions. It is not said that these hungry ones, strangers, prisoners, were Christians. The Son of Man sees in any wretch his brother; . . . his love as shepherd of Israel claims to be in solidarity with the whole of human misery in all ranges and ultimate depths" (Preiss, *Life in Christ,* p. 52). See

also Joachim Jeremias, *The Parables of Jesus,* trans. S. H. Hooke (London: SCM Press Ltd., 1954), p. 143, and Trilling, *Gospel According to St. Matthew,* 2:219. See also Jacques Dupont, "La iglesia y la pobreza," *La Iglesia del Vaticano II,* p. 427.

25. Preiss has noted that for the verb "to do" (see vv. 40, 44) Jesus must have used the Aramaic *abad* which means both "to do" and "to serve"; quoted by Bonnard, *Matthieu,* p. 366.

26. Hence the expression "ethical prophecy" (Bonnard, *Matthieu,* p. 366). From this "primacy of the ethical demand," Strecker draws certain consequences for ecclesiology: "The elect of all nations are gathered together. No attention is paid to their membership in the community; they are judged only according to their good works." Thus, "the Church and the world are put on the same footing." Both "are presented in this point of time as complex dimensions, embracing both good and bad and presupposing responsibility for human actions." This does not prevent, nevertheless, that "the community of the Lord should be the legitimate and authentic representative of the eschatological challenge in the world" (*Der Weg der Gerechtigkeit,* pp. 218-19).

27. See Isa. 58:7; Job 31:17, 19, 21; Ezek. 18:7, 16.

28. See UNEC, *Caridad y amor humano* (Lima: Tierra Entera, 1966).

29. Congar, *Situation et tâches,* p. 67.

30. Is this the perspective at the beginning of the final sequence? Does the Nazarín—in the middle of the journey carrying in his hands the material proof of an act of human and disinterested love—take up the journey again? Does he begin his life again? It is impossible not to think of the last scene of Fellini's film, *Nights of Cabiria.*

31. "Los dados eternos" in *Heraldos negros.*

32. "This human history is the only way to reach God" (Edward Schillebeeckx, "L'immagine de Dio," *Ricerca,* March 31, 1968, p. 11).

33. See Alfaro, *Teología del progreso humano,* p. 114.

34. Address of Pope Paul VI, December 7, 1965, included in Xavier Rynne, *The Fourth Session* (New York: Farrar, Straus and Giroux, 1965), p. 325. Regarding Mic. 6:8 Albert Gelin writes, "There is no doubt that the expression is orientated toward fraternal love. The Old Testament had already prepared the formula of Gal. 5:14: by loving our brothers we reach God" ("La sainteté de l'homme selon l'Ancien Testament," *Bible et Vie Chrétienne,* no. 19 [September-November 1957], p. 45).

35. "Jugément Dernier," pp. 56-59.

36. Mühlen explains this identification of Christ with the poor by using his idea of the "Great I" (*Grand Moi*). The author uses this expression to refer to what others call the "corporate personality," a notion which seems to be deduced from the Old Testament. For Mühlen this is the "central notion of the Bible" (*Esprit dans l'Eglise,* 1:118). It expresses a special relationship of solidarity between the individual and the community. It has three elements: "(a) the primitive I, the source of a community; (b) the community itself, (c) the real unity between the two" (ibid., 1:122). The community "is really recapitulated in the individual I which originates it, and on the other hand the community is the 'irradiation' and the historical 'expansion' of this individual I" (ibid., 1:134). The best expression of this notion of the "Great I" would be the "Son of Man" (Dan. 7:13). Matt. 25:31–45 refers to the Son of Man: Christ is identified with the poor and forms with them "a unity which is difficult to understand outside of the Old Testament conception of the 'Great I' " (ibid., 1:143). Thus there is neither substitution nor representation but rather identification between Christ and the poor.

37. See the comment of Christian Duquoc in *Christologie: Essai dogmatique, L'homme Jésus* (Paris: Les Éditions du Cerf, 1968), pp. 213-61.

38. See Juan Luis Segundo, "Desarrollo y subdesarrollo: polos teológicos," *Perspectivas para el Diálogo,* no. 43 (May 1970), pp. 76-80.

39. *The Wide World My Parish,* p. 124. Congar sees in this the basis for the possibility of universal salvation: "We may call it the realm of 'God in disguise': he is really met, the dialogue is really with him, but he does not call himself God and one does not know that it is he" (*Wide World,* p. 120). Javier Alonso Hernández studies the "sacramental value of history," in *Teología y desarrollo* (Lima: Centro Arquidiocesano de Pastoral, 1969), pp. 184-91.

40. "La de a mil" in *Heraldos negros.*

41. Regarding these subjects see the analyses of Emmanuel Levinas, *Totality and Infinity,* trans. Alphonso Lingis (Pittsburgh: Duquesne University Press, 1969), pp. 194-219.

42. "To love man . . . not as a means but as the first step toward the final and transcendent goal which is the basis and cause of every love" (Paul VI, Address of December 7, 1965, in Rynne, *Fourth Session,* p. 325).

43. See also Jean Cardonnel, "Dieu et l'urgence des masses," *Esprit* 36, no. 370 (April 1968): 661-76; Hugo Assmann believes that in a world "that is becoming more and more socialized we are called to recover the Biblical primacy of the people over the individual" ("Fe y promoción humana," *Perspectivas para el Diálogo,* no. 36 [August 1969], p. 181).

44. In this regard for the cases of Mexico and Puerto Rico, see the works of Oscar Lewis, *Five Families: Mexican Case Studies in the Culture of Poverty* (New York: John Wiley, 1962) and *La Vida* (New York: Random, 1966).

45. The poem of León Felipe which Che Guevara liked so much is well known. Because it was found recopied among Guevara's papers, some attribute the poem to him:

> Christ I love you
> not because you descended from a star
> but because you revealed to me
> that man has blood
> tears
> anguish
> keys
> tools
> to open the doors closed to light
> Yes! You taught us that man is God . . .
> a poor God crucified like you
> and the one who is at your left on Golgotha
> the bad thief
> is God too!

46. See José María González Ruiz, *Pobreza evangélica y promoción humana* (Barcelona: Nova Terra, 1966), p. 87.

47. We need only read Camilo Torres or Nestor Paz Zamora—to mention two who have left something in writing—to be convinced of this. It would be a mistake for theologians who might be offended by certain deficiencies of expression to ignore these efforts to penetrate what the Word of the Lord is saying to us in the Latin American context.

48. Arturo Gaete observed a short time ago the need for a "spirituality of liberation" ("Definición e indefinición de la Iglesia en política," *Mensaje* 19, no. 191 [August 1970]: 375). See also the attempt of Arturo Paoli, *Dialogo della liberazione* (Brescia: Morcelliana: 1970), to be published in English by Orbis Books. The poet Ernesto Cardenal offers us a collection of profound "Psalms" which seek and sing liberation in the midst of modern forms of oppression and exploitation (*Psalms of Struggle and Liberation* [New York: Herder and Herder, 1971]). See also the interesting ideas of Gonzalo Arroyo on the "rebel communities": "Rebeldía cristiana y compromiso comunitario," *Mensaje* 17, no. 167 (March-April 1968): 78-83.

49. See José María González Ruiz, *Dios es gratuito, pero no superfluo* (Madrid: Ediciones Marova, 1970).

50. This has been clearly pointed out in "Pastoral Concern for the Elites," no. 13, in *Medellín.*

51. If Vallejo was correct when he said "My God, if you had been a man, today you would know how to be God," it could also be said, "If you had been God, today you would know how to be human."

52. See the excellent considerations of Harvey Cox in *The Feast of Fools* (Cambridge: Harvard University Press, 1969).

53. Conrad Eggers Lan, *Cristianismo y nueva ideología* (Buenos Aires, 1968), pp. 47-48, quoted by Juan Luis Segundo, "Desarrollo y subdesarrollo: polos teológicos," p. 79.

54. See below Chapter 13. "Christians and their pastors should know how to recognize the hand of the Almighty in those events that occur sporadically—when the powerful are dethroned and the lowly are exalted, when the rich are sent away empty-handed and the needy are filled" ("Letter to Peoples of the Third World," in *Between Honesty and Hope,* p. 6).

55. This is one of the most fruitful sources for the theology of liberation: "There is great need for a spirituality of liberation" (p. 74, above). The first writings on the subject, those of Bishop E. Pironio, were followed by those of S. Galilea, L. Boff, and J. Sobrino, and many others. I myself have also returned to the theme (see my *We Drink From Our Own Wells*), developing the pages devoted to it in the present book, and enriching them with the testimonies of individual Christians and Christian communities. The soil of spirituality yields life and direction for this kind of theological reflection. For a rounded presentation of the subject, see J. Espeja, *Espiritualidad y Liberación* (Lima: CEP, 1986).

## 11. ESCHATOLOGY AND POLITICS

1. See the excellent article by Karl Rahner, "Unterwegs zum neuen Menschen," *Wort und Wahrheit* 16 (1961): 807-19, and reproduced as "Christianity and the 'New Man' " in *Theological Investigations,* 5:135-53; and more recently Harvey Cox, *On Not Leaving it to the Snake,* pp. 91-150.

2. Karl Rahner, "La nouvelle terre," *Écrits théologiques* (Bruges: Desclée de Brouwer, 1970), 10:113.

3. See above Chapter 6.

4. "Introduction," no. 4, in *Medellín.*

5. Jürgen Moltmann, "Gott in der Revolution," in *Diskussion zur "Theologie der Revolution,"* pp. 65-68. In English see "God in Revolution," in Moltmann's *Religion,*

*Revolution and the Future*, trans. M. Douglas Meeks (New York: Charles Scribner's Sons, 1969).

6. Regarding this new situation of contemporary humankind, see Edward Schillebeeckx, "The Interpretation of Eschatology," in *The Problem of Eschatology*, ed. Edward Schillebeeckx and Boniface Willems, *Concilium* 41 (New York: Paulist Press, 1969), pp. 42-56.

7. See the famous article of Léopold Malevez, "Deux théologies catholiques de l'histoire," in *Bijdragen* (1949), pp. 225-40. See also Gustave Thils, *Christian Attitudes* (Dublin: Scepter, 1959).

8. The focus of this tendency was the periodical *Dieu Vivant*, published between 1945 and 1955 and dedicated from its first issue to presenting "an eschatological conception of Christianity." In this regard see the study of Bernard Besret, *Incarnation ou eschatologie, Contribution à l'histoire du vocabulaire religieux contemporain 1935-1955* (Paris: Les Éditions du Cerf, 1964), pp. 122-44. Roger Aubert stated ironically and perceptively on this subject, "Incarnation or eschatology? Immanence or transcendence? Immanence and transcendence has been the answer. And this is very correct. But it is easier to change a conjunction and get rid of a question mark than it is to build a balanced system in which all the elements are in their proper places. Theologians today are still busy in the construction of this system, but . . . it is easy to see that the quarries are still open" (*La théologie catholique au milieu du XXe siècle* [Tournai-Paris: Casterman, 1954], pp. 69-70). And they still are.

9. See above Chapter 9. See also C. Dumont, "De trois dimensions retrouvées en théologie: eschatologie-orthopraxie-herméneutique," *Nouvelle Revue Théologique* 92, no. 6 (June-July 1970): 570. One of the first efforts to bring out the relationship between eschatology and political commitment is Georges Didier, "Eschatologie et engagement chrétien," *Nouvelle Revue Théologique* 75, no. 1 (January 1953): 3-14; the categories used say little to us today, however.

10. See "Sketch of a Phenomenology and a Metaphysic of Hope," in *Homo Viator*, trans. Emma Crauford (New York: Harper and Row, Publishers, Harper Torchbook, 1962), pp. 29-67.

11. "Theses on Feuerbach," nos. 11 and 1, in Karl Marx and Friedrich Engels, *On Religion* (New York: Schocken Books, 1964), pp. 72 and 69; italics in the original.

12. With Lukacs and Korsch, Bloch belongs to what some have called "esoteric Marxism," and to what Bloch himself prefers to call "the warm current of Marxism"— concerned with achieving the real through what today is only potential. On the Marxism of Bloch see Werner Maihofer, "Ernst Blochs Evolution des Marxismus," in *Über Ernst Bloch* (Frankfurt: Suhrkamp, 1968), pp. 112-29.

13. *Das Prinzip Hoffnung*, p. 82.

14. See Ernst Bloch, *Philosophische Grundfragen. Zur Ontologie des Noch-Nicht-Seins* (Frankfurt: Suhrkamp, 1961).

15. Quoted in Harvey Cox's prologue to a collection of Bloch's works, *Man on his Own*, trans. E. B. Ashton (New York: Herder and Herder, 1970), p. 9.

16. Bloch is concerned with the relationship between atheism and Christianity; see his *Atheismus im Christentum* (Frankfurt: Suhrkamp, 1968). In it he maintains that "only an atheist can be a good Christian and only a Christian can be a good atheist." The second part of this sentence is a reply of Moltmann used by Bloch (see Moltmann's introduction to *Über Ernst Bloch*, p. 28). For him the Bible is a profoundly revolutionary book, for it brings the good news of the limitless possibilities of humanity. The fundamental affirmation of the Bible is what is said in Genesis, "You will be like gods." This is expressed in historical figures throughout the Old Testament, it is revealed clearly

in the key event of the Exodus, and it finds its categorical realization with Christ. Nevertheless, for Bloch all this cannot be understood in its true significance except by an "atheistic interpretation" of the Bible. Therefore "only an atheist can be a good Christian." At the same time, however, Bloch opposes a dogmatic and positivistic atheism and advocates a "nonconformist atheist movement." Thus "only a Christian can be a good atheist." Although his position is fundamentally different from the Bible, it must be said that Bloch offers us a stimulating and perceptive reading of it.

17. "It is difficult to imagine a philosophy other than that of *The Hope Principle* which could be more useful in helping us to renew and elaborate the Christian doctrine of hope" (Jürgen Moltmann, "Die Kategorie Novum in der christlichen Théologie," in *Ernst Bloch zu ehren*, ed. S. Unseld [Frankfurt: Suhrkamp, 1965], p. 243; in English see " 'Behold, I make all things new': The Category of the New in Christian Theology," in *The Future as the Presence of Shared Hope*, ed. Maryellen Muckenhirn [New York: Sheed and Ward, 1968]).

18. "Perhaps Christian theology will one day have to thank Ernst Bloch's philosophy of hope for giving it the courage to recover in the full sense its central category of eschatology. . . . Bloch has taught us about the overwhelming power of the still-open future and of the hope that reaches out to it in anticipation for not only the life and thought of man but in addition for the ontological uniqueness of everything in reality" (Wolfhart Pannenberg, *Basic Questions in Theology*, 2:237-38).

19. *Das Prinzip Hoffnung*, p. 1404.

20. Moltmann, *Theology of Hope*, p. 84.

21. Ibid., p. 16.

22. Ibid., pp. 18 and 86.

23. And a "theology of universal history," Pannenberg would add, which seeks to reinterpret Christianity on the basis of history taken in its totality. On the thinking of Pannenberg, see the fine article of Claude Geffré, "La théologie de l'histoire comme problème herméneutique: W. Pannenberg," *Études Théologiques et Religieuses* 46, no. 1 (1971): 13-27; and Ignace Berten, *Histoire, révélation et foi, Dialogue avec W. Pannenberg* (Brussels: Éditions du CEP, 1969). These authors differ, however, in their way of conceiving the role of the resurrection of Jesus in history. For Pannenberg, "With the resurrection of Jesus, the end of history has already occurred" (*Revelation as History*, p. 142). Moltmann replies that the resurrection of Christ is "the source of the risen life of all believers" and that therefore "believers find their future *in him* and not merely *like* him. Hence they wait for their future by waiting for his future" (*Theology of Hope*, p. 83; see also pp. 76-84).

24. Moltmann, *Theology of Hope*, p. 18.

25. Ibid.

26. Ibid., p. 85.

27. Ibid., p. 86.

28. *Theology of Human Hope*, pp. 59-60. See also Hugo Assmann, *Teología de la liberación*, MIEC-JECI, series 1, doc. 23-24, 1970, pp. 37-38.

29. *Theology of Human Hope*, p. 59.

30. Ibid., p. 67.

31. See above Chapter 9.

32. See above Chapter 1.

33. Moltmann is aware of the danger of ignoring the present life (*Theology of Hope*, pp. 26-32), but in the terms in which this concern is expressed it does not seem to transcend the limitations which we have just indicated. His more recent works, however,

show an interesting evolution and a fruitful opening to the human historical struggle today; see the two articles we have already mentioned, "Gott in der Revolution" and "Toward a Political Hermeneutic of the Gospel," as well as "The Christian *Theology of Hope* and its Bearing on Development," in *In Search of a Theology of Development* (Geneva: SODEPAX, 1970), pp. 93-100. In this last work Moltmann establishes a rich distinction between on the one hand that which becomes, the foreseeable, the calculable, the object of futurology, which he proposes to call *future* and on the other hand that which comes, the desirable, that which cannot be calculated but only anticipated, which can be designated by the term *avenir* (in German *Zu-kunft*, which translates the Latin *adventus*, the equivalent of *parousia*; pp. 97-98). Cf. similar ideas proposed by Karl Rahner, "Autour du concept de l'avenir," *Écrits théologiques*, 10:95-103.

34. See a collection of reactions to this work, Wolf-Dieter Marsch, ed., *Diskussion über die "Theologie der Hoffnung" von Jürgen Moltmann* (Munich: Chr. Kaiser Verlag, 1967).

35. "Gott in der Revolution," p. 69.

36. See the observations of Pablo Fontaine regarding the questions which revolutionary political commitment poses to the life of faith in *El revolucionario cristiano y la fe*, MIEC-JECI, series 1, doc. 25, 1970.

37. Ludwig Feuerbach, *The Essence of Christianity*, trans. George Eliot (New York: Harper & Row, Publishers, 1957), p. 257.

38. Ibid., pp. 1-12. "If human nature is the highest nature to man, then practically also the highest and first law must be the love of man to man" (ibid., p. 271).

39. Ibid., p. 12.

40. Ibid., pp. 247-69.

41. Feuerbach was not aware of the writings of Hegel's youth. In them love occupies an outstanding position. "Religion," wrote Hegel, "is identical to love" ("Amour et religion" [Fragment of 1798] in *L'Esprit du christianisme et son destin* [Paris: J. Vrin, 1967], p. 146). Commenting on this and other similar fragments, Paul Asveld concludes, "Through love humanity rises to the level of the Absolute. In Hegel's Frankfurt writings love corresponds to the intellectual intuition of Schelling" (*La pensée religieuse du jeune Hegel* [Louvain: Publications Universitaires de Louvain, 1953], pp. 166-67). In the works of his maturity love does not seem to play the same role as in the texts of his youth (see A. Chapelle, *Hegel et la religion*, 2:62-64). Hegel speaks nevertheless of love as "the substantial bond of the world" in his *Leçons sur la philosophie de la religion*, trans. J. Gibelin (Paris: J. Vrin, 1954), part 3, p. 216; in English see *Lectures on the Philosophy of Religion*, 3 vols., trans. E. B. Speirs and J. Burdon Sanderson (New York: Humanities Press Inc., 1962).

42. See Feuerbach, *Manifestes philosophiques, textes choisis (1839-1845)* (Paris: Presses Universitaires de France, 1960), p. 200. The final lines of *The Essence of Christianity* are well known: "It needs only that the ordinary course of things be interrupted in order to vindicate to common things an uncommon significance, *to life, as such, a religious import*. Therefore let bread be sacred for us, let wine be sacred, and also let water be sacred! Amen" (p. 278; italics in the original). J. P. Osier is thus correct when he asserts that "Feuerbach is not irreligious but atheistic" (Preface to *L'essence du christianisme* [Paris: Maspero, 1968], p. 65). See the excellent study by Marcel Xhaufflaire, *Feuerbach et la théologie de la sécularisation* (Paris: Les Éditions du Cerf, 1970).

43. See Karl Marx, "Circular contra Kriege (1846)" in Karl Marx and Friedrich Engels, *Marx-Engles Werke, Ergänzungsband, Schriften bis 1944* (Berlin, 1968), 4:12-16. H. Kriege was a "sentimental communist," an emigrant to the United States, a

friend of W. Weitling, and one of the heads of "true socialism." Regarding this current see the harsh words dedicated to it in "The Communist Manifesto" (*Capital, The Communist Manifesto and other Writings* [New York: The Modern Library, 1932], pp. 349-51). When he criticizes this tendency Marx is in reality criticizing Feuerbach: " 'True socialism' with its different ramifications appears as the most authentic creation of Feuerbachian thought" (Henri Arvon, *Ludwig Feuerbach ou la transformation du sacré* [Paris: Presses Universitaires de France, 1957], p. 114; see also Xhaufflaire, *Feuerbach*, pp. 189-211).

44. "German Ideology," in *Writings of the Young Karl Marx on Philosophy and Society*, trans. and ed. Loyd D. Easton and Kurt H. Guddat (Garden City, New York: Doubleday and Co., 1967), p. 419. As Xhaufflaire correctly points out, the restoration of the "new religion" is according to Feuerbach the "praxis" which will transform the world; for him it is necessary "to change mentalities before restructuring the world" (*Feuerbach*, p. 209).

45. See Thomas J. J. Altizer and William Hamilton, *Radical Theology and the Death of God* (Indianapolis: Bobbs Merrill, 1966). See also Thomas W. Ogletree, *The Death of God Controversy* (Nashville: Abingdon, 1966). Thus it is that the so-called theology of the death of God—which some mistakenly believe to be the inevitable final phase of the process of secularization—has certain characteristics which we might dare to call "pre-Marxist."

46. The most important work of Johannes B. Metz on this subject is the address given at the International Congress of Theology at Toronto, August 20-24, 1967, "The Church and the World in the Light of a 'Political Theology.' " It is included in Metz's *Theology of the World*, pp. 107-140.

47. Metz speaks of political theology as "eschatological theology" ("Politische Theologie in der Diskussion," in Helmut Peukert, ed., *Diskussion zur "politische Théologie"* [Mainz, Munich: Grünewald-Kaiser, 1969], p. 280; see also *Theology of the World*, p. 91).

48. "The Church's Social Function in the Light of a 'Political Theology,' " *Faith and the World of Politics*, ed. Johannes B. Metz, *Concilium* 36 (New York: Paulist Press, 1968), p. 9.

49. Claude Geffré has pointed this out very well, putting political theology in the context of fundamental theology in "Recent Developments in Fundamental Theology: An Interpretation," *The Development of Fundamental Theology*, ed. Johannes B. Metz, *Concilium* 46 (New York: Paulist Press, 1969), pp. 5-28.

50. *Theology of the World*, p. 107.

51. "Politische Theologie," pp. 268-79.

52. For Metz the process initiated with the Enlightenment is of capital importance for theological reflection; see the work done with Moltmann and Willi Oelmüller, *Kirche im Prozess der Aufklärung, Aspekte einer neuen "politischen Theologie"* (Munich: Kaiser, 1970).

53. "Politische Theologie," p. 270.

54. Marcel Xhaufflaire, "Les grandes lignes de la théologie politique selon J. B. Metz," in *La Lettre*, no. 150 (February 1971), p. 26. According to the author of this fine presentation of Metz's thought, the distinction to which we refer "allows political theology to be articulated in the political sphere, understood henceforth not as the sphere of the establishment of sovereignty, powers, or domination, but rather as the democratic 'public' place of the mediation of liberty or the liberation of humankind (the general welfare of society, not the particular welfare of the Church)."

55. "Politische Theologie," p. 271; italics in the original.

56. Ibid., p. 268. For the sociological aspects of their analyses, Metz and some of his disciples often take their inspiration from the works of Jürgen Habermas. See his *Strukturwandel der Oeffentlichkeit* (Neuwied: Luebterhand, 1962) and *Technik und Wissenschaft als "Ideologie"* (Frankfurt: Suhrkamp, 1969).

57. Metz, *Theology of the World*, p. 108.

58. Ibid., p. 109. Schleiermacher had already reacted in this way to the problems posed by the Enlightenment when he insisted that sentiment was the characteristic trait of religion (cf. Karl Barth, *Protestant Thought: From Rousseau to Ritschl* [New York: Harper & Brothers, Publishers, 1959], pp. 306-54). But at the opposite extreme is Hegel, who accepted the questions posed by the Enlightenment and sought to understand the relationship between revelation and reason on the basis of history.

59. Metz, *Theology of the World*, p. 110. The opposition to Bultmann is translated clearly into the neologism which expresses this first task of political theology. Metz is indeed very critical of the "existential interpretation of the New Testament," which is based on the philosophy of Heidegger and seems to Metz to imply a serious and dangerous individualism. Not unrelated to this critique is the influence of the social and historical thought of Bloch. Indeed it is his work *Das Prinzip Hoffnung* which is suggestively presented by Harvey Cox (for whom in the secular era politics ought to replace metaphysics as the language of theology; see *The Secular City*, p. 255) as the most serious alternative to the "Being and Time" of Heidegger for theological thinking ("Afterword" of *The Secular City Debate*, ed. Daniel J. Callahan [New York: Macmillan, 1966], p. 200). Bloch himself criticizes Bultmann for having stripped the faith of any social weight (*Atheismus in Christentum*, pp. 69-72). On this theological level we have a situation which is familiar to us in contemporary philosophy and can be illustrative. Marxism and existentialism have been engaged for some years in a harsh debate regarding the values of freedom and personal decision and the social and historical decisions of human existence (see Garaudy, *Perspectives de l'homme* and the letter from Sartre to Garaudy included in this work; Sartre has attempted a synthesis in *Critique de la raison dialectique* [Paris: Éditions Gallimard, 1960]). If we go a little deeper we discover the antagonistic thinking of Kierkegaard and Marx. Both are at least partially reacting to the Hegelian system which in one way or another is still a point of reference for contemporary thought. Perhaps therefore we should go upstream toward the source, that is to Hegel, to better situate the debate between political theology and "privatizing" theology.

60. "Politische Theologie," p. 272.

61. Metz, *Theology of the World*, p. 111.

62. "The so-called fundamental hermeneutic problem of theology is not the problem of how systematic theology stands in relation to historical theology, how dogma stands in relation to history, but what is the relation between theory and practice, between understanding the faith and social practice" (*Theology of the World*, p. 112).

63. Ibid., p. 114.

64. "Politische Theologie," p. 289.

65. *Theology of the World*, p. 114. The expression *eschatological proviso* (*réserve eschatologique*) had already been used in a sense similar to Metz's by Heinrich Schlier, *Le temps de l'Église* (Tournai: Casterman, 1961), pp. 19-20.

66. Metz, *Theology of the World*, p. 116; the italics are ours.

67. Ibid.

68. Ibid., p. 120.

69. Robert Spaemann believes that the political action of Christians has no need of a theological benediction; see "Theologie, Prophetie, Politik. Zur Kritik der politischen Theologie," *Wort und Wahreit* 24 (1969): 491.

70. See Karl Lehmann, "Die 'politische Theologie': Theologische Legitimation und gegenwärtige Aporie," in *Diskussion zur "politische Theologie,"* pp. 185-216.

71. See Henri de Lavalette, "La théologie politique allemande," *Recherches de Science Religieuse* 58, no. 3 (July-September 1970): 321-50. Throughout this article the author is quite ambiguous concerning the ideas of Metz.

72. See Hans Maier, "Politische Theologie? Einwände eines Laien," in *Diskussion zur "politische Theologie,"* pp. 1-25. The author affirms the possibility—for lay people—of autonomous political and apostolic activity. But to defend his ideas Maier engages in a rearguard battle, still necessary it seems in some cases and situations, but on which the future of the Church does not depend today: the confrontation between the laity and the hierarchy. This issue has been transcended among Christians occupied with less intraecclesial problems.

73. Karl Rahner believes that "the concept of a 'political theology' is still not established in an absolutely clear manner," and he states, "I am not completely sure that I myself understand what is meant by it." And he goes on to say that he is in accord with a political theology understood as "the simple explicit valorization of the social implications of all the theological enunciations" ("L'avenir de la théologie," *Nouvelle Revue Théologique* 93, no.1 [January 1971]:24). As we have seen, Metz's effort goes beyond this. But Rahner is correct when he says that further clarification is still necessary.

74. See Trutz Rendtorf, "Politische Ethik oder 'politische Theologie'?," in *Diskussion zur "politische Theologie,"* pp. 217-30. Metz accepts this criticism and distinguishes between his effort and political ethics: "Political theology, as eschatological theology, is able to determine its orientation to praxis in an indirect manner mediated through the path of a political ethic" ("Politische Théologie," p. 280). Hugo Assmann challenges him for having adopted this distinction: *Teología de la liberación*, pp. 39-40; and "Teología política," in *Perspectivas para el Diálogo*, no. 50 (December 1970), p. 307.

75. Marcel Xhaufflaire and Frans van den Oudenrijn, "Bulletin informatif," in *Les deux visages de la théologie de la sécularisation*, pp. 74-75.

76. K. Levéque, "De la théologie politique à la théologie de la révolution," *Frères du Monde*, no. 46 (1970), p. 34.

77. This experience is fruitful for theological reflection; see Juan Luis Segundo, "Desarrollo y subdesarrollo: polos teológicos," pp. 76-80.

78. In this regard see the studies included in *Les deux visages*.

79. See above Chapter 6.

80. Another thing which must be avoided is that the new political theology contribute to an evasion of real and effective commitment to the historical present. A certain theoretical recovery at the level of language of the problems of the world today as well as the abstention which the term *eschatological proviso* (*Vorbehalt*) seems to imply—against the manifest intention of the author—are both an invitation to this.

81. Since the early 1970s political theology has deepened its first intuitions and has opened new perspectives. The dialogue between political theology and the theology of liberation has likewise become closer and more fruitful. See J. B. Metz, *Faith in History and Society: Toward a Practical Fundamental Theology* (New York: Seabury, 1980), and *The Emergent Church: The Future of Christianity in a Postbourgeois World* (New York: Crossroad, 1981). On the similarities and differences between modern or progressive theology and the theology of liberation, see my "Theology from the Underside of

History," in *The Power of the Poor in History* (Maryknoll, N.Y.: Orbis Books, 1983), pp. 169–221, and the polemic book of Ch. Duquoc, *Liberation et progressisme* (Paris: Cerf, 1987).

82. *Théologie de la révolution* (Paris: Éditions Universitaires, 1970), p. 236.

83. See Robert Eisler, *The Messiah Jesus and John the Baptist* (New York: The Dial Press, 1931), which makes Jesus a Zealot. S. G. F. Brandon, *The Fall of Jerusalem and the Christian Church* (London: S. P. C. K., 1951), does not go to this extreme but does strongly emphasize Jesus' ties with the Zealot movement. Oscar Cullmann perceptively and carefully analyzes the matter in *The State in the New Testament* (London: SCM Press Ltd., 1957). Because of contemporary concerns regarding the political sphere this matter has been taken up again with a new vigor; see Martin Hengel, *Die Zeloten* (Leiden: E. J. Brill, 1961), and Samuel Georg Frederick Brandon, *Jesus and the Zealots* (Manchester: Manchester University Press, 1967); this author believes that the Gospels, especially Mark, have a tendency to depoliticize the life of Jesus. See also Oscar Cullmann, *Jesus and the Revolutionaries*, trans. Gareth Putnam (New York: Harper & Row, 1970); Martin Hengel, *War Jesus revolutionär?* (Stuttgart: Calwer Verlag, 1970); and Georges Crespy, "Recherche sur la signification politique de la mort du Christ," *Lumière et Vie* 20, no. 101 (January-March 1971): 89-109.

84. *State*, p. 17. See the demonstration of this assertion, pp. 14-17. See also Crespy, "Recherche," pp. 100-01, and Brandon, *Jesus and the Zealots*, pp. 203-05.

85. This act of Jesus is considered as a Zealot gesture by Étienne Trocmé, "L'expulsion des marchands du Temple," in *New Testament Studies* 15, no. 1 (October 1968): 1 ff., cited by Cullmann, *Jesus and the Revolutionaries*, p. 18, no. 5.

86. Regarding these concurrences, see Cullmann, *Jesus and the Revolutionaries*, pp. 8-10. This author believes that Jesus rejected anything which might give a triumphal and political character to his entrance into Jerusalem; thus he rides on an ass and not a horse "in the manner of a warlike Messiah" (p. 43). But Crespy, following W. Vischer, *Die evangelische Gemeinde Ordnung-Mattheus 16, 13-20, 28* (Zurich: Evangelische Verlag, 1946) points out that if to understand its meaning Mark 11:10 is translated from the Greek to the Hebrew the text could be, "Save us! Blessed is he who comes in the name of the Lord. Blessed is the kingdom that comes, the kingdom of David, our Father. Save us from the Roman!" With this correction, writes Crespy, the text would be coherent: "The kingdom of the Son of David comes through victory over the pagan occupier. On the other hand, the relationship of the forms explains the translation 'in the highest,' and the softening of the text is based on an identifiable grammatical fact." The cry of the people would then be a seditious, *Zealot* act; this would help explain the fear and the reprobation of the priests and scribes according to Matt. 21:16: "Do you hear what they are saying?" (pp. 101-02).

87. The Jewish historian Josephus presents the movement created by Jesus as a Zealot movement; see Cullman, *State*, p. 49.

88. "In relation to this plan," writes Comblin, "it is clear that the Zealot is essentially conservative. What did the Zealots want? To assure Israel complete political independence, to isolate the Jews from the others in a most complete fashion, to achieve an extreme Judaism, an extreme isolationism. . . . To follow the Zealots was to adopt a regression into the past" (*Théologie de la révolution*, pp. 240-41).

89. See Matt. 4:1-11. In this regard Cullmann correctly points out that "one is tempted only by the things which stand near him" (*State*, p. 24). Regarding the meaning of the temptations of Jesus, see Duquoc, *Christologie*, pp. 52-71. "Jesus rejects a political messianism. But he confronts the political power; he takes a stand in relation to

it; and his message has inevitable political implications" (Augustin George, "Jésus devant le problème politique," *Lumière et Vie* 20, no. 105 [November-December 1971]:5).

90. See Pierre Benoit, *The Passion and Resurrection of Jesus Christ*, trans. Benet Weatherhead (New York: Herder and Herder, 1969), pp. 176-77; and Lucien Cerfaux, *Jésus aux origins de la tradition* (Paris: Desclée de Brouwer, 1968), p. 199.

91. *State*, p. 43; see also p. 12; and *Jesus and the Revolutionaries*, p. 31; as well as Crespy, p. 99.

92. *State*, pp. 47-48. Heinrich Schlier speaks of Barabbas as "a Messianic revolutionary" (*The Relevance of the New Testament* [New York: Herder and Herder, 1968], p. 221). Paul Blanquart, in an exegesis which is unique to him, believes that "by entering the prison which he enabled the *guerrilla* Barabbas to leave, Jesus, in the same action, entered into his death and resurrection . . . and liberated politics—in the person of Barabbas. . . . He enabled it to be itself, by entrusting it to the reason and love of human beings" ("L'acte de croire et l'action politique," *Lumière et Vie* 19, no. 98 [June-July 1970]: 26).

93. Regarding the "trial of Jesus" see Josef Blinzer, *The Trial of Jesus*, trans. Isabel and Florence McHugh (Westminster, Md.: The Newman Press, 1959); X. Léon-Dufour, *Supplément au Dictionnaire de la Bible*, s. v. "Passion," cols. 1419-92; Benoit, *Passion and Resurrection*; and the fine treatment of the state of this question in Wolfgang Trilling, *Jésus devant l'histoire*, trans. Joseph Schmitt (Paris: Les Éditions du Cerf, 1968), pp. 175-88. See also S. G. F. Brandon's most recent study, *The Trial of Jesus*, 2nd ed. (London: Paladin, 1971), which claims for Jesus a place of honor in the long history of martyrs of Israel (p. 14). See the interesting observations of Augustin George, "Comment Jésus a-t-il perçu sa propre mort?" *Lumière et Vie* 20, no. 101 (January-March 1971): 34-59. This article also includes a copious bibliography on this theme.

94. "Recherche," p. 105.

95. Schlier, *Relevance*, p. 215. This is also Bultmann's position in his interpretation of the Gospel of John. A good number of authors undertake to demonstrate that Jesus was innocent of the charges that were imputed to him (See Blinzer, Léon-Dufour, Benoit). It is not clear what the object of these attempts is. Innocent before what justice? Before the justice of the power groups of the Jewish people and the Roman oppressors, Jesus was guilty precisely because he challenged their legitimacy, in the name not of some partisan option, but of a message of love, peace, freedom, and justice. This message undermined the very bases of religious formalism, unjust privileges, and social injustice which supported the order of the power groups of the Jewish people and the Roman authority.

96. *Jesus and the Revolutionaries*, pp. 20 and 51.

97. Ibid., p. 13; italics in the original.

98. Ibid., p. 55. Cullmann qualifies these somewhat abrupt conclusions with considerations on the need for Christians to commit themselves to the world of today. But the basic thrust of this commitment is given by what we have just recalled. For example, he had said, "We could extend Jesus' line of thought and show that the social question would actually be solved already in this age if every individual would become as radically converted as Jesus demands" (p. 28). This makes us fear that there has been no real understanding of the political sphere. This certainly influences his interpretation of the attitude of Jesus in this regard.

99. See Werner Georg Kümmel, *Promise and Fulfillment: The Eschatological Message of Jesus* (London: SCM Press Ltd., 1961). Contrary to Albert Schweitzer, Cullmann believes that Jesus foresaw a time between his death and the parousia, a time

which he had calculated, nevertheless, at the most in decades. See his work *Christ and Time*, rev. ed., trans. Floyd V. Filson (Philadelphia: The Westminster Press, 1964), pp. 148-50.

100. Bultmann also affirms the belief of Jesus in a proximate arrival of the end of time, but he thinks that this is secondary. The important thing would be the present personal decision for the Kingdom. The "difficult" texts are Matt. 10:23 and Mark 9:1 and 13:30. Rudolf Schnackenburg concludes a study of these texts by affirming: "We have arrived at the following position. A broad stream of tradition testifies that Jesus announced the coming of God's reign, and correspondingly of the Son of Man, for a near future but without further specification of the time, indeed with an explicit refusal to provide more precise details. Against this, only a few passages contain a definite time reference, to the generation then alive. It was not possible to explain these passages. It would seem that the early Church was uncertain how to fit these awkward pieces neatly into the eschatological discourse of Jesus. This attitude of the Church may well point to the best method for ourselves: namely, to nourish a living eschatological hope from the urgent prophetic preaching of Jesus without drawing false conclusions about that prophecy from individual passages" (*God's Rule and Kingdom*, p. 212). See also Trilling, *Jésus devant l'histoire*, pp. 143-66.

101. See Anton Grabner-Haider, "Zur Kultkritik im Neuen Testament," *Diakonia* 4 (1969): 138–46.

102. See above Chapter 10.

103. "In my opinion," writes Crespy, "it is too early to speak of the political meaning of the life and death of Jesus without equivocation" ("Recherche," p. 89). In reality it will always be too soon—and too late. Indeed for some time now a political meaning has been given to the life and death of Jesus; the problem cannot be avoided by speaking of the matter in the name of his alleged apoliticism. Exegetes are not always aware of the political presuppositions of their interpretation of Scripture. Notwithstanding his initial assertion, however, Crespy proposes an interesting reflection on the political meaning of the testimony of Jesus.

104. Wolfhart Pannenberg, "Die politische Dimension des Evangeliums," in *Die Politik und das Heil* (Mainz: Matthias-Grünewald, 1968), p. 19.

105. See above Chapter 9. See also the observations of Jacques Guillet in "Jésus et la politique," *Recherches de Sciences Religieuses* 59, no. 4 (October-December 1971): 544.

106. Gustav Landauer was perhaps the first to consider—although in a perspective which suffered from a certain romanticism—the notion of utopia in our time. Landauer distinguishes between "topia"—stabilizing and even reactionary, "a broad, general conglomeration of common life in a state of relative stability"—and "utopia"—revolutionary, "a conglomeration of aspirations and tendencies of the will," which overturns the "topia," the previous order. See his work *Die Revolution* (Frankfurt: Rütten and Loening, 1907); the quoted texts are taken from the Spanish translation, *La revolución* (Buenos Aires: Proyección, 1961), p. 27. See also the classic work of one of the creators of the sociology of knowledge: Karl Mannheim, *Ideology and Utopia*, trans. Louis Wirth and Edward Shils (New York: Harcourt, Brace, and World, 1966); this work was first published in 1929. Regarding the notion of utopia, its impreciseness, its theoretical difficulties, and the present state of the question, see the texts gathered and presented by Arnhelm Neüssus in *Utopia* (Barcelona: Barral, 1971); this work also contains a copious bibliography on the subject. Orlando Borda has attempted to interpret Colombian history from the perspective of utopian thought: *Subversion and Social Change in Colombia*, trans. Jacqueline D. Skils (New York: Columbia University

Press, 1969). Paul VI has recognized the role that utopia plays in "the political problem of modern societies" (*Octogesima adveniens*, no. 37).

107. See Jean Servier, *Histoire de l'Utopie* (Paris: Éditions Gallimard, 1967).

108. Referring to the misunderstanding regarding this notion of utopia and the new conditions created in our time, Herbert Marcuse writes, "I believe that this restrictive conception must be revised, and that the revision is suggested, and even necessitated, by the actual evolution of contemporary societies. The dynamic of their productivity deprives 'utopia' of its traditional unreal content: what is denounced as 'utopian' is no longer that which has 'no place' and cannot have any place in the historical universe, but rather that which is blocked from coming about by the power of the established societies" (*An Essay on Liberation*, pp. 3-4).

109. Regarding the work of Thomas More see Concilium General Secretariat, "*Utopia,* The Problem of Eschatology," *Concilium* 41, pp. 149-65, which also includes a copious bibliography on the subject.

110. "Education as Cultural Action: An Introduction," in Louis M. Colonnese, ed., *Conscientization for Liberation* (Washington, D.C.: Division for Latin America, United States Catholic Conference), p. 119.

111. *Essay*, p. ix; regarding Marcuse see above Chapter 2.

112. See the works we have already cited by Ernst Bloch as well as an earlier one, *Geist der Utopie* (Frankfurt: Suhrkamp, 1964); this was first published in 1917. On this aspect of Bloch's work see P. Furter, "Utopia e marxismo segundo Ernst Bloch," in *Tempo Brasileiro*, October 3, 1965.

113. Thus José Carlos Mariátegui proposes with a certain amount of irony "to classify persons no more as revolutionary and conservative but rather as imaginative and without imagination" (*El alma matinal*, 2nd ed. [Lima: Empresa Editora Amauta, 1959], p. 39).

114. Paul Ricoeur, "Tâches de l'éducateur politique," in *Ésprit* 33, no. 340 (July-August 1965): 91.

115. Paul Blanquart, "A propos des rapports science-idéologie et foi-marxisme," in *Lettre*, nos. 144-45 (August-September 1970), p. 36.

116. "Utopia is present, though in a hidden way, in scientific production itself whose dynamism it constitutes; it does not appear under normal circumstances but rather in periods of crisis, between two moments of science: the one worn out, insufficient, and the other yet to be made, more satisfactory. Thus in the same movement it is the expression of the inadequacy of the existing theoretical instrument and the crucible of the new reason" (ibid.).

117. Ibid., p. 35.

118. Ibid.

119. See Hans Barth, *Wahrheit und Ideologie* (Zurich: Manesse Verlag, 1945); and Mannheim, *Ideology and Utopia*.

120. Louis Althusser has pointed this out very clearly; see his *For Marx* and *Reading Capital*, coauthored with Etienne Balibar, trans. Ben Brewster (New York: Pantheon Books, 1971). Althusser has taken up this theme again, trying to elucidate the relationships between ideology and the category of subject; see "Ideologie et appareils ideologiques d'État," in *La pensée*, no. 151 (June 1970), pp. 3-38.

121. Mannheim's distinction between utopia and ideology is well-known. Utopian are those "orientations transcending reality . . . which, when they pass over into conduct, tend to shatter, either partially or wholly, the order of things prevailing at the time" (*Ideology and Utopia*, p. 173). On the other hand, those ideas are ideological which are

appropriated for determined stages of existence "as long as they [are] 'organically' and harmoniously integrated into the worldview characteristic of the period (i.e. [do] not offer revolutionary possibilities)" (ibid., p. 174). This does not mean that ideology cannot place the existing order into a relationship with ideals which are not found within it; but what is characteristic of ideology is that it does so in such a way that these ideals do not provoke real transformations in the established order. For a critique of Mann- heim's thought see Franz Hinkelammert, *Ideolgías del desarrollo y dialéctica de la historia* (Buenos Aires: Editorial Paidos, 1970), pp. 85-89.

122. As Blanquart points out, this distinction between utopia and ideology is not found in Althusser ("Science-ideologie et foi-marxisme," p. 36, and "Acte de croire," p. 20). For Althusser there is only ideology and science; the "epistemological rupture" between the works of Marx's youth and his maturity, which Althusser justifiably points out, are seen as the precondition for the transition from ideology to science. Althusser has vigorously and correctly indicated that what is proper to Marx is to have created a science of history. It is a question of a healthy reaction, thanks to an effort of true mental hygiene, against any interpretation of Marx's thought which is ideologizing and claims to be "humanistic." But the rigidity of this position and the consignment of every utopian element to ideology prevents seeing the profound unity of the work of Marx and consequently duly understanding his capacity for inspiring a radical and permanent revolutionary praxis. Ernest Mandel has shown the evolution, and therefore the conti- nuity, of the notion of alienation in Marx (*The Formation of the Economic Thought of Karl Marx*, pp. 154-86); Althusser considers this notion pre-Marxist. Blanquart pro- poses the concept of appropriation (a notion taken from Henri Lefebvre, who presents it as the appropriation of nature and of his own nature by social humanity in *Marx: Sa vie, son oeuvre* [Paris: Presses Universitaires de France, 1964], p. 71), the negation of alienation, to signify the utopia that runs throughout Marx's work (Blanquart, "Acte de croire," p. 20).

123. See "Tercer Mundo y teología, in *Perspectivas para el Diálogo*, no. 50 (December 1970), pp. 304-05.

124. See above Chapter 2.

125. "Acte de croire," p. 25. The theologies of revolution and violence do not escape this danger. If at a given moment they presented a certain attraction it was because they were a useful attempt to break with the conception of a faith spontaneously linked to the established order (see the presentation of this theme in M. Peuchmaurd, "Esquisse pour une théologie de la révolution," *Parole et Mission* 10, no. 39 [October 1967]: 629-62 and the works already cited of Richard Shaull). But these approaches easily tended to belittle the theological and political questions involved. They also ran the risk— notwithstanding the intention of their initiators—of "baptizing" and in the long run impeding the revolution and counterviolence, because they furnished an *ad hoc* Christian ideology and ignored the level of political analysis at which these options are in the first instance being exercised. Here we are far from the theology of revo- lution. Our attempt at theological reflection moves within another frame of refer- ence.

126. "The evangelical message," writes Schillebeeckx, "gives us no direct program of social and political action, but, on the other hand, is socially and politically relevant in an indirect way, namely, in a 'utopian' sense" ("The Magisterium and the World of Politics," *Concilium* 36, p. 32). See also "Dio e 'colui che verrà,' Per una nuova immagine di Dio nel mondo secolarizzato," in *Processo alla religione*, p. 155. Blan- quart, who has worked out precisely the notion of utopia, is more categorical: "In this

space of utopia, faith and political action enter into relationship: it is the point of contact, the place of (paschal) Passover and of Covenant" ("La foi et les exigences politiques," in *Croissance des jeunes nations*, June 1969, p. 25; see also "Acte de croire," p. 29).

127. See above Chapter 6.

128. Connected with this perspective is the role which Che Guevara gives in economic activity to moral stimulus: "sense of duty, the new revolutionary consciousness," as opposed to material stimulus, "the residue of the past," which "comes from capitalism" and "will have no part in the new society."

129. "Tâches de l'éducateur," p. 90. Today this approach, according to Ricoeur, is twofold: "on the one hand, to affirm humanity as a totality; on the other, to affirm the person as a singularity"; the first aspect is "the horizon of all our debates regarding inequality in the world"; the second aspect is important "regarding the anonymity and dehumanization of relationships among individuals in the midst of industrial society" (ibid., pp. 90-91). In a similar vein, Blanquart believes that utopia, "constitutive of reason in our times," can be expressed in the formula "the integral and complete development of every person and of the whole person" ("Acte de croire," p. 22). This specifies the utopian notion of appropriation, the basis of "the only action which is really revolutionary; in the face of a single and diversified system, it can be only total and multiform; that is to say, it is at the same time universal (against exploitation—inequalities, injustice, segregations) and integral or multidimensional (against dehumanization)" (ibid., p. 21).

130. This is clearly affirmed by Blanquart in the articles cited. The vocabulary is less resolute in Schillebeeckx; see the works mentioned in note 125.

## SECTION 2. THE CHRISTIAN COMMUNITY AND THE NEW SOCIETY

1. Paul Blanquart correctly points out that "the problem underlying this crisis of the Church is the problem of politics and its relationship to the faith. We should not be surprised: if politics is a new problem for humanity, why should it not be for the Church?" ("L'acte de croire," p. 29).

2. We refer to only one of the studies representative of this concern: Henri de Lubac, "L'Église dans la crise actuelle," *Nouvelle Revue Théologique* 91, no. 6 (June-July 1969): 580-96.

3. "It seems to me," said Althusser in a "diagnosis" of the Church, "that the crisis in the Church is going to become worse. On the one hand, the decadence of theological thought is manifest and irremediable. It is not the 'theologies of revolution' or the 'theologies of violence' that can restore a *genuine* theological *thinking* which is now moribund. On the other hand, the political and ideological crisis is evident. With its structures inherited from a long past having a political role at the service of the ruling classes and the whole tradition resulting from this, *one cannot see how the Church can 'reconvert' to the service of the workers in the class struggle" (Lumière et Vie* 18, no. 93 [May-June 1969]: 29; italics in the original).

4. As regards Latin America, see above Chapter 7. For other aspects of this process, see Cecilio de Lora, José Marins, and Segundo Galilea, *Comunidades cristianas de base* (Bogotá: Indo-American Press Service, 1970), and Edgard Beltrán, *Pastoral de conjunto y comunidades de base* (Bogotá: Indo-American Press Service, 1971); for an excellent theological reflection see Eduardo Pironio, *La Iglesia que nace entre nosotros* (Bogotá: Indo-American Press Service, 1970).

## 12. THE CHURCH: SACRAMENT OF HISTORY

1. The theme has been studied especially in missionary circles. See the provocative article of Joseph Comblin, "Le but de la mission: sauver l'homme," *Spiritus* 9, no. 34 (May 1968): 171-79.

2. See above Chapter 9.

3. "Church of the World," in the work written in collaboration with Nikos A. Nissiotis and Philip Maury, *Discerning the Times: The Church in Today's World*, trans. Sister Agnes Cunningham, SSCM (Techny, Illinois: Divine Word Publications, 1968), p. 150.

4. Let us recall, for example, the words of Gregory of Nazianzen at the death of his father, who was a Christian convert: "Even before he entered our fold he was one of us. Just as many of our own are not with us because their lives alienate them from the common body of the faithful, in like manner many of those outside are with us, in so far as by their way of life they anticipate the faith and only lack in name what they possess in attitude. My father was one of these, an alien branch, but inclined toward us by his way of living" (*Funeral Orations by Saint Gregory Nazianzen and Saint Ambrose*, Fathers of the Church, vol. 22 [New York: Fathers of the Church, Inc., 1953], no. 6, p. 123).

5. "It is the law of mankind and the natural right of each individual to worship what he thinks proper" (Tertullian, "To Scapula," in *Tertullian, Apologetical Works, and Minucius Felix, Octavius*, Fathers of the Church, vol. 10 [New York: Fathers of the Church, Inc., 1950], p. 152). "It is in religion alone that liberty dwells. . . . No one can be made to adore what he does not wish" (Lactantius, "Epitome divinarum institutionum," 54, in *Patrologiae Latinae*, 6:1061).

6. Ambrose of Milan expresses this idea very clearly: "Where the preacher has not been present, the sound and the report of his voice has come" ("Commentaria in epistolam ad romanos" [10:17-18] in *Patrologiae Latinae*, 17:146b).

7. This helps us to understand the famous distinction between pagans and Jews, who have not had access to the faith, and heretics, who have abandoned it after having accepted it. For the former there is the necessity of a free acceptance of the faith, and so there will be a more tolerant attitude. The latter, on the other hand, will be considered culpable for turning their backs on the truth after having received the gift of faith; for them, severe treatment is appropriate. This position is summarized in a well-known text of Saint Thomas: "Acceptance of the faith is a matter of the will, whereas keeping the faith, when once one has received it, is a matter of obligation" (*Summa Theologica*, II-II, q. 10, a. 8, ad 3).

8. This is the real reason why the popes of the nineteenth century opposed religious liberty: to proclaim the civil equality of truth and error is to go against human salvation. See the texts reproduced in Giovanni Lo Grasso, *Ecclesia et Status: Fontes selecti* (Rome: Apud Aedes Pontif. Universitatis Gregorianae, 1952).

9. This "uncentering" begun by the Council has been emphasized by many, including G. Martelet, "Horizon théologique de la deuxième session du Concile," *Nouvelle Revue Théologique* 86, no. 5 (May 1964): 449-68, and Edward Schillebeeckx, *L'Église du Christ et l'homme d'aujourd'hui selon Vatican II* (Le Puy: Éditions Xavier Mappus, 1965), pp. 122-35.

10. Here we have been considering ideas more thoroughly treated in Gustavo Gutiérrez, "Libertad religiosa y diálogo salvador," pp. 13-43.

11. Han Urs von Balthasar writes in this respect, "Centuries of wasted opportunity are being made good; and fundamental Christian truths are being formulated which once expressed appear so right and obvious, that it is difficult to conceive how they can have been overlooked or forgotten for so long. Bridges which should never have been severed are being re-built. . . . Consequences that should have been drawn long ago are being drawn from premises which have always been there: for example, that if all men are called to supernatural salvation, grace must be active in them in some sense or other; that a dialogue between Christian and non-Christian is possible and necessary within that grace. . . . Truths such as these appear overwhelmingly great to the Christians of today and so they are. But that they should appear new is, for anyone who knows the Fathers, for example, somewhat surprising; for at bottom they are not new" (*Love Alone* [New York: Herder and Herder, 1969], pp. 122-23).

12. In this regard the most important texts are *Lumen gentium*, nos. 1 and 48; see also nos. 9 and 59; *Gaudium et spes*, no. 45; *Sacrosanctum concilium*, nos. 5 and 26; and *Ad gentes*, no. 9.

13. "In our opinion, the most important milestone of Vatican II in the field of dogmatic theology is to have designated the Church as 'sacrament,' that is, as a visible sign of salvation through the Holy Spirit sent by Christ" (H. Mühlen, "Das Verhältnis zwischen Inkarnation und Kirche in den Aussagen des Vaticanum II," *Theologie und Glaube* 55 [1965]: 171). Karl Rahner says that Christians of tomorrow, when they study the history of the Council, "will be astonished that this statement was made at the Council quietly and spontaneously without opposition, without surprise, without any-one's appearing to notice just what was being said. *Sacramentum salutis totius mundi*: sign of the salvation of the world" (*The Christian of the Future*, p. 82). Years before the Council Otto Semmelroth had dedicated a substantial study to this theme: *Die Kirche als Ursakrament* (Frankfurt: J. Knecht, 1953); and Rahner himself had also provided a valuable contribution: *The Church and the Sacraments* (New York: Herder and Herder, 1963). Nevertheless, this approach did not win the acceptance of all theologians, for it was feared that it would lead to "reducing ecclesiology to the study of outward elements" (Jerome Hamer, *The Church is a Communion* [New York: Sheed and Ward, 1964], p. 88; the point is treated on pp. 87-90).

14. See Metz, *Theology of the World*, p. 81, and *Risposta dei teologi*, p. 62. Along the same lines see Karl Rahner, *Risposta*, pp. 61-62.

15. See the old but important study of D. Deden, "Le mystère paulinien," *Ephemerides Theologicae Lovanienses* (1936), pp. 405-42.

16. The decree *Ad gentes*, in one of the texts of greatest theological importance of Vatican II, links closely the plan of salvation and the Church's task in that plan to the Trinitarian missions (nos. 1-5).

17. Juan Luis Segundo, *Nuestra idea de Dios* (Buenos Aires: Lohlé, 1970), p. 91; English version, *Our Idea of God*, 1974, was published by Orbis Books as one in the series entitled *A Theology for Artisans of a New Humanity*.

18. See Edward Schillebeeckx, *Christ, The Sacrament of the Encounter with God* (New York: Sheed and Ward, 1963).

19. See Mühlen, *Esprit dans l'Église*, 2:84-114; Piet Smulders, "La Iglesia como sacramento de salvación"; and Edward Schillebeeckx, *La mission de l'Église*, pp. 42-48.

20. "The Church," writes Christian Duquoc, "does not give human love its worth; rather it proclaims and signifies its eschatological dimension" (L'Église et le monde," *Lumière et Vie* 14, no. 73 [May-July 1965]: 65).

21. Clement, "Ensayo de lectura," *Iglesia en el mundo*, p. 663.

22. "Church and world definitely should be situated in dynamic terms within one salvific plan as two stages or two times" (Liégé, *Église de Jésus-Christ*, p. 164). "The decisive relationship between the Church and the world is not spatial but temporal" (J. B. Metz, *Theology of the World*, p. 94). From a somewhat different viewpoint Gustave Martelet had already attempted a fruitful reinterpretation of the temporal-spiritual distinction according to *Lumen gentium*: "La Iglesia y lo temporal: hacia una nueva concepción," *La Iglesia del Vaticano II*, 1:559-77; French version: "L'Église et le temporel," in *L'Église de Vatican II*, 2: 517-40. See also Lucio Gera, "La Iglesia y el mundo," *La Iglesia y el país* (Buenos Aires: Ediciones Búsqueda, 1967), pp. 9-19.

23. "The Church, if only she be rightly understood, is living always on the proclamation of her own provisional status and of her historically advancing elimination in the coming Kingdom of God" (Karl Rahner, "The Church and the Parousia of Christ;" in *Theological Investigations*, vol. 6 [Baltimore: Helicon Press, 1969], p. 298).

24. "Dio e 'colui che verrà,' " in *Processo alla religione*, p. 151.

25. The Exodus and the Covenant form a single unity. The God who established the Covenant is the same God who brought Israel "out of Egypt, out of the land of slavery" (Exod. 20:2; Deut. 5:6). As we have already recalled (see above Chapter 9), this liberation is above all a political act. On the basis of this liberation we can interpret correctly the meaning of the Exodus and the Covenant which are celebrated in the paschal meal. Joseph Blenkinsopp can therefore write that an "effect of this better understanding of the political dimension of early Israel's faith is that scholars are less inclined to accept the historical separation between covenant-traditions and exodus-tradition proposed by Von Rad." And he continues, "The founding event begins with a community in an intolerable economic and political situation and deals in the first place with their economic and political salvation—'Yahweh brought them out from there' " ("Scope and Depth of Exodus Tradition in Deutero-Isaiah 40-55," *The Dynamism of Biblical Tradition*, ed. Pierre Benoit and Roland E. Murphy, *Concilium* 20 [New York: Paulist Press, 1967], pp. 41-42).

26. See Joseph Ratzinger, "La destinée de Jésus et l'Église," in *L'Église aujourd'hui*, ed. Yves Congar (Paris: Desclée et Cie, 1967), pp. 43–45; Luc Dequeker and William Zuidema, "The Eucharist and St. Paul (1 Cor. 11, 17-34)," in *The Breaking of the Bread*, ed. Pierre Benoit, Roland E. Murphy, Bastiaan van Iersel, *Concilium* 40 (New York: Paulist Press, 1969), pp. 48-59. Blenkinsopp notes that the theme and the language of the Exodus are applied in the New Testament to the life and death of Jesus ("Scope and Depth," p. 50).

27. See J. M. R. Tillard, "L'Eucharistie et la fraternité," *Nouvelle Revue Théologique* 91, no. 2 (February 1969): 113-35.

28. C. H. Dodd believes that this episode "corresponds to the Synoptic account of the Last Supper," and he explains its omission in John "probably because the evangelist will not divulge the Christian 'mystery' " (*The Interpretation of the Fourth Gospel* [Cambridge: The University Press, 1955], p. 393).

29. "Eucharistie," p. 121. Rafael Ortega has pointed out with solid Biblical basis the threefold meaning of the sacrifice of the cross: paschal sacrifice, the liberation from all servitude (Exod. 12; 1 Cor. 5:6-8; 1 Pet. 1:18); sacrifice of Covenant which restores the former pact of union between God and the people (Exod. 19:5; 24:1; Gal. 4:4; 1 Cor. 11:25; Heb. 9:15-28); and sacrifice of expiation, of the elimination of sin (Lev. 16; 1 John 2:1-2; Rom. 3:23-25), in *Biblia y penitencia, Cuestiones litúrgicas*, no. 8 (*Medellín*); see also Stanislas Lyonnet and Léopold Sabourin, *Sin, Redemption, and Sacrifice* (Rome: Biblical Institute Press, 1970), pp. 170-74.

30. This is one of the few texts attributed to Jesus which Bultmann considers authentic; see *Theology of the New Testament*, trans. Kendrick Grobel (New York: Charles Scribner's Sons, 1951), 1:17ff.

31. This text is found in the declaration made public by Camilo Torres on June 24, 1965. He asked to be relieved from his "clerical obligations," and this was granted. In this idea Camilo found the basis for his pathetic decision of sacrificing "one of the rights that I love most dearly—to be able to celebrate the external rite of the Church as a priest—in order to create the conditions that make the cult more authentic" (Camilo Torres, *Revolutionary Writings*, pp. 163-64). This act by Camilo unmercifully revealed a reality hidden beneath a mountain of words and good intentions. And it also helped give birth to the hope of building a Church that does not present this kind of a dilemma to the best of its members.

32. Schillebeeckx, "Dio e 'colui che verrà,' " p. 150. L. M. Alonso Schökel has recalled the bond between the redemptive work of Christ and human solidarity in "La rédemption oeuvre de solidarité," *Nouvelle Revue Théologique* 93, no. 5 (May 1971): 449-72.

33. "Les biens temporels de l'Église d'après sa tradition théologique et canonique," in *Église et pauvreté*, pp. 247-49.

34. "The hour has come," declared a group of Ecuadorian priests, "for us as servants of the People of God in Ecuador, to unite our voices to the cry of the people and the voice of the apostle Paul: we cannot continue calmly to celebrate the event of liberation in the Eucharist, in which the oppressors and the oppressed eat the same bread and drink the same wine—without any true reconciliation" ("Declaración de la segunda convención nacional de presbíteros del Ecuador," *NADOC*, no. 204 [May 1971], p. 169).

35. "In Latin America the awareness is spreading—even among Christians—that Christianity has contributed to producing the cultural alienation that is seen today. The Christian religion has served, and continues to serve, as an ideology justifying the domination of the powerful. In Latin America Christianity has been a religion at the service of the system. Its rites, temples, and works have contributed to channeling popular dissatisfaction toward another world totally disconnected from this one. Thus Christianity has checked popular protest against an unjust and oppressive system" (*Juventud y cristianismo en América Latina*, final document of the seminar on the problems of youth organized by the Department of Education of CELAM [Bogotá: Indo-American Press Service 1969], p. 22).

36. Responding to accusations that the Church was "meddling in political affairs," the bishops and the Presbyteral Council of Lima stated that "every human action has an inescapable socio-political dimension. Evangelical preaching and witness, without entering into technical or partisan aspects of political activity, have a deep human duty to transform society by promoting the establishment of true justice among persons" (statement of May 13, 1971, in *El Comercio* [Lima], May 14, 1972, p. 10).

37. The observations made by Arend van Leeuwen at lectures given in Buenos Aires concerning the loss of the influence of Christianity in the revolutionary spirit of the West are not entirely valid for Latin America (*Desarrollo y revolución* [Buenos Aires: La Aurora, 1967], p. 155; in English see his *Development through Revolution* [New York: Charles Scribner's Sons, 1970]).

38. This is a controversial point in Latin America; see above Chapter 8 and Assmann, *Teología de la liberación*, pp. 44-45.

39. In this service the Church—even the groups in the Church which might be

considered in the vanguard—must avoid regressing toward any kind of politico-religious messianism, the danger of which we indicated at the end of the last chapter. As the Church must be aware of its responsibilities in these matters, so too it must be aware of the limit of its activity. As Hector Borrat correctly indicates, "Every word, every action of the Church that appears to be a 'pronouncement' in political matters has the weight and the presumed objectivity of an institution which by its very nature can claim no power; but it also has the weakness that by itself it cannot fully achieve what it seeks. . . . The Church is not an alternative to power, but this does not mean that it does not participate in the political process" ("¿La Iglesia para qué?" *Cristianismo y Sociedad*, no. 22 [1970], pp. 13-18).

40. In this regard, although in a different social context, see the perceptive observations of Marcel Xhaufflaire, "L'Église de demain," *Lumière et Vie* 19, no. 99 (August-October 1970): 133-54, especially pp. 139-45.

41. See Carlos Alvarez Calderón, *Pastoral y liberación humana* (Lima: CEP, 1970).

42. The pastoral activity of the Latin American Church is moving more and more in this direction; see Segundo Galilea, *La vertiente política de la pastoral* (Quito: Instituto Pastoral Latinoamericano, 1970), pp. 7-16. "Here we must observe," J. B. Metz points out, "that the Church, insofar as it is a historico-social phenomenon, always has a political dimension. This is so even before it sets up criteria by which it guides its activity and before taking a stand with regard to specific situations. To insinuate, as is being done today, that the Church is and ought to be a priori 'neutral' either manifests a lack of critical judgment or serves only to camouflage existing political alliances" ("Presencia de la Iglesia en la sociedad," *Concilium* [December 1970], p. 248).

43. "Amore cristiano e violenza rivoluzionaria," *La violenza dei cristiani* (Assisi: Cittadella, 1969), p. 110.

44. "There has still not emerged," writes Pedro Negre from Bolivia, "a Church in the center of oppression and margination" ("Biblia y liberación," *Cristianismo y Sociedad*, tercera y cuarta entrega [1970], p. 70).

45. In this regard see the perceptive observations of Hector Borrat, "¿La Iglesia para qué?," pp. 26-29.

46. Moreover, these modalities will be different according to their situation in the People of God. In the case of the ecclesiastical magisterium it will be necessary to accept that, given the issues involved, there will be some positions taken which will be very much marked by the specific characteristics of given situations. It is a question of being situated at the level of historical decisions without claiming to establish rigid norms based on abstract principles which can be applied to any situation. Rather than diminishing the value of the actions of ecclesiastical authority, this will make them more fruitful. The texts of the bishops' conference at Medellín are a good example of trying to interpret the Word of God *today* and in a *given situation* as well as trying to preach it opportunely and at the same time "inopportunely." "In the meantime," writes Schillebeeckx in an article dedicated to this point, "*this* specific pronouncement will hold *here and now* for the ecclesiastical community" ("The Magisterium and the World of Politics," *Concilium* 36, p. 37).

47. Lucio Gera, "Reflexión teológica," *Sacerdotes para el Tercer Mundo* (Buenos Aires: Ed. del Movimiento, 1970), p. 141. Later he writes, "Prophecy not only desacralizes every place, temple, race, or nation; it also desacralizes every time. It does not set up as the final and definitive goal any empire that supplants another, any level of civilization—no matter how Jewish or Christian it might be—or any political, economic, or social system" (p. 142).

48. Schillebeeckx has pointed out this dual function of the faith which both relativizes and radicalizes the building of the human city; see "Foi chrétienne et attente terrestre," *L'Église dans le monde de ce temps* (Tours: Mame, 1967), pp. 151-58. See also W. Kasper, "Faut-il encore la mission extérieure?" *Église et Mission*, no. 180 (October 1970), pp. 180-92.

49. This statement does not apply only to the church in Latin America; see, for example, the final report of the Extraordinary Synod of Bishops in 1985. The term "poor" embraces a complex reality. Perhaps the best way of describing this reality is to say that the poor are those who are unimportant, those who are given no consideration by society and whose most elementary rights to life, liberty, and justice are continually violated. When I speak of social conflict, I put the emphasis primarily on the element of membership in a social collectivity, for this is what makes the whole subject such a difficult one.

50. In his opening address to the Puebla Conference John Paul II spoke of "mechanisms that . . . lead on the international level to the ever increasing wealth of the rich at the expense of the ever increasing poverty of the poor" (III, 4).

51. In a famous letter Marx says: "As for me, mine is not the merit of having discovered either the existence of classes in modern society or the struggle between them. Long before me bourgeois historians described the historical development of this class struggle and bourgeois economists studied its economic anatomy." Marx considered that his own contribution was to have shown the connection between this reality and economic factors (and the dictatorship of the proletariat) (letter to J. Weydemeyer, March 5, 1852, in Karl Marx and Friedrich Engels, *Etudes philosophiques* [Paris: Editions Sociales, 1951], p. 151). Economic factors are often described as historically determined. I am not interested here in the important debate to which this view has given rise, or the interpretations it has produced even within Marxism; it is enough to say that the determinist approach based on economic factors is completely alien to the kind of social analysis that supplies a framework for the theology of liberation.

52. It was for this reason that I said at a meeting sponsored by CELAM in 1973: "The problem facing theology is not to determine whether or not social classes are in opposition. That is in principle a matter for the sciences, and theology must pay careful attention to them if it wishes to be au courant with the effort being made to understand the social dimensions of the human person. The question, therefore, that theology must answer is this: If there is a class struggle (as one, but not the only, form of historical conflict), how are we to respond to it as Christians? A theological question is always one that is prompted by the content of faith—that is, by love. The specifically Christian question is both theological and pastoral: How are Christians to live their faith, their hope, and their love amid a conflict that takes the form of class struggle? Suppose that analysis were to tell us one day: 'The class struggle is not as important as you used to think.' We as theologians would continue to say that love is the important thing, even amid conflict as described for us by social analysis. If I want to be faithful to the gospel, I cannot disregard reality, however harsh and conflictual it may be. And the reality of Latin America is indeed harsh and conflictual!" (*Dialogos en el Celam* [Bogotá, 1974], pp. 89–90).

53. Further on, when discussing socialism and the differences between it and communism, Pius XI maintains that "if *the class struggle* abstains from enmities and mutual hatred, it gradually *changes into an honest discussion* of differences founded on a desire for justice, and if this is not that blessed social peace we all seek, it can and ought to be the point of departure from which to move forward to the mutual cooperation of the

industries and professions" (*Quadragesimo Anno,* 114; emphasis added). The claim is a far-reaching one, for it is not limited to a description of facts but indicates a possible development: when the class struggle is approached in a way that takes into account the basic Christian requirement of the exclusion of hatred, it can change into "an honest discussion."

54. Letter signed by Alfred Ancel, auxiliary bishop of Lyons, in *Documentation Catholique,* vol. 65, no. 1528 (November 17, 1968), p. 1950.

55. When Medellín describes the social tensions at work in Latin America, it says that the opposition is more intense "in those countries characterized by a *marked biclassism,* where a few have much (culture, wealth, power, prestige), whereas the majority has very little" ("Peace," 3; emphasis added). Following the lead of John Paul II, Puebla speaks of structural conflict.

56. We are indeed faced with a "social fact," and it is precisely as a fact that I speak of it. For this reason, what I say has nothing to do with a more philosophical approach that talks of social conflict, and specifically of class struggle, as "the force that drives history" or "the law of history."

57. See above, p. 31.

58. The history of theological reflection on war, that deadly scourge of humanity, is an eloquent example of what I mean. European theologians have an extensive and direct experience in this area, which persons in other parts of the world do not always understand in all its details. Even so, European theological thinking on the subject has never been entirely satisfactory, because of the sensitivity and slipperiness of the subject itself. Theological reflection on war is always tentative and in process. The divergent and in some ways opposed positions recently taken by the North American and European episcopates on nuclear weapons are examples of what I am saying.

59. In this area John Paul II has made a clarifying distinction. Speaking of social conflict, the pope says: "This conflict, interpreted by some as a socio-economic *class conflict,* found expression in the *ideological conflict* between liberalism, understood as the ideology of capitalism, and Marxism, understood as the ideology of scientific socialism and communism, which professes to act as the protagonist for the working class and the worldwide proletariat. Thus the real conflict between labor and capital was transformed into *a systematic class struggle,* conducted not only by ideological means but also and chiefly by political means" (*Laborem Exercens,* 11). The "real conflict" is one thing, its ideological transformation into "a systematic class struggle" as the sole political strategy is quite another. In my approach I refer to the former, not to the latter.

60. Worth citing in this context is an interesting passage from Karl Lehmann, theologian and now archbishop of Mainz: "Situations can undoubtedly arise in which the Christian message allows only one path to be followed. In these cases, the church has an obligation to take sides in a decisive way (think, for example, of the experience of Nazi dictatorship in Germany). In these circumstances, an attitude of unqualified neutrality in political matters contradicts the commandment of the gospel and can have deadly consequences" ("Problemas metodológicos y hermeneúticos de la teología de la liberación," in International Theological Commission, *Teología de la liberación* [Madrid: BAC, 1978], p. 37).

61. For an analysis of this point, see my "El Evangelio del trabajo," in *Sobre el trabajo humano* (Lima: CEP, 1982).

62. There are times in the struggle for justice when opposition seems to exclude respect for others. Speaking of labor unions, John Paul II says: "They are indeed involved in the struggle for social justice, for the just rights of workers in accordance

with their individual professions. However, this struggle should be seen as a normal endeavor 'for' the just good: in the present case, for the good that corresponds to the needs and merits of workers associated by profession; but it is not a struggle 'against' others." He goes on to say: "Even if in controversial questions the struggle takes on an *aspect of opposition* toward others, this is because it aims at the good of social justice, not for the sake of 'struggle' or in order to eliminate the opponent" (*Laborem Exercens*, 20, emphasis added). In these difficult situations there may in fact be opposition among individuals, but even then the Christian response is to reject any hatred.

63. Peruvian Episcopate, *Justicia en el mundo* (August 1971), no. 24.

64. See Lucio Gera, "Reflexión teológica," in *Sacerdotes para el tercer mundo* (Buenos Aires, 1970), p. 125: "As long as the church is on pilgrimage in this world, it is indeed one, but it nonetheless always does penance for the imperfection of its unity and strives for greater unity. Unity, like peace, is something that must be continually achieved."

## 13. POVERTY: SOLIDARITY AND PROTEST

1. This chapter summarizes a series of classes given at the University of Montreal in July 1967 on "The Church and the Problems of Poverty." The ideas have been revised and the bibliography has been brought up to date.

2. Radio Message of September 11, 1962, in *The Pope Speaks* 8, no. 4 (Spring 1963): 396.

3. "We will not respond to the truest and deepest demands of our time nor to the hope of unity shared by all Christians if we treat the theme of the evangelization of the poor as one of the many themes of the Council. This is not a theme like others; in a way, it is *the* theme of our Council" (speech of Cardinal Lercaro, December 6, 1962; the text is in *La Documentation Catholique* 60, no. 1395 [March 3, 1963], col. 321, n . 2).

4. Most of the references are to be found in *Lumen gentium* (sixteen) and *Gaudium et spes* (fourteen). The most important text is *Lumen gentium*, no. 8.

5. See the Medellín document on "Poverty of the Church" and the other statements of the Latin American Church quoted above in Chapter 7.

6. See, for example, the works of Pie-Raymond Régamey, O.P., *Poverty: An Essential Element in the Christian Life*, trans. Rosemary Sheed (New York: Sheed & Ward, 1950); R. Voillaume, *Seeds of the Desert* (Notre Dame: Fides Publishers Association, 1955); Paul Gauthier, *Christ, the Church and the Poor*, trans. Edward Fitzgerald (Westminster, Md.: The Newman Press, 1965).

7. "The uncertainties regarding poverty are such today that it is necessary to reconsider the question from the beginning" (A. Hayen and Pie-Raymond Régamey, "Une anthropologie chrétienne" in *Église et pauvreté*, p. 83).

8. In reference to the society of the future Mounier wrote perceptively, "After we have experienced poverty of the spirit amid material poverty, perhaps humanity is called to the difficult task of practicing it amid material abundance" ("La révolution personaliste" in *Oeuvres complètes*, 1:413).

9. In religious life poverty is often very closely linked to obedience. To be poor is to have no *personal* control over economic goods; on a *communal* level, things are very different, as we know.

10. See the remarks concerning the notion of the evangelical counsel in Hayen and Régamey, "Anthropologie," pp. 106-12. See also H. Feret, *L'Église des pauvres, interpellation des riches* (Paris: Les Éditions du Cerf, 1965), pp. 201-28; Yves Congar,

O.P., "Poverty, in Christian Life amidst an Affluent Society," *War, Poverty, Freedom*, ed. Franz Böckle, *Concilium* 15 (New York: Paulist Press, 1966), pp. 52-53; and Karl Rahner, "Théologie de la vie religieuse" in *Les religieuses aujourd'hui et demain* (Paris, 1964), p. 71.

11. These two lines of thought were indicated and studied by Albert Gelin, P. S. S., in his pioneer work, *The Poor of Yahweh*, trans. Mother Kathryn Sullivan, R.S.C.J. (Collegeville, Minnesota: The Liturgical Press, 1964); they are treated with great clarity by González Ruiz in *Pobreza evangélica*.

12. I have returned to the biblical idea of poverty in my *El Dios de la vida* (1988), chapters 6 and 7. In that study I was greatly helped by the extraordinary work of J. Dupont, *Les Béatitudes* (Bruges: Abbaye de Saint-André; Louvain: E. Nauwelaerts, 1958-69).

13. Regarding the terminology, see Gelin, *Poor*; A. George, "Pauvre," in *Supplément au Dictionnaire de la Bible*, 1966, cols. 387–406; Jacques Dupont, *Les béatitudes*, vol. 2, *La Bonne Nouvelle* (Paris: J. Gabalda et Cie Editeurs, 1969), pp. 19-34; Ernst Bammel, "Ptokós" in *Theological Dictionary of the New Testament*, ed. Gerhard Friedrich, trans. and ed. Geoffrey W. Bromiley (Grand Rapids, Mich.: Wm. B. Eerdmans Publishing Company, 1968), 6:885-915; Jesús María Liaño, "Los pobres en el Antiguo Testamento," *Estudios Bíblicos* 25, no. 2 (April-June 1966): 162-67.

14. *Rash* is used twenty-one times in the Old Testament, especially in Proverbs.

15. See Gelin, *Poor*, p. 19.

16. *Ebyôn* is used sixty-one times in the Old Testament, especially in the Psalms and the Prophets. See P. Humbert, "Le mot biblique ébyôn," *Revue d'Histoire et de Philosophie Religieuse* (1952), pp. 1-6.

17. *Dal* is used forty-eight times in the Old Testament, especially in the Prophets, Job, and Proverbs.

18. This is the most common term; it is found eighty times in the Old Testament, especially in the Psalms and the Prophets.

19. *Anaw* is found twenty-five times in the Old Testament (only once in the singular), especially in the Psalms and the Prophets.

20. *Ptokós* is used thirty-four times in the whole New Testament; in most cases it refers to the indigent person, one lacking what is necessary. Only on six occasions does this term have a spiritual meaning, but even then the poor person is found at the side of the blind, the mutilated, the leper, and the sick, providing a very immediate concrete context.

21. "Poverty was never something to which the prophets could be indifferent. When they spoke of it, they protested against the oppression and injustice of the rich and the mighty. Naturally, they found expressions consonant with their feelings" (Van der Ploeg, "Les pauvres d'Israël et leur piété," in *Oudtestamentische Studiën* 7 [1950]: 258, quoted in Gelin, *Poor*, p. 19).

22. "You ought to give judgement for the weak and the orphan, and see right done to the destitute and downtrodden, you ought to rescue the weak and the poor" (Ps. 82:3-4).

23. See Gelin, *Poor*, pp. 17-18.

24. See also Deut. 23:16-21; 24:5-22.

25. Roland de Vaux, O.P., *Ancient Israel: Its Life and Institutions*, trans. John McHugh (New York: McGraw-Hill Book Company, Inc., 1961), p. 175. The author believes, however, that there is little indication that this legislation was faithfully observed (pp. 175-77).

26. Exod. 1:9-14 speaks of a dominant class that benefits from the dehumanizing work of the exploited masses.

27. Gelin, *Poor*, p. 16.

28. See Von Rad, *Old Testament Theology*, 1:139–48; and C. Spicq, O.P., *Dieu et l'homme selon le Nouveau Testament* (Paris: Les Éditions du Cerf, 1961), pp. 179-213.

29. See above Chapter 9.

30. See above Chapter 10.

31. "Neither wealth nor poverty . . . ," Thomas Aquinas said long ago, "is in itself human good" ("Neque divitiae neque paupertas . . . est secundum se hominis bonum"; *Summa Contra Gentiles*, 3:134).

32. "Poverty belongs to the sphere of privation and want and is an intolerable scandal" (González Ruiz, *Pobreza evangélica*, p. 32).

33. Gelin points out that in the Bible there are also other, less important lines of thought regarding poverty. The relationship between poverty and sin and the ideal of an intermediate state between wealth and poverty are both considered (*Poor*, pp. 23-26). Nevertheless, the dominant theme is the one we have indicated; moreover, it alone provides the basis for an adequate interpretation of the secondary themes.

34. Ibid., p. 26.

35. "Words that once denoted a sociological reality came to mean an attitude of soul" (ibid., p. 26). Something similar occurs with the term *justice*; in the Bible it first designates a social situation. Gradually—without losing its original sense—it is enriched by a spiritual meaning: justice as a synonym for sanctity.

36. George, "Pauvre," col. 393.

37. "Spiritual poverty is above all this power of being open to the will of God" (Pierre Ganne, "Aujourd'hui, la béatitude des pauvres," *Bible et Vie Chrétienne* 37 [January-February 1961]: p. 74).

38. This idea has been strongly emphasized by Bonhoeffer in *The Cost of Discipleship*, rev. ed. (New York: The Macmillan Company, 1963).

39. Jacques Dupont, *Les béatitudes: Le problème littéraire, Le message doctrinal* (Bruges: Éditions de l'Abbaye de Saint-André, 1954), pp. 82 and 122-23, and L. Vaganay, *Le problème synoptique* (Tournai: Desclée & Co., 1954), pp. 255 and 291-92, believe that Luke is closer to the sources. Gelin, on the other hand, holds for the archaic character of the text in Matthew (*Poor*, p. 107).

40. "Does this mean that we must believe that Jesus 'beatified a social class'? ... [The Gospel] canonizes no sociological state, nor places it in direct relation with the Kingdom" (Gelin, *Poor*, p. 107). See Dupont, *Béatitudes* (1954), p. 242. See also the references to the hypothesis of ebionism and "socialism" in Luke on p. 215, n. 1. Léon-Defour also seems to situate himself in this line of interpretation; according to him if the exegete "selects only Luke, he tends to beatify a sociological condition; if he selects only Matthew, he runs the risk of having the Beatitude evaporate into a spirit of poverty, which the rich are supposed to possess" ("L'exégète et l'événement historique," *Recherches de Sciences Religieuses* 58, no. 4 [October-December 1970]:559).

41. "In the Beatitudes of Luke, the basic perspective . . . is that of retribution after death. . . . [Luke] sees in Christianity the inescapable obligation of choosing against the present life and for the future life" (Dupont, *Béatitudes* [1954], pp. 213-18).

42. Gelin, *Poor*, p. 108. The author has a clear tendency to spiritualize the Biblical theme of poverty. For a similar perspective see George, "Pauvre," col. 402. Dupont, *Béatitudes* (1969), pp. 141–42, refutes—and rightly so—a variation on this interpretation: that the poor—materially speaking—will be blessed because in them there occur

more easily certain spiritual dispositions toward acceptance of the Kingdom. Karel Truhlar, S.J., notwithstanding the title of his article, also puts himself in a "spiritualist" perspective: "The Earthy Cast of the Beatitudes," *The Gift of Joy*, ed. Christian Duquoc, O.P., *Concilium* 39 (New York: Paulist Press, 1968), pp. 33–43.

43. The term *poor* (*ptokós*) occurs ten times in Luke (4:18; 6:20; 7:22; 14:13, 21; 16:21, 22; 18:22; 19:8; 21:3). The meaning we have just considered is seen very clearly if we keep in mind the context in which the expression occurs. Moreover, the first three Beatitudes in Luke form a unity and should be interpreted as a whole. "The afflicted" and "the hungry" are very concrete realities not subject to spiritualization (see Dupont, *Béatitudes* [1969], pp. 49-51 and 139).

44. See above Chapter 9.

45. Dupont includes the prophetic perspective in his interpretation of the text in question (see *Béatitudes* [1954], p. 212). But he believes that Luke departs from it to adopt the point of view of the wisdom tradition (p. 213). Nevertheless Dupont seems to modify this position in his most recent work (*Béatitudes* [1969]).

46. Although he is speaking in a somewhat different context, Régamey remarks with lucidity and realism that "the spiritual fullness of the Beatitudes does not replace its messianic meaning. . . .Christianity will always have the mission of taking on itself the hope of the poor. The task of the Messiah becomes the task of Christians. It is of utmost importance to maintain at the very core of the meaning of the Beatitudes their messianic significance. This must be translated to fit the changing circumstances which offer the challenge of fulfilling—according to Christ—the just aspirations of all persons, just as the Beatitudes announced the fulfillment of the just aspirations of the Jews twenty centuries ago" (*Le portrait spirituel du chrétien* [Paris: Les Éditions du Cerf, 1963], p. 26).

47. "Perfection, however, does not consist in the renunciation itself of temporal goods; since this is the way to perfection" (Thomas Aquinas, *Summa Theologica,* II-II, q. 19, a. 12).

48. "Los pobres y la pobreza en los Evangelios y en los Hechos," *La pobreza evangélica hoy* (Bogotá: Secretariado General de la CLAR, 1971), p. 32.

49. The Medellín document on "Poverty of the Church" distinguishes among three meanings of the term *poverty* and describes the mission of the Church in terms of that distinction. It might be useful to quote here the entire paragraph: "(a) Poverty, as a lack of the goods of this world necessary to live worthily as men, is in itself evil. The prophets denounce it as contrary to the will of the Lord and most of the time as the fruit of the injustice and sin of men. (b) Spiritual poverty is the theme of the poor of Yahweh (cf. Zeph. 2:3; Luke 1:46-55). Spiritual poverty is the attitude of opening up to God, the ready disposition of one who hopes for everything from the Lord (cf. Matt. 5:3). Although he values the goods of this world, he does not become attached to them and he recognizes the higher value of the riches of the Kingdom (cf. Amos 2:6-7; 4:1; Jer. 5:28; Mic. 6:12-13; Isa. 10:2 et passim). (c) Poverty as a commitment, through which one assumes voluntarily and lovingly the conditions of the needy of this world in order to bear witness to the evil which it represents and to spiritual liberty in the face of material goods, follows the example of Christ Who took to Himself all the consequences of men's sinful condition (cf. Phil. 2:5-8) and Who 'being rich became poor' (cf. 2 Cor. 8:9) in order to redeem us.

"In this context a poor Church:—Denounces the unjust lack of this world's goods and the sin that begets it;—Preaches and lives in spiritual poverty, as an attitude of spiritual childhood and openness to the Lord;—Is herself bound to material poverty. The poverty of the Church is, in effect, a constant factor in the history of salvation" (nos. 4-5).

50. In this regard it is necessary to rethink seriously the meaning of the assistance that the churches of the wealthy countries give to the churches of the poor countries. This assistance could very well be counterproductive as regards the witness to poverty that these poor churches should be giving. Moreover it might lead them into a reformist approach, resulting in superficial social changes which in the long run serve only to prolong the misery and injustice which marginated peoples suffer. This assistance can also provide a satisfied conscience—at low cost—for Christians who are citizens of countries which control the world economy. In this regard see the famous article of Ivan Illich, "The Seamy Side of Charity," *America* 116, no. 3 (January 21, 1967): 88-91.

# INDEX OF BIBLICAL REFERENCES

# GENERAL INDEX